Marketing the American Creed Abroad

This book examines the interaction of domestic and foreign issues in the lives of ethnic Americans. Arguing that the damaging impact of ethnic influences on U.S. foreign affairs has been overstated and misrepresented, Shain brings a new dimension to the public debate on multiculturalism by exploring its transnational aspects. Ethnic groups, despite residual attachments to their homelands, do not betray American political values and ideals, but, on the contrary, their involvement in homeland-related affairs has been instrumental in disseminating those values inside and outside the United States. Shain evaluates ethnic groups in the United States from a broad theoretical and comparative perspective, and his case studies include, among others, Arab-Americans, Mexican-Americans, and African-Americans.

Yossi Shain is Associate Professor and Chairman of the Department of Political Science at Tel-Aviv University. He is the author of *The Frontier of Loyalty: Political Exiles in the Age of the Nation-State* and coeditor (with Juan Linz) of *Between States: Interim Governments and Democratic Transitions.* He is also editor of *Governments-in-Exile in Contemporary World Politics* and coeditor (with Aaron Klieman) of *Democracy: The Challenges Ahead.* He has been a visiting professor at Yale University, St. Antony's College, Oxford University, Wesleyan University, The Fletcher School of Law and Diplomacy at Tufts University, and Middlebury College.

D0139475

Marketing the American Creed Abroad

DIASPORAS IN THE U.S. AND THEIR HOMELANDS

YOSSI SHAIN

CAMBRIDGE
UNIVERSITY PRESS

PUBLISHED BY THE PRESS SYNDICATE OF THE UNIVERSITY OF CAMBRIDGE
The Pitt Building, Trumpington Street, Cambridge, United Kingdom

CAMBRIDGE UNIVERSITY PRESS
The Edinburgh Building, Cambridge CB2 2RU, UK   http://www.cup.cam.ac.uk
40 West 20th Street, New York, NY 10011-4211, USA   http://www.cup.org
10 Stamford Road, Oakleigh, Melbourne 3166, Australia

© Yossi Shain 1999

First published 1999

Printed in the United States of America

Typeface Janson Text Roman 10.25/13pt.   *System* DeskTopPro$_{/ux}$®[BV]

*A catalog record for this book is available from
the British Library*

Library of Congress Cataloging-in-Publication Data

Shain, Yossi, 1956–
Marketing the American creed abroad : Diasporas in the U.S. and their
homelands / Yossi Shain.
p. cm.
Includes bibliographical references and index.
ISBN 0-521-64225-6 (hb) – ISBN 0-521-64531-X (pb)
1. Minorities – United States – Political activity.   2. Immigrants –
United States – Political activity.   3. Ethnicity – Political
aspects – United States.   4. Nationalism – United States.
5. Pluralism (Social sciences) – United States.   6. United States –
Foreign relations – 1989 – Citizen participation.   7. United States –
Foreign relations – 1989 – Social aspects.   8. United States –
Ethnic relations.   9. United States – Race relations.   I. Title.
E184.A1S565   1999
323'.042'08691–dc21   98-11676
                                                                        CIP

ISBN 0 521 64225 6 hardback
ISBN 0 521 64531 X paperback

To Eytan and Emily

Contents

Preface and Acknowledgments   *page* ix

1   U.S. Diasporas and Homelands in the Era of
    Transnationalism   1
2   U.S. Ethnic Diasporas in the Struggle for Democracy and
    Self-Determination   51
3   Arab-American Identity and New Transnational Challenges   92
4   Transnational Influences on Ethnoracial Relations in the
    United States: The Case of Black-Jewish Disputes   132
5   "Go, but Do Not Forget Me": Mexico, the Mexican
    Diaspora, and U.S.-Mexican Relations   165
    Conclusion: Diasporas and the American National Interest   196

Notes   211
Bibliography   255
Index   279

Preface and Acknowledgments

This book focuses on the interaction of domestic and foreign issues in the lives of ethnic Americans and seeks to add a new dimension to the public debate on multiculturalism by exploring its transnational aspects. Thus, the book examines the effects of this transnational nexus on questions of politics, culture, identity, and loyalties inside the United States, as well as on countries of origin or symbolic homelands, in an attempt to better understand and conceptualize the impact of homelands and ethnicity on U.S. domestic and foreign affairs. In other words, what is being sought is a broadening of analytical scope to reflect the internationalization of these issues.

Throughout American history, U.S.-based ethnic diasporas have been involved in the affairs of their countries of origin or of their symbolic homelands, and ethnic lobbies are known to be an integral part of American politics. There has been a great deal of analysis of individual theories and case studies of ethnic involvement in U.S. foreign policy, and many observers have pointed to the ability of ethnic lobbyists to influence U.S. foreign policy makers on issues related to their ancestral homelands. This ability is broadly perceived to be on the rise, especially after the end of the cold war and the collapse of the Soviet Union, and with the declining power of the traditional professional elites who had dominated U.S. foreign policy since the end of World War II. Indeed, in recent years, scholars, journalists, and politicians have given greater attention to the role of ethnicity in U.S. foreign affairs, with differing interpretations as to its impact on the U.S. national interest.

Although many observers agree that U.S. diasporas are increasingly influential in shaping America's international relations, there are in fact only limited studies and inconclusive findings as to whether and how diasporic dedication to homeland political affairs affects U.S. foreign policy and bears on American interests abroad. Even less attention has been paid to the issue of how ethnic involvement in homeland affairs impacts on U.S. civic culture and ethnic relations, and on the character and politics of the home country itself. Moreover, there have been few attempts to integrate the various relevant aspects of diasporic political activity, ethnic identity, and politics inside the United States.

My major argument is that the damaging impact of ethnic influences in U.S. foreign affairs has been overstated and misrepresented. Ethnic involvement in U.S. foreign affairs may be seen as an important vehicle through which disenfranchised groups may win an entry ticket into American society and politics. Indeed, one of the signs that an ethnic group has achieved a respectable position in American life is its acquisition of a meaningful voice in U.S. foreign affairs. Yet in order to obtain such a role, ethnic officials must first demonstrate their determination to advocate the principles of pluralism, democracy, and human rights abroad. In fact, in the aftermath of the cold war and with the advent of a more unipolar, ideological world order that favors democracy and the free-market economy, ethnic lobbies are likely to become mobilized diasporas. They are "commissioned" by American decision makers to export and safeguard American values abroad and are expected to become the moral conscience of new democracies or newly established states in their homelands. Such commissioning, in turn, further legitimates the ethnic voice in America's external affairs and enables diasporas to push American policy makers to adhere to America's neo-Wilsonian values of promoting democracy and openness around the globe, even when such policies seem to obstruct ad hoc strategic interests.

Another central argument of my book is that the new foreign-policy role of ethnic groups is likely to reflect positively in American civic culture by reinforcing the values of democracy and pluralism at home. Contrary to conventional wisdom, I maintain that diasporic politics has the potential to temper, rather than exacerbate, domestic ethnic conflicts, because it discourages tendencies toward balkanization inside the United States. In many ways, then, the participation of ethnic diasporas in shaping U.S. foreign policy is a force of social integration and political inclusion.

Thus, this book introduces a new perspective on the debate over multiculturalism and the changing character of American society, concentrating on the various aspects of relations between U.S. ethnic diasporas, their American environment, and their countries of origin or symbolic homelands. This nexus has deep historical roots in the United States as a country of immigrants with a legacy of racial exclusion. It is also a product of the changing nature of American politics and society and the empowerment of ethnoracial groups in electoral systems, as well as the growing foreign-policy role of individual members of Congress and even local governments.

In "the era of multiculturalism," when the demographic makeup of America is changing dramatically, when American institutions no longer impose cultural assimilation on citizens, and when diasporic elites are less inhibited by charges of disloyalty in promoting ancestral identities among their constituencies, the role of diasporas in American politics gains in intensity and importance. The openness of the American political system to ethnic voices has allowed many newly organized diasporas to acquire a meaningful role in U.S. foreign policy, especially on issues concerning the nature of the regime and the economic policies of countries of origin or symbolic homelands. Alongside the more established groups of Greek, Armenian, Irish, and Jewish descent, the more recently empowered diasporas of African, Arab, Cuban, Dominican, Filipino, Haitian, Korean, and Mexican origin have discovered that they can unite and mobilize their community abroad more effectively by pursuing causes directly relating to their homeland, than when engaged in factional struggles for ethnoracial leadership within the United States, especially when such struggles involve intractable sociopolitical and economic issues. Indeed, many countries of origin have discovered the critical role of ethnic lobbies in the United States, and these countries' leaders are taking action to build and sustain their U.S.-based compatriots' loyalty and attachment in order to further their own interests. Such policies of diasporic recruitment and rapprochement may also force changes of political behavior and even identity inside the countries of origin.

The various dimensions of the diaspora-homeland nexus have developed over time as functions of a changing American identity. These include American self-definition, the nature of the diaspora, the goals of U.S. foreign policy, and, most recently, the increasing impact of the international flow of capital and the development of transnational modes of transportation and communication. All of this leads us to the working assumption that domestic conflicts regarding American identity and the homeland factor among American ethnic groups are inextricably linked.

This book presents primary research and specific cases on diasporic politics in an attempt to arrive at a more comprehensive understanding of "homelands" as both a domestic factor and an international element in American society. Particular experiences are addressed in detail to illuminate and inform the theoretical underpinnings of the book. They therefore provide a narrative but also a basis for thorough analysis and further investigation.

Over the past few years, many people have asked me what it is that motivates a native Israeli to work on American politics and culture? I am probably not sufficiently reflective or self-analytical, but I truly never considered my personal life as relevant to the writing of this book. One of the manuscript's referees expressed his surprise that a foreigner would write about American ethnic identities, and strongly suggested that I "write a preface that lays out aspects of . . . personal biography and intellectual evolution that are relevant to the study." When my editor then made the same request, I decided to try to provide an answer.

I was born and raised an Israeli, with all of the benefits and the "baggage" that comes with that identity. I grew up believing firmly in the historical and political vision of Zionism, which treated diasporic life as a lesser existence. In spite of the Zionist effort to negate diasporic life and envision the "New Jew" as an antithesis to Jewish life in the *Galut* (exile), the Galut features of Jewish life in Israel have persisted and intensified. Moreover, despite the strong presence of socialist elements in the early years of the Jewish state, from the outset American tradition, culture, and spirit were seen by Israelis as political and social models worthy of emulation. Israel's ongoing efforts to assimilate diverse waves of Jewish migration into a melting pot, its pioneering spirit, and its biblical connections, as well as the adoption of democratic principles, were perceived and presented as analogous to the American experience. To the extent that Israelis looked outward, it was always to the "American dream" as a point of reference. This link was reinforced in my childhood experience by the special military and political relations that have created a certain perception in the Israeli public that we are something of an extension of America, our big brother.

In 1983, I left Israel to pursue a Ph.D. program at Yale. I was just turning twenty-seven and had very little sense of the world outside of Israel. My formative American experience was what Eva Hoffman has called the problem of "Lost in Translation." The scope of the project ahead of me, including the large amount of reading and writing required in a foreign language, was almost overwhelming, yet at the same time challenging, exhilarating, and almost addictive. Yale's Sterling Memorial Library became my second home – perhaps even my first – and the more I became comfortable with reading and writing English (an ongoing, indeed lifelong, process), the more I became engaged in American life, interested in its history, and fascinated by its dynamics.

I became an avid consumer of American news and culture, from daily and weekly newspapers and magazines and late-night TV shows, to more literate commentary on American history and culture. Although I constantly evaluated my American experience through the Israeli prism, I found myself becoming more and more at home in my temporary adopted country. From Rogers Smith I learned about American identity. From my instructor, the late Joseph Hamburger, and my friend Steven Smith I studied the philosophy of the founding fathers and discovered Tocqueville. Robert Dahl and David Mayhew taught me about the workings of American politics and government. Juan Linz, my mentor, gave me the comparativist perspective when studying American institutions. It was during my years at Yale that debates on multiculturalism began to take center stage in American intellectual life. As I became embroiled in the political and scholarly debates over the growing assertion of ethnicity, I felt uneasy about the focus on America's domestic agenda and the absence of a transnational dimension. Richard Rodriguez's *Hunger of Memory* provoked my thought about bilingualism in a country of immigrants. I always felt that the recovery of Hebrew was the single most important factor in the Zionist revival, yet I bemoaned the intense pressure that had been exerted on my parents' generation to reject other languages as remnants of a despised diasporic existence. Joan Didion's *Miami* shifted my growing interest in exile and diasporic politics from the European to the American scene.

I began studying diasporic politics when I wrote my dissertation on the politics and the loyalty dilemmas of opposition groups in exile. The writing of Alexander Herzen taught me more about the subject than any subsequent readings. When in 1986 people across America were mobilized by African-American leaders to protest apartheid, I became convinced that "multiculturalism" is a deeply transnational phenomenon, which ties U.S. identity to international politics and transnational movements. When in 1990 Khachig Tölölyan asked me to join him in establishing *Diaspora: A Journal of Transnational Studies*, I was happy to find a friend with whom I have continued ever since my intellectual discovery. Professor Tölölyan's comments on this manuscript and our numerous discussions have enriched my work greatly.

I was always certain that my life in America was only a temporary stage before returning to my homeland. With my American wife Nancy Schnog, however, I felt that the "threat" of losing Zion was real. "Will my children ever know what Israel is all about?" Am I bound to send them to a Jewish Sunday school, which seemed to me, at the time, so diasporic – that is, lesser in comparison to Israel's "authentic Judaism." My early reluctance to take American citizenship, even when I was entitled to it, was certainly out of fear of confusing my identity and loyalty. It was Raymond Aron's writings on citizenship that reinforced my belief that citizenship largely defines one's national loyalty in interaction with members of other nation-states and denotes which government is responsible for an individual's security. In this respect, loyalty cannot be split. Yet, in recent years, with the declining role of nation-states as the sole determinant of national identity and the growing fusion of cultures across frontiers, I am no longer certain about the possibility of sustaining political or cultural uniformity, certainly not my own.

It was Nancy, a scholar of American Studies, who taught me more than anyone else about America. Her love of New England and her constant encouragement of me to read American literature have contributed a great deal to my understanding of America. The more I stayed in America, the more I became sensitive to and knowledgeable about Jewish issues (an effort I had never felt the need to make as a secular Israeli), and fascinated by the special character of diasporic institutions. I was also surprised to find myself so entrenched in American politics and society, almost an American patriot, defending the country's global importance in front of my academic friends, who were gloomy and could only see its international faults. Remember – those were the Reagan–Bush years.

Both my children, Eytan and Emily – to whom this book is dedicated – are American and Israeli citizens, speak English and Hebrew at home, and from the first day of their lives have felt natural in this duality. For years we lived in a perpetual state of transnational movement, shuttling between Middlebury, Vermont, where Nancy became a professor of American studies, and Tel-Aviv.

The idea of this book grew and developed during these years of wandering. Myron Weiner inspired me to think about the role of American diasporas when he invited me to talk about the subject in the context of regime change at the Center for International Studies at MIT in December 1991. His comments on an early draft and insightful remarks by Nathan Glazer helped me in rewriting an essay for Weiner's book, *International Migration and Security*, a version of which appeared in *Political Science Quarterly* (1994–95). This essay became the basis for Chapter 2 of this book. I wrote parts of Chapters 1, 2, and 4 when I was a visiting professor at Middlebury College. I am indebted to Murray Dry, Noah Pickus, Russell Leng, Mark Williams, and Michael Kraus, my colleagues at Middlebury, for perceptive comments and information. Michael Levin and Christina Yim, my students at Middlebury, provided valuable research assistance. Christine Dulongue, my research assistant, provided critical help when I began studying Mexican-Americans. I am also indebted to the International Fulbright Foundation and the American Council of Learned Societies for their generous financial support. Some early findings were published in *Diaspora* in spring 1994.

While I was a visiting professor at the Fletcher School of Law and Diplomacy, I began researching and drafting the materials for Chapters 3 and 4. I thank my student Yves-Rose Saint-Dic for teaching me about Haitian-Americans. Peter Berkovitz always provided an attentive ear. My analysis of Arab- and African-Americans as players in American foreign policy appeared in *Foreign Policy* in the fall of 1995. A generous fellowship at St. Antony's College enabled me to broaden my understanding of diasporic politics through the lens of the European experience. I remain indebted to my colleagues at St. Antony's as well as the people at the Center for Refugee Studies at Oxford for allowing me to share with them my thoughts. The Tami Steinmetz Center for Peace Research provided the financial backing for my research on Arab-Americans. During this research, I enjoyed the knowledge and hospitality of many people in Dearborn, Michigan, above all Ismael Ahmed, Sally Howell, Andrew Shryock, and Kay and Osama Siblani. I am also grateful to Yehudit Barsky, who provided valuable materials and the benefit of her ideas and views. Marc Kaplan provided valuable information for Chapter 4. I have gained a great deal from conversations with Philip Mattar, Nabeel Abraham, Michael Suleiman, Martin Kramer, Joshua Teitelbaum, and Barry Rubin. An early version of Chapter 3 was published as a monograph by the Tami Steinmetz Center, and a much shorter version appeared in the *Journal of Palestine Studies* (April 1996).

It was in England, surprisingly, that I began finding strong research links to the Mexican-American–Mexican relationship. The Mexican ambassador to the United Kingdom (and previously Mexican consul in Los Angeles), Andres Rozental, opened doors to sources in Mexico and provided important documents. Rodolfo O. de la Garza broadened my intellectual scope and directed my attention to many sources. The Mexican ambassador to Israel, Jorge Alberto Lozoya, who was personally involved in the Mexican Foreign Ministry's early diasporic plans, carefully read my work and provided excellent comments. Lozoya referred me to Professor Jorge Bustamante, the leading intellectual who facilitated the rapprochement between Mexico and its diaspora. His writings and our subsequent correspondence further benefited my analysis. Finally, Carlos Gonzalez Gutierrez, Director de Asuntos Comunitarios in the Mexican Foreign Ministry, who made use of my early findings in his own writing, enriched my own with his latest analysis of the Mexican diaspora. A version of Chapter 5 will appear in *Political Science Quarterly*.

Elizabeth Feingold, Wadia Abu-Nasser, Irit Tau, Guy Ben-Porat, and Shlomo Berman were excellent research assistants. They provided materials, helped in translations from Arabic and Spanish, and made critical comments. Many of my colleagues at Tel-Aviv University deserve my gratitude for reading, listening, and advising. David Vital posed many important questions early on. Avi Ben-Zvi shared with me his unparalleled insights into Israeli-American affairs. Aharon Klieman never forgot me when he came across relevant information, and he enriched my knowledge of U.S. foreign affairs. Azar Gat and Gil Merom made important comments and provided much-needed collegial support. Alberto Spektorowski helped in translating Spanish documents. Itai Sened, Gad Barzilai, Martin Sherman, Shaul Mishal, Eyal Chowers, and Neil Diamant offered their learned perspectives. Ety Lenman, my administrative assistant, was, as usual, indispensable. I am grateful to my editor, Alex Holzman, for his encouragement and enthusiasm throughout this process. Alex read the entire manuscript and his comments in the later stages contributed a great deal. The two anonymous readers of this manuscript provided great encouragement but, most important, astute criticism and illuminating comments.

My greatest thanks go to Barry Bristman. Barry's contributions cannot be overstated. They span the domains of research, editing, rewriting, typing, and, above all, thinking. He has kept me going at a time when I assumed an administrative responsibility as chair of the department, and he never failed to alert me to my intellectual shortcomings and factual mistakes. Barry read this manuscript numerous times, and I remain indebted to him for his preciseness.

Obviously, I remain solely responsible for the content and analysis of this book.

1

U.S. Diasporas and Homelands in the Era of Transnationalism

[T]he manner in which a state conceives and conducts its foreign
policy is greatly affected by [its] national particularities.
    Arthur M. Schlesinger Jr., *The Cycles of American History*, p. 5

Both the involvement of U.S. diasporas in the politics of their countries of origin (whether they be independent states or aspiring to
statehood) and their attempts to shape or at least influence American
diplomacy directed at their homelands have been long-standing preoccupations of American scholars and politicians. Students of American ethnicity and U.S. foreign affairs have debated how diasporas
shape American perceptions of what the U.S. national interest is and
have questioned whether diasporic identification with ancestral
homelands has hindered America's national cohesion and civic culture.[1] Although many scholars agree that U.S. diasporas are increasingly influential in shaping America's international relations, there
are in fact only limited comparative studies and inconclusive findings
as to whether and how diasporic dedication to the homeland's political affairs affects the American state and its culture.[2]

The uncertainty and lack of consensus on these questions are best
manifested in the changes over time found in the works of Louis
Gerson, among the pioneers in the study of American diasporas. In
The Hyphenate and Recent American Politics and Diplomacy, Gerson
alerted Americans to what he viewed in 1964 as the perils of ethnic
politics:

> Many ethnic leaders have been increasingly successful in making
> many Americans believe that they and their children and their
> children's children are duty-bound to act in their interest of their

ancestral land – that the emotional umbilical cord can never be severed. A belief is thus being perpetuated that the United States is a multinational state which cannot and should not be fully united. The doctrine, "once hyphenated, always hyphenated," is a threat to American unity, but it is more than a threat to the majority of immigrants and their descendants, whose loyalty and devotion to America – a sanctuary from the ills of their homelands – is unbounded.[3]

Thirteen years later, even though the civil rights movement had stirred the political activity of previously excluded groups, Gerson seemingly reversed himself to echo and share early twentieth-century author and playwright Israel Zangwill's optimism concerning the American melting pot. Such an optimism does not fear the emergent ethnic activism as a threat to continued ethnic integration:

> American culture and society have continuously been reinvigorated and shaped by successive waves of immigrant groups and their descendants. Without exception, all immigrants who decided to settle in the United States wanted to be integrated into the American society and gain full access to its values. This stands in sharp contrast to the experiences of ethnic minorities in other societies.[4]

Gerson's optimism has been questioned by some recent critics of the growing presence of "ethnic zealots" in American politics and culture, as well as by others who are troubled by what they see as alarming manifestations of intolerance and balkanization in America's big cities.[5] Journalist Tamar Jacoby has argued that

> in the past twenty years, in part with the sanction of the liberal establishment . . . we've come to think that we owe our primary allegiance to our particular small communities, that the big community is ill-defined, hard to get our hands on, and that underneath we are really different. We have a benign idea of a mosaic, but it never remains benign. It invariably degenerates into "us vs. them." There is a basic polarization and distrust that leads to friction on every issue. One wouldn't want to end all particular allegiances, but the pendulum has swung too far.[6]

Such critics of the rising tide of ethnicity are often rearticulating an old American fear that the devotion to ancestral homelands further exacerbates domestic ethnic strains and endangers the fabric of American society.[7] They point to numerous instances of domestic ethnic rivalries prompted or fueled by diasporic relations with ancestral lands; of these, the most salient current examples are taken to be the heated feuds between African- and Jewish-Americans and American Serbs and Croats. Equally relevant are the tensions between Hispanics and blacks in Miami, which grew primarily out of local struggles over cultural, economic, and political domination, but were heightened after the summer of 1990, when Miami Cuban-Americans snubbed South African civil rights leader Nelson Mandela for embracing Castro. In return, African-Americans declared a boycott of tourism that cost Miami's economy about $50 million and was lifted only in the summer of 1993.[8]

The fear of balkanization is not predictably or merely rhetorical, a cover for various forms of racism, though it can be that. Many observers sincerely wonder whether Americans remain united in their commitments and distanced from the politics of other countries, a distance that is regarded as essential for domestic stability. Their anxiety is characteristic, in that it replaces earlier American fears about the wars and discords of the rest of the world, which the United States sought to keep at bay and from which it made attempts to isolate itself, both by distance and, if necessary, by the coercion of its own citizens. Today, as various forms of state breakdown (e.g., the Soviet Union, Yugoslavia) multiply the number of countries aspiring to join the United Nations and also multiply wars and misery, Harvard's Charles S. Maier writes:

> The same tides of fragmentation that have overwhelmed the Balkans and the old Soviet Union also lap at Western democracies. Navigating this turbulent current in national and international politics requires a balancing commitment to *civic universalism*. If Americans wish to construct a new framework of international principles, they must take care not to encourage the same centrifugal impulses that contribute to conflicts they find so appalling abroad.[9]

In the past decade, questions of identity and culture have also been fueled by, and become an integral part of, the growing debate over immigration and America's absorptive capacities, with concern over the economic impact of migrants often serving as a pretext for consideration of more fundamental issues of national identity and civic culture. The ethnic makeup of the United States is changing very rapidly, as "almost all the recent migrants [have come] from Asia, Mexico, Central America and the Caribbean,"[10] a result of the lowering of immigration barriers since the 1960s, and especially since the mid-1980s. U.S. census figures released in 1992 indicate that 8.6 million immigrants were admitted to the United States during the 1980s,[11] and "[al]though migrants add less than 0.5 per cent to the U.S. population each year, immigrants and their offspring are expected to be responsible for almost two-thirds of the net population increase over the next 50 years." This would mean 70 million out of an overall increase of 106 million between 1990 and 2040, bringing the total U.S. population to 355 million.[12] In Los Angeles, the nation's second largest city, by the end of the 1980s "49.9 per cent [of residents] spoke a language other than English at home; 25.3 percent spoke Spanish."[13]

There is a strong American tradition of making political use of such statistics, with those expressing nativist sentiments portraying each successive wave of "unassimilable" immigrants as a prelude to imminent national disaster. Myron Weiner, noting John Higham's comments, writes that

> in 1888, the American Economic Association offered a prize of $150 for the best essay on the theme "The Evil Effects of Unrestricted Migration." . . . [its president] argued that migrants created unrest in the labor force and were a threat not only to American prosperity but also to social and political stability. He further voiced the fear that the immigrant flows consisted of people who were unassimilable to American values. "The entrance into our political, social and industrial life of such vast masses of peasantry . . . degraded below our utmost conceptions, is a matter which no intelligent patriot can look upon without the greatest apprehension and alarm."[14]

Despite what may charitably be described as the weak predictive ability of such doomsday prophecies, they have frequently resurfaced and continue to have a strong political impact, as demonstrated in 1994 by the overwhelming passage of California's antiimmigrant Proposition 187. Although fear of immigrants in the 1990s is sometimes couched in more sophisticated terminology than its nineteenth-century precursors, the message remains the same: "Immigration in general is a threat to the 'nation' that is conceived of as a singular, predominantly Euro-American, English-speaking culture."[15]

A somewhat new variation on an old theme is concern over the growing "transnationalism" of many immigrants, meaning that, far more than their predecessors, they keep "one foot" in their home country and the other in the United States. Improvements in transportation and communication and easier access across frontiers have increased immigrant mobility and contact with home countries, helping immigrants to remain a powerful political, economic, and social force in their homelands, and enabling political actors abroad to mobilize and vie for their support. When leading South Korean politicians rushed to Los Angeles after the 1992 riots promising financial support and diplomatic pressure to secure relief for Korean store owners who had suffered losses, they reinforced the image of Korean-Americans as a "colony" of the homeland.[16] At the same time, countries such as the Dominican Republic, Mexico, and Israel have extended or are considering extending voting rights to their diasporas. In March 1998, Mexico also opened a five-year window allowing emigrants who had lost their citizenship upon becoming U.S. citizens to apply to regain their economic and social rights as Mexican "nationals," a status more distinct in name than in substance from that of "citizen."[17] This is expected to result not only in significant numbers of naturalized U.S. citizens reclaiming Mexican nationality, but also in more Mexicans resident in the United States – no longer under threat of losing their rights as Mexicans – applying for American citizenship.

Some observers maintain that immigrants are far less likely to make efforts to assimilate or to acquire American citizenship due to their continued cultural attachments to their country of origin and the problems they face at home caused by renouncing their original citizenship. "American citizens further worry that even for those newcomers who do become citizens, group-oriented policies like the amended Voting Rights Act and bilingual education encourage them to identify as members of racial and ethnic groups rather than as members of the entire American people."[18] When the number of new immigrants seeking to acquire citizenship diminished, there were concerns over their lack of attachment to the United States. However, when large numbers rushed to become citizens in 1996–

97 because of new legislation limiting social benefits to noncitizens, concern was expressed over whether the motivation for acquiring citizenship was proper – that is, with America's national interest in mind.

The question has been raised as to whether the newcomers, who often hold dual citizenship, can be reconciled with the republican vision of citizenship in the United States. New U.S. citizens must swear that they "renounce and abjure all allegiance and fidelity to any foreign prince, potentate, state, or sovereignty, of whom or which [they] have heretofore been a subject or citizen." Yet the U.S. government does not compel "naturalizing citizens to prove that their renunciation is legally effective in the country of origin and does not prohibit native-born citizens from becoming citizens of other nations."[19] This, in effect, leaves space for multiple loyalties on the part of both native-born and naturalized American citizens. Regardless of whether immigrants take citizenship or choose to avoid it, proponents of immigration reform claim that "transnational immigrants threaten a singular vision of the 'nation' because they allegedly bring 'multiculturalism' and not assimilation."[20] In addition to being perceived as a threat to the cultural coherence of the United States, transnationalism has even been described as a challenge to the very sovereignty of the country. Massive immigration from Mexico and the new trend toward rapprochement and reconciliation between the Mexican government and Mexican-Americans have raised unfounded anxiety over Mexican political separatism.[21] "More than 7 million Mexican-born immigrants reside in the United States, and their U.S.-born offspring add up to millions more." Mexican-Americans make up the majority of the U.S. Hispanic community, projected to become the largest ethnic minority in the country within the next decade. "In Houston, the nation's fourth-largest city, Hispanics have overtaken 'Anglos' as the city's largest ethnic group, largely because of immigration from Mexico."[22]

Transnationalism has long had important political implications in the United States, with candidates at every level of government making "electoral pilgrimages" to places such as Israel, Ireland, and Italy. The destinations are changing, however, reflecting new demographic trends, particularly in America's large cities. For example, one of the candidates in the race for the 1997 Democratic mayoralty nomination in New York City visited the Dominican Republic in

November 1996 as part of her effort to gain the support of the 4 percent of voters of Dominican background, "the fastest-growing ethnic group in the city." In close elections like recent New York mayoralty races, such new communities can play a decisive role. "An estimated 100,000 voting-age adults [were] naturalized in the New York area in [1996]."[23]

The idea of a transnationalist threat to American unity has received new theoretical backing from Samuel Huntington's much-debated thesis, which stresses the expanding dominance of "civilizations" in world affairs and the persistence of "kin-country" and "diaspora" loyalties that run much deeper than assimilationists are willing to admit. In the post–cold war era, diasporic communities which are intensely involved in prolonged conflicts of their kin countries and/or communities muster considerable political influence over their host governments, redefine their national interest, and affect perceptions of identity in both their old and new countries of residence.[24] This thesis has particular bearing on the American context, where contemporary nativists and right-wingers have objected to immigrants from foreign countries as the "bearers of foreign and less desirable cultural values."[25] Given that by 2050 white America is expected to lose its majority to Hispanics, Asians, and blacks, Huntington wonders whether the trend toward "the de-Westernalization of the United Sates . . . means its de-Americanization in the democratic sense." He warns that, if the pillars of American identity – the democratic liberal principle and its European heritage – are further eroded, the United States might find itself, like the former Soviet Union, falling "onto the ash heap of history."[26]

Today, when the United States is searching for a new sense of purpose in its foreign relations, and multiculturalism has heightened concerns over the nature of American identity, it is time to reevaluate the international and domestic effects of U.S. diasporas. What is the role of U.S. diasporas in American foreign policy? Do their voices threaten to balkanize the American national interest, or are they constructive? What is the relationship between a diasporic group gaining an effective voice in U.S. foreign policy and its adoption of American political ideals? What function do ethnic lobbies serve in America's global role as the champion of democratic ideals? Does ethnic commitment to ancestral countries impede U.S. domestic cohesion and encourage subnational loyalties? And how do ethnic

Americans affect the identity and politics of their country of origin or symbolic homelands?

This book will examine all of these questions. It will be argued that the negative impact of ethnic involvement in U.S. foreign affairs has been exaggerated and even falsified. Involvement in U.S. foreign policy is in fact often one of the clearest indications that an ethnic community has "arrived" in American society, and that it has demonstrated its willingness not only to reinforce and uphold American values such as democracy and pluralism inside America, but to promote these values abroad. The marketing of values such as democracy, human rights, free-market economics, and religious pluralism is likely to reflect positively on U.S. civic culture by marginalizing contrary forces of isolationism and separatism, and discouraging tendencies toward domestic balkanization. In addition, by involving themselves in the affairs of their ancestral countries, U.S. diasporas become critical players in defining the national identity and political ethos of their homelands.

In this book, "diaspora" will be defined as a people with common ethnic-national-religious origin who reside outside a claimed or an independent home territory. They regard themselves and/or are regarded by others as members or potential members of their country of origin (claimed or already existing), a status held regardless of their geographical location and citizen status outside their home country. Members of a diaspora are called upon periodically by ethnonational elements inside or outside the home country's territory to subscribe to a particular cause or group as an expression of their ethnonational loyalty.[27]

Historically, diasporas in the United States have been highly dedicated to political causes in their country of origin, often seeing themselves as representatives of their old country abroad. Some older diasporas, like Jews, Greeks, and Italians, have often lived vicariously through their ancestral home countries, rather than actively trying to change their governments. Politics in the home country is important for their political identity in America, and they are more likely to support existing regimes whose policies coincide with American liberalism and/or U.S. foreign objectives and actively oppose those which do not. They tend to embrace their homeland in a way that is not threatening to their identity within the parameters of American pluralism, but they must always defend themselves against the charge of divided loyalties.

For example, the Jewish lobby in the United States has always portrayed its devotion to Israel (the symbolic homeland) as an extension of its allegiance to American democratic values and strategic interests. Jewish organizations have a relatively strong track record in terms of influencing U.S. government policy. Yet they have found themselves torn increasingly between their obligations to the symbolic homeland and the United States.[28] This conflict of interest derives from the Jewish position inside the United States vis-à-vis other ethnoracial and religious groups,[29] as well as the government. This discord is also compounded by the growing divergence in terms of culture and values between Israeli society and large segments of American Jewry.

During the last decade or so, the often acrimonious debate among orthodox Israeli Jews and their non-orthodox American counterparts over the status of Reform and Conservative Jewish conversions and religious observance has strained and confused American Jewish ties with Israel, shifting alignments of religious and political loyalty. The orthodox hegemony in Israel is no longer acceptable to the majority of American Jews, who have come to see in it a danger to their own identity as Jews. Consequently, we have witnessed a new campaign by American Jews to change religious practices inside the state of Israel by encouraging the growth of pluralistic denominations. This process, although still in its early stages, may very well have significant consequences for Israel's redefinition of its Jewish identity. Altogether, American Jews continue to maintain strong relations with Israel, a fact used by both the U.S. and the Israeli governments to advance their respective agendas. Indeed, the vulnerability of diasporas to the charge of dual loyalty is a lever that either home or host country can use to motivate or stymie diaspora political activity. Thus, diasporas may function as pawns used to communicate between the United States and their native countries.

The nature and range of diasporic involvement in the home country's affairs depend largely on the size and diversity of the overseas community and are highly affected by the ability of diasporic institutions to generate and sustain a sense of communal identity. Ethnic cohesion is a complex and multidimensional factor. It relates to levels of interaction among group members as well as their connection with outsiders. Laurence Kotler-Berkowitz has written that "interaction among ethnic group members occurs in social, political and economic structures; occupation, residence, education, politics, family and friendship networks, social organizations, and institutions are specific structural spheres within which ethnic group members interact. The more ethnic group members interact frequently and non-conflictually in structural spheres, the higher the level of ethnic cohesion."[30] Although on the face of it ethnic cohesion is the best condition for ethnic mobilization, cohesion that is insular can impede the ability of the group to break into positions of influence in the larger society and into mainstream political institutions. Altogether, it is often difficult to assess the size of the diaspora, its composition, distribution, and especially its propensity to engage in home country politics.

To gauge diasporic makeup and political tendencies, one must take into account different waves of migration and degrees of assimilation and identity in the host country, as well as the migration politics of the home country. As a scholar of overseas Chinese has recently observed, diasporic identities are constantly undergoing transformation, influenced by factors such as race relations in the United States, American relations with the home country, and the home country's policies toward its overseas constituencies.[31] Moreover, the durability of diasporic institutions and their success in appropriating and activating old identities (ethnic, cultural, religious, or national) is greatly influenced by factors in plural societies that drive ethnic group members "to break with cultural traditions and develop different cultural activities and patterns, leading to cultural division."[32] The host government's view of the home regime (friend or foe) as well as the host society's changing perception of ethnic diversity is also a critical factor in sustaining diasporic identity and politics. For example, despite their rapid Americanization, by 1914 German-Americans still remained "by far the best organized of all foreign elements"[33] in the United States. However, war frenzy and growing suspicion of German-Americans' alliance with the pan-German movement in Berlin prompted American demands for total assimilation and unqualified renunciation of past loyalties. By 1940, the few remnants of German identity and institutions that had survived the anti-German phobia of World War I were completely suppressed, never to be revived (see Chapter 2).[34]

Older diasporas in the United States are composed mostly of naturalized and American-born citizens who are by now an integral part of the American ethnic mosaic. More recent diasporas, however, may consist of large segments of non-American citizens, including illegal and resident aliens, refugees, and political exiles. The latter group's involvement in the home country's politics is often more intense, though it is restricted legally and politically and has distinct implications vis-à-vis the homeland. Yet even this broad dichotomy between diasporas whose host state is their country of citizenship and diasporas whose home state is the state of nationality is far from precise. In fact, the status of a temporary resident, an immigrant, a refugee, a U.S. citizen, or an exile is always in flux, changing according to the individual's self-identification in the United States and the home government's legal and ideological denotation of overseas nationals – primarily issues concerning dual citizenship and naturalization rules among states, that is, *ius soli* (birthplace) or *ius sanguinis* (blood) – as well as political and social developments in the home country.

For analytical purposes, one can identify, following Alicja Iwańska, three ideal groups involved in diasporic politics: "core members" or organizing elites who are intensively active in diasporic affairs; "rear guard members" or past diaspora activists who have drifted away; and all other "silent" members whom diaspora elites, host governments, or home governments consider as potential recruits for diasporic politics.[35] While core and rearguard members are more accessible to empirical scrutiny, members of the third group are mostly part of an "imagined community," to use Benedict Anderson's expression, often existing only in the mind of diasporic political activists, as well as home or host governments. Some members of the imagined community "can identify with their perception of the old country or homeland, transforming it into a symbol which leaves out its domestic or foreign problems";[36] others may reject any attempt to identify them as diaspora constituents. Some diasporic elites are made up of political exiles who are contestants for power in the homeland, whereas other diaspora leaders do not seek power in the homeland and their commitment is not to a particular political program. Rather, they see themselves as supporters of the home country's national interest as a whole.

Early Challenges

For most of its history, American public life was dominated by its Anglo-Saxon elite, which aspired to homogeneity and hegemony. Of course, the country was never homogenous: at first Native Americans and African-Americans, then German-Americans and, after the 1840s, Irish-Americans and others made that homogeneity a fiction. But at least until World War I, the dominant culture represented white Americans of northwest European origin as generally superior, culturally and even biologically, to all other races and civilizations. Protestantism was also represented as God's chosen religion, morally and politically superior to Catholicism, Judaism, or Islam.[37] Despite the Revolution against the British and the War of 1812, during the long period of successful domination Anglo-American elites molded American foreign policy to affirm the greatness and to promote the interests of Anglo-Saxon America, which was perceived to be part of a greater English race.[38] Indeed, although Anglo-Americans were often divided in terms of state loyalties during the period between the Revolution and the Civil War, they still retained a strong sense of their common ethnocultural identity and saw themselves "as members of an Anglo-Saxon diaspora in North America."[39]

The genealogy of ethnic involvement in U.S. foreign policy should be traced back to the first time this British orientation resulting from the glorification of the Anglo-Saxon race was confronted and challenged. After the potato blight, the mysterious fungal disease of the mid-1840s that, combined with British incompetence and indifference, caused a famine killing about 12 percent of the Irish population (more than one million people) and spurring a massive exodus to American shores,[40] a politically active Irish diaspora emerged. The famine and the consequent emigration remains the defining event of the Irish-American experience until this day, and its impact on American society in general was also profound. The large influx of migrants it generated gave the country its first large urban underclass and created "the first great ethnic 'minority' in American cities."[41] It "ended forever [America's] white Anglo-Saxon

Protestant complexion. And it established America's cities as places of ethnic strife."[42]

The dominant Anglo-American population at the time of the famine was unwilling to accept Irish-American expressions of religious and cultural differences as being consistent with American national identity. The self-conception of Anglo-American Protestants and the role assigned to England "as the homeland of Protestant reformation and political liberty"[43] excluded Catholics: "When Irish Catholics sought to have their children excused from reading the King James Bible in public schools, evangelical Protestants concluded that there was a papist plot to remove the Bible from the schools. The anti–Irish Catholic Philadelphia riots in May and July 1844 were among the most violent events before the Civil War. Not until the middle of the twentieth century did a majority of Protestant Americans come to believe that there was no conflict between Catholicism and American identity."[44]

By the 1850s, Irish-Americans began to engage in significant efforts to drive a wedge into the British-American alliance and to challenge Anglo-American hegemony, an effort further emboldened by the sympathy that the textile-manufacturing British commercial elite showed for the cotton growers of the secessionist South during the Civil War. Many of the Irish immigrants regarded themselves as *political* exiles, victims of " 'British misgovernment,' 'Protestant ascendancy,' and 'landlord tyranny.' "[45] Irish militants, particularly the Fenian Brotherhood, ventured to advance from afar the idea of an independent Irish Republic by dragging Washington into a war with the British Empire: in fact, "the United States presented Irish nationalism with a second front."[46] In 1866, in the first clear instance of direct Irish-American influence on U.S. policy toward Great Britain and Ireland, President Andrew Johnson allowed "the United States to be used as a fundraising center and staging ground for an Irish-American invasion of Canada."[47] Johnson acted in order to secure the votes of New York City Irish-Americans in midterm congressional elections, with "the added benefit of pandering to lingering American resentment over Britain's aid to the Confederacy during the Civil War."[48] The Fenian conspiracy to "liberate" an Irish zone in Canada as a symbolic expression of independence ended in a fiasco, however, and British-American differences arising from the Civil War were resolved in an 1871 treaty.[49]

The Great War and the Fear of Transnational Loyalties

During and immediately after World War I, when it seemed likely that the dismemberment of the old empires (Habsburg, Tsarist, and Ottoman) would create at least some new countries, Americans of east European descent became preoccupied with the fate of their homelands. Woodrow Wilson's proclamation of the principle of self-determination further fueled the political commitment of Poles, Czechs, Slovaks, Ukrainians, Lithuanians, Armenians, Albanians, and Croats. They all lobbied vigorously for American recognition of and support for the postwar independence and border designation of their homelands, carefully trying to blend into their campaigns the home country's agenda and the interests of the United States, and always stressing their own impeccable record as American loyalists. It should be noted, however, that President Wilson's genuine sympathy for the independence of many European peoples was nevertheless closely related to his personal political ambition. The president, who was vying for reelection, tolerated "hyphenates if they could bring him political benefit."[50] His support of Polish independence and of Zionism was largely a matter of political expediency. In recent years, the resurgence of nationalism and the revival of secessionist claims in eastern Europe and the former Soviet Union have also stirred many of the eastern European diasporas in the United States, whose members have campaigned vigorously on behalf of their homelands' right to independence.

Throughout American history, immigrant groups have asserted their identification with their native lands in large part as a result of their communal experiences in America. In many cases, they have become more fervent nationalists in the United States than they ever were in their countries of origin.[51] They have also often found that they could unify and mobilize an American diaspora more effectively by pursuing goals overseas, relating to their homeland, than when struggling over domestic and community issues in the United States.

Around the turn of the twentieth century, "hyphenated American" was a term of contempt used by nativists to question the allegiance of immigrants.[52] In response, immigrants used "hyphenism" mostly as an emblem of communal pride. When ethnic

Americans saluted and celebrated their homeland, their ancestral identity was not incompatible with their loyalty to America. Yet
the events of World War I revealed and underscored the possibilities and perils of hyphenation and the risks posed by affinity
with the homeland, even for assimilated groups, for example, whose
countries of origin "opposed America's war efforts."[53] Thus, "the
fact that Norway had remained neutral in the struggle between the
United States and Germany, meant that many Norwegian-American
leaders . . . were eager to demonstrate their group loyalty to America."[54] Moreover, while eastern Europeans were permitted and even
encouraged to display their attachment to their homelands, which
were to a large extent ruled by Germanophone nations, war frenzy
and growing suspicion of German-Americans' possible allegiance
to the pan-German movement prompted demands for their total
assimilation and unqualified renunciation of past loyalties. Toward the end of the war, German-Americans, the largest and
most organized diasporic lobby in the United States prior to World
War I, dropped the hyphen and disavowed their earlier commitments.[55]

War and the fear of transnational alliances sharpened the ever
present debate over American identity and loyalty. An earlier racism
was rekindled and thrived in the nativism of the 1920s, "itself an
encore [of] the hyperpatriotism and attacks on hyphenates that had
marred the war years."[56] Of course, "Americanism" (and its extreme
version, nativism) had always been at least as dominant as the liberal
and republican conceptions of American citizenship,[57] but, with the
racist exception of the Chinese Exclusion Act of 1882, during the
later nineteenth century this nativism had not led to numerous restrictions on applicants for immigration.[58]

Despite certain misgivings on the part of native-born white Americans over the potential negative impact of newcomers on American
society, Noah Pickus has written that the turn of the century was
generally characterized by broad confidence "in the assimilative powers of American culture."[59] This spirit, manifested in Israel Zangwill's popularization of the image of the melting pot, did not, however, manage to survive the general suspicion of several national
groups created by World War I. The "Great War" eroded the
vestiges of many people's confidence in "America's absorptive capac-

ities" and made room for the expression of both genuine anxiety and racist anger over the assimilability of people of color and of southern and eastern Europeans.[60]

The best-known criticism of the "reverberatory effect of the great war" on the American belief in the melting pot came from Randolph Bourne in his famous 1916 essay, "Transnational America." This essay was the first serious effort to deal with the strong nexus of relations between the "homeland factor" in the lives of ethnic America and the changing nature of the American national identity. Bourne attacked the Anglo-Saxon demand that assimilation and the melting pot concept required the abandonment of cultural attachment to homelands. He called on Anglo-American conservatives to recognize the wonderful advances American society enjoyed as the result of the arrival of new people who "save us from our own stagnation."[61] According to Bourne, the stigmatization of hyphenation and attempts to homogenize Americans destroyed the true spirit of America – to "Anglo-Saxonize" newcomers was to inhibit America's future:

> It is not the Jew who sticks proudly to the faith of his fathers and boasts of that venerable culture of his who is dangerous to America, but the Jew who has lost the Jewish fire and become a mere elementary, grasping animal. It is not the Bohemian who supports the Bohemian schools in Chicago whose influence is sinister, but the Bohemian who has made money and has got into world politics. Just so surely as we tend to disintegrate these nuclei of nationalistic culture do we tend to create hordes of men and women without a spiritual country, without taste, without standards but those of the mob. We sentence them to live on the most rudimentary planes of American life. The influences at the center of the nuclei are centripetal. They make for the intelligence and the social values which mean an enhancement of life. And just because the foreign-born retains this expressiveness is he likely to be a better citizen of the American community.[62]

Bourne sharply disagreed with those who believed that homeland cultural maintenance on the part of newcomers posed a threat in terms of national loyalty. He perceived a greater problem in what he saw as excessive Anglo-American loyalty to Britain and its culture:

> There may be a difference between these earlier and these later stocks, but it lies neither in motive for coming nor in strength of

cultural allegiance to the homeland. The truth is that no more tenacious cultural allegiance to the mother country has been shown by any alien nation than by the ruling class of Anglo-Saxon descendants in these American States. English snobberies, English religion, English literary styles, English literary reverences and canons, English ethics, English superiorities, have been the cultural food that we have drunk in from our mothers' breasts. The distinctively American spirit – pioneer, as distinguished from the reminiscently English – that appears in Whitman and Emerson and James, has had to exist on sufferance alongside of this other cult, unconsciously belittled by our cultural makers of opinion. No country has perhaps had so great indigenous genius which has had so little influence on the country's traditions and expressions.[63]

Bourne was a true champion of the dynamism of American nationalism: "Whatever American nationalism turns out to be, we already know that it will have a color richer and more exciting than our ideal has hitherto encompassed."[64] John Gerard Ruggie has written that in the time since Wilson expressed his fear that American involvement against Germany "might unleash serious domestic clashes" inside the United States, concern over "potential instability in domestic ethnic politics" has prompted foreign-policy decision makers to favor "multilateral organizing principles for constructing/reconstructing the international order" over specific policies that favored ethnic Americans' homelands.[65]

Interwar Nativists and the Predicament of Japanese-Americans

In 1917, Congress began the process that by 1923–24 led to the adoption of "national origins quotas," which banned virtually all Asians and permitted European immigration only in ratios preserving the northern European cast of the American citizenry.[66] The limitation on the influx of European immigration accelerated the assimilation of those groups that had come earlier.[67] Indeed, the decades following World War I were marked by the silencing of ethnic expression and minority politics, as recalled by Michael Walzer:

I remember, for example, how in the 1930s and 1940s any sign of Jewish assertiveness – even the appearance of "too many" Jewish names among New Deal Democrats or CIO organizers or socialist and communist intellectuals – was greeted among Jews with a collective shudder. The communal elders said, "Sha!" Don't make noise; don't attract attention; don't push yourself forward; don't say anything provocative. They thought of themselves as guests in this country long after they became citizens.[68]

The timidity of ethnic minorities also meant the downplaying of affinities with homelands, especially those perceived as enemies or as otherwise incompatible with American self-definition or national interests. Americans of all nationalities were expected to manifest their clear loyalty to the United States. In the 1920s, "the atmosphere of civic ceremonies and anniversaries was charged with the celebration of patriots and ancestors. Stimulated by the unprecedented efforts of the Wilson administration during the war to excite sentiments of loyalty and devotion to the state and the nation, the twenties and early thirties witnessed a number of extremely large historical celebrations that made a definite impact on the entire nation."[69] Ethnic leaders of this period made efforts to incorporate homeland elements into this celebration of American identity, commemorating ethnic homeland heroes who were in fact political activists, but who were usually also cultural figures (such as poets) and therefore more acceptable to the American "mainstream."[70]

During the interwar period, American radical nativism persisted and as many as five million Americans joined white supremacist groups like the Ku Klux Klan.[71] The Great Depression further fanned the flames of nativism. Unemployment, which generated economic pressures against immigration, compounded with nativist restrictionism, facilitated the mass expulsion of hundreds of thousands of people of Mexican origin, including naturalized citizens. Mexico, which at the time was eager to receive a supply of workers with U.S. job experience, collaborated in effecting this massive repatriation (see Chapter 5). In the case of Jews seeking to flee Nazism, American xenophobic feelings were also compounded by widespread anti-Semitism. Thus, despite direct personal appeals by prominent Jews to the president and Congress to open the gates to Jewish refugees, "The Abandonment of the Jews" became a major feature of this period of American restrictionism.[72]

World War II and the attack on Pearl Harbor elevated the suspicion of ethnic diasporas to new heights. The American government's magnified and indeed exaggerated fear of divided loyalties among citizens of German, Italian, and especially Japanese descent produced a series of policies intended to "adjust, accommodate, and reconcile the ancestral emotions" of the diasporas to their new country.[73] The traumatic relocation and internment of over 110,000 Japanese-Americans in the 1940s is the most dramatic chapter in the U.S. annals of racial prejudice and discrimination on the basis of alleged loyalty toward an ancestral homeland.[74]

Like many other diasporic populations in the United States, Japanese-Americans exhibited strong emotional and cultural homeland affinities. In comparison with European-origin diasporas of the inter-war era, Japanese-Americans' ties to their homeland were even more significant relative to their involvement in the "American mainstream," in large part due to physical differences, which were the focus of racist attitudes. Japanese-American social, cultural, and political organizations of the first part of the twentieth century included some that maintained contact with, or even received financial support from, Japan,[75] but most Japanese-Americans focused on assimilating into the broader American culture, despite constraints imposed by white American attitudes. "Whatever the hold of the Japanese government over Japanese aliens . . . its influence over American citizens of Japanese ancestry was undoubtedly limited to a relatively small group."[76]

The suspicion and charges of disloyalty against the west coast Japanese in the years leading up to and during World War II were based to some extent on issues of dual citizenship status. Japanese diplomats often interceded on behalf of their nationals living in the United States, as was the case in other homeland-diaspora relationships, but this did not have any great relevance to the political loyalties of the overwhelming majority of Japanese-Americans.[77] This was really a pretext for, and a rationalization of, official racist behavior in the United States, rather than a legitimate basis for concern, but it was used nevertheless. Japanese legal reforms in 1916 and 1924 significantly relaxed the rules of citizenship acquisition and renunciation by Japanese born or living overseas, changes that had been requested by Japanese-Americans.[78] Dual citizenship among Japanese-Americans dropped from 47 to 25 percent from 1930 to 1943, according to one account.[79] As a result, when the United States entered World War II after the attack on Pearl Harbor, Japanese-

Americans found themselves caught between an identity they had sought to leave behind (Japanese citizens) and one that was being denied them (fully "accepted" U.S. citizens) because of presumed loyalty to their homeland. Popular charges of disloyalty may still be used against ethnic groups, even in the 1990s, as Arab-Americans experienced in the wake of incidents such as the bombing of New York's World Trade Center in 1993. One difference in recent years has been that the "system" is much more careful in its response to such accusations, as demonstrated by President Clinton's 1995 warning to the American public not to draw hasty, race-based conclusions about the identity of the perpetrators of the federal building bombing in Oklahoma City. In the first hours after the bombing, fingers were already being pointed by some at Arab-Americans (see Chapter 3).

At a special gathering of practitioners and scholars on American identity held at Duke University in 1997, some scholars expressed the view that the growing tendency toward dual nationality prevailing in the United States does not really raise serious "questions of disloyalty . . . only of interests and identities and of different modes of social contribution."[80] Others argue, however, that "formal membership in two nations threatens the fragile sense of national unity that makes possible the integration of all those other identities."[81] Both sides of this debate agree that the growth of transnational connections makes the proliferation of multiple national identities virtually unstoppable. What remains to be seen is how American society will cope with multiple individual loyalties in times of crisis or conflict with other nations.

The Slow Opening

With the end of World War II, dominant public opinion again began the slow shift that would eventually favor a genuine pluralism of race, ethnicity, and diaspora. Of course, official racism lingered into the mid-1960s, when the quota system ruling immigration was finally repealed, but the American participation in the war against Nazism and its ideology of Aryan supremacy "had [already begun to make] racial segregation at home and pejorative references to race in public a serious embarrassment" before then.[82] This statement most convincingly applies to the Jewish community, for which the postwar period was a golden age, as anti-Semitism was no longer respectable and "had to be tucked away in private clubs, locker rooms, bars."[83] Just as Jewish ethnicity slowly ceased to be a barrier in socioeconomic life, so also a diasporic activism on behalf of the emergent state of Israel became first acceptable and eventually influential, providing the potent example of combined domestic toleration and foreign policy influence to which other ethnic groups would eventually aspire.

When David Ben-Gurion declared Israel's independence on May 14, 1948, the United States immediately extended de facto recognition to the newborn state. This act has long been viewed as the result of pressure by Jewish voters, and as the beginning of the rise of "Jewish power" in U.S. foreign policy. While Jewish lobbying and electoral pressures undoubtedly played important roles in President Truman's decision, other factors were involved, including the knowledge of impending Soviet recognition of the new state, and Truman's assessment that Israel would indeed survive its war of independence to become a significant actor on the Middle Eastern political stage. Recognition of Israel was an aberration in an American foreign policy that in general attempted carefully to avoid even the perception of partisanship in Middle Eastern conflicts. Truman endeavored to decouple the recognition decision from the general course of American policy and domestic politics, and his decision to impose an arms embargo on the Middle East (which was directed primarily against Israel), despite contrary pressures from the American Jewish community, is a major illustration in this respect.[84] The pro-Israel lobby in the United States did not really come of age politically until after the 1959 creation of the America Israel Public Affairs Committee (AIPAC), and, even then, American strategic interests continued to be by far the most important element in the making of U.S. Middle East policy.

As the containment of communism became America's chief foreign policy objective after 1945 (Kennan's classic article was published in July 1947 in *Foreign Affairs*), domestic concerns over activism by east European ethnic groups whose homelands were labeled "captive nations" receded. "In the 1952 presidential campaign, the Republicans made political capital over the alleged failure of the Democrats to keep eastern Europe from falling under Soviet control."[85] Eisenhower's previous role commanding NATO forces in Europe had given him direct experience of the then intractable Soviet grip on eastern Europe, yet his recognition of the growing importance of the "white ethnic vote" led him to the rather cynical election promise to "roll back" Soviet influence in the region. When workers rioted in East Germany in 1953 and Hungarians overturned their Stalinist regime in 1956, the Eisenhower administration made it clear to Moscow that it would not intervene. Eisenhower was very careful to do nothing that could provoke a military confrontation with the Soviet Union. This inability to keep promises to ethnic voters was balanced to some extent by cold war rhetoric on the issue of absorbing refugees from Communist countries, but many conservative Republicans and voters of east European ancestry felt betrayed.[86]

After World War II, as ethnic diversity increased both quantitatively and in terms of social permissibility, cultural pluralists and internationalists adhered to the vision of America as the "house of all peoples."[87] However, the movement toward this sort of internationalism did not develop evenly for all groups. In the 1950s, the internationalism of black Americans – which in the 1920s extended to the Caribbean and had begun to encompass pan-Africanism – faced diverse pressures not even to appear to be linked to communism, either in the emerging postcolonial African states or at home, so that it retreated as "black leaders felt obliged to confirm their loyalty to the United States and to demonstrate that their civil rights campaign was not Communist inspired, at a time when many conservative Americans were ready to believe that Communist instigation lay behind black demands for civil equality."[88] Thus, the picture remained mixed even as it improved for some ethnic groups: the assimilative and monolithic vision of American identity that stressed conformity and homogeneity on Anglo-Saxon Protestant terms had powerful effects even as it declined into the 1960s.[89]

The civil rights movement and the steadily increasing tolerance for ethnicity culminated in the 1965 Immigration Act, which "scrapped the older system of national quotas."[90] This change of immigration policy, in turn, vastly enlarged both the actual number of foreign-born Americans and the aspiring diasporic actors who would seek to influence American foreign policy. As mentioned earlier, a voice in foreign policy has been regarded by ethnic elites and the public at large as a sign of inclusion within American society, a step in the direction of affecting the national interest, and a springboard to participation and respectability in other spheres. Cynthia McKinney, an African-American Congressional representative from Georgia who has taken on a leadership role in fighting for greater U.S. investment in Africa, considers the attainment of a significant influence on foreign policy as a move critical to breaking "one of the last vestiges of the old plantation."[91]

Indeed, the recent success of ethnic diasporas in influencing U.S. diplomacy vis-à-vis their homelands is a manifestation of this process. It is made possible by and embedded in the nature of American party politics and the power of constituency politics, which often enable small, well-organized groups to greatly influence individual congressmen or to even have an impact on foreign policy through local governments. In addition, diasporas have benefited from their increasing access to U.S. and international media. For example, the Dag Hammarskjold Plaza across the street from the United Nations building has become a theater of diasporic protests; most are not reported, but those that are have a significant impact on political discussion. Above all, diasporic leverage on U.S. foreign policy has increased as ethnic groups become "less and less inhibited by fears of disloyalty and charges of 'hyphenated Americanism' from engaging in open lobbying and pressures to advance the claims of homelands or countries . . . that have become symbolic homelands."[92]

Among the newly empowered diasporas that have come to exert influence on American foreign politics in recent decades are African-Americans, Cubans, Haitians, Koreans, Filipinos, Chinese, Asian Indians, Vietnamese, Dominicans, and Mexicans. These diasporas, like Jewish-, Greek-, Italian-, and German-Americans before them, and similar to the recently reinvigorated Armenians and eastern Europeans, have also been courted by political aspirants in their ancestral countries, who try to influence U.S. policy through them. Their growing clout in U.S. domestic politics has altered homeland perceptions of these diasporas and, more importantly, has led to changes in national identity (social, cultural, economic, and political) within the homelands themselves. In the case of Mexico, for example, years of estrangement and mutual suspicion between the homeland and its U.S.-based diaspora are being replaced by a more cooperative relationship, built in large part on official Mexican initiatives to reincorporate the diaspora into a newly "reimagined" Mexican nation. According to the U.S. Census Bureau, in 1994 there were more than

6.2 million people living in the United States who were born in Mexico, 4 million of whom arrived since the late 1980s.[93] While the majority of this number were recognized as legal immigrants under the Immigration Reform and Control Act of 1986 (IRCA), by the mid-1990s millions still remained undocumented aliens or permanent residents without citizenship. When this number is added to the approximately 14 million American citizens of Mexican origin, and with the continuous influx of new immigrants, it is clear that the Mexican diaspora is fast becoming one of the largest ethnic minorities in the United States.

Since the late 1980s, when official Mexico finally recognized the potential impact of its diaspora, the Mexican government has moved to strengthen Mexican-American ties with the homeland. The diaspora's increasing influence on Mexican interests, the growing network of nongovernmental contacts across the border, and the need to give Mexican migrants greater protection all led to the creation of the Program for Mexican Communities Living in Foreign Countries (PMCLFC). The program "reshaped Mexico's foreign policy to resemble that of other countries" that maintained strong and mutually beneficial ties with their large diasporas. "Both in the immediate context of consular action, as well as in the broader context of public opinion, the PMCLFC raised the significance of U.S. citizens of Mexican origin."[94]

Although initially seen as the fulfillment of diasporic requests for assistance, the PMCLFC's importance for Mexico itself soon became apparent. The new relationship between Mexico and its U.S.-based diaspora has been used repeatedly in efforts to influence U.S. policy in a variety of spheres, including foreign policy, the most notable example being the all-out lobbying effort to secure U.S. passage of the North American Free Trade Agreement (NAFTA) in 1993. In the ongoing Mexican debate about national identity, the PMCLFC helped prompt the ultimately successful reconsideration of Mexican statutes depriving emigrants who became U.S. citizens of their home country nationality (as discussed earlier in this chapter).[95]

The Domestic and International Nexus: Cultural Pluralism and Its Discontents

As noted already, one of the signs that a diaspora has achieved a respectable position in American life today is its acquisition of a meaningful voice in U.S. foreign affairs. In the past few decades, newly empowered diasporas have endeavored to translate their clout in domestic affairs "into a beneficial foreign policy impact on their 'ethnic homeland' societies."[95] Yet Alexander DeConde, a senior diplomatic historian, has recently argued in *Ethnicity, Race and American Foreign Policy* that despite their apparent successes, newly empowered diasporas have in fact had little impact and are able to affect U.S. policy only within the parameters dictated by an abiding Anglo-American elite. Although DeConde acknowledges that "ethnoracial concerns have always been, and still remain a prominent determinant of American foreign policy,"[97] he maintains that diasporic influence is being greatly exaggerated. He concludes that the impact of newly empowered diasporas is much more crucial in the domestic arena, where the Anglo-Saxon elite's cultural domination has been in decline.[98] This observation, however, is in tension with and indeed seems to run counter to DeConde's assertion that there is a strong correlation between the changes in American identity and in challenges to Anglo-Saxon domination of U.S. foreign policy.[99]

The important question that is immediately posed by this disparity is, therefore, whether there truly is such a discrepancy between ethnic clout in domestic and foreign affairs. How is it possible, in other words, that domestically America is becoming a multicultural state while in foreign affairs it remains unicultural? Is the divergence in Anglo-Saxon hegemony the product of different power structures in the domestic and foreign domains, or is it the outcome of different sets of interests and values that rule each sphere?

To begin to unravel these complicated issues one must start by examining the correlation between the dominant ideals in American foreign and domestic policies. Domestically, American society became politically freer and ethnically more diverse with each new wave of migration and the elimination of racial restrictions. Consequently, the Anglo-Saxon assimilationist vision, which generally treated American culture and values as static and Anglicized in nature,[100] has given way in recent decades to the pluralist one, encompassing those of non-European descent. There are, of course, different interpretations as to the nature and impact of such pluralism (to what extent it breeds either unity or balkanizing tendencies). In principle, the pluralist vision holds that America as a singular union must respect the smaller plural unions that it contains, even though it still refuses "to endorse or support their way of life or to take an active interest in their social reproduction, or to allow any of them to seize state power."[101] In other words, emergent American pluralism held that liberal civic democratic values, which are universalist, remain superior to the values of the plural ethnic unions. As Steven C. Rockefeller has written recently, the singular union critically evaluates the plural unions

> in the light of the way they give distinct concrete expression to *universal* capacities and values. The objective of a liberal democratic culture is to respect – not to repress – ethnic identities and to encourage different cultural traditions to develop fully their potential for expression of the democratic ideals of freedom and equality, leading in most cases to major cultural transformations. How diverse cultures accomplish this task will vary, given the rich variety worldwide of the forms of democratic life. Cultures can undergo significant intellectual, social, moral, and religious changes while maintaining continuity with their past.[102]

American domestic pluralism is possible, therefore, because liberalism assumes that diverse cultures will nevertheless prefer, express, and adhere to the same democratic values when allowed to flourish and attain the best that is in them. Aside from this assumption, which is also a prescription, liberalism does not ask much of its citizens. It asks them to extend to others the same rights they themselves claim; it does not require them to exercise these rights in any distinctive manner. American ethnic identity is thus pluralistic within a wide range of possibilities, but its boundaries – enshrined in rights as understood by law – require equal rights and tolerance toward other groups. The engine for this type of pluralism is the appreciation by different ethnic and cultural groups of the freedom and opportunity accorded them, as groups, within a singular union. This vision has been called the integrationist pluralist model (as opposed to cultural pluralism). It "emphasizes the *protection of cultural practices that are compatible with liberalism*." It also discourages or forbids illiberal practices in the name of ancestral values or cultural rights.[103]

Two types of criticism of this integrationist pluralist description of American reality have been presented in recent years. On the one hand, there are those who contest the mere possibility that American society, politics, and culture are open to synchronization along the lines described in the pluralist theory, pointing to the strong hegemony of Anglo-Saxon elites. On the other hand, there are those who argue that American pluralism has gone too far and, in fact, has reached the point of cultural nationalism, which threatens the very fabric of American civic culture and democratic liberal values. Those who belong to the first school, also known as the American left, often argue that, despite the advances made during the civil rights era that reduced ethnoracial discrimination, society enshrined discrimination through other mechanisms – through psychological, sociological, cultural, and economic structures that ensure the continued hegemony of white Anglo-Saxon elites and continue to inhibit the access of minorities and their upward mobility. Ronald Takaki expresses this vision:

> Due to racially exclusionist forces and developments in American history, racial inequality and occupational stratification have come to coexist in a mutually reinforcing and dynamic structural relationship which continues to operate more powerfully than direct forms of racial prejudice and discrimination. To diminish the significance of racial oppression in America's past and to define racial inequality as a problem of prejudice and limit the solution as the outlawing of individual acts of discrimination . . . is effectively to leave intact the very structures of racial inequality.[104]

There are those who believe, however, that "the democratic cultural pluralist ideal, with its stress on tolerance of divers communal groups, tends to deprecate the importance or even the existence of a common national identity."[105] While some argue that the liberal pluralist version of America, *e pluribus unum* (out of many one), should not, in principle, conflict with the vision of America as a "multicultural society" in which the particular communities tolerate each other within the institutional boundaries described earlier, others reject the possibility of reconciling liberal pluralism with multiculturalism. Joseph Raz has written that even if certain communities and cultures "are themselves intolerant . . . [they] will face great pressure for change in [the American] multicultural society."[106] Raz also points out that the liberal pluralist version of multiculturalism "should not be seen as an opponent of the assimilationist idea that advocates the integration of one cultural group by others . . . so long as the process is not coerced, does not arise out of lack of respect for people and their communities, and is sufficiently gradual."[107] Thus, American cultural pluralism endorses selective borrowing and cultural syncretism, which are the hallmarks of open liberal societies.

This version of integrationist pluralism does not seem so benign to critics of "militant multiculturalism," however, who see the move toward institutionalizing cultural diversity as carrying the seeds of American balkanization. Liberal multiculturalism has been described by many critics as too idealistic, a false reflection of American current reality, or even as a pretext for cultural separatists who are abusing the "American way" in order to undermine the American national idea. As some critics have written, "by stressing the normative priority of ethnic group identity [multiculturalism] implies that no national creed does, can, or should exist and provides no ideological cement to combine diverse groups into a single 'imagined community.' " Consequently "multiculturalism clearly has the potential to push the United States toward [disintegration]."[108]

Indeed, many critics of heightened ethnic pluralism have argued that what began as efforts to establish a truly pluralist-liberal society that fosters genuine recognition of cultures and ethnic minorities, as well as equal access to policy decision making, has taken a twist toward "multicultural nationalism" or the creation of "national minorities." According to such critics this type of multiculturalism challenges the mere idea of an integrative "polyethnic" America, to use Will Kymlicka's term.[109] Nathan Glazer, one of the early and most-cited critics of affirmative action policies, argued that, just at the time when America had finally reached a "national consensus" regarding the eradication of racial and ethnic discrimination barriers, the policy of corrective justice interrupted "a distinctive American orientation to ethnic differences and diversity with a history of almost 200 years."[110]

Other critics agree and maintain that "nationalist" ethnic pluralism, which promotes individual groups making special claims and demanding institutionalized privileges, rejects the liberal process that granted group rights on a temporary basis and as a remedial measure to correct past wrongs. Instead, it seeks to enshrine group loyalties and privileges. Thus, for example, bilingualism, which was intended to improve access for immigrant students, or electoral redistricting, which was initially intended to elevate representation of minorities, have over time become vehicles of groups to preserve their "otherness" and enhance their separateness from traditional American civic culture.

This type of multiculturalism has often been called "extreme cultural nationalism," which allegedly undermines the very fabric of American civic culture and challenges the legacy of ongoing inclusion. By advocating the theory of permanent victimization, proponents of the so-called cult of ethnicity have violated the original goal of the civil rights movement, creating "a rigidity of ethnic boundaries and a fixity of group commitment which American life does not permit."[111]

Michael Lind has written that the vision of America as a "mosaic" of "five races or racelike communities – white, blacks or African-Americans, Hispanic or Latinos, Asian and Pacific Islanders, and Native Americans" – propagates the idea that immigrants must give up on their desire to integrate within the larger nation, and instead forces them to assimilate into bureaucratic categories (Mexicans and Cubans join Hispanic America; Chinese, Indians, and Filipinos join Asian and Pacific Islander America, and so on). Moreover, each race, in addition to preserving its cultural unity and distinctness, is expected to act as a monolithic political bloc (particularly since white Americans, according to the multicultural left, are guilty of racial bloc voting).[112]

Other scholars have written in a similar vein that the inclusion of non-European immigrants (from Asia, Latin America, and Africa) within the "multicultural movement" (which challenges the liberal-pluralist vision and the idea of color-blind society) is an unnatural imposition that conflicts with the immigrants' own desire to integrate. Peter Skerry, a scholar of Mexican-Americans, has questioned the political motives of ethnic activists when interpreting the needs and desires of their claimed constituencies:

> How are we to interpret the ironic outcome that in the past, when Mexican Americans were more likely to be treated like a racial

minority, they sought protection by denying any racial distinctiveness; while today, when they experience dramatically fewer such racial barriers their leaders are intent on defining them as a minority?[113]

Will Kymlicka has written that

> immigrants view themselves as ethnic subgroups within the larger nation, not as national minorities. And immigrants generally accept this arrangement. After all, immigrants come voluntarily (if they are not refugees), knowing that integration is expected of them. When they choose to leave their culture and come to America, they voluntarily relinquish their original cultural membership, and the rights which go with it. Uprooting oneself from one's family and place of birth is painful, and immigrants know that this decision will only be worthwhile if they make an effort to integrate into their new society.[114]

Christian Joppke argues that attempts to link black efforts to resolve race-based problems to immigrant groups' claims for special status and privileges are riddled with internal theoretical contradictions:

> Emerging in the historical context of America's civil rights revolution, multiculturalism appears as the quest for group rights, that is, as the quest for public status by or on behalf of historically oppressed "minority" groups that claim special compensation and privileges. As we will see, this requires the reinterpretation of the immigrant experience along anticolonial lines, an often strained endeavor rife with paradoxes, ambivalences, and conflicts, not least with America's premier non-immigrant minority, Blacks.[115]

Joppke also argues that the "anticolonial discourse" that underlies the black radical movement and the claims of Afrocentrists contradicts the immigrant perspective:

> To put it drastically, immigrants say "we are actors," whereas the anticolonial perspective tells them "you are victims." This is not to deny that both perspectives can move toward one another, especially after the experience of actual discrimination and in view of the benefits that affirmative-action-style minority privileges promise. But it is important to recognize that multiculturalism is in the first a movement of intellectuals, who are offering an inter-

pretation of the immigrant experience that is not necessarily adopted by the immigrants themselves.[116]

Whether or not one accepts the validity of such claims regarding the destructive power of "nationalist multiculturalism" inside the United States, the potency of these forces in U.S. foreign affairs must also be evaluated. It is particularly important to examine the role of the "homeland factor" in the ethnocultural fabric of American society, since the homeland (including the "mother tongue") is part and parcel of the ethnic identification of many Americans. In fact, what transforms *ethnic* Americans into *diasporic* communities is their connection (real or perceived) to their country of origin. As will become evident, contrary to conventional wisdom and, to a large extent, the alarmist vision of multicultural critics who see a balkanization of American culture and society, ethnic groups' affinity with homeland cultures and advocacy of home country political causes have the tendency to erode "nationalist" multiculturalism and to accentuate the liberal-pluralist vision of America. Once granted full membership, immigrants (and even refugees and exiles who have been "expelled beyond all hope of return") became law-abiding citizens, bound not only by formal obligations like paying taxes but also by cultural and political attachments to their adopted country that gradually diminish their loyalties abroad.[117] Moreover, on a basic level, diasporic attachment to homelands breaks the officially designated bureaucratic categories of race and splits "racially" defined groups into "ethnic" communities. While "the categories became political entities with their own constituencies, lobbies and vested interests that caused people to think of themselves in new ways – as members of 'races' that were little more than statistical devices,"[118] the identity with the original nationality remained stronger and continued to work in favor of a much broader pluralism. For example, Mexican-, Dominican-, and Cuban-Americans, officially designated as Hispanic, cannot fall so easily into racial boxes the moment they are mobilized on home country issues.

In addition, the dynamic divergence described earlier – that is, the positive nature of ethnic involvement in homeland-related affairs as opposed to their alleged destructive impact domestically – is not the result of the differences in ethnic influences on internal and external policies, as DeConde has suggested (domestically America is becoming multicultural, while in its foreign relations it remains basically unicultural). In fact, this dynamic exists despite the growing clout of ethnoracial lobbies in U.S. foreign affairs or indeed because of it. It can be understood as a new phase in the internationalization of American pluralism by ethnic minorities, which prior to their inclusion could not have reached such a stage because of their exclusion. It can also be explained by changes in world affairs, namely the decline of Third Worldism and the end of the cold war. This reality pertains most strikingly to African-Americans, whose struggle for full inclusion has yet to be accomplished, and who have for many years seemed to be leading critics of American interventionism. The fact that African-Americans have become leading proponents of American intervention to undermine and unseat black and African dictatorships (as in the case of Haiti and even more recently in Nigeria), thereby advocating the "American creed" of democracy and human rights, gives U.S. foreign policy makers favoring intervention in certain circumstances an "ethnic alibi" of sorts. When such intervention occurs, it can no longer be condemned as the product of white imperialism because the "ethnic brush" gives it its legitimacy.

Integrationists, Isolationists, and the Homeland Connection

As noted earlier, prior to the civil rights movement the general expectation from immigrants was conformity to the Anglo assimilationist vision and abandonment of any residual loyalty to their homeland. The general attitude of Anglo- and later Euro-American elites was that manifestations of homeland affinity represented disloyalty to America, and ethnic groups often reacted to the pressure by stressing the more benign folk aspects of their cultural practices.[119]

Separatists claim that accentuating the country of origin as a focus of loyalty existed in an organized fashion in the post–World War I era primarily among black activists who questioned the possibility that blacks would ever be allowed to integrate into American society and/or advocated a reverse theory about black racial supremacy. Black Americans' interface with Africa has been dictated by their unique history of slavery and discrimination. Their "genuine intellectual and emotional endeavors to refurbish their Africanness" in the face of American racism has often led them to what Martin

Kilson called the "dysfunctional tendency to emotionally and ideologically exaggerate the African heritage, mystifying the African heritage with a fetish of re-Africanization."[120] The most noted expression of black racial nationalism was Marcus Garvey's movement, the
Universal Negro Improvement Association (UNIA), popularly
known as the "Back to Africa Movement." This was "the only mass
movement among American blacks prior to the civil rights movement."[121] Garvey was frustrated with other blacks who tolerated their
inferior and often dangerous position in American society "rather
than go[ing] to Africa and build[ing] a black nationality."[122] His ideas
about racial separation led him to support racist white politicians
who favored sending blacks to Africa, and even to praise the race
purity ideals of the Ku Klux Klan. His association with the Klan
irritated even his supporters and divided the ranks of the UNIA.[123]

Black nationalism was an aberration among other ethnoracial
groups in terms of its ideological challenge to the mainstream vision
of America. Even among blacks, the struggle for inclusion and integration took precedence over calls for a separate African nation.[124]
W. E. B. DuBois commented in 1955 that:

> This new leadership [of black businessmen, bureaucrats, and
> white-collar employees] had no interest in Africa. It was aggres-
> sively American. The pan-African movement lost almost all sup-
> port. . . . Today the American interest in Africa is almost confined
> to whites. African history is pursued in white institutions . . . while
> Negro authors and scholars have shied away from the subject
> which [earlier had been their special preserve].[125]

Other deprived minorities, including those who suffered race-based
legal restrictions such as the Chinese-, Japanese-, and Mexican-
Americans, usually fought for inclusion within American society, a
struggle that also characterized many other immigrants.

For many blacks, inclusion seemed a remote dream, and the vision
of a color-blind society has never been a part of their reality. This
was true even as members of other groups moved up the social and
economic ladder, especially after World War II, when racism became
less fashionable. President Truman worked to improve the lot of
blacks domestically, motivated in part by his desire to keep black
leaders in line with "containment," the cornerstone of his foreign
policy, and to erode their pan-Africanism. His actions included:

empowering the President's Committee on Civil Rights to report on the forms and costs of racial discrimination; abolishing racial segregation in the armed forces; supporting the civil-rights plank in the Democratic party platform for the 1948 election; strengthening the civil-rights division in the Department of Justice; and calling for the abolition of poll taxes and the enactment of federal anti-lynching legislation.... Truman probably did more for black Americans than any preceding president had since Abraham Lincoln. Black leaders focused their attention and priorities on domestic gains and had to ask themselves if they could continue to enjoy Truman's support in further efforts to reduce discrimination at home if they opposed central aspects of his foreign policy such as containment.[126]

The spirit of black nationalism was revived in conjunction with Africa's struggle to end colonialism. Regardless of their differences about the analogies between African independence movements and their own "anticolonial" struggle, African-Americans in general "were wholeheartedly enthusiastic about decolonization in Africa. Their response to the emergence of independent African states was marked by a warm, almost intimate, pride in the achievements of peoples whose goals and sufferings many Africans felt they had shared."[127] From the late 1950s, rising black elites combined their nationalist claims against Anglo-Saxon hegemony with anticolonialist Third World ideologies, calling for a revolt against Western values. Black intellectuals differed significantly about their own "colonial" status in the United States and their respective positions impacted on their political strategy. It was at this juncture that ethnoracial nationalism also took root among nonblacks.

During the most active period of the civil rights movement, in the late 1960s and early 1970s, attitudes and activities on behalf of homelands were very much an extension or an expression of diverse domestic positions on issues pertaining to the new vision of America. Ethnic integrationists, who called for nondiscriminatory universal inclusion, stressed the primacy of their loyalty to the United States, while maintaining homeland affinities and honoring their past as an important cultural element, though clearly secondary to their American identity. Isolationists, in contrast, rejected the possibility of compatibility between homeland identification, which they viewed as paramount, and primary loyalty to the United States, a country that they often characterized as the source and perpetuator of racial injustices and other inequalities throughout the world. Contrary to the integrationists who, while recognizing racial or ethnically based inequalities, believed in the ultimate American capacity to redress these imbalances, isolationists felt that racism is a permanent feature of American society, that the United States could never become a "color-blind" country, and that it was doomed to remain Eurocentric or white-dominated. Adopting the rhetoric of anticolonialism and Third Worldism, they rejected the idea of the melting pot and the various other images of a liberal pluralist society like the kaleidoscope.

The divergence between those who sought to advance black rights within American society through the political activity of the civil rights movement and those who rejected such a stand as assimilationist, excessively deferential to whites, and less than "relevant to the daily lives of many ghetto-dwellers," was manifested most prominently in the differences between Martin Luther King Jr. and Malcolm X.[128] Those who expressed the latter view preferred more militant alternatives which "implied standing up to oppression and *taking* what was rightfully one's own, as well as refusing to accept the social, political, and cultural models of one's oppressor."[129]

Black spiritual and political leader Malcolm X shared many of Garvey's ideas. "Like Marcus Garvey, Malcolm [X] foresaw the eventual return of American blacks to the African homeland, but in the meantime they would establish complete control over the black community, by way of armed force if necessary."[130] Although Malcolm X refrained from "explicitly calling for an organized transfer of black Americans to Africa,"[131] he pursued a "re-Africanization" of black culture within the United States that stressed separateness from white society.

Indeed, when studying the question of black nationalism and American identity, it must be remembered that "race" and "ethnicity" should not be used as interchangeable terms. The fact that race (white vs. black) has been so prominent in American culture and politics has also been reflected in the ways African-Americans have related to Africa, which are fundamentally different from the ways other ethnic groups – descendants of immigrants who chose America or came as refugees – relate to their countries of origin or symbolic homelands. "For African Americans . . . [America] was a land of slavery, prejudice and discrimination from which their forebears would have fled had they been able to do so." At the same time, "many took a dim view of an ancestral land whose military and political weakness permitted its inhabitants to be carried off and enslaved." In any event, "because of an often virulent racism, over the centuries African-Americans remained structurally linked to Africa whether they had any emotional bonds to that mysterious continent or not."[132] For others who had suffered periods of exclusion, entry into the mainstream of American society became progressively more available, and race remained a secondary factor.

Extreme isolationism among other groups led to denial of U.S. government authority and calls for physical and territorial separation, as illustrated by the militant rhetoric of Hispanic groups like the Brown Berets and the Alianza, and by a number of radical Chicano political leaders who "openly refused to recognize the legitimacy of the United States–Mexican border." They discredited the American conquest and colonization of Mexican lands and expressed solidarity with Third World movements around the globe. Other Hispanic leaders expressed resistance to acculturation and advocated use of the Spanish language "as a symbol of common pride and a force for ethnic unity and power."[133] In the 1960s, many Chicano activists considered American institutions racist. They rejected the liberal-pluralist legacy in favor of a new nationalist "framework that saw Mexican-Americans as a historically and culturally rich community seeking to liberate itself from Anglo-American racism"[134] (see Chapter 5). Likewise, Palestinian- and other Arab-Americans increasingly embraced nationalism and Edward Said's views on orientalism, under the influence of pan-Arabism, and in reaction to Israel's defeat of the Arabs in the Six Day War and the occupation of the West Bank and Gaza (see Chapter 3).

In keeping with their adoption of an anticolonialist agenda and the analogies they perceived between domestic and international injustices, strongly isolationist groups confronted other U.S. ethnic diasporas, particularly American Jews, as well as members of their own community whom they regarded as accomplices in U.S. imperialist policies. Traditional black nationalists and new militants of the "black power" movement have labeled black integrationists as "collaborators with the enemy" and "resurrected the connotation of 'Negro' as being a thing, a puppet, a creation of the white man, finding it peculiarly applicable to the Negro middle class and its leadership."[135] Among other citizens, Jewish-Americans in particular became a prime target for black isolationists, who accused them of encouraging alleged U.S. international crimes by enticing the United States into an alliance with Israel, the new nemesis of Third World-ists. In the early 1970s, black radicals began to criticize Israel as an extension of American imperialism and racism, and condemned moderate black leaders who sided with Israel for betraying their Palestinian "brothers and sisters." They drew a parallel between Israel's treatment of Palestinians and South Africa's apartheid, and equated the exploitation of blacks in America with the mistreatment of Arabs by Israel (see Chapter 4).

When in the early 1970s "mainstream" black elites emerged as dominant over more radical figures, blacks calling for domestic empowerment were better able to penetrate the electoral system and the larger public consciousness. Thus, for example, when in 1975 Warith Deen Mohammed, the son of Elijah Muhammad, the founder and leader of the Black Nation of Islam, steadily distanced himself from his father's racial separatism and toward a vocabulary of tolerance, he was received as part of the American religious establishment and eventually became the first imam ever to give the invocation before the United States Senate.[136]

The tendency of moving toward the American center, which generally shapes the conduct of ethnic groups seeking empowerment domestically, also pertains to U.S. diasporas that wish to play a serious foreign-policy role. Their access to foreign decision making is in large part a function of their organizational strength and the ability of diasporic elites to cultivate solidarity among their constituencies. But, equally critical to their effectiveness, which DeConde questions, is their ability to present their cause in terms of American ideals and interests. Yet, what is the American national interest, and can it be defined by liberal legal principles?

The American National Interest: Legality and Morality

American foreign policy has in recent years concerned itself a great deal with ostensibly "Anglo-Saxon" ideals such as human rights, democratization, and liberal economic reform, which would seem to indicate the continued domination of foreign policy by "Anglo-

Saxon" elites. In the post–cold war era, however, the basis of support for these ideals within the United States (and to a certain extent internationally) has become universal, with newly empowered ethnic voices being among their most forceful and consistent articulators. Who mobilizes whom today in the American pursuit of the liberal internationalist creed is thus a major question. Madeleine Albright, who was appointed U.S. secretary of state in January 1997, stated soon after taking office that one of her principal tasks would be to build a domestic consensus in favor of a moderately activist foreign policy. What is clear, however, is that the diffusion of these ideals cannot be taken to mean that the old eastern Establishment continues its hegemony over foreign policy in the United States. In fact, even in the days when its leading figures were dominant in policy formulation, members of the Establishment were divided over international goals and the definition of the U.S. national interest. Establishment views of the world lacked logical and moral coherence, more so than those of newly powerful forces such as diasporic groups who are often criticized today for destabilizing and balkanizing U.S. foreign policy.[137]

"Establishment" figures in the U.S. State and Defense Departments and other government branches and agencies exercised a decisive influence on foreign policy throughout the cold war. Their policy prescriptions manifested an "uncompromising hostility to Communism and a determination to take any step required for the United States to 'win' the cold war. . . . global problems [were] never solved, only 'managed' to maximize American power and influence."[138] The men (as they almost exclusively were) of the "Establishment" shared a great deal in common in terms of background, training, and outlook. They were, for the most part, fairly affluent, Ivy League–educated, Anglo-Saxon professionals who "belonged to influential organizations like the Council on Foreign Relations."[139] They included Secretaries of State Acheson and Dulles and other influential policy makers such as George Kennan, Averell Harriman, and Clark Clifford. Strong believers in "American cultural values and beliefs," they embraced the concept of liberal internationalism, "espous[ing] the harmony of interests among nations and emphasizing the ideals of free trade, political self-determination, and the inviolability of public opinion."[140] Noam Chomsky, a prominent left-wing critic of U.S. foreign policy, has argued that in fact none of these "principles" were "inviolate" and that U.S. cold war foreign policy can be better explained by noting its realist geopolitical conception than by reference to liberal ideas, which he claims were betrayed by U.S. actions in Third World countries such as Guatemala, Vietnam, and Laos.[141]

The extent to which American cold war foreign policy was a product of the specific common elements shared by Establishment figures, in particular their "Anglo" origins, is in doubt. The argument has been made that a U.S. policy of neglect or even hostility toward Third World aspirations reflected a racist, "orientalist" vision, which coincided with domestic policies of racial exclusion. The lack of significant non-European ethnic voices (Arabs, Asians, blacks, Latinos) in U.S. foreign policy before the mid-1960s has been seen as symptomatic of this policy. Whatever the merit of this argument, it obviously overlooks the defining and critical element of U.S. foreign policy during the cold war, the "containment" of communism, the Soviets, and their perceived proxies, and the casting of this conflict in extreme ideological-moral terms (e.g., Reagan's labeling of the Soviet Union as the "evil empire"). The centrality of this strategy led policy makers to evaluate with suspicion Third World revolutions, social reform, and self-determination movements, which were in most cases presumed to be either Communist-inspired or at least extremely vulnerable to Communist influences.[142] "Despite his liberal professions . . . even President John F. Kennedy's 'definition of progress and self-determination was limited to regimes found acceptable by Washington – almost always not on the basis of their service to their own people but on the basis of their anti-Communism.' "[143]

This posture was accompanied by an American preference for 'friendly' authoritarian regimes whose foreign policies were perceived to be less prone to ideological uncertainty, a point of view most bluntly and memorably articulated by the Reagan administration's Jeanne Kirkpatrick.[144] Liberal isolationists or ethnic minorities criticizing America's Third World policy looked at such an approach as a reflection of a "white Anglo-Saxon" mind-set which caused the United States to act in total contradiction to its professed values and its real interests. By equating progressive governments with communism and supporting dictators, critics claim that the United States betrayed its self-declared role as the champion of freedom everywhere. Some have argued that this pattern has recurred since the end

39

of the cold war, with American opposition to Islam and support for pro-Western authoritarian governments in North Africa and the Middle East, even when Islamist parties win democratic elections, as in Algeria in 1992.

American anticommunism also dictated U.S. refugee policy. East European – American lobbies, which were very limited in their ability to push a more interventionist U.S. policy toward their former homelands, were quite successful in pressuring the U.S. government to admit large numbers of refugees from those countries. One might have argued that the gate was open as long as the arrivals were "white" Europeans, but this was soon challenged by the arrival of a large number of refugees from Cuba (who were, in fact, at first seen as temporary exiles) and later from southeast Asia. U.S. decision makers were motivated more by concern over communism and the desire to delegitimize it through American asylum policies than by ethnoracial preferences. The granting of asylum became a tool of foreign policy, as refugees and political exiles fleeing Communist countries "became touching symbols around which to weave the legitimacy needed for foreign policy."[145] Paradoxically, while "white Anglo-Saxon" domination over foreign policy may have been powerful enough to exclude "nonwhite" ethnic voices from the policy process, the policy elite's preoccupation with communism allowed American doors to open to Third World refugees and, eventually, to the views they expressed. There was, of course, no going back once communism collapsed, because in the absence of a Communist threat, renewed exclusion of the opinions and interests of those not belonging to "white elites" would have to be based on racist considerations. It is, as a consequence, more difficult today for the United States to neglect relations with the nations of Africa, Asia, and Latin America, although some U.S. government decision makers are still prone to do so.

Throughout the first part of the twentieth century, the formulation of U.S. foreign policy was largely based on "the legalistic-moralistic approach to international problems."[146] Borrowed from the legalism prevalent in the domestic arena, this approach was embedded in the belief "that it should be possible to suppress the chaotic and dangerous aspirations of governments in the international field by the acceptance of some system of legal rules and restraints. This belief unexpectedly represents in part an attempt to transpose the Anglo-Saxon concept of individual law into the international field and to make it applicable to governments as it is applicable here at home to individuals."[147] The legalistic approach was guided and reinforced, in turn, by moralistic principles about the conduct of states. These supported the belief that general criteria could be found against which the behavior of not just individuals but also states could be measured as both proper and legal. This vision also laid the foundation for the idea of an international juridical regime, such as the one signaled by the Geneva Convention and the Nuremberg trials.

In 1950 the legalistic-moralistic approach was attacked harshly by George Kennan. In his famous lectures on American diplomacy, the architect of the U.S. policy of containment maintained that America's adherence to legalism-moralism is ethnocentric, unrealistic, and politically counterproductive. By ignoring the unpredictable nature of international relations and by insisting on its own moral superiority, Kennan argued, the United States in fact "makes violence more enduring, more terrible, and more destructive to political stability than did the older motives of national interest."[148]

As the cold war advanced, it became clear that the United States would not be inhibited in its international conduct by its pledge to honor boundaries set by legalism and moralism. First, the legal and moral principles to which the United States professed itself committed, such as the right to national self-determination, respect for national sovereignty, democracy, and human rights, were not always practically reconcilable, given the U.S. definition of its own interests. Second, at times the fear of communism undercut America's own sense of its legal-moral obligations altogether. And indeed, for a few decades the two major schools of thought that vied for influence in U.S. foreign affairs, "cold war liberals" and "Wilsonian liberals," could not concur on how U.S. legal-moralistic principles should be prioritized.

Cold war liberals, the dominant school, considered Communist expansionism the greatest threat and advocated U.S. support for "moderate" authoritarian regimes as long as they remained in the U.S. sphere of influence. Wilsonian liberals denounced American encroachment on the sovereignty of other nations and "railed against American support for authoritarian regimes as a policy that compromised American values respecting human rights and self-determination."[149] The debate on the war in Vietnam brought to its zenith the legal-moral confusion of U.S. foreign policy. This, compounded with the domestic upheavals of the 1960s, provided a fertile base for challenging the legal and moral boundaries of American *domestic* pluralism; confusions in U.S. diplomacy overseas were underscored by U.S. conflicts at home, and this had a reciprocal dimension.

America's legal and moral inconsistencies during the cold war reshaped Washington's posture toward diplomatic activism and containment. Diasporic groups that contested its friendly relations with tyrants in their home countries were discouraged, and in some cases the Central Intelligence Agency (CIA) acquiesced or even collaborated in underground foreign-agent activity intended to silence dissident voices in the United States. Iranians living in the United States who opposed the U.S.-allied government of the shah, for example, were hunted by Iranian secret police (SAVAK) agents, with the acquiescence of the U.S. government. The U.S. government complained, however, when similar methods were used by the Khomeini regime, whose hostility to the United States was perfectly clear.[150]

Moreover, ethnic advocates of self-determination who supported Third World liberation movements were quickly labeled pro-Communists. Yet even when the home regime was Communist, its American diaspora's opposition was not consistently appreciated. American backing for diasporas varied as the state's changing definition of its strategic interest did; thus, Nixon's opening to China led the United States simultaneously to encourage those elements of its own Chinese diaspora that advocated and sought cooperation with Peking, while discouraging protest and opposition by other elements within the same diaspora. Peking, in turn, sought to utilize the new relations with Washington to undermine Taiwan's status in the United States by opening its borders to "our fellow countrymen abroad," who were invited home to witness the achievements of communism.[151]

After years of Nixon and Kissinger's coldly realistic approach to foreign affairs, President Jimmy Carter (1977–81) appeared on the stage as a champion of humanitarian values. Carter's rhetoric tied the national interest with the American moral code domestically and internationally, a code that had suffered greatly under the strain of the Vietnam War and the Watergate scandal. The new vision articulated in foreign affairs coincided with the idea of a more pluralistic and just society inside America.

> Jimmy Carter, who had hung a picture of Martin Luther King Jr. at the governor's mansion in Georgia during his tenure there, appointed more blacks, Hispanics, and Asian-Americans than any president before him. He routinely issued proclamations – as did his successors – extolling immigrant-ethnic groups, as when he proclaimed the celebration of Asian-Pacific Heritage Week in 1980, stressing that America's strength is in "the richness of its cultural diversity," and that "the strong and varied traditions of their Asian and Pacific homelands . . . greatly enriched our cultural heritage and institutions."[152]

Indeed, as the idealistic leader of the free world, Carter initially won wide support and even admiration among freedom fighters, dissidents, and prisoners of conscience around the globe, while becoming the nemesis of dictators. Carter won the support of African-Americans who saw Andrew Young's appointment as U.S. ambassador to the United Nations as a sign of their growing domestic empowerment. Carter also raised the expectations of U.S.-based diasporic groups who fought to overthrow authoritarian regimes in Asia and Latin America. During his tenure, African-Americans mobilized against the white supremacist regimes in South Africa and Rhodesia.

Yet Carter's inability to prevent a pro-Communist takeover in Nicaragua, the rise of Khomeini in Iran, and the Soviet invasion of Afghanistan undermined the credibility of his international leadership, as did his inconsistency with regard to human rights in Iran, South Korea, the Philippines, and elsewhere. "Carter himself, the presumed number one human rights crusader, was soon found visiting authoritarian nations, selling them arms and saluting their leaders. . . . Washington was fearless in denouncing abuses [only] in countries . . . where the United States had negligible strategic and economic interests."[153] Moreover, Carter's "strategic incoherence" and his failure to obtain the cooperation of Congress led to the disappointment of diasporic activists who had considered him to be a strong advocate of their causes. Carter came to be regarded as a sellout in the case of the Philippines (see Chapter 2) and even African-Americans lost confidence in him when he remained silent following the forced resignation of Andrew Young, after the latter's meeting with the Palestine Liberation Organization's UN representative Zehdi Terzi in contravention of U.S. policy (see Chapter 4).[154]

By the end of Carter's term in office, U.S. foreign policy had to a significant extent retreated back to the cold war realist approach favored by earlier presidents, a trend confirmed and strengthened under the administration of President Ronald Reagan. Reagan shared Carter's earlier commitment to upholding morality in foreign policy, but defined morality in different, more ideological terms. His administration's posture "elevate[d] 'totalitarian' violations to a higher plane than 'authoritarian' [human rights] violations."[155] "Moderately repressive" right-wing regimes were portrayed as less morally offensive than left-wing governments and more open to eventual democratic development.

The differences between the Carter and Reagan approaches were manifested clearly in how each president treated the case of leading South Korean dissident (and later president) Kim Dae Jung, who came to the United States after Carter interceded personally with the Korean government to prevent Kim's execution.[156] When Carter mentioned his intervention to Reagan after the 1980 election, Reagan's only comment was to express "with some enthusiasm his envy of the authority that Korean President Park Chung Hee had exercised during a period of campus unrest, when he had closed the universities and drafted the demonstrators."[157] Reagan's administration allied itself closely with President Chun Doo Hwan's dictatorship, a stand criticized to no avail by Kim during the two years he spent in the United States (1982–84) working to build a popular diasporic opposition movement. He warned the United States that if it continued to remain silent in the face of authoritarian abuses, it stood to lose the backing of the Korean people.[158] Despite these admonitions, the Reagan administration was singularly unhelpful to Kim and the other Korean prodemocracy activists, who were nevertheless ultimately successful in bringing about political reform. After the 1987 "June Revolution" forced the Korean government to accede to many dissident demands, a joke among Koreans in the United States "predict[ed] a swap between the United States and South Korea, with Koreans here going home and President Chun Doo Hwan and his followers seeking exile in the United States."[159] In reality, while Kim and other dissidents did indeed return to Korea, a number of government leaders went to jail.

By 1985, thirty-five years after he had castigated U.S. foreign-policy makers for compromising American interests because of "excessive legalism and moralism," George Kennan had reversed himself. He now blamed U.S. cold war activities for its excessive cynicism on legal and moral issues: "[T]he bewilderments of the cold war have produced strange consequences, and there are times in these recent years when I have found myself wishing that there were a bit more morality in our concepts of what is legal, and more attention to legality in our concepts of what is moral."[160]

However, the idea of reconciling legality and morality in foreign policy no longer seemed an empty vision in the late 1980s and early 1990s. As human rights and democracy became a focal point of international affairs, the American "high ground" in foreign diplomacy was no longer consistently perceived around the globe as merely impractical, ethnocentric, or imperialistic. After the breakdown of many authoritarian and totalitarian systems and the collapse of communism, many have thought that the United States has an opportunity to mold an international system more compatible with its professed values. Indeed, in recent years it has become more difficult to assail U.S. foreign policy for demanding certain universal criteria of behavior regardless of political, economic, cultural, and religious tradition. Charges against the United States of imperialism and orientalism have declined substantially, an indication of the weakening of Third Worldism and similar ideological positions.

Moreover, in the United States former cold war liberals are no longer bound by their commitment to "friendly tyrants," while Wilsonian liberals who came to recognize the defects of Third Worldism in the field of human rights protection have begun to abandon their unqualified opposition to American intervention. Both camps could now concur on a U.S. commitment to democracy and human rights. They agree that "the internal character of regimes has implications for international peace, and on [the] support [given by] international organizations to reform, and even sometimes to remove, rogue regimes."[161] This new posture also forces the U.S. government to become more disposed to hear concerns about human rights and democracy by ethnic diasporas. This is not to say that they will be heeded automatically, but they will at the very least get a better hearing. If diasporic elites become vocal against the home country, even when it is an American ally, they are likely to strain U.S.-home government relations. Their voices exacerbate the conflict in Washington over how to balance human rights and strategic concerns.[162] One example of such a dilemma is seen in the various efforts to restore to power the first democratically elected president of Haiti, Jean-Bertrand Aristide. These were in significant part motivated by African- and Haitian-Americans who pressured the Bush and Clinton administrations. The scale, duration, and impact of the U.S. efforts on Aristide's behalf would have been unimaginable in the era of inertia vis-à-vis formal democracy and human rights in the Third World (see Chapter 2).

The End of the Cold War

The apparent triumph of liberalism and democracy at the end of the cold war initially seemed to offer American policy makers a unique opportunity to remake the international system in their own image. Broad agreement on principles and methods of implementation within the foreign-policy establishment, coupled with the absence of significant external opposition, should have set the stage for a consistent and determined effort to extend further the global reach of American beliefs and policies. In reality, however, U.S. post–cold war foreign policy suffers from deep confusion in both theory and practice. The disappearance of the ideological coherence of the cold war era, with its sharp distinctions between allies and enemies, and the decline of the traditional political elites who have charted American foreign policy since 1945, have led to uncertainty over the core principles and goals of U.S. policy.

Classic American political concerns such as democratization and human rights are the dominant themes in world affairs in the 1990s, with a wide range of American commentators from "various ends of the political spectrum"[163] proclaiming their central importance to U.S. foreign policy. Many observers agree that "conventional Cold War categories such as liberal and conservative, interventionist and isolationist, realist and idealist, and free trader and protectionist, have lost their predictive power in the post–Cold War world."[164] During the 1990s, both Republicans and Democrats have been among the principal exponents of an American international activism based on both morality and the pragmatic pursuit of "national interests."[165] Yet decision makers seem unsure about the degree of U.S. responsibility in promoting "American" principles abroad, and about whether the attainment of such goals is compatible with an American national interest whose definition is currently in transition and is equally unclear.

There is also no agreement over whether support for human rights, democratization, and market economies in the abstract should result in actual intervention. Writing midway through President Clinton's first term, Tony Smith argued that Clinton should be encouraged to demonstrate the courage of his humanitarian and democratic convictions, especially in U.S. relations with Latin America. It is in the U.S. national interest to help other Western Hemispheric countries such as Haiti overcome the legacy of decades of political turmoil and oppression, Smith claims, not only because of the potential benefits to people living in those nations, but because active American participation in the development of stable and prosperous democracies throughout the region "serve[s] at once America's commercial interests, the need to control its borders, and the goal of creating a community of feeling that might one day rival that which now exists with much of Europe."[166] Michael Mandelbaum, on the other hand, eschews such high-minded interventionism, arguing that the United States has no place and no interest in acting as the political world's "Mother Teresa."[167] As David C. Hendrickson has noted, "That American foreign policy stands in disarray and confusion is one of the few propositions on which a consensus exists in the country today."[168]

There is no real argument over the fact that, regardless of where American foreign policy moves along the continuum between extremes of isolationism and interventionism, the United States cannot involve itself in every dispute outside its borders. There is even less incentive to do so in the absence of a clear and present danger such as that formerly posed by the Soviet Union. The question is to what extent and under what conditions should the United States pursue international aims such as democratization, the creation and maintenance of peace and stability, and universal respect for human rights in situations or in regions where its own immediate interests are not clearly involved?

There are definite international limits to the possibilities of U.S. intervention. Insistence on improvement in China's human rights record may be completely defensible in principle, for example, but there is no practical way for the United States to impose its views on Beijing. In addition, principles that seem incontestable in their legitimacy and morality (of which more will be said later) when discussed on their own, often conflict with one another in the real world. The evidence is mixed at best, for instance, on whether democracy and self-determination will really bring peace and stability to various parts of the former Soviet Union.

The contrary pressures on American foreign policy and the challenges in developing a clear and consistent basis for policy are embodied in George Kennan, whose 1995 article marking his ninetieth birthday[169] wrestles with the same problems of reconciling principles with reality as his previous writings in 1950 and 1985. Kennan is very skeptical about the U.S. ability to actively promote democracy and human rights. He invokes John Quincy Adams' (at the time secretary of state to President Monroe [1817–25], and later president himself) belief that the United States should be "the well-wisher to the freedom and independence of all" but remain "the champion and vindicator only of her own."[170]

Many have argued that the confusion in U.S. foreign policy is not entirely driven by external influences, however, and that internal changes have also contributed to this situation. These developments include but are not limited to the growing importance of individual members of Congress and even local governments in foreign-policy formulation, concerns over domestic economic issues such as unemployment (which ties into debates over the effects of international trade liberalization), and, perhaps most importantly, the rise of ethnic voices in every sphere of American political life. Michael Clough asserts that the "globalization of American society has made the idea of national interest more elusive. . . . a fresh constellation of domestic forces creates its own global policy."[171] Clough sees the ascendance of grass-roots, ethnically based lobbying as a potentially divisive development, which "could well lead to the balkanization of the foreign policy making process . . . [and even] cause a bitter and prolonged domestic struggle over America's role in the world, undermining its ability to lead in the era now dawning."[172] Bruce D. Porter takes a similar line with his view of a United States being broken apart by subnational loyalties, increasing ungovernability, and the dissipation of "American values."[173] Jack Citrin et al. have written that "the changing character of American society is another source of discord about the country's foreign policy. . . . the dwindling of consensus about the American international role follows from the waning of agreement on what it means to be an American, on the very character of American nationalism."[174]

While some political observers have concluded that the reality of the growing number of ethnic groups creating their own foreign policy is at the core of Washington's failure to articulate a more coherent national interest, others reverse the causal order and argue that the exacerbation of U.S. domestic divisions is rooted in America's new international posture. Accordingly, America's loss of its cold war enemies has undermined political leaders' ability to rally the nation around a unifying cause. In the absence of well-defined policy challenges, Americans are turning inward to debate domestic problems. It is a process that encourages the flare-up of dormant culture wars and the renouncement of a common national identity. Many, therefore, worry that the fragmentation witnessed abroad is also affecting the United States. Indeed, whatever the order of causation in the interaction between domestic and international forces, it is almost cliché to argue that "foreign and domestic policies can no longer be neatly separated [and] ideological confusion has spilled over into domestic politics."[175]

It is clear that the new ideological convergence in world affairs and the lack of a coherent foreign policy in the post–cold war period has provided ethnic diasporas, whose power has increased domestically, with unprecedented opportunities to influence decision makers. Yet their clout is not automatic or without logical consistency or responsibility. Indeed, the greater the opportunity, the greater the challenge. The dynamic of diasporic influence in foreign-homeland related affairs seems to have established a clear pattern. On the one hand, they are more likely to affect U.S. external policy when it becomes clear that they are prepared to become a vehicle for spreading American principles abroad, such as human rights, democratization, and market economies. On the other hand, if they wish to confirm their credibility as exporters of democratic values as currently defined, then diasporic activists must be ready to challenge the peoples and governments in their homelands when these digress from norms acceptable to the United States.

In the next chapter, we will explore the changing role U.S.-based diasporas have played in undermining dictatorial regimes and in advocating democratic regime change, often as part of the struggle for self-determination. While American decision makers have spoken a great deal about democracy and democratization in the post–cold war era, they are still reluctant to push this agenda when the cost seems too high. This reticence has been even more evident in connection with the question of national self-determination. Although it is generally perceived to be a national right of all peoples, U.S. decision makers have often vacillated in their response to such campaigns, in eastern Europe, the Far East, and elsewhere, fearing international instability or other destructive effects of potentially extreme nationalism. These uncertainties in U.S. foreign policy are giving well-organized diasporas no longer inhibited by cold war considerations opportunities to present themselves as messengers of American values abroad and thereby gain a voice in foreign policy in Washington.

We will now turn our attention to this dynamic. It must be noted that diasporas are, of course, not always committed to goals compatible with the values mentioned here. The small elites of activists who mobilize on international issues sometimes play a counterproductive role, maintaining an "exile mentality" – holding attitudes frozen in time that are not conducive to democratic reconciliation in their countries of origin. Their ability to manipulate decision makers inside the United States, however, is not clear.

2

U.S. Ethnic Diasporas in the Struggle for Democracy and Self-Determination

Nathan Glazer and Daniel Patrick Moynihan observed as early as 1975 that ethnic influences have become "the single most important determinant of policy."[1] Notwithstanding the empirical accuracy of this observation, it is a fact that the ability of U.S.-based diasporas to affect American policy toward their homelands has grown over the past few decades and is likely to expand further in an international environment where distinguishing between America's friends and foes has become more complex in the wake of communism's collapse. This trend is being reinforced by the declining influence of traditional professional elites, who dominated U.S. foreign affairs throughout the cold war. In addition the global surge of national independence and the "third wave" of democratic transitions have awakened older diasporas in the United States and energized the more recently organized ethnic communities. Both these groups now play an increasingly important role in providing support for democratization and self-determination abroad.

This chapter examines how this role has changed over time, particularly in the post–cold war era, how diasporas attempted to restructure the politics of their homelands, and to what effect. It also explores the repercussions of ethnic foreign political activity on the American domestic scene, emphasizing the dilemma of divided loyalties so inherent in diasporic external politics. A diaspora's ability to play a serious foreign-policy role is a consequence of several factors: the U.S. liberal-democratic ethos, which enfranchises individual citizens regardless of place of birth; the expanded recognition of ethnic diversity; the institutional reality of a fragmented U.S. foreign-policy establishment that empowers individual members of Congress; and the impact of a powerful media. The fact that Congress, and therefore constituency politics, has an important voice in U.S. foreign policy, compounded with the ready access of ethnic groups to American and thus global media, provides a fertile base for an organized and strongly committed diaspora which may transform itself into a powerful political player with transnational implications. Yet in engaging in the politics of the country of origin (home country), diaspora activists and organizations may become entangled in conflicting allegiances. They must justify their actions in terms of American national interests and values, answer to their U.S. ethnic compatriots, and prove their loyalty to their home country.

The chapter first discusses American diasporas' involvement in the struggles for self-determination in their countries of origin. Special attention will be given to recent diasporic responses to the breakaway republics in eastern Europe and the former Soviet Union at a time when Washington has displayed a lack of decisiveness in responding to the renewed proliferation of nation-states. Next I examine diasporas' contribution to the creation and consolidation of new democracies. Then, by way of conclusion, I analyze the bearing of U.S. diasporas on the movement for self-determination and/or democratic regime change through the prism of African-Americans' contribution to the black struggle in South Africa and to the democratic transformation of black African tyrannies. Their mobilization against apartheid has demonstrated the powerful force of a diaspora in altering U.S. foreign policy and has highlighted the political responsibility that comes with such successes. Finally, the activity of African-Americans underscores how diasporic involvement in U.S. foreign affairs affects the evolution of American identity.

Diasporas and National Independence

Diasporic communities of stateless nations have historically played an integral part and often led in the struggle for political independence in their claimed homelands. The current trend toward self-determination has revived similar involvement. In the 1860s, Irish-American nationalists "were more concerned with the plight of their ancestral home than with their new country."[2] Many of them who were veterans of the American Civil War worked to draw the United States into a war with the British Empire. The climax of their activity was the Fenian Brotherhood's ill-fated attempts to liberate an Irish zone in Canada,[3] which strained relations between Britain, Canada, and the United States. Canada was angered by Washington's refusal to suppress the Fenian raids. Indeed, "few politicians dared alienate the Irish vote,"[4] even during a time of great tension between the United States and Britain. As relations improved and more Irish-Americans began to focus their lives in the United States instead of the ancestral homeland, the tensions between Great Britain and the United States lessened, but the Irish-American factor continued to be significant.[5]

President Bill Clinton's first term in office marked the first time since 1866 that Irish-Americans were able to have an impact on the foreign-policy decisions of the U.S. executive branch in a way that significantly compromised the traditional alliance between the United States and the United Kingdom. In a departure from the Bush administration's policy of deliberate noninvolvement in Northern Ireland issues, Clinton became an "active player" in the search for solutions to the region's problems.[6]

The first indication of a major change in U.S. executive policy came in a turnaround on the issue of granting an entry visa to Gerry Adams, leader of the Irish Republican Army's (IRA) political wing, Sinn Fein. In accordance with State Department policy that a visa could not be granted until Sinn Fein renounced the use of violence, Clinton initially failed to honor his 1992 campaign promise to let Adams visit the United States. The president did not maintain this position for long, however. In the wake of the December 1993 Downing Street declaration, which indicated British willingness to compromise on Northern Ireland, Adams was invited along with representatives of other participants in the conflict to a February 1994 forum in New York. Overriding both British and State Department objections, Clinton responded to pressure from forty congressional members and the Irish-American U.S. ambassador in Dublin by granting Adams a limited visa to attend the conference. Clinton's expectation of a renunciation of violence by Adams during his U.S. visit, as a "quid pro quo for the visa," did not materialize. When the IRA Council did vote for a unilateral, unconditional cease-fire at the end of August, it cited as major reasons "the power of the Irish-American lobby" and its view that "Clinton is perhaps the first US president in decades to be substantially influenced by such a lobby."[7]

Adams was granted subsequent visas and Clinton also "lift[ed] the ban on official U.S. contacts with Sinn Fein."[8]

Joseph O'Grady attributes Clinton's increased support for what might be called a pro–Irish Catholic position on Northern Ireland to a number of domestic and international factors, with the foremost internal influences being Irish-American lobbying efforts and the lack of a competing domestic U.S. lobby for the British or the Irish Protestants. The Irish-American population continues to grow, strengthened by additional recent immigration from Ireland. Americans who are not Irish Catholics do not see U.S. policy on Northern Ireland as a significant political issue, and most American descendants of Ulster Protestants had long ago assimilated into the Anglo-American mainstream, which does not identify as strongly with Britain as it did in the middle of the last century. On the international scene, the end of the cold war greatly reduced the strategic basis for the "special relationship" between the United States and the United Kingdom. "America's interests no longer coincided with Britain's interests . . . Thus Clinton's need to reach for the Irish-American vote in both 1992 and 1994 could be satisfied without any fear of causing damage to an American national interest."[9]

The final days of British Prime Minister John Major's Conservative government were difficult ones for political compromise on Irish matters, given the pro-Unionist tilt of many Conservatives and the government's reliance on Ulster Unionist MPs for a majority in the House of Commons. The election of a Labour government under Tony Blair in 1997 made Clinton's task of constructing a policy satisfying both Irish-American demands and the needs of the American-British relationship somewhat easier. Blair made key concessions, including some of those long sought by Irish-American activists such as prisoner releases and greater Irish government involvement in northern affairs, moving quickly toward a peace agreement ultimately supported by a majority of both Catholic and Protestant voters in Northern Ireland and the Irish Republic. American and British policies on this important issue once again found common ground.

Pre- and Post-Communist National Reawakenings

With the outbreak of World War I, ethnic Americans became increasingly preoccupied with their native countries.[10] While for some diasporas World War I served to intensify already significant nationalist bonds with their countries of origin, for the Polish community the events leading up to and during the war marked the first occasion where Polish-Americans of disparate social backgrounds were unified and mobilized in support of a homeland cause. Although the upper classes and educated members of "Polonia" (the Polish-American community) had long exhibited strong nationalist attachment to the homeland, the prewar links between Polish-American "peasant" immigrants and Poland were primarily familial, and immigrants identified with their community or region of origin; nationalist consciousness or solidarity with other social classes of Polish immigrants had yet to develop as serious forces.[11]

Leaders of Poland's independence movement worked to overcome this absence of unity and nationalism by appealing to the concern felt by less affluent Polish-Americans for the families and communities they had left behind, and by encouraging them to see the foreign powers occupying Poland rather than the indigenous upper classes as the cause of Poland's problems. Most importantly, "representatives of the social classes who had completely ignored the peasant as a conational in the home country and in Polonia's past now offered many symbols of attention and forms of status. . . . improvement of the status of Polonia in America was promised with the reestablishment of Poland as an independent European power."[12] By the time war broke out, Polish-Americans' various financial contributions to the movement totaled over $87 million, and during the war itself, 28,000 Polish-American volunteers served in a division as part of the Polish Army in France. Polish-American leaders, along with members of the government-in-exile, successfully pressured President Wilson to include Polish independence as part of the postwar settlement. Thus Polonia came to be identified by Polish leaders as the "fourth province of Poland."[13]

Relations between Polonia and Poland declined following the war, as Poland concentrated on internal challenges, while Polish-

Americans found that their participation in the war effort was not being rewarded in terms of respect or recognition. The most significant factor, however, was the cultural divergence that was the natural result of Polonia's evolution as a community geographically separate from the homeland. Immigrants and their descendants became "Americanized" to a greater extent, while Poland underwent changes of its own. At a 1934 convention of Poles living outside of Poland, the demand that diaspora members "swear allegiance to Poland was met with indignation by the Polish-Americans. The delegation refused to sign such a pledge, declaring that Polonia was an 'inseparable, harmonious part of the American nation, however tied to Poland by feeling, traditions and cultural ties.' "[14]

By the time World War II began, with the German invasion of Poland, Polonia was not prepared to respond to homeland pleas for assistance in the same manner as it had during World War I. Relief supplies were sent, but the level of diasporic commitment was not the same, a difference made clear by the smaller number of men volunteering for military service in the Polish Army.[15] Even though Polish-Americans expressed vehement opposition to the "sellout" of Poland at Yalta and continued to press U.S. administrations to intervene more forcefully on Poland's behalf against communism, their concerns were subordinated to more general strategic considerations in America's cold war foreign policy. They were courted at election time by U.S. politicians, who gave verbal support for freeing Poland and other eastern European "captive nations," but this support did not translate into meaningful action. The years of communism in Poland have led to a growing cultural gap and even ignorance between Poland and its diaspora, a gap narrowed somewhat by the constant influx of immigrants from Poland to the United States, who have kept the memory of the homeland fresh.[16]

The advent of the Solidarity movement in 1980 and the eventual transition to democracy in 1989 revived Polish-American nationalist attachment to the homeland, strengthened the "Polish voice" on Capitol Hill, and encouraged diasporic financial investment in the homeland. Overall, though, the involvement of the diaspora in Polish affairs has not been as thorough or as intense as in the cases of other eastern European diasporas, such as the Croats or the various Baltic communities, as the Polish situation lacked the critical element of a struggle for national self-determination and its recovery after many years of foreign domination. Yet, Polish-Americans have lately "returned home" in increasing numbers. The dramatic opening of borders and markets in the post-Communist era has resulted in a meteoric rise in the number of Americans resident in Poland, jumping from 13,000 in 1990 to 148,000 in 1997. Included in these figures are many Polish-Americans looking for new markets, and older people whose Social Security benefits go much farther in the Polish economy than in North America.[17]

The Slovak League Legacy

Among the most influential diasporic contributions to homeland independence in this century were those made by Czech-and Slovak-Americans, who played a pivotal role in the dissolution of the Hapsburg Empire and the creation of modern Czechoslovakia in 1918. From the beginning of the war, Czech and Slovak groups provided much of the anti-Hapsburg agitation, furnished material assistance for domestic opposition, and lobbied forcefully both the president and Congress on behalf of Czech and Slovak liberation. These efforts were particularly effective following the American entry into the war. The Slovak League of America and other émigré Slovak associations in the United States were vital in reaching an agreement with Tomas Masaryk on the nature of independent Czechoslovakia. Masaryk, the exiled Czech nationalist leader, traveled at that time to the United States to mobilize his compatriots' and Woodrow Wilson's support. The so-called Pittsburgh Agreement, signed on May 30, 1918, represented a Slovak retreat from an earlier Slovak-Czech document (the Cleveland Agreement) that advocated the federal union of the Slovak and Czech nations in an independent state. In the Pittsburgh Agreement, the American Slovaks yielded to the Czechoslovakian orientation by accepting autonomy for "Slovakia" while avoiding any reference to the "Slovak nation."[18]

The dissolution of Czechoslovakia into the Czech Republic and Slovakia on New Year's Day 1993 was one of the more unusual episodes in the post-Communist nationalist transformation of eastern Europe. Three years after the "Velvet Revolution" ended Com-

munist rule in Czechoslovakia, the country's two constituent republics embarked on separate political paths, despite the fact that
opinion polls continued to show that most people on both sides
opposed the split. The emergence of independent Czech and Slovak
republics, while undoubtedly driven by critical national and regional
factors such as inter- and intragovernmental disputes over constitutional, diplomatic, and economic issues, was also to a large extent the
product of intensive efforts by a small coterie of North American
Slovak diasporic activists to reassert Slovak national identity.

Similar to the pattern elsewhere in eastern Europe, diasporic academics and businessmen from North America became very involved
in the political and economic life of Czechoslovakia in the early
1990s. Truly, Czechs and Slovaks in the United States (mostly third-
or fourth-generation Americans) were more preoccupied with personal matters stemming from the collapse of communism than with
the question of secession. Many of their groups were united in 1990
under the Free Czechoslovakia Fund in protest against the decision
by the Czechoslovakia Federal Parliament to exclude American citizens and other Czechoslovak nationals abroad from entitlement to
restitution of private property confiscated and expropriated under
Communist rule. Thousands of diaspora members petitioned the
U.S. authorities to "protest the arbitrary discrimination against
American citizens and promote a respect for private property rights
in Czechoslovakia."[19] Yet, Slovak nationalists in the United States
and Canada also played an important role in encouraging the separatist drive inside Slovakia.

These nationalists viewed their involvement as the rightful restoration of historic bonds between Slovakia and its diaspora. Slovak-
American professor and activist Mark Stolarik visited Slovakia in
August 1990 and spoke with university students in Bratislava: "I told
them about Slovaks in the United States, their long-lost cousins
whom the communists had tried to erase from their memories."[20]
Just as the American government saw its role in eastern Europe as
facilitator of the introduction (or reintroduction in certain cases) of
"American values" such as democracy and free enterprise, many
diasporic activists endeavored to further this mission on a more
personal level. Yet others were concerned more with the nationalist
aspirations of their compatriots than with promoting democratic
practices.

Diasporic activists hearkened back to the pivotal role played by American Slovaks in the establishment of the Czech-Slovak federation at the end of World War I. Stolarik encouraged "the descendants of these largely successful Slovaks in the United States [to] once again work to uplift their poorer cousins in Slovakia."[21] Fundraising campaigns were launched in the Slovak-American community to help rebuild the faltering economy of the motherland.[22]

Indeed, what these diasporic leaders had in mind, as early as the spring of 1990, was more than economic reform or merely another round of constitutional wrangling with the Czechs. "Sovereignty" was their ultimate goal, and they were instrumental in eventually providing the Slovak nationalist movement with sufficient momentum to achieve independence. The meaning of "sovereignty" as expressed by Slovak leaders at home and abroad was not defined in exact terms, although many of them made a clear distinction between "sovereignty" and a complete break with the Czech republic. The call for Slovak sovereignty was expressed in emotional terms, a venting of long-held grievances against perceived Czech-perpetrated injustices. Stolarik described "Slovakia without Czechoslovakia [as] a sovereign state with its own identity in control of its own destiny. No more orders from Prague, no more mistaking us for Czechs, no more diverting of Western investments to the Czech lands."[23]

Suspicion of Czech motives and machinations extended to North America, where the Slovak League sought to combat what it viewed as the competing political influence of Czech and Hungarian diasporic organizations, as well as the effects of Czech President Václav Havel's strong international prestige. One Slovak-American activist even alleged that Slovaks were somehow being denied American media access to make their case.[24]

Although the Slovak community in the United States is demographically insignificant in comparison to more politically prominent groups such as Mexican-, Jewish-, and Irish-Americans, Slovak leaders on both sides of the Atlantic saw American (and international) recognition of their nationalist aspirations as important to their success. The American-based Slovak League worked hard during this period to convince the U.S. government of the justice of the Slovak case and of its compatibility with American values and the U.S. national interest.[25]

As early as February 16, 1990, the first postrevolution broadcast dealing with Slovak national identity issues appeared on Slovak tele-vision. The show featured Igor Uhrik of the Slovak League Executive Committee, who proclaimed Slovakia's international invisibility. It began with a four-minute montage of U.S. network news reports repeatedly and indiscriminately using the term "Czech" in describing local events, including those occurring in Slovakia. The program concluded with a call for national self-assertion: "Isn't it about time we let the world know who we are? Let's stop being ashamed of our name. Let's stop being ashamed of being the Slovaks!"[26]

Slovakia was far from being a hotbed of prosovereignty sentiment at this time. Sovereignty was simply not on the agenda of politicians and activists in Bratislava. On the same day as the groundbreaking television broadcast, Canadian Slovak nationalists distributing leaflets (in Austria, near the Slovak border) advocating Slovak independence failed to convince Slovaks to take them seriously.[27]

The visually compelling Slovak-American broadcast had a greater impact, however. It generated extensive press commentary and was followed by a large number of additional media appearances by dias-poric notables calling for Slovakia to reclaim its national sovereignty, with most favoring a loose confederation with the Czech republic. Slovak league leaders spoke in terms of "nation building" and warned "democratic" political parties in Slovakia to adopt sover-eignty as part of their platforms in order to avoid a resurgence of communism in nationalist disguise.[28]

The Slovak League leadership continued its publicity and lobby-ing efforts on behalf of Slovak sovereignty over the next two years, both in Slovakia and abroad, its calls for sovereignty and expressions of opposition to Czech political behavior becoming increasingly stri-dent. In a March 1991 interview with the Slovak journal *Smena*, Igor Uhrik stated that although he preferred the achievement of sover-eignty within the context of a "confederation," he was pessimistic about its viability. He claimed that the Czechs were trying to force Slovaks into a choice between subordination as a Czech-dominated province or total independence.[29]

Diasporic activists saw the June 1992 Czechoslovak elections as an opportunity to advance their sovereignist agenda. During the cam-paign, "leaders of the Slovak League traveled to Bratislava to declare their backing of all Slovak proponents of self-determination."[30] The elections resulted in a prosovereignty government in Slovakia, but also in political confusion and stalemate within the federation. Sovereignty remained an ambiguous term, with Slovak Prime Minister Mečiar proposing "a confederation of two states with each having international recognition and Slovakia getting sovereign and equal status."[31] How this differed from independence was not apparent. Meanwhile, Slovak parliamentarians prevented Václav Havel from being reelected president of the federation, helping to scuttle any remaining chance of a political settlement within an even loosely unified Czech and Slovak confederation.

On August 26, an agreement was reached between the Czech and Slovak governments setting January 1, 1993, as the date for the formal separation of the two nations. According to Henry Brandon of the *New York Times*, Slovakia had overplayed its hand in trying to extract concessions from Prague. By the time of the elections, Václav Klaus's Czech government was quite eager to be rid of economically depressed Slovakia, even offering to help Slovakia pay its domestic debts.[32]

The role played by what was in fact a very small number of Slovak diasporic leaders in this situation is quite striking. In working to create a space and an opportunity for Slovakia to reawaken its national identity, diasporic leaders helped set in motion a series of events over which they could exercise virtually no control. Determined to set and maintain the political agenda, they were instead overtaken by events. At the same time, it may be said, the leaders of Slovakia's government were "taken in" by their erstwhile federation partners, whose superior bargaining position may not have been properly appreciated. Thus, the Slovak diasporic activists fell into the unique position of helping their homeland attain what most national liberation movements consider to be their ultimate aim – full independence – but which the majority of their compatriots did not want.

The diaspora's extensive involvement in Slovakian affairs continued after independence. Indeed, as was the case elsewhere in eastern Europe, some diaspora members became government officials. Igor Uhrik, for example, returned to Slovakia and was elected vice-chairman of the Slovak National Party in 1993. In March 1994, he became an adviser to the Slovak minister of privatization.

The initially warm relationship between Slovakia and its diaspora has cooled somewhat in the last few years, however, as both sides have discovered that the other is not everything it had hoped. Diasporic Slovaks have been disappointed by Slovakia's halting progress on democracy and economic reform, while their "American-ness" is no longer seen by the ruling elite as a virtue.[33]

Ukrainians and Armenians

During the heyday of the cold war, when the assertion of diasporic interests in the homeland was lessened due to vulnerability to charges of disloyalty, "the only homelands that were recalled were those under communist domination. Interest in captive homelands usually served to reinforce the ideology of the American nation and its Cold War interests . . . rather than ethnic pride in the [ancestral] land."[34] Since 1989, the revival of secessionist claims in eastern Europe and the former Soviet Union, which reawakened dormant diasporas, initially received a cool reception at the White House. During 1990–91, the Bush administration viewed quests for self-determination with doubt and apprehension and only belatedly came to recognize their powerful force. On his visit to Yugoslavia in June 1991, Secretary of State James Baker said that the United States would not recognize the then would-be breakaway republics "under any circumstances."[35] During a speech in Kiev in August 1991, President George Bush portrayed the secessionist movement in the Soviet Union as "suicidal nationalism."[36] However, when in November 1991 Ukraine moved decisively toward independence, the United States was forced to admit its underrating of the separatist drive and to acknowledge the inevitability of the Soviet Union's demise. The decision to shift U.S. diplomatic support away from Mikhail Gorbachev's effort to preserve the Soviet Union just days before Ukraine's independence referendum was partially motivated by President Bush's desire to score domestic points among the 1.5 million Ukrainian-Americans and among other eastern European diasporas. The president disclosed to diaspora leaders his decision to recognize Ukraine in the hope of winning the hearts of a sizable voting bloc that was traditionally Democratic.[37] There are signs, however, that Ukrainian-Americans are losing their zeal for the nationalist cause since the attainment of the primary goal of Ukrainian independence. Among Ukrainian-Americans who have become personally involved in rebuilding post-Soviet Ukraine, for example, disillusionment with corruption, inefficiency, and lack of official cooperation have caused some Ukrainian-Americans resident in "the homeland" to question the reasons why they stay. After three years in Kiev, John Hewko, an American coauthor of the Ukrainian constitution, reflected on his personal journey as a nationalist activist: "Now I treat [Ukraine] not as a mission, an ethnic thing, but just as another country to work in."[38]

Until the end of 1991, the United States withheld recognition from the self-proclaimed independent republics which had broken away from the Soviet Union, even though they elected democratic governments. The United States saw the disintegration of states as a source of global instability and favored loose federal arrangements and accommodations. The early recognition granted to independent Baltic states was an exception, because the United States and other countries had never recognized the incorporation in 1940 of the Baltics into the Soviet Union. In the case of the Baltics, the consistent nonrecognition posture of the United States in the postwar era may be attributed, at least in part, to the strong diasporic lobby, especially of Lithuanian-Americans, who were behind the institution of an annual vigil of congressional and presidential reaffirmation on the national holidays of the three states. These symbolic gestures were difficult to ignore when the Baltics declared independence.[39] To the extent that the White House had contacts with diaspora communities before the American decision in December 1991 to establish relations with the splintering parts of the Soviet Union, it tended to encourage their leaders to uphold the U.S. cautionary posture, or at least to remain quiet on the issue of secession. Yet, by adopting Washington's initial posture or by taking a wait-and-see attitude, diaspora activists, particularly those interested in returning home, risked compromising their credibility inside their homelands.

For example, Armenian-Americans' initial support of Washington's position resulted in the loss of their leaders' anticipated political role as the navigators of national life in the former Soviet Armenia. This leadership role had been expected because of the intense involvement of leading Armenian organizations in the United States, which had raised and channeled support and money to needy Armenians throughout the seventy years of Communist rule. In 1989, when the diaspora's leaders called on the home nation to reach an agreement with Gorbachev without secession, they were perceived at home as reinforcing the Communist line. When leading diaspora members of the Dashnag Party – which ruled the independent Armenian Republic (1918–20) and since Armenia's reoccupation served as a "government-of-exiles" – belatedly responded to Armenia's declaration of independence and returned home to compete for the presidential elections (October 1991), they suffered a humiliating defeat.

Although the Dashnag Party remains a contender for power in Armenia proper, it is now clear that since independence a new diaspora-home division of labor has been drawn. Armenian authorities have asked the U.S.-based diaspora to take a back seat on political issues inside the homeland, though it is still expected to extend its technocratic expertise and economic services as an expression of national commitment. Indeed, in recent years, Armenian-Americans (roughly one million) have been key supporters of Armenian demands for independence in Nogorno-Karabakh, an Armenian-populated region in Azerbaijan.[40] The Armenian lobby in Washington was also instrumental in the U.S. Congress's 1992 Freedom Support Act that had earlier blocked aid to Azerbaijan,[41] "and made Armenia the third largest per capita recipient of U.S. assistance. This backing from abroad was essential to Armenia's survival and appropriately earned it the sobriquet of 'The Israel of the Caucasus.' "[42] Finally, Armenian lobbyists have focused U.S. legislative and foreign policy attention on the Armenian Genocide, and have in many instances thwarted Turkish efforts to deny responsibility for (or even the occurrence of) the massacres and expulsion of over one million Armenians during World War I.

The Fall of Yugoslavia

How far are diaspora organizations and leaders willing to push the cause of their homeland's independence against the official U.S. position? Certainly, when appealing to an unsympathetic administration, diasporas must work hard, usually through Congress and the media, at persuading decision makers to shift their position. They must pledge interest in what preoccupies the U.S. government and redefine their cause to relate to those preoccupations. When the Bush administration had not yet moved to support secessionist moves (1990–91), eastern European diasporas cooled their self-determination rhetoric while accentuating the U.S. moral commitment to support those who chose freedom, democracy, and a market economy.

How to address the American indifference toward self-determination was at the center of debate among Croatian-Americans, who in the early 1990s witnessed with horror the destruction of their homeland by the former Yugoslav federal army. The struggle between the Serbs and the Croats has long been a feature of the American political scene. Rather than promote a sense of unity and accommodation, the two diasporas to some extent encouraged the home rivalries. During World War II, when the Yugoslav government-in-exile in London was trying to keep its own unity intact in the face of reports of Croat atrocities against Serbs in Croatia, it turned to its diaspora in the United States as a source of moderation. But the diaspora soon mirrored the schism at home. A pro-Serbian Pittsburgh newspaper, *American Sroboran*, accused the Croats of betrayal and was portrayed by Miloš Trefunonvic, then minister of education in the exiled government, as the organ that "set out on the road of national separatism."[43] As the acrimony among the various national groups and publications escalated, the U.S. Office of War Information intervened, unsuccessfully trying to solicit all groups' commitment to unity.

Fifty years later, the national rivalries that have torn Yugoslavia apart were again mirrored in the respective diaspora communities in the United States. The recent dispute among American Serbs and Croats was largely dominated by charges and countercharges over past and present wrongs. During the war, Croatian-Americans along with the authorities in Zagreb made special efforts to lure Jewish-American groups to their cause. In numerous letters, publications, and pamphlets, they emphasized their aversion to old anti-Semitism and stressed the new Jewish-Croatian alliance in the homeland, in the hopes that "Jewish power" would sway opinion in Washington.[44]

Since June 25, 1991, when Croatia and Slovenia proclaimed their independence and the Yugoslav civil war erupted, their overseas nationals have been mobilized to promote their causes abroad. Croatian-American groups helped establish the Office of the Republic of Croatia in Washington, D.C., and formed a branch of President Franjo Tudjman's Croatian Democratic Union party (HDZ) in Cleveland. Numerous Croatian organizations launched lobbying campaigns in the White House and Congress, organized large demonstrations in Washington and at the United Nations, and used the American media to focus public attention on their people's suffering. In their initial campaign following Croatia's independence proclamation, Croatian-Americans responded to Washington's hostility toward the new proliferation of nation-states by downplaying the rhetoric of self-determination. Instead, they stressed the symmetry between cherished American values and their homeland's commitment to democracy, human rights, and a market economy. Toward the end of 1991, however, with the increased bloodshed at home and in light of Germany and other European Community (EC) members' decision to proceed with diplomatic recognition of Croatia and Slovenia (rebuffing pleas of the United States and the United Nations to refrain from extending recognition to the breakaway republics), Croatian-American organizations became more aggressive in their efforts to obtain U.S. recognition.[45] Croatian-Americans have also organized the shipping of medical supplies and clothing, which were brought into the republic via Italy, Austria, and Hungary through the American Red Cross. In the summer of 1991, Croatian-American members of OTPOR, an organization affiliated with the Croatian National Resistance, were arrested in Miami and charged with violating the Arms Export Control Act for plotting to ship millions of dollars worth of weapons to the Republic of Croatia.[46]

Diasporas and Democratic Regime Change

By and large, matters concerning the integrity and sovereignty of the ancestral homeland or the safety of the scattered nation are likely to trigger a more intense diaspora involvement than matters concerning the homeland's domestic political struggles. In the first instance, the dichotomy between "us" and "them" is evident, and the question of where the national interest lies is rarely in contention. However, when the principal rivals in the interpretation of national loyalty are national contestants for power in the homeland, each vying to represent its own interpretation of the national interest, diaspora members may shy away from the home country's politics. Allegiance to an aspirant opposition under a nondemocratic rule, in particular, may prove to be too costly. The inconsistency of diasporic commitment to democracy was particularly evident during the cold war, when

American foreign policy often preferred friendly tyrants over unpredictable "democrats" whose opposition to communism was not as certain.

The fact that U.S.-assimilated diasporas are more likely to engage in home country affairs of a national friend-foe nature than in domestic politics concerning democratization is best demonstrated in the discrepancy between the Greek-Americans' vigorous campaign to move Congress to impose an economic and military embargo on Turkey following its 1974 invasion of Cyprus,[47] and their acquiescence and collaboration with the military junta at home. Greek political exiles operating from the United States and Europe to overthrow the dictatorship in Athens (1967–74) had to face the fact that many Greek-Americans were fervent anti-Communists and in many respects potential allies of the colonels' regime. Only a few were willing and able to devote their time and effort to the struggle for democracy.[48]

Greek-Americans have been highly successful in projecting their American loyalty and ethnic identity "within the agora of American multiculturalism,"[49] and have in general maintained a strong sense of connection with their ancestral homeland. The community organizational structure of the Greek Orthodox Church has reinforced these ties, as have the galvanizing effects of perceived threats to Greek sovereignty and culture, like the 1974 Turkish invasion and occupation of northern Cyprus, and the adoption of the ostensibly Greek name "Macedonia" by one of the newly independent fragments of former Yugoslavia.

Greek-Americans have acted as a political conduit for both Athens and Washington. The U.S. government has made successful use of the community leadership's lobbying efforts on issues such as Greek reentry into NATO and dialogue with archenemy (but NATO partner) Turkey, as well as on U.S. military bases in Greece.[50] The Greek government, with less success overall, has looked to Greek-Americans to influence U.S. positions on Cyprus, Macedonia, foreign aid, and Aegean Sea disputes with Turkey.

The height of the Greek community's influence in Washington is generally thought to have come during 1974–75, when the United States imposed an arms embargo on Turkey after the latter's invasion and occupation of the northern part of Cyprus. Although U.S. arms sales to Turkey resumed very quickly thereafter, the fact that the

U.S. House of Representatives voted eight times in favor of an arms embargo has been attributed in part to the lobbying efforts of the Greek-American community.[51] Yet its apparent success in moving Congress to impose sanctions on Turkey after its invasion of Cyprus backfired when the perception prevailed in public that "Congress acted irresponsibly" by capitulating under the pressure of an ethnic group.[52]

Almost twenty years later, Greek-American lobbyists in Washington mobilized on behalf of Athens's attempts to diplomatically isolate the newly independent former Yugoslav Republic of Macedonia (known in Greek circles by the name of its capital, Skopje). Greek-American community leaders echoed Greek accusations that irredentist tendencies were indicated by their northern neighbor's adoption of the honored ancient name of Macedonia and various historical symbols Greece claims as its own. In June 1992, Greece persuaded the European Community to deny recognition to the new republic until it agreed to use a less offensive name. President Bush also supported that position.[53]

These successes did not last long. According to Hitchens, the Greeks mismanaged their diplomatic campaign by focusing on symbolic issues and by unrealistically "denouncing the Skopje nationalist-conservative regime as a tool of communism."[54] Despite Greek community opposition, the United States has since recognized Macedonia.

By any reasonable standard, Greece and its diaspora have failed to move the U.S. government on any substantive issue over the past twenty years. Cyprus remains divided, with the United States exerting little pressure on Turkey to either remove its troops or arrive at a political compromise. Turkey and Greece continue to clash sporadically over disputed parts of the Aegean, again without apparent significant U.S. interest. Greek-American efforts to downgrade American defense ties with Turkey have failed completely.

The Diasporic War Trap

The pattern of unequivocal diaspora support for the home nation as a whole excludes the unusual circumstances when the home country and the host country are at conflict or war, a situation that brings the bewildering diaspora loyalty dilemma to its extreme. In wartime, when "a particular prefix . . . coincides with the name of an enemy nation [it tends to] . . . stigmatize rather than Americanize its bearer."[55] Under such difficult tensions, diaspora members may be called upon to make the excruciating choice between their identities. During World War I, German-Americans "swatted the hyphen" and dropped the umlaut, as other Americans made clear their hostility to all things German. "German books were removed from the shelves of American libraries, German-language courses were canceled in the public schools, readers and advertisers boycotted German-American newspapers."[56] During the Gulf crisis, Arab-Americans found themselves on the defensive when their home compatriots gave passionate support to Saddam Hussein.[57] When Serbs began to appear to be the villains in Bosnia, American Serbs lowered their profile, wavering between support for Serbs' "historical rights" and condemnation of President Slobodan Milošević. Within this context of international isolation, Belgrade's ruling Socialist Party offered the post of prime minister of Yugoslavia to a Serbian-born natural-ized American, Milan Panić, in an attempt to deflect U.S. pressure.[58]

At first, many Serbs regarded Panić as Milošević's puppet, while others considered him an entrepreneurial hero for making a fortune in pharmaceuticals in the United States. Right-wing Serb nationalists labeled him a CIA agent, pointing to the fact that he had to get U.S. government clearance to serve in a foreign government. Soon after he assumed his post as prime minister, Panić became Milošević's major opponent. He blamed the president and other militant Serb nationalists for the war and called for a compromise with the succes-sor republics. When he decided to contest the presidential election against Milošević, Panić became a target of the state-controlled me-dia, which launched an unremitting assault on him as a Serbian traitor and an agent of the CIA. After his defeat in Milošević's rigged elections in December 1992, Communists and nationalists combined forces in the federal parliament to oust Panić from his post as prime minister. He was declared "a foreign agent who should be jailed for embezzlement and for acting against the interest of the Serbian people."[59] Panić and his entire Serbian-American staff were sent back to America, where Panić became a leading opponent of Serbian policies.

It must be remembered that home governments usually enjoy the advantage over other contestants for power in the state in establishing standards for loyal and disloyal behavior. Their prescribed criteria for loyalty do not stop at the borders of the state. Nondemocratic regimes also tend to denigrate their political opponents as "nationally disloyal," a designation that licenses the home regime to impose psychological and material penalties on constituencies at home and abroad who oppose the regime. The yardstick for "nationally loyal" conduct fluctuates with the regime's changing definition of the national interest. Hence, governments may include or exclude interchangeably conationals abroad from the national community as a cost-benefit mechanism to ensure national loyalty. The fear of being branded disloyal is one of the reasons why people who flee their native country often refrain from attacking it while abroad or from acquiring foreign citizenship. Moreover, despotic regimes – vulnerable to foreign criticism and pressure, and dependent on U.S. economic or military support – that perceive a threat in the diaspora's ability to foster and channel international animosity toward them may use a variety of means to discredit, deter, and silence overseas opponents, including retraction of citizenship, restriction on visitation, confiscation of property, withdrawal of academic awards, persecution of relatives in the homeland, and, in extreme cases, kidnapping and political assassination.[60]

Diasporas and Exile Politics: Campaigns for Aristide and against Castro

In many instances, the struggle of overseas communities to unseat authoritarian regimes in the home country is led by political exiles who, prior to their departure, were engaged in antiregime activity at home or were regarded by the home regime as troublemakers. The more immediate pool from which this core elite may draw followers is that segment of the national diaspora forced to flee the country for political reasons. Another fertile source for overseas recruitment is foreign students. Organizing abroad along national lines, foreign students are prone to demonstrate against nondemocratic practices at home. Iranian students in the United States played a pivotal role in repudiating the shah's regime in the United Nations, in the U.S. Congress, and in the media. In the past few years, Chinese students have been in the vanguard of the opposition to the Communist authorities in Beijing. After the violent suppression of the democratic movement in 1989, Chinese leaders grew frustrated with their inability to put the Tienanmen Square massacre behind them. In an attempt to break the impasse in relations with the United States, they devised a plan to win back overseas Chinese and to curtail opposition abroad. Since 1990 Beijing has conducted a campaign to discredit and split the overseas Chinese dissident movement and rebuild the Chinese Communist Party's (CCP) underground movement in the United States. In what has been reported to be a leaked secret party document, it was revealed that the Chinese authorities targeted the student community in the United States to be pressured by the CCP organization abroad to assert their loyalty to the regime at home or suffer the consequences. According to this report the strategy is "organizing those who remain firm on our side, maintaining contacts with those who are wavering, and removing those who are reactionary." The alleged document further revealed attempts to bribe the politically loyal, the "patriotic" passive, and the less committed dissidents to return home and obtain governmental preferential treatment in jobs and housing; active exiles, however, would be punished by financial penalties, suspension of scholarships, and restrictions on their relatives' travel abroad. The exiles' leaders and organizers who circulate antiparty views and encourage others to testify before Congress against the home government were targeted for withdrawal of their passports, banishment from the homeland, character attacks, and sanctions against family members at home.[61]

The most recent example of an exile leader employing a diaspora to oust a rival despotic regime was the campaign to restore to power Haitian President Jean-Bertrand Aristide. During Aristide's three years in exile (1991–94), the Haitian-American community mobilized to reverse the September 1991 military coup that had deposed him. As a democratically elected president who had received close to 70 percent of the vote, Aristide enjoyed a legitimacy many previous Haitian leaders had lacked, an important consideration in the post–cold war era where the export of democratic values and respect for human rights were stated primary objectives of U.S. foreign policy.

Aristide established his government-in-exile in Washington, D.C., and energized the diaspora through radio broadcasts and public appearances. He addressed diaspora members as Haiti's "tenth department" (Haiti is divided into nine), to which they responded enthusiastically, lobbying their American political representatives and demonstrating in support of U.S. intervention to unseat the junta in Port-au-Prince.[62]

Pro-Aristide campaigners had little influence on President Bush, however, whose government officials and Republican congressional allies were generally opposed to Aristide as a leftist whom some branded mentally unstable. Bush and other Republicans favored rees-tablishing democracy in Haiti without Aristide, but could not escape the fact that only Aristide had a democratic mandate. The diaspora remained firm in its support of the exiled leader and insisted on his restoration, voting overwhelmingly in 1992 for Democrat Bill Clin-ton, who promised to work for Aristide's return to Haiti.

The Haitian diaspora soon gained politically powerful allies among African-American community leaders,[63] both inside and out-side the U.S. government, including members of the Congressional Black Caucus and TransAfrica's Randall Robinson, whose later twenty-seven-day hunger strike is widely recognized as having tipped the balance in favor of President Clinton's ultimate decision to inter-vene in Haiti. Despite many Haitian-Americans' desires not to be identified with other blacks, whom many Haitians perceived as so-cially and economically inferior, the two communities experienced common race-related difficulties in the United States, and African-American leaders saw the Haitian plight as a case through which they could advance their own struggles for social justice and political empowerment. As a result, the campaign for forceful U.S. action on Haiti became "racialized" as a cause embraced by politically active black Americans regardless of homeland origin.[64]

Bill Clinton's win in November 1992 encouraged Haitian diaspora members to believe that their political agenda was advancing, but Clinton balked initially at intervention and also backtracked on promises to reverse Bush's policy of returning boat people to Haiti. By late 1993, Haitian-Americans, Black Caucus members led by Kweisi Mfume, and key white Democratic politicians such as Joseph Kennedy Jr. and Christopher Dodd began to press Clinton to respect his commitments. A statement signed in November 1993 by forty-four prominent African-American "politicians, college professors, la-bor leaders, lawyers and others," called on Clinton to impose "a total embargo on Haiti until the military permits Aristide to return."[65] Presenters of the document, who were among its signatories, were also prepared to consider the possibility of direct U.S. military intervention, arguing that "there is no more compelling social justice issue in the world community today than the crisis in Haiti."[66] Ironically, Black Caucus members and white liberal Democrats had been among the staunchest opponents of U.S. military intervention during the cold war era.

Clinton's cabinet and other government officials were mostly opposed to intervention in Haiti, with those having greater foreign and defense policy experience, particularly with reference to Haiti, being especially adamant. Clinton's political advisers, however, such as George Stephanopolous, were more attuned to electoral considerations and favored direct U.S. action on Aristide's behalf. Christopher Caldwell claims that the political staff was responsible for marginalizing and, in certain cases, removing from decision-making responsibilities State Department and other bureaucrats opposed to American action on behalf of Aristide. Caldwell views as particularly significant the replacement of State Department Haiti expert Lawrence Pezzullo, an ardent opponent of U.S. intervention, by former Pennsylvania representative and Black Caucus member William Gray. "At State, area expertise was traded for political savvy."[67]

The fact that the United States eventually did intervene to restore Aristide to power in 1994, despite such strong opposition in professional governmental circles, is a testament to the combined political strength of the African-American and Haitian-American communities, who turned Aristide into a cause célèbre. To a large extent, the Clinton administration was compelled by a successfully mobilized diaspora and its allies to act on the U.S. government's own stated principle of spreading democracy, when the president's own foreign and defense policy experts advocated restraint and an avoidance of direct commitments.

Since large diasporas are often products of different migration vintages and of different political circumstances at home, the diaspora pool will rarely consist of a homogeneous population holding similar views or retaining the same militancy toward the home government. Thus, even among Cubans who fled after Fidel Castro's revolution, we must differentiate between the militancy of the earlier wave of refugees and the post-1964 émigrés. Although both groups opposed the regime in Havana, the latter came to the United States principally for economic gain and was increasingly depoliticized. In the 1970s, some Cuban-Americans started to look for normalization of relations with Havana. This accommodating spirit, which was encouraged by the Carter administration, resulted in a dialogue with Castro on the reunification of families and led to Havana's changing its labeling of the diaspora from "traitors" to "members of the Cuban community abroad."[68] But the *dialogo* came to a quick end with the disastrous 1980 Mariel boat lift, and with the help of the militant Cuban exile group Omega 7, which resorted to terrorism to deter conciliatory diasporic tendencies. More than a decade later, two Cuban exile participants in an April 1993 conference with Cuban government representatives were later murdered after threats from the exile paramilitary group Alpha 66.[69]

The establishment of the conservative Cuban American National Foundation (CANF) in 1981 by active and financially generous supporters of the Republican Party coincided with the rise to power of Republican President Ronald Reagan, an ideological crusader against communism who could be counted on not to repeat Carter's earlier conciliatory stand toward the Castro government. Reagan's desire to rid the Western Hemisphere in particular of Communist influence was shared by the vast majority of Cuban-Americans, especially those living in Miami. Unlike other U.S.-resident Hispanics, Cubans were overwhelmingly conservative in political orientation and supported Reagan strongly on most foreign-policy issues, including defense spending and aid to the Nicaraguan Contras.[70] As Damian J. Fernandez wrote, "the success or failure of Cuban foreign policy efforts are dependent on the Executive branch. . . . If [an] ethnic group's goals and worldview coincide with those of the White House, the Executive will support the group's proposals, will use the group as evidence of popular backing, and, whenever appropriate, as a mechanism to pursue presidential goals."[71] This was certainly true of CANF, which reached the peak of its influence on U.S. foreign policy during Reagan's years in office. More liberal voices in the Cuban-American community that had been significant under Carter were rendered effectively mute by the alliance between CANF and the Reagan administration.

The collapse of the Soviet bloc in the late 1980s and early 1990s isolated Castro internationally and further weakened the Cuban economy, raising expectations in the Cuban-American community that Castro's fall was imminent. While community members were united in their opposition to the Castro government, they diverged on which measures were appropriate to help achieve the end of the only nondemocratic regime left in the Western Hemisphere. Washington was divided over similar issues in the wake of the disappearance of its major strategic threat, the Soviet Union. The clear cold war era identity of interests between the Cuban community and the U.S. foreign-policy establishment in fighting communism was replaced by confusion among U.S. policy makers over the degree of intervention that could be justified to export democracy.

Exiled militants, members of paramilitary groups in southern Florida who refused to wait for Castro's demise, urged President George Bush to grant them the right to use force to oust the regime in Havana. Their combative mood was heightened further when, in January 1992, as part of Castro's unyielding posture, Cuba executed a member of the shadowy Miami-based exile paramilitary group Alpha 66, who was captured with two other exiles after landing on the Cuban coast. Other Cuban-American leaders advocated more moderate tactics, such as selectively tightening the economic squeeze, enhancing the diplomatic pressure in the United States and abroad, and continuing the campaign over Radio and TV Marti.[72] In October 1992, Cuban-Americans scored a diplomatic coup as transnational actors when President Salinas de Gortari of Mexico acceded to U.S. pressure and met with two of their prominent leaders, including the controversial chairman of the Cuban American National Foundation and the would-be president of Cuba, Jorge Mas Canosa, who passed away during the writing of this book. Salinas acknowledged the potential importance of Cuban-American support to the congressional passage of the North American Free Trade Agreement and departed from Mexico's traditional diplomatic support for Cuba.[73]

The efforts of the Cuban-American lobby to unseat Castro have generally concurred with U.S. objectives. Yet the lobby's clout has demonstrated that even American presidents may be forced to compromise their position in the face of a well-organized diaspora that poses an electoral threat. Over one million people of Cuban origin live in the United States, with most concentrated in Florida and other electorally important states on the east coast such as New York and New Jersey. In the months leading up to the 1992 presidential elections, with polls showing a close race in Florida between Democratic nominee Bill Clinton and Republican President George Bush, Mas Canosa pushed Congress to pass the controversial Cuban Democracy Act, which tightened the American economic embargo of Cuba. Despite Bush's concerns that the bill would alienate U.S. trade allies, the president yielded in the face of Bill Clinton's early endorsement of the measure. Consequently, the *New York Times* wrote that Mas Canosa had become "one of the most effective power brokers in Washington."[74]

It is important to note, however, that the Cuban community centered in Miami is not the same as it was thirty-five years ago, in the early days after the revolution. New and more Americanized generations conceptualize their identity more and more in terms similar to those of other immigrants to the United States, rather than clinging to the exile as the defining characteristic of their existence. Although they "grew up in the Heart of The Exile, [they are] emotionally and culturally distant from it."[75]

Indeed, militant political groups within the exile community have had greater difficulty maintaining the same zeal for an uncompromisingly hard line on the current Cuban government in the face of such demographic shifts, and in competition with more moderate attitudes brought in by subsequent waves of arrivals from Cuba. This has been especially true of two new groups in the early 1990s, artists and other cultural figures who still maintain some of the ideals of Castro's revolution, and poorer and more racially mixed immigrants who have a keener sense of the suffering caused in Cuba by U.S. economic pressure. They do not identify with the rhetoric of the older activists whose commitment to democracy they may also question, and who often appear to them to be more interested in reestablishing lost status and power for themselves than in bettering the lives of Cubans who have remained on the island. These divisions raise the question of how accurately organizational leaders such as Mas Canosa represent Cuban-American opinion. Canosa viewed himself as a potential successor to Castro, but the right-wing views he espoused are no longer as prevalent among Cubans in the United States.

Despite these profound changes in the U.S. Cuban community, traditional Cuban-American lobbyists continue to exert substantial influence on U.S. foreign policy, as demonstrated during the 1996 presidential campaign. Cuba's downing of an unarmed American plane with Cuban-Americans on board earlier in the year brought to a halt a nascent conciliatory shift in the Clinton administration's position toward Cuba. American outrage over the event translated politically into support for new congressional legislation (the so-called Helms-Burton law) to increase economic pressure on Havana by, among other things, allowing for suits to be brought in U.S. courts against third-country companies and their executives who benefited financially from nationalized Cuban property claimed by exiles in the United States. While the Clinton administration recognized the problems this would cause with other countries, many of them allies, the president signed the legislation, conscious of the large number of electoral votes in Florida and other states with substantial Cuban-American populations. Clinton's ambivalence was displayed by the fact that he suspended implementation of certain provisions twice, the last time after his reelection.[76]

Clinton, after all, initially opposed Helms-Burton and in 1995 "in effect . . . repeal[ed] the Cuban Adjustment Act of 1966," removing "without warning [the] special status" Cubans had enjoyed in the United States as exiled refugees from communism.[77] This was done in reaction to the impending arrival of more than forty thousand Cuban boat people in Florida, and was followed by instances where the United States Coast Guard actually returned would-be immigrants directly to Cuba. David Rieff writes that in the Miami Cuban community "there was a devastating sense of shock. For it was clear that whatever Cubans in South Florida believed, the Clinton administration was declaring that the 36-year-old collaboration between the U.S. government and the Cuban exile community was over. Cubans would be considered an ethnic group, one whose original members had come as political refugees, but whose relatives were immigrants for whom no special treatment would be accorded. In other words, for Washington the exile was over."[78] Yet, the strong romantic sense of the homeland, the history of exile and displacement, and the symbolism of Castro as the enemy of democracy all ensure the continued importance of the exile voice both in Cuban-American diasporic politics and in American foreign-policy decision making.[79]

Diasporas and the Changing Importance of Democracy in U.S. Foreign Relations

As noted earlier, the propensity of diasporas to take part in a campaign to overthrow and replace a nondemocratic regime are greatly affected by the official U.S. posture toward the home government. In the case of postwar east European diasporas, for example, though the United States shared their ultimate goal of freedom and independence for their captive nations, the U.S.-Soviet understanding on spheres of domination rendered diasporas' activities ineffective, with the exception of symbolic successes. In the 1960s, in the face of Communist impermeability and their own impotence, east European exile institutions were largely transformed into American ethnic organizations.[80] From the 1950s until the mid-1970s, support for human rights and democracy in other countries was secondary in American foreign policy to containing the power and influence of communism. The granting of asylum became a tool of foreign policy, as refugees and political exiles fleeing Communist countries "became touching symbols around which to weave the legitimacy needed for foreign policy."[81] During the Nixon-Ford-Kissinger years, realpolitik and "de-ideologization of foreign relations became the order of the day." The United States "accepted without visible disgust despotic governments of both right (Greece, Portugal, Brazil, Chile) and left (Russia, China, Romania, Yugoslavia)."[82]

Whereas Henry Kissinger sought to eliminate the "moral exuberance"[83] of American foreign policy, Jimmy Carter endeavored to restore its idealistic dimension by placing the promotion of human rights at the top of his international agenda.[84] Yet, even during the Carter years, U.S.-based diasporic campaigns for democratization in the homeland that did not coincide with U.S. short-term goals were ignored or even obstructed. In 1979, the U.S.-based opposition to Ferdinand Marcos, which sought to capitalize on Carter's declared human rights policy, became dispirited when the president was quick to shelve criticism of Marcos after the United States secured a new agreement on U.S. military bases in Manila.

President Reagan and his administration officials, while officially promoting a gradual democratic regime change in Communist and non-Communist countries, often invoked democratic rhetoric rather cynically. In August 1981, on his visit to Manila, then vice-president

Bush went as far as praising President Ferdinand Marcos for his "adherence to democratic principle and to the democratic processes."[85] Consequently, when leaders of the U.S.-based Filipino democratic opposition were implicated in the 1981 series of bombings in Manila, Marcos was able to convince the Reagan administration to crack down on his overseas opponents.[86] In 1988 Steve Psinakis, one of Marcos's leading opponents in the United States, accused the Reagan administration of duplicity in dealing with political exiles:

> The United States government, at the request of the Philippine dictator Ferdinand Marcos, targeted for investigation and prosecution the leaders of the US-based movement to restore democracy to the Philippines. The government did so at the same time that it was not only tolerating but actively supporting the actions of private groups in the United States to provide arms to the Nicaraguan Contras, and other foreign resistance movements. Congressional investigation of the Iran-Contra affair . . . make[s] it clear that whether . . . a group supporting efforts in opposition to [a] foreign government is encouraged, on the one hand, or prosecuted, on the other, depends on whether the group's political position is supported by the current administration.[87]

Only toward the mid-1980s, after some years of "democratic ambiguity," did the Reagan administration become genuinely committed to democratic transformation around the globe.

Despite many obstacles, the experience of recent years shows that diasporas may contribute significantly to democratic change in their native countries. They do so by challenging the home regime's attempts to suppress or co-opt its opposition, contesting the regime's international legitimacy, exposing human rights violations, combating the home regime's foreign propaganda, obstructing friendly relations with the United States through effective lobbies, and, finally, assisting and actively participating in the struggle of the domestic opposition. In many instances political exiles and other diaspora members have returned home in the aftermath of regime transition to occupy top private and public posts. The anti-Marcos campaign of Filipinos abroad has been one of the most successful and multifaceted diasporic efforts to unseat a nondemocratic regime, and it became a model for Korean-American groups who organized to protest Chun Doo Hwan's authoritarian practices.[88] Shortly before his death, in an attempt to clear his name, Marcos published an essay in which he maintained that the chief reason for the shift in the U.S. friendly posture toward his regime was "the contrived image of the Philippine reality" cultivated "by the articulate and well-financed representatives of the anti-Marcos expatriates residing in North America." He further argued that "the committee hearings in the US Congress were given the widest circulation by the American press; [and that] the wildest charges [against him] were given credence."[89]

A major reason for the success of diasporic communities in affecting U.S. diplomacy vis-à-vis the home government is the nature of American politics and especially the power of the individual Congress member – which makes a unitary foreign policy unlikely. Today, even immigrants and refugees without citizenship status may find easy access to Congress and the media and build other networks that influence American foreign policy. Moreover, American party politics has been increasingly dominated by ethnic groups that have pushed their domestic and homelands' concerns to the center of political party platforms.

For example, in 1988, just a few weeks before Mexico's 1988 presidential elections, an international controversy erupted when members of the California Democratic Party Chicano caucus recommended a condemnation of human rights violations in Mexico in the California platform for the Democratic national convention. Although the Mexican opposition hailed the motion, associates of President Salinas strongly criticized the proposal "as interventionist and filled with stereotypical generalities and false assertions."[90] This incident represented a growing involvement of Mexican-Americans in Mexico's domestic affairs in the previous decade (see Chapter 5).

In the aftermath of the cold war, when the principles of democracy and human rights reign supreme, it has become more difficult for the United States to overlook dictatorial practices of friendly regimes. This development has enabled diasporas to become more effective in pushing policy makers to adhere to America's values of promoting democracy and an open society around the globe. Such pressures may be critical when ad hoc strategic interests seem to take precedence over the promotion of democracy. Certainly, in recent years the U.S. government is more disposed to hear concerns of ethnic Americans who endeavor to influence American diplomacy toward their country of origin if and when they promote democracy and human rights.

As Myron Weiner has pointed out in his study of the impact of Asian-Americans on U.S. foreign policy,

> because immigrants and human rights activists are likely to be vociferous when the [transgressing] . . . country is an ally of the United States, their demands will invariably create strains in US relationships with [home] . . . governments. These demands will further generate conflicts within Washington over how we should weigh human rights against strategic considerations.[91]

Naturally, the ability of the United States to drive a government to improve its human rights practices and to democratize its political system increases with the home regime's vulnerability to diplomatic and economic pressure. However, diasporas that play the card of economic sanctions imprudently risk being seen as insensitive to indigenous national concerns. When in 1983 the United States negotiated the renewal of its bases in the Philippines, the leaders of the U.S.-based opposition to Marcos faced a dilemma. As nationalists, they wanted the United States to pay rent for the bases without dictating how the money should be spent; but as opponents of the regime they feared Marcos would misuse the funds to strengthen his rule. In testimony before Congress, diaspora leaders "grit their teeth and suggest[ed] that it be given in aid, rather than rent, and if possible all non-military aid."[92] Post-Tienanmen Chinese exiles who advocate U.S. sanctions have become vulnerable to the Chinese government exploiting their image as traitors "living off the fat of the land in exile."[93]

Cultural Impediments: The Chinese Experience

The "loyalty baggage" is particularly heavy for a political exile who is awaiting return. He is more susceptible to a home regime's charges of disloyalty than the immigrant who works to establish himself abroad, and "must try to identify his cause with the national interest, and give himself the psychological support to survive the constant political and socioeconomic pressure pushing him to abdicate his exile status."[94] The issue of loyalty from afar is also compounded by culture. Overseas Chinese, for example, have been traditionally ineffective in host and home politics and have preferred to concentrate on their internal affairs.[95] Moreover, some post-Tienanmen Chinese intellectual exiles still retain Communist ideological residues; and even more critical, they are culturally dedicated to the Confucian political heritage that commands their highest allegiance to their country and nation. These exiles' fears of the "pluralist chaos" in the United States and their desire to escape the trap of "extreme individualism" make them highly vulnerable to the home government's depiction of them as traitors. Thus, they become hesitant in their opposition efforts and are more inclined to return home on Beijing's terms. In light of these tensions, one scholar of Chinese politics has questioned the democratic commitment of some post-1989 exiles.[96]

In examining the role of U.S. diasporic communities in bringing about the demise of communism in eastern Europe, it may be said that the effect has been cumulative rather than direct. Probably one of the most significant diasporic contributions to the weakening of Soviet communism was made by Jewish-American lobbies, which were pivotal in focusing the spotlight on the conditions and rights of Soviet Jewry. Jewish-Americans became personal emissaries of *refuseniks*. Working against the Nixon administration's official position, they lobbied vigorously for the Jackson-Vanik amendment, which linked the USSR's most-favored-nation trade status to its willingness to allow freer emigration. Overall, postwar east European émigrés were ineffective in their struggle to free their captive nations, with some exceptions, such as the Polish-Americans' support of Solidarity since 1981.[97] The relative weakness of the east European lobbies had little to do with questions of loyalty. The diasporas considered their home Communist governments as enemies of their nations and stooges of a foreign regime, a position reinforced by America's aversion to communism. This mutual reinforcement in fact eased the integration of eastern Europeans in the United States. The host country did not demand their abandonment of home country loyalty, but rather helped them to redefine their outward patriotism to include and emphasize freedom and democracy. This is also why so many diaspora members felt a swell of pride in the political and economic changes taking place in their native countries. On their visits to the United States, east European leaders like Lech Walesa, Václav Havel, Vytautas Landsbergis, and Sali Berisha of Albania have made direct patriotic appeals to their respective diasporas, offering them citizenship and encouraging their economic and political support. Many diaspora members have assumed the role of cultural and political ambassadors between the United States and their native countries, others were offered key economic positions, and others even emerged as leaders and candidates of political parties (including a presidential candidate) in the old countries. In the homelands, diaspora members initially enjoyed added credibility and moral authority by virtue of being untainted by suspicion of collaboration and complicity with the former regime. One of the latest manifestations of this phenomenon was the January 1998 election of Valdas Adamkus as president of Lithuania; Adamkus spent almost fifty years in the United States before returning to his native country. However, there has also been some evidence of east European resentment toward diaspora members, whose quick rise to the top in home country affairs is not always seen by residents as legitimate or beneficial.

Finally, the crafting of new democracies often demands patience and reconciliation, rather than revenge or an arbitrary "settling of accounts." It also requires courageous leadership on the part of both outgoing authoritarian regimes and their democratic opposition, and a broad understanding among supporters of democracy that not everything can be achieved quickly. Diasporic forces that push for immediate results at the expense of long-term political healing and viability may therefore compromise or endanger the political "progress" they seek to encourage. This is particularly pertinent to the case of exiles whose personal experiences of war and injustice prior to their departure, and their commitment to continue the struggle while abroad, have left them frozen in time, "dwell[ing] in the past . . . locked inside hates and angers of the past," and unable to adapt to new political realities. "They treat today as if it were still an evil yesterday with which one could not compromise."[98] Indeed, these opinions find fertile ground in influential, primarily conservative American political circles, which tend to portray political realities in stark black and white, while trumpeting the American example as the acme of democratic purity. These forces are prone to demand quick democratic fixes without regard to the particular circumstances or nuances of societies undergoing transformation. Yet, overall, the American experience of an open society has a strong propensity to moderate even political exiles over time and erodes the special status that initially created the appearance of barriers between them and other immigrants in American society. At the end of the cold war, when U.S. foreign-policy makers are less quick to designate enemies with the same ideological zeal, this propensity against "diasporic democratic extremism" increases.

African-Americans and the Global Context

One of the most effective diasporic efforts to alter world politics in recent years was conducted by African-Americans.[99] Through mobilization and protest action against apartheid, they managed to generate a historic shift in U.S. foreign policy toward Pretoria, which helped bring about change in South Africa toward a nonracial democratic polity. The success of African-Americans in influencing U.S. foreign policy is all the more remarkable given their unique historical experience as a "race" and not an "ethnic group." They are, in the words of George Frederickson, the

> only minority [which] has been consistently thought of as a "race" in the full and invidious sense. . . . Most other persecuted minorities were eventually considered candidates for assimilation and were denounced and abused when they chose to remain culturally distinctive. Blacks, on the other hand, were regarded for centuries as inherently unassimilable, because, as subhuman, they lacked a developed or refined human culture and were deemed incapable of having one. Consequently, every effort was made to keep them from taking a full part in American society.[100]

This profound historic and cultural legacy of domestic disempowerment and failed efforts at integration have led some observers and black activists to reject positioning African-American politics within the spectrum of the debate on multiculturalism, which is, at its core, they argue, a debate between pluralist and assimilationist visions of America. For them, blacks have never had either option. It is therefore critical that, when it comes to the diasporic sphere of activity, African-Americans have exhibited the same characteristics as other groups, which in and of itself offers evidence that even American racism is not an irresistible force. The importance of diasporic and transnational politics in the U.S. foreign-policy process provided space for African-Americans to have a strong impact on America's stand on South Africa.

By the 1980s, the antiapartheid movement had reached far beyond its roots as a black ethnoracial cause to become a broadly based grassroots movement of unprecedented size, diversity, and impact on U.S. foreign policy. Black leaders had succeeded in making apartheid an "American" issue as opposed to an exclusively ethnoracial one, involving fundamental issues of justice, human rights, and equality. The 1986 Comprehensive Anti-Apartheid Act (CAAA), which Congress passed over President Reagan's veto, was critical in pushing South Africa to release Nelson Mandela and other prisoners, legalizing antiapartheid organizations, lifting the state of emergency, enabling the return of exiles, repealing key apartheid laws, and entering into negotiations with black organizations on the transition to democratic rule. These reforms, in turn, led to the termination on July 10, 1991, of most U.S. economic sanctions by President Bush, initially to the consternation of African-American leaders who insisted that a number of the conditions set by the CAAA had yet to be fulfilled.[101]

The active involvement of African-Americans in South Africa is part and parcel of the evolution of their community and politics inside the United States. In this case, the importance of diasporic politics is beyond the mere relevance of ethnoracial leverage over U.S. foreign policy. It represents a significant step into the long-sought and yet unattained vision of African-American integration. The involvement in the South African struggle allowed African-Americans, perhaps for the first time, to change American mainstream politics and values, as the diaspora lobby succeeded in establishing a symmetry between its own agenda and the American creed of freedom and democracy, thereby challenging the Reagan administration on its own rhetoric. By exploiting the growing legitimacy of the ethnic voice in U.S. foreign policy and by portraying their homeland's cause as an all-American concern, African-Americans were able to move one step forward toward their own domestic inclusion.

Indeed, the 1960s represented black America's growing belief that "what happens to blacks in Africa has implications for blacks at home."[102] However, over the next few years, despite the success of the civil rights movement in breaking many social and economic barriers, black Americans were unable to translate their stake in Africa into an effective foreign policy lobby. This failure was the result of a schism between the emergent class of mainstream blacks, represented by the formation of the Congressional Black Caucus (CBC) in 1971, and the marginalized radical nationalists, Pan-Africanists, black Muslims, and Marxists, all of whom rejected the possibility and the desirability of integration into the larger polity.

In 1974, in an essay entitled "Can the Blacks Do for Africa What the Jews Did for Israel?" Martin Weil argued that though American blacks have had little impact on American policy toward Africa, "[s]ooner or later the United States will have to confront the emergence of powerful pressure hostile to American policy in Africa."[103] He further argued:

> To be successful, a black movement for reform of American policy toward Africa must be perceived as a vehicle for exporting *American* ideals. It must be an affirmation of black faith in the United States and a demonstration of black ability to manipulate the fine structure of American politics with the astuteness and finesse of previous practitioners. Blacks as blacks may identify with Africa, but it is only as Americans that they can change United States policy in Africa. . . . To aid the revolution abroad, blacks must first join the establishment at home.[104]

Weil's prediction began to be realized in the mid-1970s. First, the extremist movements were shunted to the periphery of black politics, while the mainstream discovered the "secrets" of influencing American foreign policy, "an electoral threat, . . . a lobbying apparatus, . . . and a successful appeal to the symbols of American nationhood."[105] During the 1976 U.S. presidential election campaign, African-Americans made their mark on the Democratic Party's platform by pushing the issues of independence for the white minority-ruled states of southern Africa while African foreign policy in Washington was still centered around the East-West conflict. Most significant for the institutionalization of black political power in the U.S. foreign-policy arena was the July 1977 establishment of TransAfrica, a black American foreign-policy lobby focusing on African and Caribbean issues led by lawyer Randall Robinson. Under him, the organization enlisted the support of many mainstream organizations like the NAACP and Africare and began a grass-roots outreach program to mobilize African-American support for TransAfrica's foreign-policy initiatives, especially with regard to South Africa. Dovetailing with the self-proclaimed pro-African interests of the Carter administration, TransAfrica's goals of mobilizing the African-American electorate enjoyed modest success.[106]

The link between the civil rights movement and the antiapartheid struggle was reinforced during the years of President Reagan, who was perceived by the black leadership to be insensitive to civil rights issues in general, and uncaring on apartheid in particular. Black leaders were initially divided on how to respond to Reagan's challenge, especially since the president's popularity in the early 1980s rendered him "unassailable." But with the unfolding of an extended crisis situation in South Africa and in response to Pretoria's imposition of a partial state of emergency, apartheid provided a focus and power to attack the administration from the back door. Apartheid became a rallying cry for reviving the spirit of the 1960s, although this time not in the form of a domestic battle. Here, black Americans organized as insiders to set the conscience of American values back on track. Though the American Committee on Africa, the first antiapartheid organization in the United States, was founded in 1953, it was only during the 1980s that "civil right activists discovered in the fight [against apartheid] an effort they could throw themselves into with gusto – and little moral ambiguity."[107] In the mid-1980s, therefore, black leaders could no longer be labeled disloyal. But as long as the reality of Mikhail Gorbachev's "new political thinking" was not seriously apprehended, there was a temptation to label those sympathetic to the African National Congress (ANC) as pro-Communists.

The strategy of escalating the antiapartheid campaign was devised by TransAfrica. The wave of protests, sit-ins, and voluntary arrests caught like wildfire across the nation. Apartheid became a principal political concern for local governments, towns, media, and universities pressured by black organizations to rid themselves of holdings that involved U.S. and foreign companies with interests in South Africa. The impact on elected representatives and the public at large was dramatic, and the political momentum paved the way for an unprecedented congressional coalition in the House and the Senate, which adopted the sanctions legislation. Then Senate majority leader Bob Dole acknowledged that the issue of sanctions "has now become a domestic civil rights issue."[108]

It is not surprising that the mobilization of the black diaspora against apartheid coincided with a renewed search for black identity in the United States – expressed by the move to change the group appellation from black to African-American. Such alterations in terms had been introduced at various junctures of the struggle for black liberation and equality in the United States even before the Emancipation Proclamation.[109] Yet in the 1980s the lobby for "African-American" epitomized a strong perception that integration and political power at home had much to do with an alliance with a country and culture abroad. When in 1988 black leaders announced their preference for the term African-American, Jesse Jackson declared: "Every ethnic group in this country has a reference to some land base, some historical, cultural base. African-Americans have hit that level of maturity."[110]

The link between African-Americans and South Africa was accentuated further in 1990 during Nelson Mandela's first visit to the United States, after his release from prison. Mandela enjoyed a hero's welcome. One observer stated:

> He fires the pride of African Americans and touches a deep desire in the psyche of Americans. . . . For the sometimes dispirited American civil rights coalition, Mandela provides . . . a rallying point and common cause. For the many blacks who have begun to call themselves African-Americans, he is a flesh-and-blood exemplar of what an African can be.[111]

Ultimately, the identification with black South Africa became one of the critical tests for political allegiance to domestic black causes. When New York Mayor David N. Dinkins landed on South African soil on November 12, 1991, and proclaimed himself "finally home," an editorial in the *New York Times* stated that "Mr. Dinkins seemed to be speaking as much to Brooklynites as to any listeners [in South Africa]."[112]

The success of the African-American lobby is an additional testimony to the power and legitimation of "hyphenated" groups in the United States. But the leverage of ethnicity places new challenges on diasporas that wish to affect American foreign policy at a time when the U.S. government has been more disposed to concerns over human rights and democratization. The struggle for self-determination tends to galvanize diasporic unity – using the American rhetoric of democracy and freedom – against undisputed ethnonational foes. However, the attainment of homeland independence, when not in

accordance with democratic principles, forces diasporas to make agonizing choices. If the homeland is ruled undemocratically, the diaspora may be required to make a clear break with the home government, side with its democratic opposition, or even cut its ties with
home compatriots, with all the actual and psychological ramifications
of such action. If the diaspora chooses to cooperate with a nondemocratic home regime, however, it risks undermining its U.S. domestic
reputation and loyalty status, especially if the prevailing American
mood toward the home government is hostile.

The African-Americans' antiapartheid struggle largely parallels
the self-determination model of diasporic politics, as the white minority represents the obvious foe. Such is also the case for the majority of Arab-Americans who endorse Palestinian self-determination
and consider Israel to be the adversary (see Chapter 3). But to sustain
a democratic reputation a diaspora may have acquired in its campaign
for a homeland's independence, it must continuously demonstrate its
hostility to nondemocratic practices of a home regime. During the
cold war, black American organizations, which were often criticized
for accentuating the grievances of apartheid while overlooking abuses
of black regimes, could vindicate their support of African governments that were ideologically hostile to democracy as a way of coun-
tering U.S. "imperialist intervention" via nondemocratic proxies.
This was the case in Angola, where African-American organizations
sided with the Angolan Marxist government against the United
States–sponsored UNITA rebels. However, in the aftermath of the
cold war, when the prevailing perception in the United States is that
the continued support of dictatorships or military surrogates in regional conflicts is economically and politically imprudent, the rationale for siding with or acquiescing in the rule of black despots, or
alternatively supporting one-party revolutionary regimes, is rapidly
disappearing for the White House and for African-Americans alike.
Accordingly, the U.S. State Department, seemingly motivated by
TransAfrica's lobbying, is now pressing African countries to embrace
democracy quickly or otherwise suffer economic penalties. Since
1991, African-American leaders have moved steadily to redefine their
pro-Africa crusade along the democratic theme of urging the U.S.
government to get serious about promoting democracy and human
rights in Africa. In his testimony before the Senate Foreign Relations
Committee in May 1991, TransAfrica's Robinson called for a new

U.S. foreign policy in Africa "contingent on respect for human rights and progress toward political and economic reform."[113] Bolstered by its striking success in influencing American policy on Haiti, in 1995 TransAfrica launched a national campaign to restore democracy in Nigeria. TransAfrica led daily picketing at the Nigerian embassy and organized petitions and media ads denouncing Nigeria's rulers. Robinson, supported by some members of the Congressional Black Caucus, urged the White House to take a more confrontational posture toward the military junta by refusing to buy Nigerian oil.[114] This campaign was the first display of a strong African-American protest against the abuses of a black African regime. The campaign has been applauded by some Nigerian opposition leaders, such as former foreign minister Bolaji Akinyemi.[115] The Nigerian government and some Nigerian interest groups in the United States, however, charged Robinson with exploiting the Nigerian political tragedy to promote TransAfrica's fund raising and warned that Robinson's crusade "will ultimately batter our national pride, and cause harm to the image of the black man,"[116] as one such group stated. President Clinton's historic visit with Jesse Jackson to Africa in 1998 focused on the new, more democratic face of several African countries as a source of pride and inspiration for African-Americans.

Without diminishing their contribution to the recent U.S. campaign to push African countries to embrace democracy, it must be remembered that for African-Americans the opposition to black dictatorial rule is relatively safe, as the homeland is symbolic and the consequences of a home government's retaliation are virtually nonexistent. This is not the case for diaspora communities directly tied to homelands whose regimes tend to hold insiders and outsiders hostages to their repressive rule. To become a meaningful and reliable voice for human rights, democracy, and self-determination, such diasporas need courageous leaders who are willing to take risks and make personal sacrifices.

The dynamic described above will be highlighted further in the next chapter through an in-depth examination of Arab-American politics and identity in recent decades. Arab-Americans are an amorphous community consisting of numerous religious and national groups. Their identity and politics inside the United States have been shaped largely by developments in the Middle East, particularly those related to the ongoing Arab-Israeli conflict over Palestine. This conflict, which draws great attention in the United States, in part because of Jewish-American involvement, has at the same time served as a source of mobilization for self-designated Arab-American elites. Their views and activities on issues concerning American domestic affairs and their conception of their own identity as Americans have become inseparable from their foreign policy concerns. How this dynamic came about and how it has evolved in recent years in the wake of Middle East peace agreements, the rise of militant Islam, and other international developments will be explored. As will become evident, the internal dynamics in the Arab-American (and Arab Muslim) communities are shaped by the different voices in the Middle East and are constantly affected by developments in the region's political processes.

3

Arab-American Identity and New Transnational Challenges

Middle East and other international developments have long influenced the identity and politics of Americans of Arab and Muslim descent (by no means identical groups, though obviously overlapping). Since the early 1990s, the Arab-American community and its mainstream institutions have been grappling with a new crisis of identity and political purpose in response to global changes, including the Gulf War, the collapse of the Soviet Union, the Arab-Israeli peace process, the escalation of intra-Arab struggles (primarily between militant Islamists and failing nationalist regimes), the war in Bosnia, and the "third wave" of democratic transitions. These developments are forcing Arab-American institutions and leaders to redefine their domestic and foreign-policy strategy.[1]

For the past three decades, the agenda of U.S. Arabs has been monopolized by the Arab-Israeli conflict and the Palestinian "cause." Indeed, given the diversity of the community – in terms of quasinational homelands, religions, and ideological persuasions[2] – the Palestinian cause could be said to have provided the very foundation for pan-Arab ethnic identity in America. In the wake of peace treaties and other diplomatic advances in the Middle East, one of the questions is, if Israel could no longer be singled out as the Arabs' principal antagonist, what would take its place? Which issues can best foster Arab-American solidarity and command the attention of American politicians and media, if indeed the peace process is ultimately successful and the Palestinians finally gain independence?

To some extent, the challenges facing Arab-Americans are similar to those now facing American Jews. In view of the Middle East peace process, the reality of Israel as a strong and affluent country, and the growing gap between increasingly assimilated American Jews and

Israeli culture and life, Jewish-American organizations are grappling with the "burden of peace."[3] Will their strong connections with Israel persist in the same manner as when the Jewish state's very existence was in undisputed jeopardy? Some Jewish activists no longer perceive such a danger (an issue that dominated diaspora life for decades) and are searching for new sources of communal identity inside the United States. However, even those American Jews who seek to become completely assimilated and avoid association or identification with Israel sometimes find themselves influenced by events in the Middle East, as was the case with the upsurge of American Jewish pride after the Six Day War or, on a more minor scale, after other dramatic events in the region. "Israel's acts, or even existence, might seem to implicate them involuntarily in far more responsibility"[4] than they would initiate on their own. In this there are similarities with Arab-Americans. Others, especially Orthodox Jews (who tend to express the greatest degree of attachment to the land of Israel, though not always to the state), and who have generally rejected the Oslo peace process, have grown more isolated in terms of connections with their non-Orthodox (Conservative and Reform) kin. Jewish religious extremists have questioned the legitimacy of Israeli democracy and have advocated violence against its government. Some Orthodox rabbis (Americans among them) even decreed that it was "halachically" correct to assassinate Prime Minister Rabin. Notwithstanding the growing divergence and divisiveness among American Jews and between their communities and the increasingly fragmented population of Israel, Israel remains a major focus of Jewish ethnoreligious life in the United States and a prime source of solidarity.[5]

In contrast, many American Arabs, qua Arab-Americans, have never resolved the issue of their transnational identities and allegiances. For example, Americans of Iraqi descent are troubled primarily by the suffering of their families under Saddam Hussein, Yemenites by periodic turbulence in their home country. Certainly, Arab-Americans have yet to establish a strong ethnocultural or political presence within America's multicultural society.[6] Indeed, Arabs in the United States are a highly diverse and contentious community whose members arrived in distinct migration waves over a long period of time and for a variety of involuntary and voluntary reasons. Their disparity has been deeply influenced by Middle East intra-

Arab enmities, which often split Arab-Americans down to the level of families.[7] Yet even as Middle Eastern realities led to the stigmatization of U.S. Arabs (and Muslims) on various occasions, at the same time they also reinforced their solidarity and invigorated their political energies. Israel's 1982 invasion of Lebanon, more than any other event, "catalyzed [Arab-Americans] into collective action that cut across all religions, classes, and generations."[8] This unity proved fragile, however, as mobilization failed to translate into concrete political gains. Then, in September, came the horrible reality of the Sabra and Shatila refugee camps where Christian Arabs killed Muslim Arabs. Although some Arab-American organizations were able to build up their structures during this short-lived mobilization, the long-lasting effects were slight.

The Palestinian *intifada* in the Israeli-occupied territories revived the sense of identity and pride among young Arab-Americans. In fact, the Palestinian cause had long provided the foundation for pan-Arab ethnic identity in America. It became the yardstick by which many Arabs and Muslims in the United States have gauged the world and afforded the ideological core to almost all Arab political and religious groupings. Attitudes toward "the cause" became "the subconscious cue" in evaluating the behavior of outsiders toward the Middle East: "a friend is he who supports the Palestinians; and an enemy is he who opposes them."[9]

For many Arab-Americans, the support for the Palestinian struggle and the protest against America's friendly relations with Israel became a unifying battle into which they could throw themselves with little moral ambiguity. U.S. Arab activists of different descent and conflicting ideologies could apply their own particular narrative to the cause. Ethnic, national, and religious identities became intertwined in the struggle for Palestine.

The more left-leaning diasporic activists, primarily Palestinian-Americans, adopted the narrative of colonialism and American imperialism. Inspired by Palestinian intellectuals and scholars-turned-activists, they draped the cause in the mantle of Third World rhetoric and secular humanism. In the late 1960s and in the 1970s the cause became a struggle against Western colonial domination, represented in their view by the Zionists and their American allies. Supporting the Palestine Liberation Organization (PLO) was an imperative. After all, as Fawaz Turki has written, "Palestinians became the PLO, and the PLO became, in an age that looked romantically at such things, a national liberation movement."[10]

For devout Arab Muslims, the cause was not born of Arab nationalism; instead it represented a religious crusade to recover the Holy City of Jerusalem (al-Quds).[11] Palestinians were perceived to be sacrificial lambs in the struggle for the Holy City. This notion was magnified whenever violent clashes took place on the Temple Mount – October 8, 1990, for example. Moreover, many Muslims in America (Arabs and non-Arabs) have viewed U.S. support of Israel as part of the Western assault on Islam. Yvonne Haddad, a scholar of Muslims in America, has argued that the U.S. Middle East policy "has had the most profound influence on Muslim identity [in the United States]," accounting for the reluctance of many Muslims to integrate.[12]

Proponents of Arab-American integration, by contrast, articulated their support for the cause in terms of cherished American values, such as self-determination, human rights, and freedom. They couch their objection to U.S. foreign policy in the Middle East in terms of "America first" and have presented their case as part of a concern for the U.S. "national interest."

Despite these differences in orientation and regardless of deep-seated and long-standing divisions within the Arab-American community, the cause served many Arabs in America as a litmus test to distinguish clearly between "us" and "them." The resounding exceptions have been the Lebanese Phalangists – archenemies of the Palestinians and strong opponents of Arab unity – represented by the American Lebanese League and the Maronite clergy.[13] As a unifying "glue," the cause was somewhat effective, but its days seemed to be numbered. The display of Arabs fighting Arabs during the Gulf War, the historic handshake between Rabin and Arafat in September 1993, the Israeli-Jordanian peace treaty, ongoing Israeli-Palestinian negotiations (despite disturbances and interruptions), and increasing intra-Arab violence (especially between Islamists and proponents of Arab nationalism) have all left Arab-American diasporic solidarity in grave need of a new source of cohesion.

This chapter examines how various Arab-American groups have coped with these challenges. It focuses on the rhetoric and actions of mainstream Arab-American activists and the more left-leaning camp led by Palestinian intellectuals. It also examines the rhetoric and actions of Islamic groups, though the analysis in that part is quite preliminary. Spokesmen of these groups define the agenda of Arab-Americans to the outside world. Yet, as is the case with other ethnic groups in the United States, it is difficult to assess their real power and influence among American-Arabs or to determine whether they are truly representative of their claimed constituency – to whom they are not accountable by clear and customary procedures.[14]

The intent herein is to analyze how these activists have defined and responded to the link between events abroad and the challenges facing the Arab community inside the United States. What has been the impact of the Mideast peace process on Arab-Americans? Are they likely to assume a greater role in U.S. foreign policy? How do they respond to the acrimony between Islamists and proponents of Arab nationalism? Finally, how have events abroad affected relations between Arab-Americans and American Jews?

Arab-Americans as a Mobilized Diaspora

As noted before, the engine behind ethnic community involvement in domestic and international affairs is comprised of "core members" or intensively active organizing elites who are often, but by no means always, connected to and financed by elements in the country of origin. These activists draw on the loyalties of "rearguard members" or occasional recruits whose commitment fluctuates with the turn of events. The vast majority of them, whose size is always difficult to gauge (in the case of Arab-Americans, two to three million), are silent members, considered to be potential recruits by the elites of both home and host countries.[15] This assessment is often mistaken. Some "silent members" may identify with symbols of the old country without maintaining an interest in its domestic or foreign affairs; others may not identify at all as members of the community or with homeland symbols or issues.[16]

In the case of Americans of Arab descent, the notion of pan-Arab ethnic solidarity and the appellation "Arab-American" took hold only after the 1967 Arab-Israeli war. Before that war, Arab-American identity was amorphous and dormant. Arab-American political organizations were virtually nonexistent. As members of many subnational and religious groupings with unclear ethnic boundaries,

American Arabs generally either assimilated as individuals or retreated to their ethnic and religious communities. Most of them were second-generation Christians of Syrian-Lebanese origin who, while often retaining some sentimental affinity toward the countries and villages of their parents' or grandparents' birth, remained apolitical.[17]

Prior to the establishment of the PLO and the 1967 Arab-Israeli War, Arab-Americans had no ideological core, national political organizations, or funding. Even Palestinian-Americans who came to the United States after 1948 with a strong sense of homeland loyalty did not retain a broad Palestinian identity. They focused primarily on family and village networks and were largely incognizant of the Palestinian cause as a whole.[18] Moreover, until 1967 Arabs in America "generally refrained from identification with Arab issues, considering that the [American] political process was closed on such issues, and fearing that they would be subject to social and economic repercussions by challenging Zionist and pro-Israeli sentiments."[19] Finally, many Arab Muslims in America concealed their religious identity in a society that considered Protestantism God's chosen religion.[20]

The ethnopolitical awakening of Arab-Americans coincided with the civil rights movement and the increasing tolerance of ethnicity in American society after the 1965 Immigration Act. Its real impetus, however, was the traumatic defeat of the Arabs in 1967, Israel's occupation of the West Bank and Gaza, and the spread of anti-Arab sentiment in America. Edward Said maintains that it was only after the Six Day War that "Arab-American identity came to a crisis of collective self-knowledge. There would [be] no Arab-American organization had it not been for 1967."[21]

Since the late 1960s, many American Arabs have begun to assert their ethnic origin and to attempt to present a united front to non-Arabs. In the 1970s and 1980s, activists developed a minority consciousness that reflected frustration with the caricature of Arab culture and the Muslim religion in America. They established Arab-American institutions that focused the ethnic self-affirmation and pride of their kinfolk and made their identity visible to all.[22] In their effort to gain political influence in American domestic and international affairs, Arab-American activists drew heavily on the energies and frustration of the post-1967 Palestinian immigrants and refugees "with the homeland still fresh in their minds [who] were ready to be foot soldiers in the tedious, frustrating task of lobbying U.S. policy makers."[23]

As the Middle East conflict intensified and the U.S.–Israeli alliance solidified, Arab-Americans felt the heat. The increasing power of the pro-Israel lobby, the 1973 Arab oil embargo (and subsequent series of OPEC price hikes), PLO terrorism, and the U.S. boycott of the organization in 1975 all worked to exacerbate anti-Arab feeling in the United States. The 1978 FBI Abscam operation, in which FBI agents disguised as Arabs sought to corrupt members of Congress, galvanized many Arab-Americans politically. As activist James Zogby said, "while Palestinians [in the United States] were absorbed with issues 'over there' [in Palestine], we [Americans of Arab descent] were mainly concerned with issues 'over here' [in America]."[24]

In 1980, former U.S. senator James Abourezk founded the American-Arab Anti-Discrimination Committee (ADC) which subsequently became the most important Arab-American grass-roots organization. Its primary goal was "combating the negative stereotyping of Arabs in the media and discrimination against Arab-Americans in employment, education and political life."[25] The theme of the ADC's first national convention was "Arab Americans Come of Age," reflecting a desire "for a concerted effort by Arab-Americans to make their presence felt in the United States; to emerge from the shadows and cease being a 'hidden minority.' "[26]

Israel's invasion of Lebanon in 1982 was a watershed in terms of Arab-American public protest. Many were recruited by the ADC and the National Association of Arab Americans (NAAA) – the Arab-American foreign policy lobby, which was founded in 1972 – to protest the Israeli assault on Beirut, the Sabra and Shatila massacre, and America's perceived silence. The summer of 1982 may have been the diaspora's "finest hour," but the failure to translate communal mobilization and the American public's support into political gains – such as congressional condemnation of Israel's role in Sabra and Shatila, a halt in the arms flow to Israel, or a cut in aid – led to disillusionment and retreat.[27] Gregory Orfalea, an Arab-American writer and former ADC activist, described the grim mood of fellow activists during this period as follows: in the face of "the complete dismemberment of Lebanon, not only by Israel, but by Syria, Iran and fifty factions . . . American public interest faded or became jaded.

In the wake of 1982, Arab Americans turned inward, brooding, or simply turned away. To many, all the emotional fervor and selfless energy had in the end resulted in little more than shiny offices and brazen internecine scuffles." Moreover, "the irrefutable fact . . . that Lebanese themselves – Fualangists [*sic*] and others – carried the guns and the knives into the [Sabra and Shatila Palestinian] camps and did the killing, . . . hit home at the souls of Arab Americans, [and] precipitated a decline of Arab American political involvement in the Middle East conflict."[28]

Arab-Americans' Grievances

Americans of Arab descent who have elected to downplay their ancestral affinities have found assimilation in the United States to be firmly within reach.[29] Yet Arab-Americans who have ventured to stand out ethnically or religiously (as Muslims) have faced difficult times finding their way in America's multicultural society.

The loyalty of Arab-Americans as a group has been called into question on many occasions.[30] After Israeli sportsmen were kidnapped and eventually killed at the 1972 Munich Olympic games, the Nixon administration issued directives to investigate Arab-Americans who might be connected to PLO terrorism.[31] During the Gulf crisis, a law professor at American University compared the plight of Arab-Americans with that of Japanese-Americans during World War II.[32] In the wake of the 1993 New York World Trade Center bombing, and immediately after the April 1995 bombing in Oklahoma City, Arab- and Muslim-Americans were held collectively accountable, or in the latter case, collectively accused, for the repudiation of American culture and values in their countries of origin. Indeed, the implication of recently expatriated Arabs and Muslims in terrorist attacks inside the United States "devastated the efforts of American Muslims to show the good face of Islam," to cite Abdurahman Alamoudi, the head of the American Muslim Council.[33] Islamic terrorism also hindered both the American Muslim and the Arab-American communities' ability to rally popular support and to influence American foreign policy in the case of the beleaguered Muslims in Bosnia.[34] In the aftermath of the World Trade Center bombing, an editorial in the *New Republic* referred to a "culture of incitement" that it believed to be prevalent among Arab-Americans and which brought "foreign grievances to be fought on American streets."[35]

U.S. Arabs have protested against the crippling impact of prejudice by association. In pamphlets, street demonstrations, and scholarly writings, they have denounced the portrayal of their culture and kinfolk in the U.S. media and in motion pictures as uncivilized, violent, anti-American zealots.[36] In the wake of the World Trade Center bombing, diaspora leaders asked President Clinton to "go on record disassociating Arab-Americans and Muslims from any individuals arrested" and to warn against anti-Arab hate crimes; they also protested the FBI "harassment" of communal leaders.[37] When the Oklahoma bombing spurred congressional action on antiterrorism legislation intended to limit U.S. fund raising for foreign causes (primarily militant Islamic groups in the Middle East) and ease deportations, diaspora leaders called for the measure's defeat, saying it would target their community for social discrimination and political persecution.[38]

Certainly, the two basic and related concerns expressed by Arab-American institutions are their own status in American society and politics and the relations between the United States and the Arab world – primarily the U.S. position on the Israeli-Arab conflict. The responses of diasporic leaders to these concerns have been shaped by their different perceptions about the nature and mores of the American society (and their position within it), and by the belief in the ability of the American political system to transform itself, domestically and internationally. This outlook also has been shaped by ideologies and internal compulsions, such as the initial inclination (or actual success) of the Arab immigrant to integrate into American society, or his religious inhibitions about integrating based on Islamic dictates.

Another important concern has been how to sustain the internal integrity and cohesion of the Arab-American community, which have always been ephemeral.[39] Indeed, leading Arab-American institutions have been struggling constantly for funding and membership. Since they do not count on grass-roots financial support and have always relied on foreign funding, primarily from the Gulf countries, they have often compromised their political independence.[40]

Confronting Marginality

In his excellent analysis of Arab-American politics between 1967 and the mid-1980s, anthropologist Nabeel Abraham identifies the different reactions of organized Arab-Americans to their domestic marginalization and exclusion from the formulation of American Middle East policy.[41] The two main approaches are isolationism and integrationism. These positions, in reality quite fluid, manifest themselves in ideology and action and define the nature of diasporic involvement in U.S. domestic and foreign affairs. I introduce and develop Abraham's argument in an attempt to explain the current challenges facing the Arab diaspora in America.

In general, ethnic isolationists in the United States consider their culture, religion, or tradition as alien – and often superior – to American or Western culture. They deliberately avoid acculturation, reject assimilation, and at times promote a cultural war against the dominant European heritage. For example, the "Constitution" of the U.S.-based Muslim Arab Youth Association (MAYA) declares the values of American society the enemy of "Islamic civilization [which] is based upon principles fundamentally opposed to those of Western civilization."[42] Extreme isolationists may promote secession and violence. In many respects, isolationists are the silent allies of Anglo-Saxon nativists, as they endorse the latter's position that membership in American society should be limited to those who are part of a particular Anglo-Saxon culture.

Adherents of isolationism have been present on both the left and the right of the Arab-American political spectrum. On the right they include Muslim advocates of ethnoreligious exclusion; on the left, mostly Palestinian proponents of Third Worldism espousing a narrative of colonialism and American imperialism. Although these groups differ dramatically in their philosophies and ultimate political goals – the latter is, in principle, secularist and universal, the former, religious and parochial – their criticism of U.S. foreign policy and American society and their views on their diasporic kinfolk have been quite similar at times.

Isolationist proclivities have been dominated by an exile mentality, inward-looking or limited "*ad hoc* coalitions with sympathetic, mostly marginal groups such as those on the American left, and occasionally on the extreme right."[43] Fearing the encroachment of the American mainstream or abandoning the goal of transforming America's civic culture, isolationists tend to retreat to their own ethnic and religious clubs, which become social sanctuaries. Muslim refugees who resist assimilation tend to put particular pressure on females, who are perceived to be "the transmitters of culture. Keeping them in traditional mode becomes a mechanism for resisting the powerful assimilationist vision found in America."[44] Some Sunni religious Muslims have insisted on distinguishing between themselves and Muslim Shiites. They also separate Muslims from Arabs and reject any political union with Arab Christians.

Integrationists, by contrast, protest their exclusion but believe that their situation can, and will in time, improve. They identify themselves as Americans and as proponents of American values. Their leaders nonetheless encourage their constituencies to cling to their ancestral roots as part of their ethnic American identity, and advance the idea that what happens to their kinfolk abroad has a profound effect on their lives in America. While integrationists may resist assimilation into a dominant Anglo-Saxon culture, they still endorse the vision of a pluralist democracy. They believe that American culture is dynamic, that it does not have a European essence, and that it may be utilized to enhance their own cultural affinities. In other words, although they deny the notion that every community in the United States has already achieved a level of cultural identity sufficient to enable it to blend into a multicultural society, integrationists still seek to become part of American society. Accordingly, they demand cultural and political recognition from American mainstream institutions. When it comes to foreign affairs, integrationists present their case in terms of America's best "national interest," and establish political lobbies to compete for their own interpretation.

Left-Leaning Isolationists

The embodiment of left-leaning isolationism is the Association of Arab-American University Graduates (AAUG). Established after the Six Day War, the AAUG was made up primarily of Palestinian students and professors – the "brain drain" Arab immigrants of the late 1940s and early 1950s.[45] They included Professors Ibrahim Abu-Lughod, Hisham Sharabi, and Edward Said. With a limited membership, the group did not try to establish itself as an American organization. It preached against assimilation and was largely perceived "as a foreign voice in America."[46] Animated by a Third World credo, the AAUG generally supported the goals of the PLO and regarded the United States as a captive of the "Zionist bias." America's mistreatment of Arab-Americans was presented as "an illustration of the failure of the concept of the secular, pluralistic, and democratic nation state."[47] Altogether, the AAUG failed to attract the attention of the American media or politicians. It did, however, receive significant coverage in the Arab world.

The AAUG discovered American sympathizers among the marginal groups of the American left, like the Black Power movement. In the 1960s and early 1970s, black nationalists, for example, characterized Israel as an extension of American imperialism and racism and denounced black leaders who supported the Zionist state as collaborators in the oppression of "our Palestinian brothers and sisters." The Black Panther Party, the radicalized Student Nonviolent Coordinating Committee, and the Nation of Islam (Black Muslims) denounced Zionism as racism and equated South Africa's apartheid and the exploitation of blacks in America with Israel's mistreatment of Arabs and Sephardic Jews. The black-Arab compact was one of a number of factors that led to the disintegration of the civil rights alliance between blacks and Jews.[48]

Followers of the Arab-American left immersed themselves in pan-Arab ideology that came to denote primarily the revolutionary struggle of Palestinians. Third Worldism became a convenient position for U.S. Palestinians, Christian and Muslim alike. They could repudiate the United States in a manner that combined attacks on what they saw as America's imperialist policies and its anti-Islamic bigotry. The charge of "Orientalism," explicated by Edward Said as a Western form of domination, was presented in terms of a Western assault on both the Arab culture and the Muslim religion.[49] Third Worldists, therefore, could also present themselves as defenders of Islam.

Influenced by Palestinian-American academics and intellectuals, many left-leaning isolationists were enlisted in the service of the PLO. Edward Said, who became the most prominent Palestinian spokesman in the United States, was asked to translate Yasir Arafat's 1974 speech to the United Nations, while Palestinian-American writer Fawaz Turki was recruited as its editor. Professor Ibrahim Abu-Lughod became a member of the 1975 PLO delegation to the

United Nations. Turki also went on to join the Palestine Congress of North America (PCNA) and became its director of writing and research. Sponsored by the PLO, the PCNA "was intended to be the ultimate authoritative voice of Palestinian-Americans, with an executive committee, a board of directors, and fifteen full-time officers. Their aim was to represent the Palestinian community in America, to disseminate information about the cause, and to help Palestinians [in the United States] become acquainted with their constitutional rights."[50]

In his firsthand account of the PCNA, Fawaz Turki describes an organization befouled by a culture of corruption and nepotism, dominated by unscrupulous PLO apparatchiks who could hardly speak English, were unfamiliar with America, lived in million-dollar homes, flew the Concorde to Europe, and generally dedicated their revolutionary energies to power, money, and sex, all in the name of the Palestinian "disinherited."[51] Yet Turki, like other Palestinian intellectuals, endured silently. He wrote: "I am a Palestinian activist now. So regardless of all the manifestations of neobackwardness, corruption, and opportunism I am to see from here on, I'll turn a blind eye and a deaf ear. It's good for me to do that and to go on believing in the 'people.' "[52]

The sociologist Lewis Coser has written that "self-conscious exiles among refugee scholars" in America tend to orient themselves "to points of reference across the ocean." Yet even those who "started out with [the] mentality of exiles . . . were gradually caught up within the network of American cultural life, so that, wittingly or unwittingly, they were sooner or later absorbed into the American intellectual world."[53] This observation captures the evolutionary course of many Palestinian refugee scholars in the United States. The most prominent among them are exiles from the war in 1948 (by now in their sixties or early seventies). They became the PLO's ideologues and spokesmen abroad and were appointed to the Palestine National Council (PNC). To a large extent they have been responsible for the separation between the Arab-Israeli and the Palestinian-Israeli conflict in the American mind. They were also instrumental in shifting public discussion in the United States from strategic terms to terms of human rights and self-determination. Palestinian scholars in America also advanced the cause in academia and through research centers.[54] In 1979 Edward Said wrote: "there is not the remotest chance that any alternative Palestinian leadership [to the PLO] will ever emerge; the PLO is too legitimate and representative a body for that to happen."[55]

Although many Palestinian scholars began as Third Worldists, over the years they became entrenched in Western culture and to some extent exporters of its values in the Middle East. The decline of their revolutionary ardor in the late 1980s has been largely the result of their own assimilation into American society, the general decline of Third Worldism, and, above all, their disillusionment with the PLO and Arafat. Hisham Sharabi, Georgetown professor of European intellectual history, is a case in point. He started his revolutionary career as a member of the Syrian Social Nationalist Party, which rejected the then-popular theory of pan-Arabism. After 1967 he became a supporter of George Habash's Popular Front for the Liberation of Palestine (PFLP) and in the 1970s moved closer to Yasir Arafat and the PLO mainstream. He also became more involved in Arab-American affairs, and took part in the 1972 founding of the NAAA.[56] Sharabi also served as editor of the *Journal of Palestine Studies* and as chairman of the Washington-based Center for Policy Analysis on Palestine.[57]

By the time Israel and the PLO signed a Declaration of Principles (DOP) on September 13, 1993, Sharabi was ready to embrace the historic compromise and urged AAUG's members against a new isolationist posture.[58] Within months, however, he was worrying that Arafat and his "cronies" would create "a new Arab dictatorship." Like many other Palestinian intellectuals, Sharabi has indicated little sympathy for the PLO or its chairman Arafat: "We have tried to reform the PLO from within, but each time our efforts were deflected. We found a brick wall. . . . There was no point in going public earlier. . . . The PLO was all we had."[59]

For Sharabi, the "Palestinians are [still] the key to understanding the Third World. . . . They are the last Colonial project." Yet he no longer articulates an anticolonial ideology. He speaks more as a passionate humanist and as a social liberal emphasizing the urgent need for quick democratic Palestinian elections, and for asserting the rights of Arab women. In 1994 he predicted a grim future for the Palestinians if free elections, which would include women, are delayed, and warned Palestinians "not to use Islam in a fanatical manner." He further asserted that only a Palestinian social democracy could usher in the road to "the liberation of the Arab world."[60] By 1995, Sharabi, almost in despair, became involved with Haydar 'Abd al-Shafi's efforts to found a Palestinian secularist progressive party as "an eleventh-hour attempt to challenge both Arafat and the Islamic movement in free elections. . . . If we fail we may have to go alone with the devil," he said.[61] In the wake of Arafat's sweeping victory in the 1996 Palestinian Authority elections and Sharabi's marginalization, his political options appeared quite limited.

Even as relations between Palestinian-American intellectuals and the PLO foundered, the former continued to praise Arafat in public until the early 1990s. Edward Said and Ibrahim Abu-Lughod – the PLO's representative in North America as early as 1964 – remained members of the PNC even after the Gulf War, and Said was involved in Palestinian preparation for the Madrid Conference before breaking ties with the PLO. Both were instrumental in establishing the 1988 dialogue between the PLO and the Reagan administration.[62]

After the signing of the Declaration of Principles, Said became Arafat's major intellectual opponent. He declared the accords an "instrument of Palestinian surrender, a Palestinian Versailles," and denounced Arafat as the man "who sold his people into enslavement." According to Said, Arafat was seeking the approval of the United States more than pursuing his people's interests. The PLO "just wanted the white man to say they were okay. That's all."[63] When asked why it took him so long to recognize Arafat's defects he replied: "It is my fault. . . . The autocracy, profligacy, the corruption, the stupidity. . . . We were always aware of them, but we didn't think they would get so out of hand, we all felt and thought we will take care of that later. . . . It was a question of priorities."[64]

Underlying the profound disillusionment of much of the older generation of the Palestinian-American left is the pain of irrelevancy after a lifetime devoted to a cause that has changed. By the early 1990s the old Palestinian-American left had lost its allure. While some of its followers have remained hostile to the idea of Arab integration inside the United States and are irritated by the activities of Arab-American integrationists, they suffer increasing marginality due to the loss of their ideological core. In fact, even the AAUG could be said to be moving closer to the center. Its officials are members of the Council of Presidents of Arab American Organizations (analogous to the Conference of Presidents of Major Jewish

Organizations) and have taken part in meetings with senior members of the American administration, while the organization has been giving greater attention to the sensitive issue of dictatorial Arab regimes and denouncing the situation of women in the Arab world.[65]

Finally, scholars who belong to the younger generation of the Palestinian-American intelligentsia are committed just as fully to their life in the United States and to the American Creed as they are to the Palestinian cause. Many of them welcomed the peace process. As part of the younger American-born and/or American-educated generation, scholars like Rashid Khalidi and Philip Mattar based their initial criticism of the DOP or Arafat in nonideological terms, pointing to procedural shortcomings and raising doubts about the PLO's ability to lead the way in nation building and democratization. Rashid Khalidi, a prominent Palestinian scholar and activist, began criticizing the PLO's decision-making process after the 1982 war in Lebanon where he witnessed firsthand Arafat's actions in the face of Israel's siege of Beirut.[66] In late 1993, he said: "The peace process has already exhausted our energies. . . . Can we sustain a rule of law? Can we build a healthy economy and a functioning bureaucracy? I am not sure . . . maybe I am too pessimistic."[67]

Islamic-Leaning Isolationists

Is the designation "Muslim-American" a contradiction in terms or an accurate characterization of a minority within the American multicultural reality? This question has various answers, reflecting different theological interpretations and conflicting sociological observations. To begin with, the Qur'an is open to interpretation according to the demands made on the lives of various individuals and groups.[68] Moreover, observant Muslims in the United States vary widely in their culture, language, ethnic, and national affinities, as well as in the ways they practice Islam – for example, Shi'a or Sunni, Wahhabi or Sufi. Indeed, significant differences exist even among Muslim Arabs in the United States, by all accounts a small minority of the growing American Muslim community.[69] In addition to their division along religious affiliation and national-ethnic lines, Muslim Arabs have also split according to their loyalty to their sponsoring Arab states. Countries like Saudi Arabia, Libya, and Kuwait have exercised political and religious clout over American Islamic communities that are dependent on their financial support.[70] Thus, for example, in the months leading up to the Gulf War, Muslim activists in Los Angeles who undertook to protest the United States' impending attack of Iraq failed to mobilize local Muslim leaders who were economically dependent on the Saudis.[71]

The majority of Muslim Arabs in the United States are "secularists." They pursue integration, even as they fear that a society that professes a "Judeo-Christian" heritage may never fully embrace them.[72] Like non-Arab Muslims who are active in religious life, Muslim Arabs differ in the degree of orthodoxy required in their Islamic practices: how much should they participate or assimilate into the American mainstream, how should they interact with other Americans, particularly Christians and Jews, and to what degree should their spiritual traditions remain sacrosanct? In reality, only a minority (although a growing one) adopts an orthodox (sometimes extremist) theology of isolation and withdrawal. Members of this group generally reject the idea of Muslims laying claim to Arab ethnicity or nationalism and are likely to avoid participation in American mainstream politics. They are also skeptical about entering politics in collaboration with Christian Arabs.[73]

Despite their growing numbers, Muslims in the United States have hitherto been unable to unite as an effective lobbying force and remain poorly represented in American politics and culture.[74] In the absence of a single, unified Muslim denomination or a supreme clerical hierarchy in America, religious leaders, or Imams, tend to build their own following. Mosques are set up and split along ancestral lineage (national or local), religious overtones, political persuasions, race, or class.[75] But the failure to establish an effective Muslim lobby is not just the product of a fragmented community. It is also the result of an orthodox religion that allows only limited pluralism.

In the history of Islam, the Hijra (the emigration of Muhammad and his followers from Mecca to Medina) marked the beginning of a Muslim community. The Prophet refused to stay under pagan rule in Mecca and migrated to a place where he and his followers could create a Muslim polity and live a Muslim life. The Hijra is the transformative event in Muslim history from the "pre-Islamic pagan past to a divinely guided and centered world in which tribal kinship was to be superseded by membership in a community (*ummah*) bound together by common religious belief."[76]

Islamic traditional teachings interpreted the Hijra experience in different ways. Above all, Hijra became associated with the precept that a believer must retreat from a Muslim territory that falls under non-Muslim rule. The orthodox view holds that a Muslim could not accept a middle ground between Islam and a pagan way of life or the life of those ignorant of the faith (*jahiliyya*).[77] The Islamic injunction, therefore, obliged the fully faithful to emulate the Prophet and move to another Muslim territory as an act of temporal retreat until "in God's good time, [he] or [his] descendants would return to reconquer the lands which had been lost."[78]

Thus Islamic law and traditions reject, in principle, the notion of Muslims building a minority life in a non-Islamic country. Bernard Lewis has written that the early interpreters of the Qur'an never considered the possibility of a Muslim moving voluntarily to settle in a non-Muslim land. Islamic orthodoxy took into account only the prospect of a Muslim being forced out of his religious domain.[79] Yet if he is forced to reside in a land of nonbelievers, the Muslim is obliged to propagate the Call of Islam and try to bring the infidels of his new home into the House of Islam. Thus, while the Islamic corpus (which views the world outside the faith, particularly Christianity, as the House of War) dictates retreat from persecution and idolatry, it also establishes a more moderate interpretation of Hijra, one that sanctions migrant life in a non-Muslim society as long as the Islamic community can develop and thrive.[80] To put it differently, the minimum requirements of the believer forced to reside under non-Muslim rule is to be able "to manifest the signs of Islam."[81] His ultimate obligation, however, is to transform his new society by converting unbelievers to Islam through *da'wa* (religious outreach, proselytism, or propaganda).[82]

With this theological background in mind, one may approach the complexity of Islamic life in the modern Christian world and assess the challenges faced by Muslim communities, primarily in Europe and North America, where they are fast becoming large minorities. It is the totality of Islam that imposes on orthodox adherents of the faith the greatest challenge: how does one live as a believer and preserve the faith under Western democracies where, in the words of Amer Haleen of the Islamic Society of North America, the "system [was] organized by design to elevate the will of man above the will of God"?[83]

Indeed, orthodox followers of the Muslim faith cannot, in principle, integrate into a system that requires loyalty to a liberal democratic state.[84] Nor can they accept the idea of being granted a minority ethnic status, for example, as Muslim Arabs. The idea of the *ummah* repudiates national identities, ethnic solidarity, or any concept of an Arab culture that is distinct from Islam. Ethnicities, like tribes, undermine Islam as a total way of life, and as the only legitimate source of communal identity for the followers of the faith.[85]

The tension between Arab identity and Islam in the context of the diaspora was the subject of study by the Palestinian-American Muslim scholar and activist Ismail R. al-Faruqi. Initially, he advocated a natural blending of Islam and Arabism. The latter (Arabism or *'urubah*) was defined as more inclusive than the former because it is said to include not only Arabic-speaking and non-Arab Muslims – by virtue of Arabic being the language of the Qur'an – but also all non-Muslim Arabs who adhere to the "Arab consciousness."[86] In his later years, however, Faruqi discovered that by trying to combine three distinct groupings – Arab Muslims, non-Arab Muslims, and non-Muslim Arabs – he may himself have become an accomplice in the process of fragmenting the *ummah*. In order to save Islam from modern forms of tribalism (*shu 'ubiyya*) – that is, nationalism and ethnicity – Faruqi advocated that Islam should become "the primary referent in all aspects of life."[87]

The clash between Arab nationalism and Islamism that has beset the Arab world in recent years is also reflected in the life and activities of Muslims and Arabs in the United States. At the core is the distinction between "Arab-American," a denotation of ethnic identity, and "Muslims in America," a religious definition of a way of life. This distinction is the key to discerning the desire and ability of diasporic institutions to develop a voice in U.S. domestic and foreign affairs. In general, while the term "Arab-American" has been invoked by Christian Arabs who decry cultural and political discrimination but wish to integrate into American mainstream politics and society, many religious Muslims in America are reluctant to portray themselves as Arab-Americans. They fear they may be viewed simply as another ethnic group and become integrated. The ideal of many devout Muslims in the United States is the establishment of a religious community detached from the larger American society, to some extent analogous to ultraorthodox American Jews, for whom the open nature of American society threatens their communal boundaries, and for whom Zionism and the politically secularized state of Israel are anathema to Judaism.

Muslim isolationists actively oppose the idea of ethnicizing Islam by turning it into a "cultural token, occasions for celebration, a folklore." They denounce the life-style of "passive Muslims" who try to blend ethnic and religious identity, and reject the notion of a Muslim political lobby.[88] For them, the "*kufr* (unbelief) system [of the] American government cannot give rise to an Islamic state."[89] The less religious may consider partial involvement, directed mainly toward educating non-Muslims, while retaining "purity outside the American system." Still others may consider joining ad hoc political coalitions with Arab-American organizations, mainly on foreign affairs, despite their concern about being "coopted into Christian Arab-American political designs."[90] Community members holding these views joined with Arab-American organizations in endorsing the presidential candidacy of the Reverend Jesse Jackson, who was perceived as a genuine supporter of the Palestinians and a courageous challenger of American policy toward Israel. Activists in Dearborn, Michigan, have told me that many devout Muslims helped in electing Arab-American Michigan Senator Spence Abraham in 1994, which the activists interpreted as a sign that an Arab-American identity exists even among orthodox Muslims.[91]

As in the Middle East, religion has undergone a revival among Arab-Muslims in the diaspora.[92] In Dearborn (home to one of the largest concentrations of Arab Muslims in the United States), as in many other Arab Muslim communities across America, the growing presence of religion manifests itself in the stress on female modesty (Islamic dress for women in public), increased mosque attendance, and the display of photographs of religious leaders in people's homes.[93] Islamic revivalism is also evident on many American campuses. Thousands are attending the conventions of the Muslim Arab Youth Association, which has become "an umbrella organization for militant Islamic groups around the world."[94] In the Shi'a congregations in Dearborn, the "Sharia minded" institutions have triumphed over the less strict leadership in setting up standards of Islamic behavior for the community. New mosques are led by Shi'a shaykhs who are inspired by revolutionary Iran and the radical Hizbullah movement in Lebanon. They emphasize "pure Islam" and reject the idea of adapting the religion to American surroundings.[95]

The increase in militant Islamism has split the Arab Muslim community and prompted greater scrutiny by the U.S. government. The radicalization of American Muslims has been inspired by exiles from Arab countries and the West Bank and Gaza, and is inflamed by occasional visits by leaders of radical Middle Eastern groups. Some of these Muslim evangelists have used the United States as a safe haven for plotting against Arab regimes and Israel, as well as against targets inside America. The most famous of these groups has consisted of followers of the blind Islamic cleric Sheikh Omar Abdel-Rahman of the al-Salaam mosque in Jersey City, who was arrested and later convicted in connection with the bombings of the World Trade Center.[96] The exiled radicals have reportedly adopted the strategy of agents provocateurs, deliberately fomenting divisions between ordinary Muslims and the American government, in an attempt to increase "nativist pressure on local Muslims" and thereby "reinforce [among Muslims] the sense of victimization and oppression."[97]

Israeli scholar Martin Kramer has observed that Muslim fundamentalism has become a hothouse for poor disenchanted Arab immigrants who have found it difficult to assimilate in "the land of unbelief."[98] These young men have found escape and solace within the walls of newly established mosques, where the politics of anti-American resentment is preached. In recent years, there have been numerous media reports about the growing number of Islamic terrorist organizations that have established infrastructures in the United States. *CBS Evening News* reported on October 3, 1994, that much of the funds supporting terrorist activities of the Palestinian Hamas movement, which violently opposes the PLO-Israeli accords, has come from Muslim sympathizers in Virginia, Texas, and Chicago. Yasir Arafat complained: "I have the right to ask how they get money from the U.S." Steven Emerson's sensational television investigation, "Jihad in America," uncovered numerous Muslim groups throughout the United States that fund and actively support groups like Hamas, Islamic Jihad, and Hizbullah. These groups "found that the United States was the best place to raise funds, disseminate propaganda and build up their political organization."

Though Emerson qualifies his report by saying that the "overwhelming majority of [U.S.] Muslims are not members of militant groups [which are the] extremist and violent fringe," he still warned Americans against the culture of violence that is now instilled among American Muslim children.[99] On October 24, 1994, after a bus bombing in Tel Aviv, Secretary of State Warren Christopher promised to seek new legislation to cut the flow of dollars from Hamas backers in the United States. The ADC was quick to denounce the administration for suggesting that Hamas is funded by the Arab-American community.[100] On January 24, 1995, President Clinton issued an executive order entitled, "Prohibiting Transactions with Terrorists Who Threaten to Disrupt the Middle East Peace Process."

By all accounts, radicals comprise only a small portion of the Arab Muslim community. In other quarters of the community, there have been calls for greater Muslim participation in American politics and society. Arab and Muslim groups also collaborated with American Jewish organizations in protesting the assault on Muslims in Bosnia.[101]

One of the leading advocates of a Muslim integrationist approach is the American Muslim Council (AMC), which set up a Washington office in 1990. Eritrean-born executive director Abdurahman Alamoudi has written that Muslims in the United States "want to dissociate [themselves] from what goes on internationally" and "want to live as Americans." We "would like to be recognized as another positive group that wants to be part of the system and culture. We want to be part of this great nation."[102] In February 1995, Alamoudi announced a national campaign to register Muslims to vote in the 1996 presidential elections. He said that he could foresee a day when American Muslims "become a swing vote."[103]

The Message of Arab-American Integrationists

Arab-American integrationists have attempted to build a pan-Arab ethnic identity that could forge solidarity among members of different immigration waves, diverse descent, and different religions. They have called on American Arabs to turn away from assimilation or religious identification as Christians or Muslims, and join together in ethnic cooperation as Arab-Americans. The tapping of Arab-

American ethnicity has been in line with the growth of multiculturalism in the United States and is perceived as the only way to achieve
domestic empowerment. This assertion of pan-Arab identity con-
trasts with Middle Eastern realities, where pan-Arab nationalism has
been in decline since the early 1980s.

Integrationist spokesmen for the Arab-American diaspora (by no
means a harmonious camp) have maintained that the "twisted images" of Arabs and Muslims in the American mind, anti-Arab hate
violence, and the exclusion of U.S. Arabs from the political arena
constitute forms of "political racism," defined by Helen Hatab Samhan as a form of stigmatization that "takes prejudice and exclusion
out of the arena of personal relations into the arena of public information and public policy."[104] This stigmatization was blamed, in
large part, on Zionism and the pro-Israel lobby, and the allegedly
Jewish-controlled media that encourage anti-Arab and anti-Muslim
sentiment. The Jewish lobby was also accused of discrediting pro-
Arab activists as "foreign agents," hindering their civil liberties by
using illegal spying operations against them, and constraining their
participation in the political process by pressuring elected officials to
return Arab-American donations.

Many have concluded that the only remedy for the diaspora's
domestic distress is the cessation of the Middle East conflict, which
would advance its status in American society, boost its influence on
U.S. decision makers, and improve its relations with American
Jews.[105] They have therefore advocated a more "balanced" U.S. foreign policy in the Middle East and called for a rapprochement between the United States and the PLO. Some Lebanese Arab-
Americans also reason that "a solution to the civil war [in Lebanon]
is inseparable from the solution to the problem of a Palestinian
homeland, which would, in their view, result in a withdrawal of Israel
from Lebanese territory and the restoration of Lebanese sovereignty."[106]

All the leading integrationist organizations are therefore deeply
involved in Middle Eastern affairs. To counter the powerful pro-
Israel lobby, they consciously modeled themselves after leading pro-
Israel groups.[107] The National Association of Arab Americans
(NAAA) – the Arab-American foreign policy lobby – molded itself
after the American Israel Public Affairs Committee (AIPAC). NAAA

founders came mostly from the earlier immigrant groups. They "re-alized that they could only re-establish themselves within American society if they dealt with the problem which so affects their own lives, the Arab-Israeli question."[108] The NAAA budget came mainly from U.S. corporations doing business in the Middle East and, indi-rectly, from Arab governments which advertise in its organ, the *Middle East Business Survey*.

Like AIPAC, the NAAA presents its case to the American public in terms of U.S. national interests. In 1985, NAAA officials described their organization's goals as follows: "Arab Americans are deeply proud of their culture and heritage. They seek to promote the closest possible relations between the United States and the Arab World. ... They are American first, last, and always. Their approach to lobbying, therefore, is to identify America's national interests in the Middle East and to promote those interests through advocacy and education."[109]

The NAAA emphasized the following points: (1) opposition to Israel's occupation of the West Bank, Gaza, and the Golan Heights, and the "attendant violations of human rights of their inhabitants"; (2) the need to cut U.S. aid to Israel to prevent the "establishment of illegal settlements and annexation of occupied territories, includ-ing Jerusalem"; (3) the need to enforce American laws especially pertaining to the Arms Control Act "with reference to Israel's misuse of United States supplied military equipment for attacks on Leba-non"; (4) the need for a Palestinian state and recognition of the PLO.[110] Indeed, the NAAA was instrumental in establishing an ear-lier dialogue between the United States and the PLO.

The Arab American Institute (AAI), which officially concentrates on empowering Arab Americans in the electoral system, and the American-Arab Anti-Discrimination Committee (ADC), whose pri-mary goal has been to organize Arab-Americans at the mass level to combat "anti-Arab racism," have also given much of their attention to the Palestinian struggle. ADC's publications devote ample space to charges against human rights abuses by Israelis, almost never mentioning questions of democracy and human rights in Arab coun-tries. The ADC's position has lurched to the left steadily. The orga-nization failed to endorse the PLO-Israeli accords and its former President Albert Mokhiber vowed to "continue putting daily pressure on Israel to make new concessions."[111] Many in the Arab-American community have described the ADC as a "Syrian mouth-piece."[112]

By 1990, Arab-American national organizations had already established considerable visibility in U.S. politics and the media. They drew heavily on Palestinian suffering during the *intifada*. The AAI, for example, considered its most meaningful political accomplishment up to that point the breaking open of the debate on Palestinian rights and the Middle East peace process on the floor of the 1988 Democratic National Convention in Atlanta. In this debate, AAI's President James Zogby announced, "Today we respond to the Palestinian people. We address . . . the violation of their basic human rights, the killing and the beating, and agonizing expulsions, the daily humiliations of being a people without a state."[113] Although Jewish delegates sought to downplay the impact of the open debate, some Jewish-American officials called it "the Arab-American intifada," drawing a parallel between the belated response of Israel to the eruption of the Palestinian uprising in the occupied territories and the American-Jewish community's initial "numbness" in the face of the Arab-American electoral threat.

A 1991 Anti-Defamation League report on "The Anti-Israeli Lobby" concluded that U.S. Arab groups "have made clear strides in effectively communicating their views to the American public and promoting their goals among Washington policy makers."[114] These accomplishments notwithstanding, Arab-Americans' entry into the American political arena remained circumscribed by events in the Middle East and the actions of extremists in the diaspora.

The Persian Gulf War and the Rise of James Zogby

The Persian Gulf War resulted "in one of the worst setbacks for the Palestinians in modern times."[115] In the United States, the diaspora organizational structure was shaken and the "perils of hyphenation" reached new heights as leaders of the Arab-American community were questioned by the FBI about their knowledge of international terrorism.[116] In reality, the diaspora was highly polarized on the question of American intervention in the Gulf. A survey of Arab-Americans during the first week of February 1991 showed that the

notion of Arab-American ethnic convergence on foreign policy matters was more myth than fact. "Arab-Americans of Muslim [*sic*]
religion were one and one-half times as likely to oppose the war than
non-Moslems," and "those of Jordanian or Palestinian origin were
more than twice as likely to oppose the war than other Arab-
Americans."[117]

With Arab-American loyalty and patriotism called into question,
Osama Siblani, the publisher of the Detroit newspaper *Sada al-
Watan* (*Arab-American News*) declared, "For Arab-Americans, this is
their first country. America is where they chose to live. They fled
persecution, oppression and poverty."[118] Faced with the agonizing
reality that Arab unity was illusory and frustrated by the Palestinian
embrace of Saddam, diaspora activists were torn between the pressure to affirm their American allegiance and their concern for events
abroad. Moreover, "the Ambassadors of the Gulf countries in
Washington made sure that of the [Arab-American] groups they
assisted in various ways, only those leaders and those organizations
which supported their political position in the crisis were allowed
to remain in operation."[119] Thus AAI and NAAA, heavily dependent
on their Gulf connections, maneuvered uneasily between supporting
U.S. intervention to restore the government of Kuwait, and requir-
ing American "consistency" toward Israel and the Palestinians.[120]
ADC scored some political points among the grass-roots community by opposing the American buildup in the Gulf.[121] Palestinian
intellectuals, true to form, were "virtually silent about missed opportunities and PLO corruption and blunders, including in the Gulf
crisis."[122]

For years, diaspora organizations had stifled serious dialogue
about intra-Arab conflicts or on Arab authoritarianism: clinging to
the Palestinian cause was comforting, and it remained the preemi-
nent litmus test of loyalty. After the Gulf War and the beginning of
the peace process launched in Madrid, some integrationists concluded that their domestic political empowerment could no longer
remain in the sole service of Palestinian interests. In a speech delivered to a meeting of the Democratic National Committee's National
Platform Committee in Cleveland, Ohio, in May 1992, James Zogby
declared that Arab-Americans should not be considered "a single-
issue constituency," that they want to be heard not only on the

Middle East but also on multicultural education and the broad subject of ethnic relations in the United States.[123]

The AAI adjusted its message to suit the changing direction of the "American creed," both domestically and internationally. Zogby modified his tone to conform to the zeitgeist of multiculturalism and the international political spirit that grew out of the global wave of democratic transition. By the early 1990s, Zogby emerged as the most energetic, sophisticated Arab-American lobbyist, and the one who has received more attention from American politicians and the media than any other. Yet his mainstream positions on the Middle East made him the target of left-leaning Palestinians who labeled Zogby a "collaborator."[124] Indeed, Zogby has been the archetypal example of a mainstream diaspora activist.[125] A former codirector of the ADC, Zogby left the organization in 1984 after a falling out with former Senator James Abourezk. His departure along with some of his loyalists disrupted ADC's operations.[126] In 1985, he established the AAI "to focus not on Israel but on getting Arab-Americans politically organized."[127] His cofounder was George Salem, an assimilated Palestinian-born Washington lawyer who had headed Ethnic Voters for Reagan/Bush in 1984 and later served as solicitor at the U.S. Department of Labor, making him the highest ranking Arab-American in the administration at that time.[128] The AAI sought entry into the American party system. Salem's advantage was among Republicans, Zogby's among Democrats. Both ventured to "create a political climate where Arab-Americans – Republicans, Democrats, and Independents – can run for political office and win, while wearing their ethnicity on their sleeves."[129] Arab-Americans "want their [cultural] heritage preserved and treated with respect, they want their fair share of jobs. They are tired of being locked out."[130]

Zogby's understanding of the American political system and the power of electoral politics, and his ability to project himself as a diasporic leader who offered an "American" solution to the Israeli-Palestinian conflict, helped him to penetrate U.S. political institutions and impress American Jews. "He speaks to America as part of America," and "He sounds like Peace Now," I was told by an official of one of the Jewish organizations. From its inception, the AAI has drawn a direct link between the empowerment of Arab-Americans inside the United States and the defusing of the Middle East conflict.

In 1987, AAI deputy director Helen Hatab Samhan wrote that "anti-Arab prejudice in America will continue to confront the Arab American community as long as the Arab-Israeli conflict remains unsolved."[131] Samhan, Zogby's closest assistant, said that with the signing of the Israel-PLO accords, "the zero sum game between Jews and Arab Americans no longer exists. . . . we will no longer be seen only as Anti-Israeli and will be welcomed to the table. . . . Once you de-mystify the Arab-Israeli conflict as being the driving force in Arab-American politics, Arab-Americans will automatically overcome tremendous hurdles in becoming an effective voice," she said.[132]

By the late 1980s, one scholar wrote that the AAI was already "on its way to creating a viable political organization with bases in several large metropolitan areas."[133] Yet Zogby's entry into the American political arena remained circumscribed by developments in the Middle East. For years Zogby fought the pro-Israel lobby, describing the pressure it exerted on Congress as an "intrusive, destructive vehicle that inhibits debate and ultimately does a disservice to everyone involved, Jews as well as Arab Americans."[134] Yet in the aftermath of the Gulf War, the AAI could no longer settle for a showdown with American Jews. In reality, some forms of Arab- and Jewish-American cooperation had already appeared in the 1980s, as more and more Israelis and American Jews called for a "two-state solution" to the Israeli-Palestinian conflict. Adopting the American jargon of opportunity, fair play, and anti-discrimination, Zogby called in 1988 for reconciliation and cooperation with American Jews:

> Just as it is anti-Semitic to complain of a Jewish financial cabal that is ruling American institutions, it is equally wrong to incite against Arab Americans because of an imagined "petro-dollar conspiracy" to buy up America or a "terrorist" connection to any and all advocacy work for the Palestinians. Just as exclusion or discrimination have in the past been painful to Jewish Americans, today they deeply hurt my people. . . . We do understand Jewish fears and the need for security felt so deeply by Israelis. Now I urge you to understand realities like Palestinian nationalism and the emergence of an Arab American political constituency.[135]

The AAI presented the case of Arab-American exclusion in the political arena as a "unique form of racism," in large measure the result of American Middle East policy, "which supported a climate that many perceived to be anti-Arab and anti-Islamic."[136] Arab-Americans were depicted as "victims of disenfranchisement."[137] Yet by the early 1990s, Zogby, acting on strong political instinct, decided to depart from the narrative of Arab victimology. In 1992, he encouraged Arab-American optimism when he publicized the story of his entry to Bill Clinton's 1992 presidential campaign. Zogby pleaded the case of Arab-Americans' exclusion with Democratic Senator Joseph Lieberman. Lieberman, an Orthodox Jew, petitioned Clinton's people, and Zogby was subsequently invited to Little Rock. *Washington Post* columnist David Broder quoted Zogby as saying that "only in America would an Arab American call a Jewish American to call a Greek Orthodox [Clinton's communications director George Stephanopoulos] . . . to let us help a Southern Baptist get elected President."[138] The entry of Arab-Americans into the Clinton presidential campaign and the role played by the community in electing Clinton were hailed by Zogby as a great diasporic step toward political inclusion. The subsequent appointment of Arab-American Donna Shalala as secretary of Health and Human Services signified, in Zogby's words, Clinton's genuine commitment to "diversity and inclusion."[139]

When Zogby approved President Clinton's appointees to key Middle East positions – most notably Martin Indyk, former director of the pro-Israel Washington Institute for Near East Affairs, appointed to the National Security Council; and former ambassador to Israel Samuel Lewis, appointed to the State Department Policy Planning Council – even though they seemed to favor the pro-Israel lobby, he found himself awash in a storm of criticism by fellow Arab-American leaders.[140] The Palestinian newspaper *Al-Fajr* published articles by its Washington correspondent assailing Zogby for his betrayal.[141] Hala Maksoud, then president of the AAUG, announced that Zogby and other heads of Arab-American organizations – referring to Khalil Jahshan of the NAAA, who refused to condemn Zogby or Indyk directly, but only criticized the "phenomenon" – "don't any longer represent the community, nor do they have a will of their own; they are basically agents of these Arab governments which also have no will of their own." Muhammad Hallaj, from the Center for Policy Analysis on Palestine, denounced Zogby and Jahshan as " 'self appointed *makhateer* (leaders),' who establish offices and 'proceed to speak in the name of the Arab American community. [They] have [not] been chosen by anyone, nor are they accountable to anyone, and therefore it is a fraud to think of them as leaders.' "[142] Zogby was also denounced by the ADC and the American Federation of Ramallah, Palestine.

Going Out on a Limb: Arab-Americans in the Era of Peacemaking

The "Zogby-Indyk" affair reflected the AAI's new position that the Palestinian cause should no longer jeopardize Arab-Americans' domestic empowerment. Zogby held the view that only from within the American system could stigmatization be reduced and charges dispelled that Arab-Americans were primarily "anti-Israel." Zogby blamed his attackers for failing to grasp the delicate position of Arab-Americans and for forsaking the liberal-pluralist values that underlie diasporic politics in the United States.[143] He argued that working within American institutions should be a precondition for becoming an effective voice in U.S. foreign affairs, and urged his critics to adopt the values of plurality and tolerance if Arab-Americans wish to remain politically viable. He also maintained that empowerment in the United States could not be achieved by resentment and political avoidance:

> We at AAI are proud of our record of achievement in advancing the cause of Arab-American political empowerment and bringing the issue of Palestinian statehood to the center of the debate in the Democratic Party. We have done so out of a commitment to principles and within the framework of our strategic vision on how to approach American politics. . . . If our community is to grow and to become more powerful politically, it is essential that we practice the old formula for co-existence; we must agree to disagree and to continue working on those areas where there is a consensus.[144]

The attacks on Zogby in the Arab-American community grew in intensity after the signing of the Israel-PLO accords. Like many other Arab- and Jewish-Americans, Zogby was jubilant. Zogby's AAI considered the accords "an opportunity for Arab Americans to achieve full empowerment and assimilation into the mainstream of

American culture and life."[145] Zogby went so far as to declare that "anybody who raises the question of cutting aid to Israel puts the peace process at risk."[146] His passionate endorsement of the accords and his subsequent partnership with Jewish-American leaders in "Builders for Peace," a joint venture aimed at developing the private-sector economy in the West Bank and Gaza, led to Zogby's denunciation as a "collaborator."[147] Edward Said, who in recent years made Zogby a regular target for his attacks, declared that Zogby and NAAA's Khalil Jahshan had been "bewitched" by the Clinton administration and the Jewish lobby.[148] Certainly, anyone who receives so much attention from Edward Said is a player of consequence.

In the aftermath of the Israel-PLO accords, while the AAUG and the ADC were paralyzed, trying to figure out what to do with their slogans, the AAI and the NAAA were ready to assume a pivotal foreign-policy position. As late as February 1994, Albert Mokhiber, at the time president of the ADC, accused the AAI and the NAAA of "rushing to legitimate Israel" by inviting Israeli ministers to speak in their forums.[149] Zogby and, to a lesser degree, NAAA's Khalil Jahshan could not wait. They could finally wear two hats at once: one in the service of the Palestinians and one all-American. While many started to lash out at Arafat for "selling out to the Jews" in the accords, Zogby and Arafat found in each other mutual support. Zogby could prove his fidelity to the Palestinians by bringing foreign investors to the West Bank and Gaza.[150] As an American of Lebanese Christian heritage, Zogby finally felt freed of the divisions among Palestinians and could rise above their criticism. His "Builders for Peace" enterprise was designed to achieve three concurrent objectives: mobilizing the support of the American administration, playing the role of a loyal Arab by receiving the endorsement of the PLO chairman, and establishing a strong link to the Jewish-American mainstream.

With Arafat and the American administration on his side, Zogby confronted his diasporic kinfolk: the frustrated AAUG, some of the embittered intellectuals, and the crippled ADC. "They all remained in the old paradigm," remarked Helen Samhan. "How could the ADC claim to represent Arab-Americans and remain mute when it comes to the peace accords?" she wondered.[151] Philip Mattar, the executive director of the Institute of Palestinian Studies, expressed a similar view: "The intellectuals are subject to their own myths that all Israelis are vicious and conspiratorial." "None of them can lead the way," he said.[152]

As it turned out, by the end of 1994, in the face of repeated setbacks in the PLO-Israel negotiations, and the growing discrediting of Arafat, the intellectuals and the other critics of the accord seemed to have strongly influenced Palestinian-American opinion.[153] Palestinian-American businessmen who sought to contribute to Zogby's Builders for Peace were called traitors.[154]

Tentative Conclusions about an Uncertain Future

Even though the voice of pan-Arabism has long been in decline in the Middle East, it has been kept alive and well among Arab-Americans. Yet, by 1995, the fragile unity between different diasporic camps, which had held together under the banner of the Palestinian cause, was dissipating rapidly, thereby threatening the vitality of Arab-American institutions and complicating further the question of Arab-American identity. In theory, the Middle East peace process should have provided Arab-Americans with a unique opportunity to end their stigmatization inside the United States and to accelerate their integration into American politics. It should also have enhanced their stature as a foreign-policy lobby, as they would no longer be in constant confrontation with Jewish-Americans. However, with the passage of time we are witnessing a process of intensified diasporic fragmentation and Arab-American organizational turmoil, which weakens the political vitality of the diaspora and complicates further the question of Arab-American identity. Indeed, just as it seemed to reach its apex, the Arab-American lobby found itself in a deep crisis.

This deterioration of hard-won Arab-American solidarity is closely linked to events in the Middle East and to America's foreign policy. It also reflects important transformations within the community itself, including accelerated integration prevalent among American-born Christians and Muslims alike and, among Arab Muslims, especially the younger generation, a growing shift from Arab nationalism to Muslim identity. Islamic revival gains strength from recently arrived immigrants and exiles who tend to observe the faith more strictly as a way of asserting their sense of communal identity while abroad. Muslim groups have also drawn support from younger generation Arabs disenchanted with mainstream Arab-American politics.

Moreover, paradoxically, some of the immigrants who have sought refuge in the United States from the tumult of Islamic revivalism in their homeland find themselves, because of difficulties in assimilating into American society, drawn into a devout and often militant Muslim environment.

By mid-1995, mainstream diasporic activists were clearly anxious about the shift to Islamic identification, which leaves out the Christian Arabs, who still form the majority among Arab-Americans. "The next few years belong to the Islamists," said Khalil Jahshan, executive director of the near-defunct NAAA. When I visited the NAAA's office in April 1995, its staff had been cut dramatically after Arab governments slashed their funding. "Arab-Americans lack the cementing factors," Jahshan said. "We were unable to connect with our constituencies [while] Islam presents an appealing option especially to the immigrants," he added. Yet, he said, "Islam is lacking a national leadership to harness the feeling of frustration."[155] Other integrationists, like Zogby, express greater confidence: "We are reaching more and more young people on campuses. They are proud of their Arab heritage and wish to learn more about their ancestral cultures. . . . We are part of America." Osama Siblani, publisher of the *Arab American News* in Dearborn, argues that in the long run, even radicalized Muslims are turning into mainstream Americans. "The ADC, the AAI and the NAAA were out of touch with the community," he said. "Their failure should enable local communities to build a more genuine Arab-American identity with an American focus." "Before making a change in Washington we must affect policy in Lansing [Michigan]." Siblani also said that "Arab-Americans, Christians and Muslims, liberals and conservatives, are becoming more powerful every day."[156] Kay Siblani, his American wife, the executive editor of the *Arab American News*, was less certain: "The tribal and village mentality still dominates. . . . Power comes from family lineage and not from what you do in America."[157] Altogether, it is too early to determine how enduring is the current identity wave among Arab-Muslims from nationalism to religion. As always, political developments in the Middle East, including the Palestinians' ability to consolidate a secular-democratic political entity, will influence the trend in the United States.

Meanwhile, the Arab-American left is encountering great difficulties finding a receptive audience for its message. Far from being the rallying point it was several decades ago, it has been neutralized by the PLO-Israel accords on the one hand and the Islamic challenge on the other. On many U.S. campuses, AAUG is being ignored as Arab students join Islamic groups. As late as the fall of 1993, AAUG members were still considered the PLO's "ambassadors to the American people." In his message to AAUG's twenty-sixth annual convention – shortly after he signed the accords – Arafat expressed confidence that his diasporic foot soldiers "will spare no effort, individually, as AAUG members, and collectively as an association, to render your service whenever duty calls."[158] But as the initial euphoria of the peace process evaporated, and progress on the Israel-PLO track lagged, the left, consisting mainly of a shrinking group of Palestinians and the marginalized ADC, returned to their old mode, blaming Israel and the United States for conspiring against the Arabs and the Palestinians. Like others in the Palestinian camp who had championed Arafat and the PLO for so long, the diasporic left was ready to declare "the father of Palestine" a "traitor." Many within the AAUG feared that their organization might be compromised by Arafat's dramatic shift.

Without the umbrella of the PLO, and in the absence of any viable leadership on the Palestinian left to fill the void, intellectuals like Said could provide only limited rhetorical solace. In his presidential address to AAUG's annual convention in November 1994, Dr. Ziad J. Asali, asking "Where did we go wrong?" called upon his colleagues to reexamine their convictions:

> It will not do to lay blame solely on imperialism and Zionism to explain away the current state of disarray and degradation across the Arab world. It will not do to formulate slogans and generalization as a substitute for realistic strategies and thought out tactics. . . . The suppression of free expression across the Arab world adds an extra measure of responsibility on the shoulders of the Arab intellectuals in the West who are not encumbered by government or violent censorship. . . . For most of this century there evolved a consensus that the solution lies in pursuit of Arab nationalism and socialism. This consensus does not hold.[159]

In fact, even Edward Said seems to have undergone an intellectual metamorphosis, as he advanced a Western-type condemnation of Arab and Palestinian cultures in an interview with the *Journal of*

Palestine Studies: "[W]hy [are we] satisfied with persistence and stead-fastness, and not concerned enough with actually defining some-thing, the sort of thinking that produced the slogan 'Another Acre, Another Goat'?"[160] In a keynote address at the ADC's Eleventh National Convention, Said called on Arab-Americans to capitalize on their freedom in the United States and rescue Arab culture from Arab leaders and governments: "[They] not only abandoned their responsibilities for the care of their people, but they have also aban-doned their culture and history."[161]

Finally, many integrationists remain committed to the peace pro-cess and trying to assist their kinfolk in the West Bank and Gaza through economic ventures.[162] "I look at [our venture] as Americans working for peace, helping the economy of a region that has been war-torn," said Talat Othman, a Palestinian-American businessman and founder of the Chicago Arab-American Business and Profes-sional Association.[163] Since the 1991 Madrid conference, integration-ist leaders have called for parity between Arab- and Jewish-Americans when it comes to Middle Eastern affairs. They were encouraged when President Bush summoned their representatives to the White House in November 1991 and asked them to support his peace initiative in the region.[164] The mainstream was also gratified that Secretary of State Warren Christopher briefed them on his trips to the Middle East, just as he did the Jewish leadership.[165] Certainly, soon after the PLO-Israel accords, Arab-American integrationists seemed to be on their way to acquiring a meaningful voice in U.S. foreign affairs. Not long after the accords were signed, James Zogby noted that "never before has the Arab American community had such a constructive ongoing dialogue with a Presidential administra-tion on domestic and foreign policy issues."[166] Zogby and Jahshan accompanied American high officials like the late U.S. Commerce Secretary Ron Brown on their tours of the Middle East and were invited to be among President Bill Clinton's entourage at the 1994 signing of the Israeli-Jordanian peace treaty. Khalil Jahshan met with Israeli Foreign Minister Peres in Jerusalem even before the signing of the Declaration of Principles.

Like other ethnic diasporas in America that wish to have an influ-ence on U.S. foreign policy, Arab-Americans have been "commis-sioned" by American decision makers to export and safeguard Amer-ican values and interests abroad. They were also expected to assume the role of moral conscience of their homelands.[167] Zogby, for example, understood that in order to sustain the reliability of the AAI, the group must show greater commitment when it comes to democratizing Arab autocratic regimes. The new status of mainstream Arab-American organizations has also forced them to confront more assertively their diasporic kinfolk who advocate Islamic radicalism or left-oriented rejectionism.

In anticipation of this new role, the AAI held a January 1994 conference entitled "Challenges 94: Making Democracy Work at Home and Abroad." Zogby warned that silence on democracy issues in the Middle East would compromise Arab-Americans' political credibility, adding that "I feel deeply that this period requires a new way of thinking – a new paradigm. If the peace accords are to bear fruit then we must make every effort to begin to develop new priorities. [While] we are [still] committed to Palestinian statehood . . . [and] oppose Israel's occupation of the Arab land . . . we [also] want to see human rights and democracy in the Arab world."[168] Yet any serious call for democracy in the Arab world may alienate AAI's Arab benefactors. Indeed, Zogby has already restrained his prodemocracy oratory as he now calls for an Arab-American alliance with pro-American Arab regimes: "[Arab-Americans] are [Arab leaders'] strongest supports [sic] and our strength and theirs are intimately related to one another."[169] When asked about his apparent desertion of the theme of Middle East democracy, he hailed the democratic advances he had witnessed in his visits to Saudi Arabia.[170] This shift is unlikely to impress the many in the Arab-American community who often call Zogby an opportunist and self-promoter.

By early 1995, the near-defunct NAAA was considering a plan to redirect its energies from foreign affairs toward Arab-American issues. Khalil Jashan said in despair that "Arab governments have a simplistic and even racist view toward Arab-Americans."[171] At the same time, the ADC faced a deep crisis. Amid controversy over the direction of the organization and with serious financial difficulties, its new executive director and president Candace Lightner (who replaced Albert Mokhiber) resigned after a brief tenure. With her left former senator Abourezk, the organization's founder and chairman. In the wake of Lightner's departure, Ray Hanania, then the vice-president of the ADC Midwest Chapter, wrote in the Arab-American Chicago paper *Al-Bostaan* that the ADC "was governed by a board consisting of old-fashioned thinking Arabs who had yet to understand what being an American is all about. . . . ADC has always focused itself in the wrong direction, involving itself in international political issues that raise tempers, and ignoring in substance issues of discrimination."[172] Indeed, if Arab-Americans are to be effective in foreign affairs, they must first try to build a genuine constituency in the United States.

Finally, Palestinian-Americans (by all accounts a more distinct subgroup within the Arab-American diaspora) are reaching a critical point in terms of the relationship between their ethnic roots in the Middle East and their current and future status inside the United States. Whether they unite in committing themselves economically and politically to support for the emerging Palestinian entity is very much on their agenda. The answer will be determined largely by a combination of factors: the success of the peace process; containment of the rejectionist camp by Palestinian authorities and establishment of the rule of law in liberated territories; and good governance by the PLO-led Palestinian Authority, resulting in definite progress toward both democratization and a free-market economy.

Such positive developments in the homeland itself are likely to clarify the outlines for a new Palestinian-American identity and may foster the creation of new diasporic institutions. In constructing new relations with the Palestinian entity, this diaspora may finally reconcile and synchronize its hopes for the homeland with the American creed of democracy and pluralism. The ongoing problems of split identity experienced by Palestinians in America – by being put on the defensive because of long-standing American public support of Israel – may be resolved. Indeed, should this scenario actually materialize, it is likely that more and more Palestinians-Americans will gradually remove themselves from the more militant Islamic camp.

Epilogue

Although the primary research and writing of this chapter concluded in the summer of 1995, and its thesis regarding the Arab-American diaspora still holds, it is clearly important to place the political developments of the past three years in the context of the chapter's principal arguments. Since the signing of the second Oslo agreement in the autumn of 1995, a series of dramatic events in the Middle East

has challenged the tentative foundations of Arab-Israeli reconciliation established in the region, and consequently the course of action
and rhetoric of Arab-American activists, who have once again refo-
cused their attention on events overseas, promoting Palestinian
causes which seemed to be threatened by Israeli actions. This new
posture has also meant the decline of newfound Arab-Jewish cooperation in the United States and a return to a more conflictual
posture, as demonstrated by the collapse of the "Builders for Peace"
initiative. While some American Jewish activists have somewhat sim-
plistically charged that Arab-American mainstream organizations
that originally supported the peace process have returned to a reflex-
ive anti-Israeli position and joined the usual "American detractors"
of Israel,[173] the reality is much more complex. Although the apparent
deterioration in the Middle East peace process may cause others to
perceive the cementing of a monolithic Arab- and Muslim-American
coalition, in fact the differences among these groups remain fundamental.

A brief list gives some indication of the extent to which the confidence and good will of "moderates" on both sides of the Middle East
conflict have been tested, and to which regional political dynamics
have shifted. These events have had a great impact on the diasporic
politics of both Arab-and Jewish-Americans: the Rabin assassination;
suicide bombings by Islamic militants in the streets of Israeli cities;
the Israeli attack on Qana in Lebanon; the election of a hard-line
Israeli government under Benjamin Netanyahu; Israel's opening of a
controversial tunnel in Jerusalem's Old City; the botched Israeli
attempt to assassinate a Hamas leader on the streets of Amman,
Jordan's capital; and, above all, the stalemate in the peace process.

Solidarity among Arab-American organizations and interest in the
Israeli-Palestinian relationship was revived to some degree by the
renewed atmosphere of crisis in the Middle East. This revival began
with the Qana attack, in which over a hundred Lebanese civilians
were killed, and intensified after the election of Netanyahu who,
despite promises late in the 1996 election campaign to respect the
agreements reached by his predecessors, had been consistently hostile to the Oslo process. As late as March 1996, mainstream Arab-
American organizations publicly denounced Hamas attacks against
Israeli civilians in Jerusalem. Ray Hanania, national president of the
Palestinian American Congress, wrote in the *New York Times* that

"the majority of Palestinians detest the violence and the murder of innocent civilians. The bloodshed is unnecessary and contradicts the basic views of Christians and Muslims."[174] After the Sharm-el-Sheikh international summit on terrorism later that month, representatives of fourteen Arab-American organizations met in Washington to denounce terrorism, while calling upon the Clinton administration to take measures to build Palestinian confidence in the peace process.[175] Yet shortly after, the Israeli attack on Qana triggered demonstrations that united Arab-American Christians with Muslim-Americans who identified with the Lebanese Shi'ite Hizbullah organization. Hizbullah has been cited in U.S. congressional anti-terrorism legislation as a terrorist group, in keeping with Israeli views on the organization. The Israeli operation "elicited a virtual exculpation of Hizbullah. . . . [AAI President James] Zogby characterized it as nothing other than 'the Lebanese armed resistance.' The ADC also justified Hizbullah actions as 'legitimate resistance activities.' "[176]

The major shift, however, took place after Netanyahu's rise to power. His policies brought together Muslims, Palestinian-Americans, and other Arab-Americans, and blurred what had become clearer distinctions between supporters of the peace process and the Islamic resistance to Israel, which is categorically opposed to peace. By 1998, one could discern the positions of the major Arab- and Muslim-American parties involved. The Palestinian-American intellectual left continues its descent from marginalization to irrelevance. Arab-American integrationist organizations generally remain ineffective and continue to find rallying grass-roots support and financial backing a difficult task. AAI President James Zogby may still be the most cited Arab-American name, yet his standing among other community activists remains suspect.[177] The balance of power within the Arab-Muslim diaspora has shifted to *Muslim* activists, whose organizational base is religious rather than ethnic. Muslim organizations in the United States have made impressive strides in furthering their own agenda, and in using the new dynamics in the Middle East domestically to mobilize grass-roots support among members of the rapidly growing Muslim-American community. The Council on American Islamic Relations, the American Muslim Council, and the Muslim Public Affairs Committee are among the organizations founded within the past decade (some within the past two or three years) that have become increasingly active recently. While integrationist voices within the Arab-American diaspora such as the ADC struggle to maintain wide-based credibility and support, these Muslim organizations are on their way to becoming the leading force inside the United States for Arab diasporic activism. Even though they have often been stigmatized by their association with radical terrorist groups in the Middle East, they have made inroads in the American arena, appealing to American values on issues of religious and human rights for Muslims,[178] and have begun to establish themselves as a lobbying force in foreign affairs.[179]

In May 1998, in the midst of a deep crisis in the Middle East peace process and while tensions between the United States and Israel grew, an unprecedented meeting between President Clinton and members of the Arab-American lobby took place. Speaking as the first sitting president to address the Arab American Institute Conference, Clinton decried negative stereotypes plaguing the community, praised Arab-American values, and called upon Arabs in the United States to help spread American values abroad. Clinton made reference to the difficulties in the peace process, and encouraged Arab-Americans to mobilize on its behalf.[180] The meeting can be seen not only as a Clinton administration effort to signal to Jerusalem and to Jewish-Americans the existence of alternative U.S. diplomatic approaches to the Middle East, but also as a reminder to the Arab lobby in the United States that it must accept American diplomatic, philosophical, and political parameters in order to have a place at the table in U.S. foreign policy making.

4

Transnational Influences on Ethnoracial Relations in the United States: The Case of Black-Jewish Disputes

The experiences of Arab-Americans have shown the strong nexus between U.S. foreign policy and international developments in countries of origin on the one hand, and ethnic identity and political empowerment inside the United States on the other. This connection raises further questions as to the strength of the impact of international politics on the fabric of American society and its culture. To what extent do events abroad impede or enhance American societal cohesion? How do they hinder or promote ethnic pluralism or divisiveness?

Indeed, many have stressed how strong ties between ethnic Americans and their countries of origin have grown in recent years, and some have warned against the erosion of the American national interest as a result of the increasing domesticization of U.S. foreign policy, in part by the growing clout of ethnicity, which has taken the lead in redefining the national interest in the wake of the end of the cold war and the conceptual vacuum it has left. While assuming the combined threat of the "disintegrative effects of the end of the Cold War"[1] and the domestic growth of multiculturalism, scholars and pundits have said very little about how relations with the motherland and the influences of ethnicity on foreign affairs bear on ethnic relations inside the United States. Indeed, an examination of such impacts is critical to validate or to contradict their assertions.

This chapter, therefore, examines how ethnocultural identification with countries of origin or symbolic homelands, compounded by the increasing influences of ethnic voices on U.S. foreign policy, bears on ethnoracial relations inside the United States and on American civic culture in general. To begin such an inquiry, it seems almost

132

natural to turn to one of the most heated and durable discords in U.S. ethnoracial relations, that between Jews and blacks. The homeland factor has had a strong presence in the life of both communities, and especially in the rhetoric and action of their leadership. Moreover, since organized lobbies of Jewish-Americans have long been cited as the most powerful diasporic voice in affecting U.S. foreign policy, and since African-Americans in particular have recently made a giant leap in this domain by playing a decisive role in affecting U.S. policy toward Haiti, South Africa, Somalia, and black Africa in general, it is natural that relations between the two communities are strongly affected by transnational influences, at least at the level of diasporic elites but also in terms of popular images and perceptions.

The feuds between African- and Jewish-Americans have been among the most intense and agonizing conflicts in the recent history of U.S. ethnoracial relations.[2] To many, black-Jewish friction has been particularly disheartening because of the two communities' common history as casualties of racism, political exclusion, and marginalization, and especially in view of the strong cooperation between blacks and Jews during the civil rights era. The black-Jewish civil rights coalition disintegrated rapidly from the late 1960s due to fierce quarrels over domestic and international issues.[3] In 1995, Murray Friedman, a writer on Jewish-black relations, declared that the "alliance is dead."[4]

The sources of contention between blacks and Jews are located primarily in the context of America's domestic affairs, specifically related to issues of race, religion, and class. The acrimony of recent decades has been exacerbated by black anti-Semitism and the opposition of neoconservative Jews to affirmative action.[5] It is also fed by the general feeling among blacks that Jewish prosperity comes at their expense, and among Jewish-Americans that despite their safety and material well-being in America, black anti-Semites "are out there begrudging [their] success."[6]

For decades black-Jewish domestic quarrels have been exacerbated by disputes over external affairs, primarily over issues concerning the diasporas' symbolic homelands, Africa and Israel. Their relations were also affected by the two diasporas' positions vis-à-vis their respective kinfolk (real or symbolic) worldwide – African-Americans' affinity with blacks wherever they may be (including in Israel) or with the Third World in general, and Jewish-Americans' campaigns on behalf of world Jewry. On various occasions, Jewish-Americans faulted blacks for their hostile position toward Israel and for their indifference to the plight of Russian and Syrian Jewry, while blacks have charged American Jews with supporting Israel at the expense of their domestic responsibilities, and blamed them for compromising their moral integrity by remaining silent concerning Israel's friendly relations with South Africa, and for Israel's mistreatment of Palestinian Arabs. The Jewish-black rift on foreign affairs has also pervaded the intracommunal debate. It has often divided the African-American leadership, and has also strained relations among American Jews.[7]

In this chapter, the past impact of external affairs on black-Jewish relations will be analyzed and used to assess future prospects in light of new international developments like the Middle East peace process, the decline of Third World ideology, and the end of apartheid in South Africa. This chapter also examines how Israeli domestic affairs, especially the treatment of Ethiopian (black) Jews, factor into relations between American blacks and Jews and into Israeli efforts to influence ethnoracial relations inside the United States. The analysis suggests that even close contacts between the homeland and its loyal diaspora (as is the case of Jewish-Israeli relations) do not preclude the possibility of conflicts of interest when it comes to ethnoracial relations inside the United States. In conclusion, I offer preliminary observations about the impact of homelands on interethnic relations in America.

Diasporic Identity

Since the foundation of the Jewish state, the dominant issue for American Jewry has been protection of the state of Israel. The attitude toward Israel has been the critical litmus test American Jews have used in distinguishing between friend and foe among other ethnic groups in the United States.[8] The commitment of Jewish-Americans to Israel and the strong connection between the Israeli government and Jewish organizations have been unique in their intensity and institutional design, and have become the model other ethnic groups and their respective home governments try to emulate.[9] Although Jewish-Americans like to downplay the widely held notion about the exceptional power of their pro-Israeli lobby by pointing to other ethnic groups who act like them, as Nathan Glazer has pointed out, "the difference in the degree of involvement with homeland that marks Jews, owing to the special position of Israel, reaches to a difference in quality."[10]

Diasporic financial, political, and emotional support for Israel has been extensively documented.[11] For some American religious Jews, relocating to the land of Israel has been a tenet of their faith. The overriding commitment of many other Jews to the well-being of the state of Israel has been an imperative for their self-identity inside America. They "are proud of Israel and see its worth for dispossessed Jews, but not for themselves." They support Israel as self-assured Americans. A smaller number "have a deep sense of gratitude" to the United States for providing Jews with a safe haven but still recognize "the uncertainties and vagaries that have always attended Jewish existence in the Diaspora," and consider the state of Israel as a potential place of refuge. An even smaller segment is the group of "aberrant exiles," who identify with Israel more than with their country of domicile.[12] The fact that Israel perceives itself as the Jewish state and defines all diasporic Jews as potential members automatically entitled to Israeli citizenship further strengthens the diaspora-homeland connection.

The tie between African-Americans and Africa is more complicated and less direct than relations between Israel and the Jewish-American diaspora. In general, few African-Americans can identify their precise country of origin and "most Blacks have felt little affinity for or loyalty toward any country other than the United States."[13] Until the rise of African national movements in the 1950s, black American interest in foreign issues in general was meager, with Africa being no exception. Surprisingly, in Africa, information about America and African-Americans reached even the remotest parts of the continent.[14] Across Africa, and especially in the west, America was perceived as "God's country" and the "conscience of the world." The mythologization of America also led to the idolization of the black condition in America and the creation of an unrealistic integrationist vision that downplayed American racism and discrimination. In fact, "Africans needed a wholly positive vision of a prosperous and progressing African-American community, stripped of the unpalatable facts, in order to maintain their own hopes of advancing in a world governed by whites."[15]

Yekutiel Gershoni, in his book *Africans on African-Americans*, has documented the deep influence of African-American intellectuals on Africans' self-perception. People like Booker T. Washington, Marcus Garvey – neither of whom had ever visited the black continent or had contact with the people of Africa – and W. E. B. Du Bois grew into larger-than-life figures in Africa, and were seen as uniquely American figures, visionaries that would "lead their African brethren to freedom and progress."[16] The mythology of the black condition in the United States and the influence of African-American culture and religion that pervaded large segments of African society were critical in building African self-confidence and a belief "that the black man was not the incapable being he was taken by some to be,"[17] but rather that Africans could attain a status equal to that of their colonial masters.

Yet, in the United States, by 1957, only 1 percent of blacks, contrasted with 6 percent of whites, could name as many as five countries, colonies, or other territories on the African continent; 70 percent of blacks compared with only 55 percent of whites, could not name any at all.[18] Indeed, African-American political leaders and intellectuals generally agree that the Jewish-American tie to Israel is much stronger than the African-American tie to Africa.[19] Moreover, unlike Israel, which actively courts and works to strengthen its ties with its diaspora, African states have been slow to take advantage of the potential support base available to them within the African-American population. Instead, contact and cooperation have largely been the result of African-American initiatives, designed primarily with domestic purposes in mind. More recently, however, South Africa, under the leadership of President Nelson Mandela, has been trying to build a relationship with African-Americans and obtain their backing for greater U.S. political and economic involvement in Africa.

Despite problems in identifying direct black ancestral links with particular countries and the lack of popular black American involvement in African affairs, racism in America has made many African-Americans "remain . . . structurally linked to Africa whether they had any emotional bonds to that 'mysterious' continent or not. . . . Whenever African Americans sought equality with Americans of European descent, they were reminded that their Africanness precluded such aspirations."[20]

To a large extent, black leaders' ideas about the black transnational connection revealed more about their concerns within America – that is, the possibility of black integration in the United States – than about their ties with Africa. From Marcus Garvey, who called on American Negroes to flee the United States and return to Africa, to W. E. B. Du Bois, who protested the Negro condition with an eye to future integration, through integrationists like Martin Luther King Jr. and Roy Wilkins and their opponent Malcolm X, up to the Reverend Jesse Jackson and current ranks of Afrocentrists, certain similarities are evident. Black leaders and intellectuals, while differing sharply on whether America should be their prime object of loyalty, have always looked to Africa as "a possible external haven or zion." And they have "sought to borrow from African realities (past and present) sources of emotional, ideological, and cultural reinforcement of Black American identity."[21]

Certainly the black and Jewish diasporas in the United States have drawn heavily on their transnational attachments in constructing their American identity, although organizationally the homeland plays a significantly different role. For American Jews, Israel as a symbolic homeland has been the primary basis of community mobilization, whereas their black counterparts see events in Africa as simply one among a number of important issues facing their community. Leaders and communal organizations of both groups have utilized the symbolic homeland to galvanize and mobilize their communities inside the Unites States both socially and politically. The importance of the homeland in defining their American identity has had a significant impact on black-Jewish relations. Thus, when Israel and black Africa clashed, or when the foreign policy concerns of blacks and Jews were in conflict, the domestic friction between the two groups was aggravated. The shared nature of black-Jewish domestic and transnational discord led one scholar of Jewish-black relations to remark that any "valid discussion of African-American Jewish relations cannot focus on domestic issues to the exclusion of international affairs."[22]

Protesting Exclusion and Searching for Empowerment

In the past, discrimination and harsh conditions, including a generalized assault on Africans as savages, led some African-Americans to reject their biological and sociocultural ties to Africa through a "process of acculturation and miscegenation."[23] Yet, in recent decades, many African-Americans, in congruence with their own civil rights struggle inside the United States, have manifested their transnational sentiments by empathizing with the racial and political aspirations of blacks in other parts of the world.[24] Only a small group of blacks followed Marcus Garvey's message of racial pride and even superiority to the point of wanting to return to Africa and work for its betterment.[25] In any event, the American failure to integrate African-Americans has remained one of the strongest motivations for the African connection. Even Nathan Glazer, one of the leading intellectual opponents of affirmative action in the 1960s and 1970s, recently acknowledged that America's inability or deliberate reluctance to incorporate into its society African-Americans challenges the mere vision of America's inclusionary nature.[26]

Jews in the United States have also suffered from civil exclusion, anti-Semitism, and religious intolerance. However, as Gunnar Myrdal wrote more than fifty years ago in his classic study of blacks in America, "there is a quantitative difference between [the discrimination against the Jew in America] and the discrimination against the Negro which is so great that it becomes qualitative."[27] The great difference between the two communities stemmed from a number of sources, including the lack of clear and specific black ancestral and historical ties to particular countries or territories comparable with those of the Jews. Dramatic recent events in Jewish history, including mass migration from Europe to America, the development of modern Zionism, the tragedy of the Holocaust, and the establishment of the state of Israel, reinforced Jewish ties to an already lengthy and remarkable cultural and religious history stretching back thousands of years. This common experience unified Jews and gave them a unique perspective on persevering, indeed thriving, in the face of adversity.

The centrality in Jewish life of the symbolic homeland, the Land of Israel, and the legacy of Jewish history, had no African-American parallels. Because of the sudden geographic detachment from the cultural and historical legacy of Africa caused by slavery, and the extent to which Africa and African culture were systematically devalued in the United States, African-Americans did not have access to the strengths and ties of their own past in the same manner as Jews. It was therefore far more difficult to mobilize U.S. blacks on African or "homeland" issues than was the case among Jews and, more importantly, it was difficult to repeat the pattern of success enjoyed by Jews in America. Although most Jews who immigrated to the United States were very poor when they arrived, many were able to move up socially, economically, and politically in the United States, while the fortunes of African-Americans who, as mentioned, had very different experiences and opportunities in America, failed to improve. Integrationist black leaders were very much aware of this distinction and the lessons it held for their community. Black leader Frederick Douglass

> had urged blacks to follow the example of modern Jews in Europe and America, who by emphasizing group solidarity and pride, improved their status. Booker T. Washington also pointed to the example of the Jews, to their unity, pride, and love of their own people that would, "as the years go on," make them "more and more influential in this country." . . . [Martin Luther] King also frequently compared the situation of blacks to that of Jews, arguing that blacks could learn from the Jewish combination of ethnic traditions with social and political action.[28]

After World War II, as American racism began to lose its public appeal, primarily because of the Nazi legacy, discrimination against blacks and other minorities became an international embarrassment and was even used by the Soviets to invalidate American criticism of their own abuses.[29] In the 1950s and 1960s Jews and blacks joined forces in the civil rights struggle to end discrimination in jobs, housing, and education. Some have underrated the authenticity of the civil rights alliance, declaring it to be a temporary marriage of convenience, an outcome of ethnoracial expediency on the part of Jewish and black elites alike – blacks needed Jewish financial support and Jews needed black "moral authority" to secure their domestic advancement and international objectives.[30] However, the fact remains that "by the time civil rights became a national crusade in the 1960s the notion of black-Jewish alliance was firmly rooted in U.S. National mythology."[31]

The Jewish-black rift began widening in the 1960s, at a time when a confluence of international and internal events amplified black and Jewish ethnoracial identities and stimulated a reassessment of their role in American society. Jewish-black domestic debates concerning integration and economic mobility were intertwined with and heightened by foreign events. For blacks it was the struggle for independence by their kinfolk in Africa and the rise of Third World-ism in general that inspired a new diasporic identity. Black transna-tionalism was also fueled by the realization that the civil rights "rev-olution of rising expectations would not be rapidly followed by a revolution of rising gratifications."[32]

In the 1960s a deep divide developed between black integration-ists, who continued to believe in the idea of desegregation and the possibility of black assimilation, and black separatists, who forsook both the prospect and the desirability of black integration. The rad-icalization of many veteran civil rights leaders manifested itself most prominently in the rise of the "Black Power" movement, which found its ideological match in the global context of Third Worldism and pan-Africanism. The rise of black consciousness in the United States coincided with and was affected by the successful struggle for independence of African states,[33] and by the late 1960s the black domestic crusade was fully internationalized.[34] The message of Third Worldism to black Americans was enchanting. In the words of Paul Berman, "You, the African-Americans, are hopelessly outnumbered within the United States, and this unfortunate reality cannot be wished away by a lot of talk about liberalism and rights. But on the world scale you are no minority at all. . . . You are many, not few; strong, not weak; time will right your wrongs!"[35]

Some black intellectuals considered racial oppression inside Amer-ica as a form of "internal colonialism." Their politics of racial sepa-ratism, black nationalism, and the embracing of Islam represented the black rejection of American life and the melting pot idea. The notions of black pride and black self-determination left no room for white liberal activists, primarily Jewish civil rights organizers who "lost their place in the anti-Western front that was imagined by Black power."[36]

For Jewish-Americans, the Six Day War was a watershed. The fear of a "second Holocaust" that preceded the war and the exhila-ration of salvation that followed Israel's overwhelming victory al-tered, almost overnight, the American-Jewish universe.[37] Martin Per-etz characterized the event as "the return of power to the Jewish people."[38] Alan Dershowitz wrote that the Six Day War was the pinnacle event in his life that enabled him to express his Jewishness openly: "I never stepped back into the closet or even the shadows."[39] The famous Rabbi Abraham Joshua Herschel wrote that "America's Jews would never be the same."[40] Indeed, since 1967, many Jewish-Americans have lived vicariously through the state of Israel. To a large extent "Israel had become the new religion of American Jews. . . . Jews were to be found less often praying to God than raising funds, mobilizing support and engaging in political lobbying on behalf of Israel."[41]

Internationalizing the Domestic Rift

It has been rightly observed that Africa's awakening in the 1950s and 1960s "had the misfortune of beginning its era of independence at the height of the cold war struggle between the US and the Soviet Union."[42] The friend-foe demeanor adopted by the United States during the cold war located much of the Third World movement on the side of the enemy. This U.S. posture had an adverse impact on black-Jewish relations since black nationalists considered Zionism and Israel as extensions of American imperialism and racism, while Arabs and Palestinians were perceived as Western colonialism's latest victims. Radical American blacks condemned integrationist black leaders who supported Israel for collaborating in the oppression of their Palestinian "brothers and sisters."[43] Since they identified with all people of color, they also viewed Israel as the oppressor of darker Jews.[44] Paul Berman writes, "It was sometimes believed that Palestinian skin tone was darker than that of the Israeli Jews, as if in pigmental confirmation of the proposed new link between Palestinians and African-Americans."[45]

When in 1967 the radicalized Student Non-Violent Coordinating Committee denounced Israel for conquering "Arab homes and land through terror, force, and massacres,"[46] many Jewish benefactors of the desegregation movement felt betrayed that "the most vitriolic anti-Semitic and anti-Zionist rhetoric seemed to be emanating from those with whom we had marched hand in hand, promising to 'overcome' racism and religious bigotry."[47] Prominent liberal Jewish activists subsequently distanced themselves from the civil rights movement.[48]

Jewish-Americans, who have always insisted that their devotion to Israel was an extension of their allegiance to American democratic values and strategic interests, regarded black attacks on Israel as anti-Semitism, or at best an expression of misplaced blame. Alan Dershowitz wrote that Israel became the "surrogate for the sublime hatred [of blacks] really directed against others."[49] Although by the mid-1970s black separatism had already lost its appeal, black popular support of Israel continued to decline and Jewish-black relations to deteriorate. The background for this erosion was a combination of domestic and foreign quarrels, primarily over Jewish opposition to affirmative action, Israel's relations with South Africa, and growing black support for Arabs and Palestinians in the Middle East conflict.

Moreover, after 1967 Jewish America's disenchantment with and irritation by what they considered to be Israel bashing in black radical quarters coincided with the declining saliency of civil rights issues for many American Jews. Some observers have maintained that in their rush to consolidate their long-sought admission into the American mainstream and in their efforts to secure their middle-class status, many Jews abandoned their liberal commitments.[50] African-American scholar Adolph Reed has quoted Albert Vorspan, vice-president of the Union of American Hebrew Congregations, as saying that "Black criticism of Israeli policies which Jews liked to simplify as Black anti-Semitism, provided the pretense for Jewish withdrawal from Black concerns."[51] Jonathan Kaufman has written that "The humanitarian liberalism of the 1950s, with its focus on equal rights for Blacks, now competed with – and in some ways was replaced by – a commitment to Israel that occupied a great deal of Jewish personal and political thinking."[52]

This Jewish inward-looking stance was seen by some black integrationist leaders as a betrayal. Jewish neoconservatives' assault on affirmative action – on grounds that the policy of quotas represented a form of racism analogous to the tsarist anti-Semitic *numerus clausus* – was stamped as Jewish racism.[53] The fact that Israel had broadened its friendly relations with the apartheid regime in South Africa after the 1973 Arab-Israeli War was magnified in the American domestic debate and consequently inflamed Jewish-black tensions even further. Certainly Jewish-black relations suffered also from the outcome of the 1973 Arab-Israeli War, which shattered diaspora Jewry's belief in Israel's invincibility and caused them to focus on their own ethnic self-interest, primarily their diasporic commitment to Israel.

The Consolidation of Black Integrationism

By the early 1970s, the integrationists who had eclipsed more radical figures at the forefront of black political activity in the United States could point to some success in expanding their electoral power, with black congressional representation increasing from four members in 1960 to thirteen in 1971.[54] The newly emergent class of mainstream blacks, best represented by the Congressional Black Caucus (CBC) formed in 1971, championed the cause of integration into American plural society. A growing circle of black leaders arose at this juncture who derived their power, for the first time, from the American democratic process and were not merely black paragons dependent upon the approval of whites. As one scholar of African-Americans has pointed out, the formation of the CBC indicated "a consciousness and willingness to use that power as a lever with which to bargain."[55]

The importance of Africa to black domestic politics intensified in the mid-1970s. The unfolding of crises in southern Africa, the collapse of Portuguese colonialism, the ensuing civil war in Angola, the liberation struggle against white-ruled Rhodesia, and the Soweto uprising caused black elites to deepen their involvement in U.S. policy toward Africa.[56] Under the assumption that the fate of black Africa had ramifications for blacks in America, integrationist leaders considered a voice in U.S. foreign affairs an important entry ticket into American society and politics.[57] Accordingly, they distanced themselves from the course of black ethnocentrism, recognizing that it established "neither effective lobbying organizations nor institutions for transferring developmental resources for African countries."[58]

From the mid-1970s through the 1980s black integrationists concentrated their international campaign primarily around opposition to South African apartheid.[59] Most significant for the institutionalization of black political power in the U.S. foreign-policy arena was the establishment of TransAfrica. Dovetailing with the self-proclaimed pro-African interests of the Carter administration,[60] the group enlisted the support of many mainstream organizations like the NAACP and Africare and began a grass-roots outreach program to mobilize black support for TransAfrica's foreign policy initiatives, especially with regard to South Africa.

Despite their growing involvement in external affairs, the influence of African-Americans on foreign policy formulation remained quite limited throughout the 1970s. This trend began to change when Andrew Young, a prominent black activist, was appointed by President Carter as the U.S. ambassador to the United Nations. Under Carter's human rights foreign policy, Young – the highest ranking black in the administration – led the way in pushing for American support for majority black rule in Rhodesia and opposition to apartheid in South Africa. Alongside the CBC and TransAfrica, Andrew Young helped to foster a greater American interest in South Africa and its relations with the United States. His "diplomacy [also] reflected the desire among Black leaders to act as intermediaries between the United States and the Third World countries."[61] It was within this context that black-Jewish tensions reached their explosive moment.

The Andrew Young Affair

In the summer of 1979, Andrew Young was forced out of his post as UN ambassador after it was revealed that he was conferring with the PLO's UN observer in violation of U.S. policy that since 1975 had barred any dialogue with the organization. President Carter's vague excuse for Young's removal helped to reinforce the popular belief that Jewish and Israeli pressures were behind the dismissal and that the president was in fact powerless in the face of such pressures. The Young affair had a grave influence on black-Jewish relations.[62] It embellished the mythology of Jewish power as opposed to black weakness, and became a symbol of Jewish "affluence compared with Black poverty."[63] Moreover, the notion that Jewish control over America's international affairs was part of the wider Jewish assault on the empowerment of blacks became prevalent. According to one poll "at least 40 percent of Black respondents saw Young as a victim of both Jewish and Israeli pressures."[64] Thus the incident was seen as an expression of Jewish racism.

The Young episode helped to mend the rift between black radicals and moderates.[65] For the next decade attacks against Israel's policies in the Middle East and Israel's friendly relations with South Africa became a major African-American preoccupation and more and more black leaders and intellectuals expressed their support for Palestinian independence and called for open talks with the PLO. In the wake of Young's dismissal, African-American delegations went on visits to the Middle East and made public statements assailing Israel's belligerent practices. The snubbing of Reverend Jesse Jackson by Israel's Prime Minister Menahem Begin, in contrast with his enthusiastic reception by the PLO in Beirut, further deepened the domestic quarrel.[66] Ze'ev Chafets, who worked for the Begin administration and has written on Jewish-black affairs in America, wrote in 1993 that Begin was uninformed about the African-American community and sought the advice of the Israeli Embassy in Washington about Jackson's visit. The Embassy, in turn, consulted American Jewish "experts" who advised the Israeli prime minister to avoid the African-American leader. "Ironically [Begin's] color-blindness led [him] to miscalculate; he failed to see the Young and Jackson affairs in their true, i.e., [American] domestic, context – as a part of a nasty quarrel between the Black and Jewish establishments in the United States."[67] Notwithstanding Begin's motives, the floodgate was fully open. Andrew Young himself contrasted Begin's discourtesy with Israel's official acceptance of South Africa's prime minister, John Forster.[68] By the late 1980s, Israeli foreign policy officials would begin to seek contacts with African-Americans without the mediation of Jewish-Americans.

The Ascendance of Jesse Jackson

Throughout the 1980s the internationalization of the Jewish-black domestic quarrel was displayed most prominently in the actions and rhetoric of African-American leader Jesse Jackson and the Jewish response to them. Jackson used the dismissal of American UN ambassador Andrew Young as a springboard in his own rise to political prominence at home and abroad,[69] launching a new black posture of "not giving in to the Jews."[70] Young's departure would serve as the catalyst for blacks to rise up against what African-American scholar Adolph Reed called the "veto power that Jewish elites have held in Black interest articulation processes."[71] According to this thesis, Jewish-Zionist clout in America was so powerful that it could silence black voices with regard to the protection of Israel's "sacrosanct status," and even on matters of direct interest to the black community. In other words, Jewish dominance over American public pronouncements allegedly stifled the autonomy of black members of Congress to express their irritation with Israel's friendly relations with Pretoria and forced them to vote for U.S. aid to Israel in exchange for Jewish support for black issues domestically. In the mid-1990s, Reed still held firm to his thesis that the Jews were the gatekeeper for black access to the American mainstream. To become a legitimate black voice for the mainstream, "all it takes is the courage to square off in the white public sphere against Black anti-Semitism on the Anti-Defamation League's terms."[72] Whether Reed's thesis is true or not, the fact remains that members of the Congressional Black Caucus have almost always voted overwhelmingly for foreign aid to Israel and "kept silent" during the Palestinian *intifada*.[73]

Black sympathy for the Palestinians gathered momentum in the 1970s.[74] Jesse Jackson's outright attacks against Israeli policies toward the Palestinians and Israel's links with South Africa touched a Jewish-American nerve when Jackson embraced Yasir Arafat, Israel's mortal enemy at that time. In hugging the PLO chairman, Jackson may have intended to send "a declaration of independence from liberal Jewish tutelage."[75] More significantly, however, Jackson's controversial Middle East approach marked the beginning of blacks' aggressive quest for a voice in U.S. foreign affairs, no longer restrained by what Reed called the concern over the high cost of "potential Jewish alienation."[76] For American Jews the shift was dramatic. As one writer put it, it was as if Jesse Jackson had "placed the moral authority of the civil-rights struggle . . . at the disposal of [the] PLO."[77]

It has been argued that Jackson's resolve to preach his pro-Palestinian position regardless of the high political cost to his 1984 presidential campaign stemmed more from his moral theological creed rather than from his desire to overcome what he perceived as excessive Jewish influence over foreign policy or from his affinity with Third World have-nots. According to this argument, Jackson's creed commanded that the self-assertion of the victim is needed if one wishes to secure "mutual recognition" between someone subjugated and an oppressor. This philosophy, which Jackson allegedly wished to apply to U.S. foreign and domestic affairs, meant that mutual recognition between the PLO and Israel *should* be preceded by the Palestinians' assertion of their "Godly right" for self-determination and a homeland.[78] The advocacy of the "mutual recognition" philosophy might have earned Reverend Jackson the title of America's moral compass on Palestinian rights. Indeed, Jackson's message assured him the support of many Christian Arab-Americans and even some religious Muslim Arabs who traditionally stay away from the voting booths in American elections.[79] Yet, the prophet spoiled his message with his infamous "Hymie" and "Hymietown" slurs, which reinforced the Jewish diaspora's solidarity. Adolph Reed has written that "in one stroke Jackson sacrificed the moral authority on which he might have stood to demand a Middle Eastern policy that acknowledges the legitimacy of interests other than Israel's."[80] Jackson's failure to disentangle himself from Louis Farrakhan – the anti-Semitic leader of the Nation of Islam who in 1984 praised Hitler as "a great man" and denounced Judaism as "a dirty religion" – further eroded the credibility of Jackson's Middle East message.[81]

The internationalization of the Jewish-black rupture was dramatized fully during the emotional debate over the Democratic Party platform for the 1984 elections when a passionate break occurred between the Mondale and Jackson camps over the drafting of a foreign-policy plank on the Middle East. The failed attempt to push Jackson's program – that called for "the establishment of a Palestinian homeland" and "the readjustment of relationships in the Middle East to more 'balanced' proportions" – also led to the failure of Jackson's Africa plank, which was voted down in retaliation, even though it had been thought likely to win the support of the majority of delegates.[82] During Jackson's second presidential bid in 1988, despite his laborious attempts to erase the Hymietown stain, Jewish Democratic voters refused to forget his 1979 photograph with Arafat and "Farrakhan's omnipresent shadow behind him."[83] Yet, by the late 1980s Jackson's Middle East position had already become more acceptable to the U.S. government and even to large segments of American Jews. By 1988, "two thirds of American Jews . . . indicated that Israel should talk with the PLO if it recognized Israel and renounce[d] terrorism."[84]

As mentioned earlier, the influence of foreign policy on black self-definition became evident during the anti-apartheid campaign, when community leaders moved to replace "black" with the appellation

"African-American." In 1991, hundreds of African-American dele-gates, including educators, politicians, business, religious, and civil rights leaders, attended the first African–African-American summit in Abidjan, Ivory Coast, and pledged to "strengthen the bond of heritage and history that link Blacks in the United States and Af-rica."[85]

The fervor with which African-Americans approached their strug-gle against apartheid also meant that they could no longer remain indifferent in the face of human rights abuses by black African re-gimes. More and more African-American intellectuals disassociated themselves from the Afrocentric romanticization of Africa and dis-puted the notion of a "generic kinship" among blacks in America and in Africa. Their attention shifted toward the "quality-of-rule issue."[86] Accordingly, since the early 1990s African-American leaders have moved steadily to redefine their pro-Africa crusade along dem-ocratic lines.[87]

Israel and South Africa

The critical importance ascribed to the struggle against apartheid in building African-American identity and in mobilizing the black com-munity domestically put Israel, in the eyes of many blacks, in the camp of the enemy. Moreover, while more and more "race conflicts in Southern Africa [were seen] as surrogates for US racial issues,"[88] the ties between Israel and South Africa became a major liability for the American Jewish community.

From the late 1950s and throughout most of the 1960s Israel had close relations with most of the emerging African states. Israeli activ-ity in the black continent was intended to lift Israel out of its regional isolation in the Middle East, and was also embedded in the ideology of the Jews being "a light unto the other nations."[89] Within this context, Israel initiated and implemented numerous aid and devel-opment programs. Hundreds of Israeli experts were spread through-out the continent and at the same time Israel hosted thousands of Africans for skill-enhancement programs. In 1962 *Newsweek* com-mented on Israeli-African cooperation as "one of the strongest un-official alliances in the world."[90]

The African orientation in the Israeli Foreign Office meant that Israel accepted African demands with regard to South Africa. In 1961

Israel voted in the United Nations against the apartheid regime, to the chagrin of the government in Pretoria, which retaliated by revoking Israel's exemption from commodity and transfer restrictions. This action had direct ramifications for South African Jews, who for the next five years were unable to utilize Israel's preferential status to liquidate business assets and transfer money out of the country.[91] Certainly since then, sensitivity for the welfare of South African Jews remained an issue that affected Jerusalem's policy toward South Africa.

The Israeli victory in the Six Day War was perceived in South Africa as the victory of the West over Soviet imperialism. Despite Arab and growing Third World hostility, Israel continued to maintain a cold posture toward South Africa, hoping that its good international standing in the African continent could be preserved. Indeed, until the early 1970s, Israel was able to prevent a united African political front against it regarding the Israeli-Arab conflict. However, a change in relations occurred following the Yom Kippur War in 1973. Israel's international standing rapidly declined as a result of the Arab diplomatic assault and the oil embargo. Pressured by the Arabs, most African countries severed their relations with Jerusalem. In light of this, Israel began to develop better relations with South Africa as both countries felt themselves to be "pariah states." The real turning point in South African–Israeli relations took place after the first Rabin government hosted South African premier John Forster in 1976. Following this visit, the countries' relations increased in terms of trade, sports, tourism, and, above all, in arms sales and military cooperation, including nuclear issues.[92]

Supporters of the Israeli–South African connection argued that Israel could not afford to choose its allies at a time of international isolation. They also maintained that Israel must distinguish between politics and morality, especially since morality never dictated the actions of its enemies. Others emphasized the importance of these relations to the well-being of South African Jews, though opponents of these relations considered this explanation to be no more than a "fig leaf" masking Israel's realpolitik attitude.[93] Israeli expert on Africa Naomi Chazan wrote that "Israel has appeared to relinquish the cause of liberation in Southern Africa at precisely the same time as an international consensus has coalesced on the obsolescence of white domination in that area."[94] Indeed, the harsh international criticism of the apartheid system that spread and intensified by the mid-1980s caught Israel in the midst of an international storm.

In 1984, the "First One Hundred Days" committee, appointed by the then Labor nominee for prime minister, Shimon Peres, suggested that Israel modify its approach to South Africa. Yossi Beilin, who later became Foreign Ministry director general, designed the program "Facing Israel Back in the Context of the Third World Hinterland" to implement this policy adjustment. His emissary, Shimshon Zelniker, began searching for a connection with the black leadership in South Africa. His activities, however, were not the result of a formal governmental policy and were subsidized by liberal Jewish-Americans anxious about the effects that Israeli–South African relations would have on their own position.[95] In fact, Israel retained its close relationship with South Africa even after the imposition of American and European sanctions in 1986. Only overseas protests, heavy pressure by progressive American Jews, and the fear that the South African connection would anger Israel's supporters in Congress to the point that it might endanger American assistance brought a change of policy.[96]

In March 1987 Israel decided to curb arm sales to Pretoria and reduced official ties in other areas. Ran Kuriel, a senior political officer in the Israeli Embassy in Washington at the time, said that once Israel joined the United States and Europe and imposed sanctions, American public pressure on Israel and Jews was reduced significantly and the alliance between Jewish and black Congress members got back on track.[97] Yet tensions with blacks on the issue and the virulent criticism of Israel persisted as late as 1992.[98] According to one source, by the early 1990s Israeli ties with South Africa had become the "most divisive issue in Black-Jewish relations."[99]

There is no doubt that the Israeli–South African connection damaged Israel's image in the United States and hurt Jewish-black relations. The U.S. media characterized the Israeli–South African relations in terms of an ideological alliance and even as an "Apartheid Alliance." Despite wide criticism by Jewish liberals, Jewish mainstream organizations generally stood behind Jerusalem. Allan Kagedan of the American Jewish Committee argued that the public emphasis on the Israeli–South African relationship was very much driven by a "propaganda alliance" between the PLO, the Soviet Union, and other nonaligned states. They all singled out Israel while excluding Arab countries with equally strong ties to South Africa in an international leftist conspiracy "that sees the force of 'liberation' including the PLO and ANC, waging battle against ever new branches of imperialism."[100]

Israel's Outreach to American Ethnic Minorities

One of the more interesting developments in interethnoracial relations in the United States is the increasing awareness in countries of origin of the importance of American ethnicity to their own position. This recognition may motivate them to become involved in the shaping of these relations.[101] By the mid-1980s, in the context of anti-Israeli criticism for its friendship with the apartheid government in South Africa, and in light of the changing demography of the United States, Israeli Foreign Office officials decided to give more emphasis to the ethnic dimension in American politics. They raised the issue of how to ensure American popular support of Israel when other ethnic minorities with their own foreign policy agenda were fast becoming a dominant force on the U.S. political and social scene. This realization was summarized in the statement made by the Israeli consul general in New York, Uriel Savir: "It's an objective situation, [that] more Blacks and more Hispanics will take leading positions and will [have an] impact [on] the way Israel is viewed here."[102]

From interviews with Israeli foreign policy officials who served in the United States from the mid-1980s to the 1990s, and after reviewing diplomatic cables, it is evident that the Israeli plan to reach out to minorities was turned mostly into a campaign to win the hearts of African-Americans. One official document stated clearly that "Despite assessments that the number of Hispanics will be greater than the number of Blacks and so also their economic power, and despite the rapid increase in the Asian community, we have decided to concentrate on the Black community, the most complicated and difficult one which is undergoing a process of transformation, development, and political empowerment."[103] In the same memo, the diplomat deals with the ways in which Israel should improve its relations with African-Americans, concluding that "Israel, if at all, is on the Black agenda only because of the complex Black-Jewish relations inside the United States."[104] Consequently, the memo's author suggested practical methods to improve Israel's cooperation with blacks in ways that would separate Israel from black-Jewish tensions. The plan was to enhance Israel's prestige by presenting it as a multicultural society which absorbs black Jews and acts philanthropically toward Africa. Israel was also advised to get involved in developing community projects with blacks inside the United States.[105]

Much of the initiative for the development of Israeli-black relations was conceived and executed at the consular level inside the United States, with little direction from Jerusalem. To a large extent Israeli representatives throughout the United States worked as "ethnic entrepreneurs" with little institutionalization. Israel Peleg, the consul general in Philadelphia, for example, was behind the failed attempt to establish the Martin Luther King Jr. Forum in Jerusalem. Peleg also collaborated with former congressman Bill Gray in developing a black-Jewish project called "Operation Understanding."[106]

Above all, Uriel Savir in New York "made closer ties between Israel and minorities in the city the focus of his activities."[107] His actions in the ethnic domain enjoyed widespread attention among blacks and Jews and made national headlines. With the consent of the Israeli Foreign Office, Savir established a special unit in the consulate to deal with ethnic Americans and appointed a community relations officer to reach out to ethnic communities in an organized and coordinated fashion. Yehudit Katz-Carmeli, who headed this desk, said, "we did not accept the notion that Jewish Americans would speak on our behalf. The basis for our dialogue with Blacks was the assumption that Israel could achieve for itself greater acceptance if it could remove itself from the Black-Jewish domestic controversy."[108] This view was amplified after the Gulf War and the beginning of the Israeli-Arab peace process, and as a result of the winding down of the apartheid regime in South Africa. In fact, Jewish leaders have looked at the Israeli ethnic outreach program with ambivalence and even suspicion: "They did not trust our understanding of the American community and were quite leery about the damage that our independent work could cause them," said Katz-Carmeli.[109]

Colette Avital, the Israeli consul general in New York who replaced Savir, continued his outreach programs. When in 1994 she went on a speaking tour of black churches to build an interfaith dialogue she said: "Ethnicity . . . plays a role in politics . . . the [American] demographics are changing, and more political leadership is growing in the African-American community. . . . [we must] expose the Israeli case for them to understand what it is all about."[110] Despite these Israeli attempts to establish an independent dialogue with blacks, the connection remained entangled with and dominated by African- and Jewish-American domestic affairs. Attempts of lone foreign policy officers remained sporadic and, as Yossi Beilin, who served as the deputy foreign minister in Peres's first administration and later as a minister in the Rabin-Peres government, told me, "there is little possibility to reach out to Blacks without the Jewish-Americans. . . . Israel would not risk [alienating] Jewish-Americans when it comes to US internal affairs."[111]

"Black Jews" and the Confusion of Identity

The state of Israel provides an interesting duality in terms of its identity. Although it defines itself as an "ethnofocal" nation – and thus considers itself to be the state of the Jews including those in the diaspora, it also has strong "ideofocal" traits.[112] If Judaism is considered an ethnically homogenous feature, then in this regard Israel is indeed an ethnofocal state. If, however, the more commonly perceived ethnic traits, such as ancestral origin, social and cultural norms, mother tongue, or even physiological features are considered, then the Jewish population of Israel may be perceived as a highly diverse ethnic community, united by the ideofocal principle of Zionism. In fact, some have argued that the ethnofocal component of the Jews in modern times is more the result of global animosity and of persecution by external groups than of any inherent sense of a common national identity.[113]

In addition to the main divide in Israeli society between Jews and Arabs, multiple identity among Israeli Jews has often manifested itself in deep ethnic cleavages, primarily between Ashkenazi and Sephardic Jews. As noted earlier, the radical and at times even the more moderate black leadership have portrayed Israeli society and Jewish-Americans who support Israel as racists for their alleged oppression of Palestinian Arabs and their discrimination against dark-skinned Jews.[114] Thus when in 1984 and 1991 Israel airlifted Ethiopian Jews to Israel in "Operation Moses" and "Operation Solomon," the Jewish-American diaspora felt pride and vindication. The Israeli government exploited the airlift in a public relations campaign to improve Israel's image as a tolerant and unprejudiced state. The Israeli consulate in Atlanta organized an exhibition of pictures from Operation Solomon at the Martin Luther King Center, under the auspices of Coretta Scott King, the late black leader's widow, and the New York consulate organized a similar exhibition in the Empire State Building.

In a special brochure issued by the Community Outreach Department of the Consulate General of Israel in New York, New York's black mayor David Dinkins was quoted as saying "Israel is the first country in the world to welcome Black Africans not just as free men and women – not just as automatic citizens – but as brethren." Dr. Benjamin L. Hooks, executive director of the NAACP, issued a statement saying "the weekend airlift to safety of some 14,000 Ethiopian Jews by the Israeli government was an act of great humanitarianism unparalleled in recent memory."[115] Indeed, the circumstances surrounding the airlifts captured the imagination of the entire world, and it was said that "while the world let East Africa starve . . . the Jewish nation was saving its own."[116]

The campaign for Ethiopian Jews enabled Jewish-Americans to prove that neither they nor their brethren in Israel were racist. The Anti-Defamation League (ADL), for example, was behind the organization of special visits of young Ethiopian Jews in cities across America. ADL's project "Children of the Dream" was meant "to shatter stereotypes about Jews and to promote an appreciation of Israel." The Ethiopian Israelis "were chosen to come to the United States because, as Black Jews, they had the ability to heal the rift between the African American and Jewish American communities."[117] In her briefing before the Ethiopian Jewish delegation, the ADL's Marjorie Green said: "We want the [black] youngsters with whom you are about to meet to know that Jews come in all colors. It is also important for us to deliver a positive message about Israel. Let them know that Israel is not a country of violence, discrimination, and oppression as it is often being portrayed in the media."[118]

Israeli professor David Vital has written that "the greater Israel's reliance on the Diaspora, the more it necessarily involves the Diaspora in its affairs. The more it involves it in its affairs, the more it endangers it by leading it into conflicts and contestation of which otherwise the Diaspora might be free."[119] This diagnosis is also valid

for the Jewish diaspora's attempts to lean on Israel for its own domestic purposes. Thus, the more closely the diaspora affiliates itself
with Israeli affairs and policies, the more likely it is to be affected by
Israel's conduct. In the case of Ethiopian Jewry, Jewish-Americans
and Israel encouraged the link between their own community and
Israel's treatment of Ethiopian Jews, hoping that such a connection
would enhance Israel's image in the United States and alleviate
black-Jewish tensions. As long as their campaign strategy was effective and Israel's behavior was seen favorably, the utilization of black
Jewry was a success. Yet, when the world discovered that the life of
Ethiopians in Israel was not so rosy, the shock waves reached the
Jewish-American community.

The harmful effects of the dependent relationship that results
from the diaspora-homeland linkage came into play when disturbing
facts about the lot of the Ethiopian community in Israel came to
light during the 1996 "blood-spilling scandal," which reached international proportions. In January 1996, Ethiopian Jews in Israel rioted
after discovering that their blood donations were routinely discarded
due to their higher risk of carrying the AIDS virus.[120] Israeli blood
bank officials and the Ministry of Health explained that the motivation for the secrecy of the blood spilling was the desire to protect
Ethiopian Jews from the stigma of being ineligible to donate blood,
rather than to discriminate against them. Despite assurances to the
contrary, however, many Ethiopian Jews saw the blood spilling incident as racism, Israeli style, or at best paternalism. The considerable
media coverage of Jewish Ethiopian rioting provoked strong anti-
Israeli feeling among African-Americans. Jewish-Americans were left
to deal with the fallout. Their pride was turned into shame with the
rise of accusations that Israel's façade of egalitarianism hides an ugly
strain of Jewish racism.[121]

In July 1996 Israel appointed the first Ethiopian Jewish graduate
of its School for the Diplomatic Corps as ambassador for public
relations in its Chicago consulate. Upon her departure she said that
she does not intend to hide the grave mistakes that Israel has made
in absorbing Ethiopian Jews. Yet her message to Americans is that
"Israel is not a racist country, it is the only country in the world
which brought in Blacks not for enslavement but as equal brothers."[122]

African- and Jewish-Americans and the New World Order

As we have seen, the homeland factor has been an irritant in black-Jewish domestic relations at least since the mid-1960s. As late as 1993 African-American scholar Cornel West wrote that "without a candid acknowledgment of Blacks' status as permanent underdogs in American society, Jews will not comprehend what the plight of Palestinians in Israel means to Blacks symbolically and literally." He charged that in supporting "the inhumane policies" of Israeli governments toward the Palestinians, Jewish-Americans "tip their hats toward cold-hearted interest group calculations."[123]

In view of the dramatic international developments of recent years, including the decline of Third Worldism, the collapse of the Soviet Union, the dismantling of apartheid in South Africa, and the Middle East peace process, one may wonder whether the easing or even elimination of many conflicts between blacks and Jews over international matters, could also help resolve black-Jewish domestic disputes.[124] Indeed, the post–cold war international regime brought greater synchronization between African- and Jewish-American foreign-policy agendas. When in 1991 the United Nations reversed its 1975 resolution of "Zionism as Racism," a shift in the attitudes of many African-American leaders toward Israel also took place. Paul Berman has written that "the international pressures that made it more or less mandatory for African-Americans, if they wanted to take their place within the Third World revolutionary movement, to endorse – or, at least, abide – the anti-Zionist cause" disappeared almost overnight.[125]

In December 1992, Jesse Jackson addressed a Jewish audience in a synagogue: "When we are in coalition we almost always win, and when we are apart we are both vulnerable."[126] Just before the 1992 Democratic convention, Jackson accepted an invitation to speak to the World Jewish Congress in Brussels where he declared Zionism to be a liberation movement. "By this single act," wrote Paul Robeson Jr., "Jackson established an unbridgeable ideological gulf between himself and Minister Louis Farrakhan, for whom Zionism is anathema, and thereby intensified his personal challenge to Black anti-Semitism."[127] By 1993 Jesse Jackson assumed a double role of domestic and international healer when he took it upon himself to smooth relations between Israel and the ANC, and to help free Syrian Jews. At the same time, he became the leading force in the campaign to rebuild the civil rights alliance.[128] Certainly the historic handshake between Rabin and Arafat on September 3, 1993, took the sting out of the 1979 Jackson-Arafat photograph. Shortly after the signing of the Israeli-PLO peace accord, Jackson and other black leaders expressed their hope that Middle East peace would bring peace between Jews and blacks inside America. Jackson estimated that with the emergence of a new South Africa, critics of Israel would no longer be able to single it out as a supporter of a racist regime.[129] In his April 1994 official visit to Israel and the West Bank, Jackson was embraced by the PLO and Israelis alike. He met with Prime Minister Rabin and Foreign Minister Peres and praised the Israeli government for its peace efforts.[130] Israeli Chief Rabbi Meir Lau pronounced upon Jackson the blessing, "you can be a messenger of God."[131] In reaction to his vindication, Jackson's wife Jackie expressed her relief at a gathering of Palestinian notables in the West Bank: "This situation has been so heavy on our lives for the past fifteen years. We've suffered much because of it, it has taken an incredible toll on us."[132] Despite the difficult road ahead in the Middle East peace process, it is already evident that the subject has lost much of its vehemence as a source of controversy between American blacks and Jews.

Finally, in recent years the foreign-policy agendas of Jewish- and African-Americans have been quite compatible, and their foreign-policy lobbies have been among the leading advocates of interventionism in U.S. foreign policy. Jewish members of Congress joined with African-Americans in pressuring the White House to intervene in Somalia and Haiti.

Conclusions

For those concerned with the growing discord in American society, "the future of the relations between the Jewish and the African-American communities will tell much about the potential of US society to live fruitfully within its pluralistic structure, repudiate hatred, and secure a better future for all."[133] This chapter shows the strong connection between diasporic affinities, homeland-related affairs, and ethnoracial relations inside the United States. The internationalization of black-Jewish relations highlights the growing importance of the homeland factor for U.S. ethnic relations and American civic culture in general, at a time when relations between ethnic Americans and their countries of origin are on the rise because of forces of transnationalism and the legitimization of ethnicity in general in American public life.

As we have seen, the homeland factor is not just an objective, independent variable. It is also a subjective factor that has been interjected or brought into ethnoracial relations by ethnic activists inside the United States, elements in the home country, or other foreign actors, as well as American decision makers. All these actors may try to foster or manipulate homeland-related affairs and diasporic identities and loyalties in the service of their internal or international agendas. Moreover, homeland-related affairs may be inserted into the domestic scene by one ethnoracial elite in order to attack or connect with another ethnic group. Governments in the home countries may come to the defense of their kin diaspora when endangered by other American ethnic groups; alternatively, they may try to build bridges to ethnic Americans in order to bypass a conflict between its own kindred diaspora and another group. Indeed, homeland- and kin-related issues may be used by all actors to motivate or stymie diasporic political activity and may gain or lose significance according to developments inside and outside the United States. Such developments are related to broader issues of U.S. ethnoracial relations, changes in American national identity, and regional conflicts in parts of the world with some association to diaspora kin in the United States, as well as the basic thrust and future orientation of American foreign policy, which in the post–cold war era has become less coherent and more susceptible to pressures by well-organized ethnic lobbies.[134]

The American example, despite its idiosyncrasies, can also teach us about the internationalization of ethnic relations in other countries that have similar structural features. Such conflicts exist, for example, between Sephardic Jews and Arabs of the Maghreb in France, or between Hindus and Pakistanis in England and Canada. In the United States, some of the most intense ethnoracial conflicts were compounded by real or perceived differences related to homeland or kin diasporic issues. For example, as Nancy Abelmann and John Lie have argued, the explosion of black-Korean violence in

1992 in Los Angeles may not be reduced to simple differences of culture, ethnicity, or economics. The conflict has also drawn on homeland-related images. While Korean-Americans have in the past been stigmatized as part of the "inscrutable and unassimilable" mass of Asian immigrants, an image built in part on Korea's status as an impoverished country, in the 1980s they came to embody the image of a "model minority," benefiting from the meteoric rise of the Korean economy. Indeed, some American observers now identify "the common cultural origins of Asian and Asian-American success" with the ancestral legacy of "Confucian values" of work and education. By contrast, blacks have been characterized by some as a culturally deprived underclass, a concept that has often been reinforced by popularized denigration of Africa's repeated postcolonial failures. Blacks and Koreans have been labeled "antipodal minorities," the supposed reliance on welfare of the former differing sharply from the "entrepreneurial heroism" of the latter, an alleged parallel with the condition of the respective homelands themselves.[135] While these images are not the sources of this conflict, they certainly fuel it.

It is clear therefore that the core of most U.S. ethnoracial disputes lies in domestic socioeconomic, political, and cultural issues. This is no different for blacks and Jews. Jewish-black tensions are deeply rooted in American racial history, the character of the economic conditions of the two communities, stereotypes, and pejorative expressions on both sides. Although blacks and Jews have collaborated on numerous issues, there is a widening gap between the two communities in terms of socioeconomic and even political preferences. Although Jews, like blacks, still vote overwhelmingly for Democratic presidential candidates, this obscures the broad changes which have been taking place.

> Jews are . . . far more economically conservative than African Americans and far more conservative on crime. Yet [they are] generally alienated by the Republican Party's [nativist orientation and especially the anti-Semitic tenets of the Christian Right], so although their presidential voting patterns and party registration numbers appear at first to confirm the stereotype of [Jews] as anchors of the liberal wing of the Democratic Party, in fact [as shown by their local and state voting] they are stranded together [with Hispanics] in a fiscally conservative, culturally cosmopolitan no-man's land.[136]

It must be made clear, however, that the internal bases of these feuds cannot be fully separated from diasporic legacies or homeland-related affairs. In other words, even though U.S. ethnoracial rivalries usually originate in local turf disputes and not over foreign issues, this does not preclude American-based ethnoracial groups from becoming entangled in transnational conflicts or from being subjected to homeland actors' demands for their allegiance, active support, and full participation or, conversely, from pressures from other U.S. diasporic groups and American authorities to disengage from international commitments and deny any residual transnational loyalties.

This point must be emphasized, since U.S. ethnicity has always been an expression of blended identities generated by both American and home country experiences. U.S. diasporic identities are forged and sustained through immigrant memories, national historic experiences, and shared values with ancestral cultures. Yet they are constantly undergoing transformation, influenced by factors such as changing American perceptions of ethnoracial diversity, U.S. relations with the home country (whether the home regime is viewed as friend or foe) as well as the home country's attitudes and policies toward its overseas community. Thus, the degree of homeland attachments in the life of American ethnic groups – that is, the ways by which the diaspora's socioeconomic, political, or religious standing inside the United States are connected to, constructed by, or invented as part of the homeland – is likely to impact on U.S. ethnoracial identities and by extension on American interethnic relations.

This chapter's analysis of the black-Jewish conflict in the United States has shown that just as international disputes may exacerbate tensions, international reconciliation related to homelands or other foreign-policy issues has the potential to temper domestic interethnic conflicts. The Jewish-black conflict is long and complicated and is currently driven mainly by the mutual anxieties of both communities. Lettie Progrebin has succinctly captured the essence of this conflict when she observes: "African-Americans need relief in the form of practical economic assistance; Jews need relief in the form of normalized group and individual acceptance."[137] Indeed, each group is perceived by the other as the potential supplier of its needs.

It is beyond the scope of this chapter to assess the black and Jewish conditions in the United States or the prospects for black-Jewish domestic reconciliation. At this point it is evident that both communities are grappling with serious questions regarding their American identity and their relations toward their respective homelands. For quite some time, Jewish-American intellectuals and activists have admonished the diaspora for its failure to find internal sustenance in cultivating American-Jewish identity independent of Israel. Judaism in the United States, they have warned, has become ephemeral due to its overwhelming concentration on the Jewish state.

This Jewish-American internal conflict has been exacerbated recently because of efforts by Israeli Orthodox politicians to delegitimize the Conservative and Reform branches of Judaism, which, although they represent only a tiny minority of Israelis, comprise the majority of America's Jewish population. Prime Minister Netanyahu's efforts to allay diasporic concerns by claiming that Israeli conversion legislation proposed in 1997 merely preserves the status quo have been met with suspicion and with a sense that Israeli politicians do not understand why such laws are so offensive to many in the diaspora. The Israeli refusal to recognize conversions performed in Israel by non-Orthodox religious authorities, and the persistence of the Orthodox monopoly over marriage and burial services, and appointments to religious courts and other public bodies, not only exclude the small but growing number of Israeli adherents to non-Orthodox denominations from important areas of public life, but also imply that most American Jews practice a debased and inauthentic form of Judaism. This perception has been reinforced by leading Israeli Orthodox rabbis who have denigrated non-Orthodox practices and who have even said that non-Orthodox Judaism is a heretical sect or another religion altogether.[138]

Another significant question is how will Jews in America define their relations with Israel, if indeed Israel concludes peace agreements with all of its Arab neighbors. Despite recent diplomatic and political setbacks, this continues to be an issue. Many Jewish diasporic activists and pro-Israel lobbyists have wondered since the Oslo agreements what their new mission will be. What will be the source of their political recruitment? What will compel them to remain Jews?[139] The growing rift between Israel and American Jews over issues of religious and national identity will likely continue to be a source of antagonism and friction.

African-Americans are also facing a difficult predicament in terms of their American identity. Their domestic divisions reflect a growing class split between the black middle class and the poor in the inner cities, the failure of black mainstream institutions to present an attractive and organized leadership, as well as the changing makeup of the American multiethnic society in general. The failure of the mainstream to connect with the underclass contributed to the rise of a more radical leadership under Nation of Islam leader Louis Farrakhan, who organized the watershed million-man march in Washington, D.C., in 1995. While on domestic issues the black leadership is in disarray, on international affairs African-American Congress members and activists are emerging as one of America's strongest foreign-policy lobbies, perhaps on a par only with Jewish-Americans. Mobilization of African-Americans on the issue of South Africa and black leaders' triumph in racializing the issue of Haiti (President Jean-Bertrand Aristide's restoration) have shown how powerful foreign-policy issues are for internal mobilization. Obviously, these accomplishments are difficult to emulate in the battle to save other parts of Africa, where the human catastrophes of state collapse, tribal wars, ethnic genocide, economic fiascoes, and political corruption are widespread. Indeed, the African-American foreign lobby faces some difficult decisions about "whom [they] support and why."[140] Professor Henry Louis Gates has wondered whether, in its current condition, Africa can remain a viable reservoir from which African-Americans can draw moral or spiritual sustenance in the future.[141]

There is certainly a correlation between intra-black and intra-Jewish sociopolitical debates in the United States, and the nature of the two communities' respective foreign policy activities. Overall, the issues of diasporic politics and homeland courtship of diasporas are imbued with questions of identity and interests that constantly undergo transformation in ancestral countries and in the United States. Thus, what certain sectors of the Jewish-American community think of as Israel's needs and identity may not always coincide with the government of Israel's own agenda. Israeli perceptions of the Jewish diaspora are not monolithic and have changed substantially over the past fifty years. Likewise, African leaders and governments do not always see eye to eye with the prescriptions of some diasporic activists on "African interests."

These discrepancies took on a different character at the end of the cold war, when universal values such as liberal pluralism, open boundaries, and the globalization of markets conflicted more intensely with particularistic notions such as national security and a Third World alliance versus the West, as well as conservative social and religious traditions. Each set of values may be represented in either or both the country of origin or the diaspora in a way that militates against unity within each community, as well as between the diaspora and the national community at home. This debate goes directly to the heart of the issue of identity and loyalty of diaspora members as Americans and vis-à-vis their respective homelands.

In general, the more "universal"-oriented a diaspora, the more likely it is to support liberal-universal values at home. This is in fact the general diasporic trend. Yet, American realities of marginalization by choice or design may also foster parochial diasporic attitudes toward home-country policies. Ultra-Orthodox Jews in the United States who endeavor to escape integration into American society are most likely to oppose "liberal universalistic" leanings inside the state of Israel. Indeed, many of them consider modern Zionism and the state of Israel themselves as heretical. African-Americans who feel "separate" from white American society are less likely to support the "de-Africanization" of Africa through its integration into a Western-dominated global economy.

When Israel under Rabin and Peres sought to follow a "New Middle East" approach by signing the Oslo accords, many conservative American Jewish voices were raised against what they saw as initiatives inimical to the interests of "the Jewish people," reflecting bitter and ultimately violent differences between the two sides. Israeli representatives speaking before American Jewish audiences were often accused by conservatives of compromising fundamental interests and even of treason. Similarly, when the right-wing Likud took office in Israel in 1996 and emphasized the nationalist and religious character of the state, large, more liberal, segments of the American Jewish community judged the new government's policies to be an unfortunate retreat into atavism and parochialism.

Among African-Americans (primarily the political elites), diaspora-Africa controversy currently surrounds the issue of how much the old "colonial model," portraying America as a principal source of black and African suffering, should prevail over a newer model wherein America is helping lead Africa in the direction of liberal democracy through its determined advocacy of a free-market philosophy. Between these two positions, there is a middle road wherein America is still seen as responsible for correcting past wrongs against African-Americans through affirmative action and other redressive measures. By extension, even as believers in this path uphold the liberal American creed when it comes to Africa, they still demand greater American responsibility in regard to integrating Africa into the global economy; aid must precede free trade. These various positions found expression around the time of President Clinton's 1998 visit to Africa, when Clinton championed an African Growth and Opportunity Act liberalizing U.S.–sub-Saharan trade in exchange for African democratic and market reforms. This bill, which passed in March 1998, split the Congressional Black Caucus. TransAfrica's Randall Robinson opposed the bill on the grounds that it represented an American abdication of moral responsibility to assist Africa in its recovery from white colonialism. Jesse Jackson Jr., a junior congressman from Illinois, took this argument further, tracing the spirit of the bill back to the West's first "African trade policy," slavery. "Why should we trust the people who discriminate against us and disparage affirmative action at home to be respectful to African workers?"[142] Jackson asked. At least one African ambassador pointed out that such decisions actually rested in the hands of Africans, and not African-Americans, seeming to respond to Jackson: "What do you mean 'We'?"[143]

Finally it seems that the rapprochement between the symbolic homelands of the two communities (improvement of relations between South Africa and Israel, or Israel and Africa in general), as well as improved prospects for peace between Israel and the Palestinians, have already opened doors and to some extent have already proved themselves conducive to greater cooperation between blacks and Jews. Although deep divides remain and the homeland issue may yet again be injected into the domestic dispute, even the temporary removal of transnational elements from the domestic scene has given some observers hope "that it is indeed possible for Blacks and Jews to put the past twenty-five years of contention behind them."[144] Now that the more significant transnational grounds for dispute between the two communities have been largely resolved, there may be a chance that deep-seated domestic rifts will benefit from the healing effects of progress in international affairs.

5

"Go, but Do Not Forget Me": Mexico, the Mexican Diaspora, and U.S.-Mexican Relations

This chapter examines the changing relations between home countries and their diasporic populations in the United States, using the interaction between Mexican-Americans and Mexico as a case study.[1] It focuses on two major interrelated questions. First, how are homeland attitudes toward kin diasporas and homeland intervention in diasporic affairs being transformed over time and why? Second, how do these homeland-diaspora-related changes affect conceptions of national and cultural identities within the home country itself? These questions are particularly interesting in the context of the United States, where newly mobilized ethnic groups have gained importance in U.S. civic culture and politics, and where new types of complex and elaborate interaction between ethnic Americans and their ancestral homelands have developed as a result of the growth of transnationalism.

While other scholars have focused on the repercussions of diasporic influences on American foreign policy and a few have alluded to issues of national identity and loyalty within the United States,[2] there has been little recognition of the fact that the political, social, and cultural effects of diasporas are not confined to the host country. In Chapter 2 I have discussed the critical roles played by several U.S.-based diasporas in helping to attain homeland political goals such as national self-determination and the removal of dictatorial regimes. This chapter explores the equally important impact that diasporas have had on home country culture and society, in particular the construction and reconstruction of homeland national identity. The relatively recent rapprochement between Mexico and its U.S.-based diaspora after years of estrangement makes Mexico an interesting case study in this regard. As will become apparent, Mexico's new posture toward its diaspora and consequently its attempt to reimagine itself as a "global nation"[3] are strongly connected to (1) the evolution of diasporic conditions in the United States, including the Mexican-American community's political and economic empowerment, and its dual self-perception as both an integral part of American society and a distinct ethnic diaspora; (2) the growing economic, political, and social impact of the Mexican-American diaspora on homeland affairs; and (3) changes in U.S.-Mexico relations. The first part of this chapter examines the ramifications of the interplay between the homeland's changing perceptions of its diaspora and of itself, while the second part elaborates on the theory in view of the Mexican experience.

Homeland's Conception of Emigration and Diaspora

States and regimes adopt different postures toward their diasporic communities. Attitudes toward the diaspora and relations with its members vary significantly according to:

1. the national ethos of the country of origin;
2. its official and societal perception of emigration in general;
3. its reliance on the economic investments of diaspora members and emigrant remittances;
4. the makeup of the diaspora (emigrants, refugees, or exiles); its success in establishing itself in the new country; and the general attitude of its members toward the home regime;
5. the political role assigned by the home regime (or its opposition) to the voice of the diaspora in domestic or international affairs of the home country; and
6. citizenship laws (*ius sanguinis* vs. *ius soli*) and especially the possibility of holding dual citizenship.

All these factors may be in flux, changing according to the transformation of the home country's regime, interests and national self-perception, the material and political position of the diaspora abroad, the ways the home regime feels it can exploit and mobilize the diaspora's status and organizations, and the availability of symbolic and material means that enable home states to intervene in the life of their overseas population and enforce their will abroad.

Home governments, as prime manipulators of national symbols, use nationalist rhetoric to shape and control the attitudes and behavior of relevant constituencies vis-à-vis their rule. They tend to pose a psychological as well as an actual cost on those who reject their authority and to reward those who respect their claims as legitimate. Governments also use their power to promote and sustain the attachment of the people to the motherland and often use the national border to differentiate between "us," the insiders, and "them," the outsiders. The manipulation of loyalty boundaries often extends beyond state borders to include diaspora members who may be discredited as "outsiders," or may alternatively be considered as "insiders" in accordance with the home government's changing view of them.[4]

For example, when Mussolini came to power in Italy, he still "considered emigration a fundamental necessity."[5] Yet, in his drive to enforce the Fascist state he sought "to transform emigrants from an index of Italian national weakness into a symbol of strength."[6] Consequently, he adopted a policy of mobilizing the diaspora around the mother country's new Fascist identity and politics. In 1927, Mussolini established the Direzione Generale degli Italiani all'Estero (General Bureau of Italians Abroad) as a special agency to organize and "protect" Italian communities abroad. The term "emigrant" was replaced by "citizen" as part of the Fascist policy "to redeem the emigration from the political ineptitude and social irresponsibility of the liberal state," and to achieve "the spiritual recovery of all Italian communities spread throughout the world by strengthening those material and oral contacts between Italy and her citizens abroad."[7] Not all émigrés were seen in the same light, however. Fascist propagandists revived the medieval terms *fuoruscito* and *fuoruscitismo* as words of contempt for political émigrés.[8]

Whereas some states have defined national membership based on the formality of holding citizenship, other states have defined their nationality to include kindred populations outside their territorial confines – even if they never resided, intended to reside, or held citizenship status in the home country. Such states, by their own ideological definition, may be considered "diasporic entities." The fact that the prime criteria for citizenship in Germany is German ethnicity makes "the attainment of German citizenship difficult for aliens" while at the same time it follows that ethnic Germans may gain citizenship regardless of their place of birth outside Germany or their domicile citizenship status in other countries.[9]

Diasporic states tend to perceive national life outside the homeland as abnormal, transitory, or even theoretically impossible. Israel approximates the prototype of such a case. It calls itself a "Jewish state." By including every Jew, irrespective of his or her place of residence or citizenship, as a part of its national community, the state of Israel was unable to define nationality solely in territorial terms or to create a new nationality detached from Jewish diasporic life. By the Law of Return (1950) (which sets down the legal foundations for Jewish immigration into Israel), every Jew is automatically entitled to Israeli citizenship.

Moreover, since Zionism is based on the idea of *Shlilat ha'golah* (the negation of diaspora) the state of Israel has long perceived emigration from the Jewish state as a national calamity that threatens the national sovereignty of the Jewish people. The Israeli treatment of emigration "has been saturated with profound emotional and ideological weight, which is given symbolic expression by the accepted use of the term *yeridah* (descent), rather than the universal and neutral word 'emigration.' "[10] In 1976, the late Israeli prime minister Rabin used the expression "the fallout of the weaklings" to describe Israeli contempt for emigrants. By the following decade, however, as individualism and materialism dissipated the strong sense of social solidarity that had characterized Israeli society in its earlier years, public and official perceptions of emigration and diasporic life in general began to change. As Israel evolved into a more pluralist society, and with the decline of the hegemonic ideology of the state's early years, more Israelis began considering emigration as an action of "normal" free choice and less and less as an act of treason.[11] Ephraim Ya'ar, an Israeli sociologist, has written that, in view of the phenomenal economic success of Israelis in the United States, Israel "must seek to preserve and strengthen the network of connection between the emigres and Israeli society, both because the emigres of today might be the immigrants of tomorrow and because they might be able to help the State of Israel, just as the American Jewish community traditionally has helped. ... more advantage will be gained by encouraging their link to Israel than by making life difficult for them and calling them names."[12] A recent proposal to extend voting rights to Israeli emigrants would, if implemented, reinforce this trend of widening the transnational scope of electoral campaigns, with the votes of citizens living overseas potentially rivaling diasporic financial contributions as a factor in Israeli elections. Indeed, changing perceptions of emigration may result in different postures toward mobilizing or ignoring a diaspora, a policy that in turn impacts on the home country perception of itself and its internal politics.

Citizenship and Consular Involvement in the United States

A growing number of states regard the acquisition of American citizenship in purely practical terms. They recognize that immigrants are simply trying to improve their economic and professional prospects, and they therefore accept such behavior with few qualms over issues of loyalty. This is a significant departure from a more traditional viewpoint still found in many countries where the acquisition of nationality through naturalization is considered to be an indication of shifting allegiances "imposing on the individual the obligation to refrain not only from acts directed specifically against his country of adoption, but also from such acts as prove his firm attachment and loyalty toward his country of origin."[13]

Some countries that consider their diaspora populations in the United States to be integral parts of their own nations may treat diaspora members as regular citizens, regardless of their residential or citizenship status abroad. From the home country's point of view – even if only rhetorically – such members of their diaspora are only waiting to return home. Ideological, political, and economic factors may be intertwined in the decision of how to approach the diaspora. Such decisions may vary dramatically over time according to conditions inside the homeland and the international standing of the home government, primarily vis-à-vis the United States.

The fact that home regimes tend to manipulate citizenship as a carrot-and-stick mechanism means that naturalization and denaturalization are not always final acts; "all patriots are potential traitors" and vice versa.[14] Changes in regime are particularly critical to the approach of homelands toward their kindred communities abroad. A diasporic community consisting of refugees and exiles may at one point be considered as an enemy of a dictatorial home regime and as a result suffer from "blackmail, surveillance, threats and other intimidations abroad,"[15] as has happened to Iranians, Chileans, Filipinos, and Koreans in the United States. Over time, however, the same diaspora may come to be viewed as the key population for domestic transformation. Indeed, on several occasions, emigrants and political émigrés residing in the United States who were attacked by home country agents later became important players in the campaign to dislodge dictatorial home regimes and establish democracies.

While some countries consider emigration a national calamity, others may promote it to ease domestic economic pressures or as a means of building economic outposts abroad in the hope of enjoying the flow of remittances back home. For example, the South Korean government has sponsored programs for professional emigrants seeking to build businesses abroad, with the expectation of direct financial benefits to Korea.[16] Indeed, once South Korean communities emerged in the United States, the South Korean government treated them as a "supervised colony" and used its consulates in New York and Los Angeles to monitor and control their activities in order to further Korea's economic and political goals. "The immigrants responded positively, partly out of nationalism and partly out of economic interests, with the result that their principal organizations became subordinate to home government agencies."[17] One scholar of Korean-American concerns has written that "it is no exaggeration to say that the Korean Consulate General is the informal government of New York's Korean community and that the consul general is its mayor."[18]

The formal and informal control of the diasporic community by the South Korean state contributed to the diaspora's failure to build overseas institutions and create authentic leadership in the United States. This failure prevented an effective South Korean community response to the 1992 Los Angeles riots and necessitated the financial and political intervention of the South Korean government to deal with the aftermath. Although local Koreans appreciated this assistance, they recognized the limits of this kind of help, as well as its potential negative effects on their efforts to integrate into American society. The riots, therefore, while demonstrating the strength of Korean power over its diaspora, also led to diasporic reevaluation of ties with the home country. No doubt, a "bear hug" may provide emotional and practical protection to a diaspora, yet subordination to a distant government may also generate hostility, antagonism, and charges of foreign loyalties.[19]

The size of a diasporic community and the affluence of its members may transform U.S.-based diasporas into a major force in the economics and politics of their countries of origin. The Greek-American diaspora, for example, has had a great impact on the evolution of the Greek state.[20] More recently, newly democratized countries in eastern Europe have looked to their U.S.-based diasporas as an important source of economic investment and as important players in mediating and improving relations between the United States and the homeland (see Chapter 2).

The economic power of diaspora members has also become a critical factor in running democratic political campaigns inside homelands. Political candidates of many countries finance their domestic activities from diasporic sources – for example, by channeling funds to so-called voluntary associations that endorse political parties or oppose their rivals. The heated conflict of recent years between the Israeli left and right has been fueled not only by ideological tensions and domestic rivalries and cleavages, but also by the vast investment and political contribution of diasporic Jews, with significant impact on political results. Israeli newspapers have reported that Prime Minister Benjamin Netanyahu's critical and controversial September 1996 decision to open a tunnel near the Temple Mount in Jerusalem, which ignited an explosive Palestinian reaction costing many lives and threatening to derail the Middle East peace process, was in large part the result of direct pressure from Orthodox Jewish contributors in the United States. One of Israel's most respected senior journalists wrote shortly afterward that these events provide further evidence that Jewish diasporic financial and political influences have an overwhelming influence on Israeli affairs. She went as far as to say that Netanyahu's political reliance on the money of religious right-wing Jews abroad made diaspora sources more critical than his domestic constituency in terms of his frame of reference and his accountability.[21]

The political strength of diasporic communities in the United States has also been reflected recently in the growing phenomenon of home country candidates running elaborate American political campaigns in the hopes of benefiting from diasporic economic

weight, prestige, and political influence. In some cases where diasporic political clout and money may be critical in determining electoral results at home, candidates may even run on platforms empowering diaspora members politically in ways that may compromise the
very sovereignty of the home state. This was demonstrated during
the 1996 presidential election campaign in the Dominican Republic,
where the two main contenders, José Francisco Peña Gómez and
Leonel Fernández Peyma, targeted the Dominican community in
New York City as a critical voting bloc even though Dominican
emigrants can only vote at home. In their rush to gain the financial,
organizational, and political support of the diaspora, which sends
home over $1 billion a year in remittances (the Dominican Repub-
lic's largest single source of foreign exchange), the two candidates
went to the extent of endorsing special legislation that would enable
Dominican expatriates to vote in consulates abroad. Candidate Peña
also announced that he would sponsor legislation enabling the election of congressional deputies as direct representatives of the New
York–based diaspora. Larry Rother of the *New York Times* wrote that
if the plan to allow Dominicans abroad to vote is implemented, the
proposal would immediately "transform the New York City metropolitan area into the second largest concentration of votes in future
Dominican presidential elections, exceeded only by the Capital."[22]
Within weeks of taking over as president, Fernández delivered a
speech (later televised in New York) explicitly calling upon Dominicans in the United States to adopt U.S. citizenship in response to
tough new federal legislation denying or severely cutting various
social benefits to noncitizens: "If you, young mother, or you, elderly
gentleman, or you, young student, feel the need to adopt the nationality of the United States in order to confront the vicissitudes of that
society . . . do not feel tormented by this. Do it with a peaceful
conscience, for you will continue being Dominicans, and we will
welcome you as such when you set foot on the soil of our republic."
Fernandez himself had grown up in New York City.[23]

At the end of 1997, the Dominican government prepared to move
even further, proposing that its citizens abroad be granted the right
to vote where they live, rather than having to fly home. Nelson
Camacho, a Dominican businessman in New York, even plans to run
his upcoming campaign for a Dominican congressional seat from his
adopted city. Diaspora members spearheading the movement in sup-

port of such electoral reforms have explicitly connected their continued remittance of funds to the island republic to gaining full electoral
participation rights, echoing a historical American complaint against
"taxation without representation." Observers note, however, that the
effects of this legislation will almost certainly diminish over time, as
the process of integration into American society is well underway in
the Dominican community, and that to younger Dominican-
Americans in particular – those born or raised in the United States –
America is their home and the undisputed focus of their lives.[24]

The complex historical relationship between Mexico and its large
diaspora in the United States illustrates many of the theoretical
points outlined here. Mexican attitudes toward conationals living in
the United States have undergone several transformations since the
1840s, when the cession of half of Mexico's territory resulted in a
substantial number of Mexicans suddenly becoming residents of the
United States. Subsequent waves of migration increased Mexican
numbers north of the border, a phenomenon alternatively regarded
in Mexico with dread or optimism, or, on occasion, indifference.
Mexico's political and economic advances and setbacks over the past
150 years have been paralleled by equally dramatic changes within
Mexican-American communities, and have been reflected in Mexico's position toward its diaspora, with each side displaying profound
ambivalence toward the other. Over the past two decades, this relationship has continued to evolve as both sides reassess the meaning
of the other group to their identity and culture, their economic
status, and their political future. In light of the growing interdepen-
dence of the Mexican and American economies, which deeply affects
Mexican society, the Mexican government in particular has made a
concerted effort to build a new relationship with its diaspora, leading
to a significant reimagination of the idea of Mexican national identity.

Mexicans in the United States: Changing Perceptions

For years, scholars have given limited attention to relations between
the Mexican-Americans and Mexico, and have downplayed the role
of official Mexico in shaping the identity and loyalty of Mexico's
U.S.-based diaspora. Many writers on U.S.-Mexico relations have
stressed the disaffection of Mexican-Americans with their troubled

homeland or have underscored Mexico's indifference (even animosity) towards its kindred population across the border. Certainly, both official Mexico and many Mexicans have long considered Mexican-Americans as deserters who have "forsaken their impoverished homeland for capitalistic U.S. comforts."[25]

Since the early 1980s, the growing rapprochement between Mexico and its diaspora has led to a reexamination and slight modification of the historical portrait of mutual rejection. In the process of rediscovering the Mexico-diaspora affinity, observers have often overstated the political significance and intensity of the transborder connection and at times even romanticized the strength of the cultural bond. For example, sociologist Morris Janowitz has developed a plotlike portrait of a Mexico–Mexican-American alliance. He has depicted Mexican-Americans as colonizers who are resisting acculturation inside the United States, undermining America's Anglo-Saxon heritage and plotting irredentism. According to his account, the Mexican-Americans have been sent by the Mexican government into the southwestern United States as part of Mexico's long-term scheme to recover lands that were in the past part of Mexico.[26]

Richard Rodriguez, a more astute observer of Mexican-American relations and an advocate of Mexican-American integration into the mainstream of American society, has also overstated Mexico's attachment to its kindred population. This leading Mexican-American essayist has written that like "a true mother, Mexico would not distinguish among her children. Her protective arm extended not only to the Mexican nationals working in the United States, but to the larger number of Mexican-Americans as well. Mexico was not interested in passports; Mexico was interested in blood. No matter how far away you moved, you were still related to her."[27]

The portrayal of Mexico as an agent of Mexican-American separatism is by all accounts unfounded. In fact, "by the late 1980s, even the most extreme elements among Mexican Americans had abandoned [separatist rhetoric]."[28] Similarly, the description of Mexico as an affectionate parent extending its hand to its lost children is also quite misleading, distorting the reality of a more practical and calculating approach evident on both sides of the border. While official Mexico has always managed its relations with the diaspora to suit its own domestic goals, Mexican diasporic elites have at various times strengthened or weakened their ties to Mexico, depending on the ways they define the needs of their own communities.

Indeed, the relationship between Mexicans on either side of the border can best be characterized as ambivalent. Although the two groups share strong connections based on family ties, history, and culture, Mexico's domestic upheavals and the experiences of Mexicans in the United States have had a distancing effect, both politically and emotionally. Thus, while official Mexico has usually looked down at the diasporic existence of its kindred population, it nevertheless hurried to intervene on the diaspora's behalf whenever it felt that its mistreatment inside the United States represented a direct assault on Mexico's national pride and culture. Likewise, people of Mexican origin in the United States have often felt stigmatized by the impoverishment of their homeland and embarrassed by Mexico's political and socioeconomic failures. Although many have sought to conceal or even erase their ancestral identity, the majority have nonetheless retained homeland affinities. In fact, the discovery that their ethnocultural heritage inhibited their integration into American society helped cultivate Mexican-American ethnic pride and reinforced home country sympathy. Thus, many Mexican-Americans have looked to their mother country for emotional and cultural solace while at the same time harboring great animosity toward the Mexican state that failed them.

From the late 1970s, under President Luis Echeverria, and during the presidency of Miguel de la Madrid (1982–88), Mexico began to display a growing interest in its kin diaspora, hoping to utilize the increasing empowerment of the Mexican-American community economically and politically. This new Mexican posture of rapprochement (acercamiento) intensified under President Carlos Salinas de Gortari (1988–94), who negotiated the North American Free Trade Agreement with the United States and Canada. In the context of Mexico's attempt to extricate itself from its economic problems through growing integration with the United States, and in view of Mexico's economic reliance on huge remittances sent by workers abroad, the Mexican government sought to position itself in a way that it could reap the benefits "from improving its channels of communication with the increasingly powerful Mexican-American community."[29] In order to institutionalize its relations with its U.S.-based diaspora, Mexico's Foreign Affairs Ministry established the Directorate General of Mexican Communities Abroad (DGMCA) and the Program for Mexican Communities Abroad (PCME) in 1990.[30] In a September 1995 program report, the authors commented that in the next decade U.S.-Mexico relations are likely to be deeply affected by the Mexican diasporic community.[31] One of the important roles of the PCME has been to improve the image of Mexican-Americans inside Mexico, above all "burying" the image of the *pocho* – a derogatory term used to question the loyalty of diasporic Mexicans and ridicule their inferior culture.[32] Mexican policy also led to efforts to make Mexicans in the United States (los Mexicanos "de afuera") citizens of Mexico once again.

Mexican-Americans have responded to these overtures with some interest but also with suspicion. First, their deep mistrust of Mexico's political system and its corrupt bureaucracy have inhibited their relations with official Mexico. A 1989–90 survey found that 85.1 percent of Mexican-Americans saw Mexican corruption as the major cause of problems in Mexico, as opposed to U.S. policy toward Mexico, with 9.4 percent perceiving a combination of both as responsible.[33] Second, while community leaders have welcomed the opportunity of having connections on both sides of the border, they feared becoming pawns in the bilateral relations of their old and new countries. Above all, Mexican-Americans are wary of any action that "might raise the specter of disloyalty, and the legitimacy of their new-found status [as pro-Mexican lobbyists] would be questioned."[34] To avert such a danger, Mexican-American leaders who interact with Mexico always stress their American identity. Some of them have demanded that Mexican officials take time to better understand Mexican-American culture and the diaspora's interests as citizens of the United States.[35]

The Formative Years and the Elusive Boundary

Mexico's conflicting relationships with Mexican-Americans have been closely linked to the general state of relations between the United States and Mexico (which to some extent have themselves been shaped by the Mexican diaspora's experience inside the United States). Mexico lost half of its national territory in the Mexican-American War of 1846–48, and Mexicans who remained in the

United States were quickly disenfranchised and dispossessed by An-glo-Americans, who overwhelmed the new diaspora in numbers and who marginalized the Mexicans politically and economically through tax laws and extralegal means.[36]

In 1877, a long period of national upheaval in Mexico was brought to an end by the rise to power of General Porfirio Diaz, a leader with strong connections to business interests in the United States. As a result of Diaz's policies, by 1910, foreigners – mostly Americans – "owned about one-seventh of the land surface of Mexico," much of it located along the U.S.-Mexican border.[37] Those Americans who benefited from Diaz's economic policy became strong supporters of the Mexican leader. They lobbied on his behalf in Washington and used their connections to curb anti-Diaz forces, which at the time were agitating against the aging president from their exile bases in the American Southwest. American capitalists, some of whom were the most influential Los Angeles business leaders, became involved in Diaz's efforts to suppress his exiled revolutionary opponents, most notably the Flores Magon brothers.[38] Yet over the years, U.S. terri-tory remained a staging ground for Mexican opposition activists, some of whom succeeded in capturing power in Mexico City.

Until the early 1920s, the southern U.S. border was more theoret-ical than real in terms of migration control. In the absence of an "authentic concept of a boundary between the two nations,"[39] Mexi-cans entered and left the United States at will, without passports. The events of World War I and the general American anxiety re-garding the alleged threat to America's national identity of ethnic groups with dual allegiances sparked opposition to the influx of Mex-ican migrants. The fear of a potential fifth column among the large German settlement in Texas (suspected of collaboration with Mexi-cans in the Southwest against the United States) was heightened in 1917 when it was revealed that German Foreign Minister Arthur Zimmermann had offered assistance to Mexican Chief Venustiano Carranza in a war to free Mexican territory lost to the United States in 1848.[40] In the wake of the Zimmermann telegram, with northern Mexico becoming a base for raids across the border resulting in the death of American citizens, Mexicans in the United States came under suspicion and were the targets of racist violence. Peter Skerry has written that the memory of violent attacks that took thousands of Mexican lives in the Rio Grande led many Mexican-Americans to conceal their origins by referring to themselves as "Latin Americans" or "Spanish-speaking Americans."[41]

The Great Depression, Repatriation, and Mexican Consolidation

At many junctures in their relationship, both Mexico and the United States have used the Mexican-Americans as pawns (or even hostages) in the service of their domestic and bilateral agendas. The Mexican diaspora was mobilized or abandoned, periodically, to fit the economic and political goals of both countries. Thus while Mexico campaigned against abuses of Mexican workers inside the United States and even helped them to receive "unemployment compensation, severance pay and death benefits,"[42] the Mexican government went on collaborating with the United States in encouraging the repatriation of its kindred communities when it served its needs.

American attitudes toward Mexicans in the United States were also inconsistent, a function of differing political, cultural, and economic considerations. In the late 1910s and 1920s, American anxieties about their ability to assimilate new immigrants intensified. "Americanization" efforts concentrated mainly on southern and eastern Europeans while "the easy racial distinctions Americans made with regard to Chinese and Mexican immigrants often precluded them from considering these groups as capable of being assimilated."[43] However, despite its concern over the large influx of Mexican immigrants escaping the turmoil of the Mexican Revolution, America was apparently unable to give up on this cheap "flexible and temporary supply of labor."[44]

American-Mexican collaboration on the use of the Mexican immigrant community in the service of their respective needs became particularly pronounced after the Mexican Revolution, when Mexico began to recognize potential cultural and economic benefits in the return of Mexican-Americans. Mexican activist intellectuals of this era worked to establish a national identity that elevated the mestizos as the dominant ethnic element. The nonmestizo indigenous lower class was perceived as a threat to unity that needed to be civilized. Mexican returnees who were "modernized" in the United States could help in this task,[45] while becoming the basis of a Mexican middle class, a pool of people that would help modernize and transform the country and the nation.[46] "In this fashion, the largely rural migrants that made their way to Los Angeles became part of a larger mission of the nationalization of the 'Indian' launched by the Mexican government during the 1920s."[47] When Americanization programs seemed to threaten these plans – "steal[ing] away [Mexico's] most potentially productive nationals," Mexico became eager to collaborate with the American government in repatriating its people.[48]

Mexican President Alvaro Obregon ordered the consular offices in American cities to expand relations with the community and instructed them to preserve "the cultural integrity of Mexican emigrants through the establishment of institutions to foster Mexican patriotism."[49] It was in this context that the Mexican government organized "Honorary Commissions" made up of diasporic notables who worked in conjunction with the consulates to foster loyalty to the motherland. The emphasis was on preserving the Spanish language of Mexico abroad by supporting Mexican schools and the publication of Spanish newspapers. The diaspora was perceived to be an important ingredient in instilling a new sense of "unifying nationalism among the diverse and often unwieldy population,"[50] a forerunner of Mexican efforts to relegitimize the diaspora in the 1990s.

The Great Depression contributed to Mexican repatriation efforts, as a U.S. government concerned over high unemployment asserted greater control over the country's southern border. In 1930, when President Hoover declared that Mexicans were a major source of the economic crisis – "they took jobs away from American citizens" – the gate for large-scale deportation was opened. Deportation served the interests of both Anglo-American racist sentiment and Mexico's ambitious modernization plans. In the early 1930s, one-third of Los Angeles's 150,000 Mexican residents were repatriated, among them many American citizens.[51]

The depopulation of the Mexican diaspora during the years of the Great Depression generated a change in Mexican-American leadership. In Los Angeles, American-born Mexican-American leaders established a strong partnership with organized labor. Their fury about Mexico's cynical manipulation of them and their indignation at America's contempt for the Mexican peasant produced a dual strategy: while struggling inside the United States to protect the community's hard-won economic gains, the diaspora leaders called on their compatriots to retain their Mexican national pride. In other words, while Mexican workers organized in the United States to demand civil rights and political empowerment, they still ventured to preserve their "Mexican soul."[52]

In 1929 in south Texas, middle-class Mexican-Americans founded the League of United Latin American Citizens (LULAC), the first ethnic organization to differentiate Mexican-Americans from Mexican immigrants. Lawrence Fuchs has written that "more than any other Mexican organization, [LULAC] was typical of the immigrant-settler voluntary organizations of the 1920s, which emphasized hyphenated Americanism, combining a love and admiration for ancestral culture with commitment to American citizenship."[53] Although LULAC's members sought to disassociate themselves from native country culture and citizenry, they still engaged Mexican consuls in redressing Mexican grievances with American local authorities. LULAC's connection with Mexico led to Anglo-American charges of dual loyalty and prompted U.S. government surveillance of the Mexican-American community.[54]

Like many other ethnic Americans, U.S. Mexicans have often found themselves entangled by the question of their allegiance. Loyalty to either side – old or new country – threaten to compromise their credibility in the eyes of the other. Thus, on the one hand, Mexicans in the United States have often found it hard to rid themselves of the stigma of their national origin. Even when they displayed their ultimate loyalty to their new country, as they did through their participation in the American army during World War II, some Americans still regarded Mexican-Americans as enemy aliens. On the other hand, elements in Mexico could too easily label them as traitors. LULAC's credo of combining both cultures – "Mexican in culture and social activity, but American in philosophy and politics" – defined this problematic duality in Mexican-American ethnic life that would eventually came to dominate diaspora politics.[55]

Both the creation of LULAC, representing the integrationist middle class, and the emergence of an American-born Mexican-American leadership among the working-class population – distrustful of both American and Mexican officials – signaled the decline of the Mexican government's presence in the life of the diaspora. Although Mexico continued to protest abuses of its compatriots in the decades ahead, as happened, for example, during the famous Zoot

Suit Riots of 1943, by the mid-1930s Mexican consulates no longer played "a crucial role in organizing local leadership around goals formulated in Mexico City."[56] Moreover, while until the late 1920s Mexico "did not distinguish between Mexicanos and Mexican-Americans on the strict basis of citizenship,"[57] by the late 1930s Mexico had already established a clear distinction between Mexican immigrant workers and American citizens. In addition, Mexico's internal political and social consolidation and the pursuit of an independent foreign policy allowed it to focus on national development without reference to Mexicans living beyond its borders. Mexico's pride in its perceived postrevolutionary conversion into a "modern nation" without having to "betray" itself, in the words of renowned Mexican author Octavio Paz, was matched by an equally strong contempt for the desolate existence of Mexicans in the United States. Paz, who lived in Los Angeles for two years during the mid-1940s, expressed his country's new national ethos in his description of Mexican-Americans as empty and culturally bereft *pachucos*: "[The *pachuco*'s] whole being is sheer negative impulse. . . . [he] has lost his whole inheritance: language, religion, customs, beliefs. He is left with only a body and a soul with which to confront the elements, defenseless against the stares of everyone."[58]

Mexican contempt for Mexican-Americans was made clear in the 1940s by the popularization of the derogatory term *el pocho*, used to describe those Mexicans born or raised *de aca de este lado* (north of the Mexican border), "whose Mexicanness was suspect."[59] Jorge Bustamante, Mexico's leading expert on Mexican-Americans, has written that after World War II "there was a continual decrease in contact between organizations on both sides of the border to the point where they virtually disappeared in the 50s and 60s."[60]

El Pocho

Earl Shorris in his book *Latinos* describes the *pocho* as an individual of Mexican descent, residing in the United States (usually as a full-fledged citizen), "who has traded his language and culture for the illusory blandishments of life in the U.S."[61] Shorris expands the definition stating that, "the *pocho* lives on the cultural and racial line, . . . utterly unprotected, [and] despised on every side: too Mexican for the Anglos and too *agringado* for the Mexicans."[62] The *pocho* therefore has a "doubly marginalized" status.[63] His new country has not afforded him the equal economic and political opportunity he believed he was guaranteed, and the country he has left has disowned him, considers him a traitor, and looks down at him disparagingly as culturally inferior. As Shorris explains, "No amount of success will change the situation for the *pocho* on either side of the border."[64] Rodolfo O. de la Garza, a leading scholar of the Mexican-American experience, has written how he was rebuffed by a high Mexican official when he requested an interview in 1971. "[He told me that] I was a traitor to Mexico and other harsh criticism about the fact that I was not really a Mexican."[65] Indeed, defamation and excommunication, along with a strong burden of guilt, were often the costs of leaving one's country.[66]

For many years, Mexicans taking American citizenship were seen quite simply as collaborators with the enemy. This accusation constituted a psychological hindrance impeding integration into American society. When Richard Rodriguez's father decided to apply for American citizenship "he told no one, none of his friends, those men with whom he had come to this country looking for work. American citizenship would have seemed a betrayal of Mexico, a sin against memory. One afternoon, like a man with something to hide, my father slipped away. He went downtown to the Federal Building in Sacramento and disappeared into America. Now memory takes her revenge on the son."[67] Furthermore, in imposing penalties Mexico sought to warn its citizens against the perils of departing their native country and forsaking their culture in search of a better life in the United States. It also wished to reassure Mexicans that they were making the proper choice by remaining at home and that they would benefit from their loyalty. A Mexican may not have the material possessions of *el pocho*, but he is guaranteed the pride of belonging to a national community and the national-cultural coherence and peace of mind that are the rewards of faithful citizens.

Ironically, *el pocho* internalized the negative characterization assigned to him and reinforced it through his behavior, especially with reference to his alienation from Mexico.[68] Thus, *los pochos* living along the border tend to mistreat newcomers, especially those who come without papers. This can best be explained by the fear of many Mexican-Americans that their status in the United States is threatened by the presence of undocumented Mexican immigrants. They also fear that new Mexican immigrants will reinforce popular anti-Mexican stereotypes and result in lower socioeconomic and social mobility for themselves.[69]

Revolving Relations

Mexico's fear that American politics and economics would dominate or even totally absorb their culture and society has contributed to Mexico's reluctance to interact with its diasporic brethren. This inhibition was also augmented by Mexico's high economic growth from the 1930s to the 1970s (averaging 6 percent per year), which strengthened national self-confidence, as manifested in Mexico's identification with Third World causes, and in foreign-policy differences with the United States.[70] During this period, the diaspora itself was not politically empowered and was therefore not in a position to challenge negative Mexican assumptions about its potential usefulness. All of these elements contributed to Mexico's detached attitude toward the U.S.-based diaspora. In addition, Mexican elites wanted to avoid provoking retaliatory U.S. intervention by becoming too involved in the affairs of *pochos*, for whom they had little regard in any event.[71]

In the past three decades, however, a turnaround has occurred in Mexico's attitudes toward its U.S.-based diaspora. In the early 1970s, the Mexican left's support for the struggle of the Mexican-American *movimiento* sparked mainstream interest in the fate of Mexican-Americans. This manifested itself in the form of scholarly meetings, articles, television programs, and attention to Mexican-American-related movies.[72] External forces, including the global trend toward economic liberalization and the growing political power and organizational sophistication of the diaspora in the United States, combined with internal Mexican factors such as economic decline, political turmoil, and increased dependence on the U.S. economy (and on remittances from Mexicans across the border in particular) all contributed to the gradual rehabilitation of the diaspora within Mexico. One potentially destabilizing aspect of this dependence on the U.S. economy is the divide that has opened up within Mexican society between those who benefit from the U.S. connection and those who do not.[73]

The impact of an amended U.S. Voting Rights Act (VRA)[74] on

Mexican-American political opportunities and social mobility became clear in the 1980s, as the number of Mexican-American voters grew significantly, resulting in a sharp increase in the number of Mexican-Americans elected to local and federal positions. This phenomenon accelerated after the 1986 enactment of the Immigration Reform and Control Act (IRCA), which facilitated the rapid naturalization of 2.5 million Mexicans. The IRCA represented another important turning point in diasporic political involvement, helping to diminish the distance previously felt between native and foreign-born Mexican-Americans, and leading to an increase in Mexico's attention to the Mexican-American agenda. Mexican-American leaders began to take advantage of their newfound power and have used their positions to defend community interests, resulting in reduced discrimination and the expansion of educational, employment, and political opportunities for Mexican-Americans. Today, 150 years after half of Mexico's territory was annexed by the United States, Mexican-Americans are being incorporated into mainstream American institutions like European immigrants before them.[75]

Mexican-American political efforts were not, however, confined within the borders of the United States. Abandoning the ambivalence and political timidity of earlier years, some Mexican-American leaders began to advocate closer political cooperation between Mexico and its U.S.-based diaspora. As early as 1978, after a meeting with Mexican President Jose Lopez Portillo, LULAC chairman Eduardo Morga told reporters that Mexican-Americans "are all ready to help Mexico in the United States. . . . We feel that in the future Mexico can use us as Israel uses American Jews."[76] Mexican-Americans have also used their increased political power to work toward achieving a greater say inside Mexico. In particular, Mexican-Americans who have resided in the United States for more than one generation have discovered the political and economic power of the Latino community inside the United States and its potential in doing business with Mexico.

The hope in Mexico that it could channel the voting clout and economic power of Mexican-Americans to serve Mexican domestic and foreign interests was translated into action when the Salinas government made a concerted and systematic effort to transform Mexico's political presence in the United States. The Mexican desire to build a continental free-trade zone required greater political and economic freedom at home, as well as greater responsiveness to demands made by American environmental, labor, and human rights groups.[77]

In its effort to mobilize the diaspora and change its image at home, the government of Mexico took steps to change the abusive behavior of Mexican border officials toward returning Mexicans. The Mexican government issued a special brochure entitled *Cartilla de paisano* (brotherly document) informing diaspora members of their rights and responsibilities when interacting with hostile officials at the border.[78] In addition, Mexico began to try to influence its American neighbors to be more welcoming of Mexican immigrants and their culture.[79] Finally, those who administered the program "have undertaken the dual tasks of 'educating' . . . the members of the Mexican state and elite about how to think about the Mexicans residing in the US, and of advocating on their behalf in Mexico. Through these two tasks, the Program is attempting to teach the other part of the state and the elite surrounding it to re-imagine the Mexicans in the US as part of the Mexican nation."[80]

The Mexican government has revived the role of its consulates as an important link between Mexican immigrants and the homeland, and Mexican consulates strive to reach all Mexican-Americans and remind them of Mother Mexico's message, "Vete pero no me olvides," through the promotion of educational and cultural programs as well as consular involvement in Mexican-American community affairs. For instance, Mexican consulates are responsible for the organization of Mexican immigrants into regional clubs (Comites de apoyo a compatriotas), which serve as institutional mechanisms to build the social networks necessary for massive migration. The clubs of origin also help build bonds of mutual assistance among *paisanos* (brothers) in a "hostile" land and strengthen their self-imposed duty to help the communities they left behind.[81] The Mexican government may indeed have an interest in its stated goal of improving Mexican-American quality of life, but primarily because doing so will improve Mexico's own political and economic power.

The 1988 Mexican Elections and Mexican-American Relations

An apparent paradox of the Mexican-American situation is that as the American government tried to integrate Mexican immigrants by assuring them of their right to participate in political processes, the empowered Mexican elites became more interested in their ancestral country, mainly as a reinforcement of their identity as ethnic Americans. Thus, what may at first glance appear to be a Mexican-American rejection of the United States is in fact an indication of the Mexican-American community's integration into American politics and culture.[82] One 1989–90 poll indicated that 89.5 percent of Mexican-Americans surveyed were concerned more with U.S. than with Mexican politics.[83] As Mexican-American (*qua* Mexican-American) cultural and political self-confidence grows, interest and direct activity in Mexican affairs is less inhibited by self-doubt or external accusations of disloyalty. Mexican-American elites realize that they can wear two hats without compromising their ancestral ties or their American identity, a reality that Mexico itself, in a departure from its historic inclination, has begun to recognize and now interpret as a positive development.

The new political status enjoyed by Mexican-Americans was particularly evident during the 1988 Mexican presidential campaign between Carlos Salinas of the PRI (Institutional Revolutionary Party) and Cuauhtémoc Cárdenas, leader of the PRD (Party of the Democratic Revolution). For different reasons and opposite goals, they looked to Mexican-Americans in California and Texas for support, hoping that their clout would influence Mexican voter behavior. The need to get Mexican-American approval or support meant recasting Mexican domestic concerns for an American audience, which in turn had important effects on the Mexican domestic agenda.

Prior to the 1988 elections, Mexico's political system was known for the virtual monopoly of the PRI over political power, regularly rigged elections, and fragmented, politically timid opposition parties with little electoral support; a ubiquitous state ruled over a mixed and underdeveloped economy. However, by 1988, a new opposition had developed into a full-fledged political party, under the leadership of Cuauhtémoc Cárdenas.[84] Cárdenas advocated state intervention in the economy, vowed to defend small and medium-sized firms, demanded the immediate suspension of debt payment, and promised to rescue privatized firms that had been sold by a "treacherous regime and its party that defends foreign interests."[85] Accordingly, the PRD found support among groups that had traditionally organized themselves outside of the PRI's corporatist agenda and among the sectors that had borne the brunt of the 1982 economic crisis. Cárdenas also spoke to the frustrations of Mexican-Americans who felt disenfranchised in the United States and disregarded by Mexico. As one of his deputies explained in California, *Cardenismo* would allow people to recover their Mexican roots and at the same time live their reality in the United States.[86] The diasporic community, which until then had experienced Mexico's government as a unified entity with clear policies, was now confronted with a choice between the PRI and the PRD. The majority of those who paid attention to Mexican domestic affairs, fed up with Mexico's economic failures, endemic corruption, human rights abuses, lack of political reform, and condescension toward the diaspora, opted to support Cárdenas.

Salinas's controversial victory over Cárdenas, marred by widespread irregularities and accusations that the election had been "stolen" outright, could easily have led to a diminishment in the Mexican government's political influence in the United States. The new president, aware of this danger, adopted a new attitude toward the diaspora, attempting to redirect its energies toward the advancement of the Mexican economy, and away from political issues that threatened the PRI's hegemony. The implicit bargain offered by Salinas (and accepted by many Mexican-Americans) was that political reform would come, but only after sufficient progress had been made in reforming and modernizing the Mexican economy. Asking for support, Salinas stated that political and economic reforms "are linked, but we ought to consider the priority that economic reform has, without excluding political reform. We need to consolidate our economic reform. That demands the consensus that makes possible the decisions we have been adopting."[87]

Many of Salinas's efforts were directed at establishing a free-trade agreement with the United States, and in 1992 Salinas undertook a major effort to court diasporic and American governmental support, visiting major U.S. cities on a speaking tour. In addition, Mexican government officials and an array of top Washington lobbyists converged on the U.S. capital, repeatedly contacting a wide variety of

U.S. politicians and congressional staff in "the most elaborate, expensive lobbying campaign ever conducted in Washington by a foreign interest."[88] The Mexican diaspora was also a focus of Mexican lobbying. Hispanic members of Congress were targeted and "pro-NAFTA businesses and organizations like the Hispanic Chamber of Commerce . . . played a key role in various states to rally support for the agreement."[89] However, the importance and the strength of the Mexican government's political influence on Mexican-American leaders and the general community should not be overstated. The fact that all but one Hispanic member of Congress voted for NAFTA is not directly indicative of Mexican success in enlisting Mexican-American support on behalf of Mexican political goals. Hispanic congressional votes for NAFTA were conditional on the satisfaction of certain domestic requirements, including program funding for residents of (largely Mexican-American-populated) border regions. The NAFTA campaign made it clear that Mexico still had a long way to go in its efforts to reincorporate Mexican-Americans into its political and economic spheres and that, in many ways, Mexico needed its diaspora more than the diaspora needed its homeland.[90]

Cultural Transformation

Since the War of 1846–48, Mexico has feared losing its sense of sovereignty as a result of "the imperialist tendencies of el Coloso del Norte, or the colossus to the north, Mexico's term for the United States."[91] Mexico is wary of the United States but, in many ways, cannot do without it. The growing cross-border interaction of capital and labor in the NAFTA era has revived Mexican fears over identity loss and the risk of bicultural fusion. Not surprisingly in this context, Mexico has begun to redefine its diaspora, a cultural and economic bridge between the two countries, not as a liability or as a sign of weak national character, but rather as evidence of Mexico's uniqueness, deep cultural roots, and strong hold over its compatriots. Mexico has tried to convince itself and the outside world that not only is Mexican-American culture not degrading to the motherland, it is to be celebrated as evidence of the strength and breadth of Mexican culture.

The new Mexican ideology holds that by creating and maintaining a distinct ethnic identity within the United States, albeit different from Mexico's indigenous culture, Mexican-Americans are preserving their national heritage and proving that Latino roots are much deeper than Anglo-American influences. When asked about the risk of cultural spillovers, Andres Rozental, a Foreign Ministry official and architect of Mexico's new policy toward the U.S.-based diaspora, expressed his belief that there was little need to worry: "There's an inherent difference between our two cultures, and that is that the Mexican culture is more profoundly rooted than the American culture. . . . you don't have these 30 centuries of history and of cultural assimilation in America."[92] Similar views have been expressed (albeit with different nuances) by Jorge Alberto Lozoya, who worked on Mexican-Chicano relations under presidents Echeverria and Salinas and later served as Mexico's ambassador to Israel.[93]

Mexico has therefore begun to acknowledge publicly the value of diasporic culture and reward Mexican-American intellectuals and activists as its guardians. In 1991, Antonia Hernandez of the human rights protection group MALDEF (Mexican-American Legal Defense and Educational Fund) was awarded the Order of the Aztec Eagle, Mexico's highest honor given to a foreign citizen for his or her contribution to the advancement of Mexico or to the better understanding of Mexico abroad.[94] In 1993, an Aztec Eagle medal went to Raul Yzaguirre, president of the National Council of La Raza. Yzaguirre's comments at the time clearly demonstrate the cultural duality embraced by Mexican-Americans. He supported NAFTA, "but pretty much down the lines of what President Clinton wants – with protections for [American] workers and environmental concerns."[95] In 1995, Mexican-American poet and author Jose Antonia Burciaga was given the Premio Nacional de patrimonio Hispanico, in recognition of his literary efforts. He also emphasized his dual identity as a Mexican-American: "I would like to stress that I always felt Mexican and always American. I was never ashamed of my Mexican identity. . . . But I am also an American."[96]

As mentioned earlier, the Mexican attempt to conceptually relegitimize the U.S.-based diaspora as an integral part of the Mexican nation includes an important political dimension. Mexico legally accepted dual citizenship in early 1997, so that those who become naturalized in the United States continue to retain Mexican citizenship. Those who advocated this departure from Mexico's traditional exclusionary policy promoted it as another way to recover and sustain diasporic loyalty and attachment. Through its Program for Mexican Communities Abroad (PCME) and its other U.S.-based representatives, the Mexican Foreign Ministry seeks to convey the message to Mexicans living north of the border that acquisition of American citizenship is no longer viewed in Mexico as treasonous or as being incompatible with the retention of Mexican cultural identity. On the contrary, greater Mexican participation in American society is seen to be of great value to the motherland. Consequently, Mexico's government has declared its support for American multiculturalism as an indication of the Mexican-American community's determination to preserve its culture. American citizenship is intended to empower Mexican-Americans not only as individuals, but also as members of an interest group able to lobby American politicians on behalf of Mexico.[97]

In this context, Mexican government condemnation of the 1994 passage of California's Proposition 187, a measure intended to deny "non-emergency health care, schooling and social services to illegal immigrants," was to be expected.[98] California's Hispanic voters were, however, less inclined to echo the Mexican government's criticisms, with 31 percent actually voting in favor of Proposition 187. Even the figure of 69 percent opposing the measure is deceptive as an indication of majority Hispanic support for the rights of illegal immigrants, as most eligible Hispanic voters in California failed to cast ballots.[99] It should be noted that while, according to recent surveys, a majority of U.S. Latinos oppose denying benefits to undocumented immigrants, their support for the continued provision of assistance is based on the expectation that it will be geared toward integrating the newcomers into American society, and not as a means of sustaining a resident "foreign" culture.[100] In a press interview, MALDEF's Antonia Hernandez explained this situation to Mexicans by asserting that racism was not a sufficient explanation for the harsh American reaction to illegal immigration. Consideration had to be given to the American belief in the importance of law and the close linkage between American identity and the Constitution.[101] Ironically, Hernandez's comment illustrates not only the historic continuity in negative Mexican-American attitudes toward newcomers from south of the border, but also the realization of official Mexico's wish that Mexican-Americans assimilate the "wisdom" and knowledge of America and find a comfortable place within its society and also transmit that knowledge and wisdom back to the homeland.

The PRI Dynasty under Threat: 1994 Elections and Beyond

The ability of Mexico to recover its diaspora while presenting itself as a modern and open society has suffered a severe setback, despite Mexico's efforts. It is the discrepancy between the reality illustrated by the common Mexican phrase "todo cambia pero nada cambia" (everything changes but nothing [really] changes) and the way Mexico imagines itself that makes rapprochement an uphill battle.[102]

By the mid-1990s, the PRI's credibility had been seriously undermined by several spectacular events. First, in early 1994, Zapatistas in the southern state of Chiapas launched a military and political campaign for native rights and economic redistribution, and against government corruption and human rights abuses. They gained considerable support among the economically marginalized in other regions of the country and won international sympathy.[103] Second, the 1994 assassination of PRI presidential candidate Luis Donaldo Colosio, allegedly at the behest of rivals within the PRI, and the political disgrace of former president Salinas, now living in Ireland, underlined the extent of corruption within the PRI.[104] Third, the collapse of the peso and the subsequent controversial American bailout also dampened Mexican-American enthusiasm and reinforced the image of Mexico as a failure.[105] Despite their disappointment, however, Mexican-Americans actively encouraged American support for the peso, an effort recognized and appreciated by the Mexican government. Luis Ortiz Monasterio, Mexican consul general in Miami, was lavish in his praise for Mexican-Americans' loyalty to the motherland and their contributions to Mexico's well-being: "At this time of difficulties, I render tribute to the Mexico of the diaspora, to the migrants in the United States, to the unredeemed believer, the faithful who under the counter provide our lean finances with 3 billion dollars every year, almost the size of our current reserves in the central bank."[106]

In his book *La frontera de cristal* (The crystal border), the famous

Mexican author Carlos Fuentes describes a dialogue between Mexico and its diaspora across the border:

> Mexico asks: "Why did I raise you, nurture you, celebrate you [and] bless you with my sacrifice – so that one day you could come and ask me, why aren't you like your brother, our uncle [the United States]? Why did you have to be so poor and disgraced?" Then Mexico follows: "Do not become part of the enemy." But the *pocho* smiles and answers: "But the other side is worse. Mexico is the place of the enemy. . . . [there] there is more injustice, more corruption, more deceit, more poverty. You should thank us for being gringos."[107]

For Mexican-Americans, whose rapprochement with the motherland had been based on promises of Mexican domestic reform, the dramatic events described here called these ties with the motherland into question. Recent survey data presented by Rodolfo O. de la Garza and Louis DeSipio show that Mexican-Americans perceive Mexico as a state beset by major problems, lagging far behind on issues such as democracy, human rights, corruption, drugs, and environmental protection. These data also suggest that Mexico's condition further strengthens the "Americanness" of the Mexican-Americans, and whatever attachment they may have to their "Mexicanness" is linked to their desire to integrate fully into American society rather than remain a "transitional" ethnic community caught between two worlds, belonging fully to neither. This has been the case with Mexican-Americans' attitudes toward immigration, NAFTA, and bilingualism. In the last case, Mexican-Americans favor the provision of bilingual services only to the extent that they speed and assist newcomers' integration into American society, and not as a means of creating a permanent cultural divide.[108]

Many Mexican-Americans were particularly upset by the Mexican government's response to the Zapatista movement, and demonstrations took place at various Mexican consulates in the United States.[109] Mexico's efforts to protect Mexican-Americans from American mistreatment had the unintended consequence of placing the spotlight on Mexico's own misdeeds toward its own citizens. In response to another outrage, the Mexican police's firing on peasants attending a commemoration of the death of Emiliano Zapata, one protest leader commented: "If the government is going to demand justice for Mexicans in another country, it has to begin by protecting the rights of its own people at home."[110] Moreover, although the PRI promised substantive political reform during the 1994 election campaign, progress has been uneven under President Ernesto Zedillo's leadership. The documented involvement of top Mexican officials with major drug traffickers (which has led to the labeling of Mexico as a "narco-democracy"),[111] the perpetuation of human rights abuses by the government, and severe economic mismanagement, have all cast a shadow on Mexican political and economic reform efforts.

Mexican-Americans have reacted with disappointment and suspicion about the motherland's future prospects. However, Mexico's failures of the past several years have opened up opportunities for internal political change, which at least one author believes may result in "The Next Mexican Revolution" and an end to the PRI's presidential dynasty.[112] The recent emergence as serious competitors for state and national power of various PAN and PRD party politicians committed to wide-ranging democratic and economic reform holds out the possibility of fundamental political change,[113] a trend confirmed by the momentous results of the July 1997 midterm elections in Mexico. For the first time in over seventy years, the PRI lost its majority in the lower house of Congress, with both PAN and the PRD making large gains, and the PRD's Cuauhtémoc Cárdenas won the Mexico City mayoralty by a landslide. These defeats were the "biggest blow yet to a party [PRI] whose autocratic ways and elaborate network of corruption are an outright embarrassment to Mexicans who like to think of themselves as part of the advanced world."[114] Loss of control in the lower house likely means that the PRI will have to compromise on a variety of economic and political issues with one or both of the major opposition parties, a new experience for the PRI leadership.[115] Both Cárdenas and the PAN governor of Guanajuato, Vicente Fox, have indicated that they will stand as candidates for president in 2000.[116] The victory of a presidential candidate dedicated to new policies may help lead to a synthesis of the two types of reform encouraged (or even demanded) by Mexicans living north of the American border – economic and political – and help build Mexican-American faith in Mexico's future.

Conclusions

In recent years, the American fear of balkanization and disunity has been particularly pronounced in the case of Mexican-Americans, the fastest growing diaspora, whose homeland is in America's backyard. Yet very few have recognized that the homeland connection has in fact generated a tendency opposite to the one expected that works very much in favor of American unity. Many newly empowered diasporas are exhibiting in their ethnic assertiveness their growing Americanization rather than separatist aspirations, which has often been more evident to observers in the homeland than in the United States. Consequently, if elements in countries dependent on diasporic voices inside the United States wish to mobilize their diasporas, they must heed their diasporas' "Americanness," including their allegiance to "American values" such as democracy and human rights, and incorporate diasporic perspectives in a redefinition of the homeland. To a large extent, U.S. diasporas have emerged as the true marketers of the American creed abroad.[117] For some countries like Haiti and the Dominican Republic, their respective U.S.-based diasporas have such a large economic and political role that they have become major factors in the redefinition of the national ethos. In Mexico, even though the diasporic impact has thus far been less pronounced, its decision in late 1996 to legalize dual nationality will likely further the trend toward increasing diasporic influence on its national identity.

Fifty years ago, Octavio Paz's *The Labyrinth of Solitude* depicted a Mexico on the road to recovery, a newly modern postrevolutionary state with strong national pride and a bright vision of the future. The *pachucos*, in contrast, had sacrificed their identity for illusory economic gains north of the border, becoming like the *yordim* of Israel's earlier years, the despised "weaklings" who had given up on the national dream. Fifty years later, Paz's hopeful picture has not materialized. On the other side of the Rio Grande, however, people of Mexican origin have emerged as an important community with distinctive cultural characteristics and growing economic and political power. This discrepancy and the trend toward globalization have contributed to a crisis in Mexican national identity that Mexico is trying to resolve through a redefinition of what it means to be "Mexican."[118]

In the current situation, where large numbers of Mexicans north of the border are recent arrivals who have yet to experience the economic comforts of American life, the newcomers' attachment to Mexico can be reinforced relatively easily through the range of contacts and services provided by the Mexican government. However, large segments of the U.S.-based diaspora have successfully integrated into American society, charting their own future and creating their own identity. Mexico may continue its attempts to reintegrate this community into Mexican national life in some form by building on its concept of a "global nation," but these efforts will be limited by the fact that the Mexican-Americans have a strong sense of themselves as *Americans*, and their ethnicity is part of the American ethos. Indeed, at present the "Americanized" diaspora exercises greater cultural and economic influence on Mexico than Mexico does on Mexican-Americans, meaning that the homeland's national identity is affected more by its diaspora than the other way around.

Mexican nationalists have great difficulty accepting the notion of cultural fusion with their hated enemy to the north. Yet most intellectuals recognize the inevitability of the Mexican-American–Mexicano *acercamiento*. They remind themselves that Mexico and its diaspora are bound together by family, cultural, historical, and economic links, and their continued strong impact on one another is a given, but their different environments dictate the continued development of unique and separate identities. Some intellectuals have advocated that the cultural exchange be conducted between the motherland and its diaspora in the spirit of openness to identity transformation in both Mexico and the United States. In this context, relations between the two communities across the border are often presented as an indication of the growing integration of North and South America.[119]

The new approach toward the diaspora is often presented in Mexico as criticism of Paz's *pachuco* characterization. Yet, one must remember that even the late Paz was aware that national character is not immutable and that changes are effected by external circumstances as much as by internal development, if not more so.[120]

Conclusion: Diasporas and the American National Interest

The strong presence of ethnic groups in the United States and their significant impact on America's national identity, civic culture, and bureaucratic structures have been issues at the top of the American agenda for the past three decades. Indeed, public and scholarly debates over the limits of diversity, the threat of disunity, and America's absorptive capacities have always been a feature of American society. Yet, what characterizes such debates in the era of multiculturalism is growing erosion in the belief in the melting pot, and concerns that the changing makeup of American society, in light of the massive influx of non-European immigrants since the early 1980s, undermines America's "Anglo-European values." Even among the most ardent believers in America's inclusionary vision, who had held the view that the 1960s marked an irrevocable transition to full inclusiveness, and had shared a belief in the power of universal citizenship to change the status of victims that had been built over the course of many years, faith in the forces of inclusion has dissipated. Nathan Glazer, the most cited opponent of affirmative action in the 1970s, admits in his recent book *We Are All Multiculturalists Now* that his own belief in the possibility of achieving a color-blind society was misguided. He writes that "Multiculturalism is the price America is paying for its inability or unwillingness to incorporate into its society African-Americans, in the same way and to the same degree it has incorporated so many groups."[1] The large influx of immigrants since the early 1970s and the adoption of American citizenship by more than a million newcomers each year in the 1990s, most of them non-European, have raised concerns that citizenship is being acquired by many for the wrong reasons – less patriotic and more instrumental

196

and bureaucratic.[2] Certainly, America has always exhibited ambivalence with regard to immigration. As much as it is famous for being a country of immigrants, it has always been characterized by nativist concerns. In June 1998, President Clinton referred to such nativist sentiments as "un-American." He urged Americans to welcome immigrants, "the most restless, the most adventurous, the most innovative and the most industrious of people." The fears of native-born Americans that "the America they know and love is becoming a foreign land" are groundless, he claimed.[3]

With the growing recognition that a nexus exists between multicultural developments on the domestic front and U.S. foreign affairs, scholars have turned their attention to the fact that U.S.-based diasporas are increasingly playing a greater role in U.S. foreign policy with significant consequences for international conflicts and U.S. domestic affairs. Because of the realization that for many ethnic Americans, old and new, "former homes . . . no longer mean . . . what [they] did"[4] before the era of transnationalism, diasporic influences, albeit more legitimate in certain ways, become even more suspect, with issues of identity and loyalty complicating the already confused task of redefining the American national interest. The dramatic changes in world affairs, which left America the world's only superpower at the end of the cold war, have raised the issue of America's new national interest in the absence of a clear international adversary. The "coherence problem" or the confusion of foreign-policy decision makers has been blamed at least in part on the greater clout of ethnicity in foreign affairs. Overall, the presence of homeland interests and forces in U.S. policy toward diasporic homelands – and the impact of ethnicity on the diversification of the foreign-policy process – has come to be widely accepted as fact, although with different interpretations regarding its effects. The debate now centers on the ways in which ethnic participation affects American national integrity and the definition of the national interest. Opinions range from those which maintain that ethnicity in foreign affairs confuses the real U.S. national interest, creates and encourages subnational loyalties, and opens the door for outside foreign influences to dictate policies, to those which consider the phenomenon to be truly in the spirit of America's history, nature, and democratic values.

This is certainly not a debate without precedent. Rather, it has been a recurrent theme throughout the twentieth century, with commentators decrying the pernicious ethnic influence on national poli-cies during both world wars, throughout the various postwar periods of cold war and détente, and into our own time. In an article pub-lished in 1968, for example, Lawrence Fuchs, one of the leading scholars on ethnic America, wrote that "it may . . . be argued that minority group propaganda is emotional and narrow, and cannot help to clarify debate. The parochial claims of nationality groups are not likely to elevate public thinking. The best judge of compatibility of minority groups' propaganda and the national interest is not the minority group itself or an informed and uninformed [*sic*] public opinion but the elected and appointed officials responsible for mak-ing foreign policy."[5] In the 1990s, the debate over ethnic influences has become particularly impassioned, due to the perceived challenges posed by transnationalism to American society and, no less so, be-cause of the dramatic shift occurring in America's racial composition, largely the result of arrivals from "nontraditional" sources of immi-gration. The fact that race is a primary concern is made clear by constant references to projections that the white majority in the United States will disappear within fifty years, to be superseded by a demographic combination of blacks, Latinos, and people of Asian ancestry. Such data have led to pessimistic interpretations and opin-ions on what this will mean for democracy and other traditional American ideals.

At the time of writing, this debate has captured widespread public attention, due to congressional investigations into foreign campaign contributions to Democratic and Republican 1996 presidential and congressional campaigns – donations which are illegal – and also because of some concern over the impact of ethnic American contri-butions to particular campaigns, which arouse suspicions about mo-tivations on the part of both donors and receivers. Indeed, in many instances, funds have been given to candidates in the expectation that they will favor one foreign country over another. This was evident in the 1996 senatorial race in South Dakota, where both Republican incumbent Larry Pressler, known among Americans of South Asian origin as a supporter of India in its ongoing rivalry with neighboring Pakistan, and Democrat Tim Johnson, the man who defeated him, received "at least $150,000 each"[6] from donors identifying with ei-ther side of the conflict.

In contrast with the popular view that ethnic lobbying is damaging, former New York Democratic representative Stephen Solarz sees ethnic fund raising as "Americanism at its best . . . these people [are], by and large, interested in contributing to the development of an American foreign policy that reflect[s] the view of what our country was all about – namely a commitment to democracy and human rights."[7] Solarz's portrayal of ethnic political participation and the role of ethnic lobbies, albeit somewhat self-serving and simplistic, is quite compatible with many of the findings of this book. The analysis presented here debunks fears about the damaging impact of diasporic involvement in homeland-related affairs on U.S. domestic and foreign policies. I have argued that as the United States continues to allow for ethnic voices in the formulation of foreign policy, it recasts these groups not only as marketers of the democratic-pluralist creed abroad, but also as America's own moral compass, helping to keep a somewhat confused U.S. foreign policy true to its ideals. Yet, the importance of the diasporic factor in U.S. foreign policy runs much deeper than sheer influence on international affairs. It is my contention that diasporic mobilization on homeland-related affairs, which takes place mostly through "official channels" of U.S. foreign policy – that is, the electoral system and the lobbying of decision makers – has the potential to direct ethnodiasporan energies in ways that are conducive both to the assimilation or reinforcement of basic American values, such as freedom and pluralism, and to overall diasporic integration into American society. The successful struggle for a legitimate foreign-policy voice is a process that relieves ethnic alienation by helping to create a more positive view of the American inclusionary process and of America's absorptive capacities. Empowerment, in turn, generates new responsibilities, which come with the shedding of outsider status, involving diasporic integration into established practices and institutions.

It is true that small minorities among diasporas have in several instances involved themselves in clandestine or underground international activity through arms procurement and financial support of, or even personal enlistment in, militant groups such as the IRA, Sikh separatists, Croat militias, or religious radicals like the Palestinian Hamas or the Jewish Kahane movement, and have been critical players in armed conflicts involving their homelands. However, although some such conflicts have spilled over and played themselves out in America's domestic arena, occasionally with violent consequences, such as in the 1993 World Trade Center bombing, the impact of this phenomenon on U.S. domestic affairs and foreign policy can be easily overstated.

While during the cold war, the U.S. government gave tacit or overt support to certain diasporic groups fighting "unfriendly" regimes from U.S. territory, most notably in the case of the Cuban exiles, the end of Soviet-American global competition makes official U.S. encouragement of such activities far less likely. Furthermore, people involved in clandestine and illegal activity are, in general, doubly marginalized, unable to obtain official American support for either the nature or the scale of the intervention they seek, and also subject to denunciations and disavowals of involvement by leading, more established kin activists, who recognize that such actions may hamper diasporic efforts to influence mainstream organizations and elected officials, as demonstrated in the case of Arab-Americans. In addition, although the impact on homeland-related conflicts of diasporic members who act outside the law may be dramatic, and though they may even have indirect implications for American foreign policy, such activities clearly belong to the fringe of diasporic behavior and have no serious direct impact on foreign-policy decision-making *processes*. This is especially true when such actions conflict with American interests or laws, as made evident through the enactment of U.S. antiterrorist legislation over the last few years, which prohibits contributions to and affiliation with "terrorist organizations."

How intense or frequent diasporic interactions with homelands remain is not always evident, and issues of politics and economics inside and outside the United States may reinvigorate dormant diasporas or hinder the more organized or active ones. One pattern that seems to remain more or less constant, however, is that diasporic elites wishing to have influence on foreign policy work hard to remain within the "acceptable" parameters of the American public's view of America's global role. There are those who will argue that such boundaries are not at all clear, and that ethnic activity in the international realm helps to widen the confusion even further. Americans are clearly divided in their foreign-policy preferences, on general issues and along political and ideological lines (e.g., liberal Democrats vs. conservative Republicans) and by various sociodemographic characteristics. Yet surveys sponsored by the Chicago Council on Foreign Relations in the 1990s show that "Americans are not afloat in uncharted seas [as their decision makers seem to be]; for good or ill, their foreign policy opinions remain firmly anchored to a structure of largely internationalist beliefs that has proven remarkably resilient." Even more relevant to the findings of this book, "there are no meaningful differences in the foreign policy beliefs of whites, on the one hand, and Hispanics and African Americans, on the other."[8]

It is my contention that what defines the coherence of optimal policy options is not the ethnic heterogeneity of the American polity, but rather the coherence of the challenges and threats that are perceived to face America as a collective. Such threats are currently defined not in the clear ideological terms of the cold war, but still within a certain vision that prescribes values such as democracy, human rights, individual rights, and political pluralism as desirable, both at home and abroad. As the external threats become less coherent, so the definition of the optimal policies to contend with them becomes commensurably less evident, independent of the ethnic configuration of the polity. Truly, as America's ethnoracial makeup is rapidly changing, in conjunction with the subsiding of the perceived threat, the ethnodiasporic voice becomes more noticeable. This leads those who feel that the nation lost its compass on external affairs with the end of the cold war to believe that America will now lose its core values on the domestic front. Yet, such fears belittle the vitality of America's fundamental commitments domestically and internationally and, even more so, the power of American institutions and civic culture to sustain them.

It is true that diasporic elites do not always reflect the beliefs of their claimed constituency, especially in large and diverse communities that contain different perceptions of the proper role of homelands in the life of the community. Yet, even among the leadership, opinions and positions are not monolithic, and organized elites must constantly work among themselves to present their homeland-related demands in terms consistent with the larger interests of the country as defined by American leaders and the public at large, and always in ways that seem beneficial (or at least not too costly) to America as a whole.[9] When President Clinton wishes to demonstrate his frustration with the Israeli prime minister's position, he does not have to confront Netanyahu directly. Instead, he can call upon certain Jewish-American community leaders to mobilize their constituents in favor of particular policies and to reprimand the Israeli government for its behavior vis-à-vis the Palestinians, prodding Israel to act in accordance with America's values and national interest.

Although mobilization around the cause of the homeland is often a litmus test of the strength of ethnic leadership in the United States, Jewish-Americans, by all accounts the most organized and committed diasporas, have shown lately a greater diversity of opinion vis-à-vis Israel. In the past, the argument that pressure should be exercised to "save Israel from itself" was heard from groups or persons perceived by American Jews as hostile to Israel, such as William Fulbright, George Ball, and the Council on Foreign Relations. Now, such criticisms of Israel can be heard from those within the mainstream, indeed the backbone, of the "special relationship" paradigm.[10] What had long seemed like virtually automatic American Jewish endorsement of Israeli policy no longer exists. For most of Israel's brief history, its security was perceived by American Jews as a top priority, deserving constant and extensive diasporic community mobilization. Yet, the end of the cold war and splits within Israel regarding the direction of peace negotiations have helped divide the U.S. Jewish community in terms of both varying preferences for American policy in the region and in differing assessments of the degree to which Israel's moral claims continue to coincide with American values of democracy, pluralism, and human rights. Some "prominent mainstream American Jewish leaders . . . consider [Israeli Prime Minister Netanyahu] partly responsible for the breakdown of the peace process," and have urged U.S. President Clinton to exert "pressure on Israel. . . . They have also urged Washington to make it clear to Israel that the United States has other interests in the Middle East, such as the flow of oil and the stability of friendly Arab governments."[11] Another new but contrary source and direction of pressure arose during the Rabin-Peres years (1992–96) from right-wing and Orthodox Jews, who vigorously lobbied their allies in the United States to reject Israel's "irresponsible" peace overtures to the Arabs.

The expression of such views by major Jewish-American leaders would have been unthinkable twenty years ago. These divisions run parallel to those among foreign-policy makers in Washington, who have yet to express a clear and unified stance on several major issues, including whether the Islamic world should be seen as the West's "new enemy" and principal threat; the relative importance of the various dimensions of the "Palestinian problem," such as terrorist activity against Israelis versus legitimate Palestinian demands for self-determination; or whether Israel's democratic character – which Israel has long portrayed as an extension of American ideals – has been dangerously compromised by the Netanyahu government, perhaps necessitating a review of U.S. policy toward Israel. The two most often cited examples of behavior considered unacceptable by American Jews are the Netanyahu government's treatment of Palestinians, and its collaboration with the efforts of Israeli Orthodox religious parties to deny the legitimacy of "American-style" Conservative and Reform Jewish practices.

The thesis here, therefore, has two interrelated components. First, that ethnodiasporic leadership may in fact reflect a genuine American sentiment, as it expresses itself in pluralist debate, rather than being a monolithic, partisan force in U.S. foreign policy that undermines American goals. Second, diasporic involvement may have positive ramifications at the domestic level of political and civic culture, since the trumpeting of the "American creed" abroad further reinforces such ideas domestically. How conducive a plurality of opinion in foreign policy is to the pluralist vision domestically may be demonstrated in the behavior of African-American elites, inside and outside of Congress. Contrary to the precedents of other ethnoracial groups, blacks have gained far greater visibility and importance in the foreign-policy arena in recent decades without parallel progress in the socioeconomic life of the country. The fact that the black lobby for Africa is not a monolithic voice without limits or distinctions in terms of American interests and values was illustrated in the case of America's involvement in Somalia. The African-American lobby initially advocated intervention in Somalia to relieve the suffering of its starving inhabitants, but this effort soon suffered from internal political strains due to the rapidly escalating human and financial costs of the military operation. Congressional "Black Caucus members, like other lawmakers . . . were affected by the television images of Somalis celebrating the deaths of American soldiers and public cries for a quick end to U.S. involvement." As CBC Chairman Kweisi Mfume noted at the time, "the days of unanimity are over for the Congressional Black Caucus because of our diversity."[12] The moral imperative cited by African-American politicians in favor of helping Somalia, Haiti, and Nigeria has been applied to non-African issues as well. African-American Representative Cynthia McKinney (D-Ga.) cosponsored an arms trade Code of Conduct in 1997, which, among other provisions, "would bar arms transfers and training to governments that are nondemocratic . . . [or] fail to protect human rights."[13]

My analysis regarding the impact of ethnicity on U.S. foreign policy has been supported recently by the findings of John Ruggie, who claims that ethnic diversity has historically influenced U.S. foreign policy to be more consistent with core American principles and values as articulated by the nation's founders. Ethnic diversity and the need to maintain harmony among people of various national origins have also strengthened a U.S. foreign-policy preference for multilateralism, a favoring of "international orders of relations based on 'a universal or general foundation open in principle to everyone,' [over those based] on discriminatory or exclusionary ties."[14] Social peace at home is supported by shunning favoritism abroad, and by American decision makers striving to avoid the perception of favoring one ethnic group over another in dealing with homeland-related affairs.[15] Ruggie argues that the increased influence of transnational diasporas will enhance the appeal of foreign policies based on generalized and universal principles, rather than those built on "narrow ethnic lines"[16] (as is feared by some), leading most likely to an even stronger emphasis on multilateralism in U.S. foreign policy.

Opposition to my analysis of the nexus between homeland-related factors and U.S. domestic politics has come from both scholars on the left, such as *Social Text* editor Bruce Robbins, and from the right, including Samuel Huntington. Robbins labels my positive assessment of diasporic involvement in U.S. foreign affairs "politically naive,"[17] reflecting ill-considered biases in favor of mainstream U.S. foreign policy and U.S.-based diasporas. He rejects the possibility that diasporic involvement in U.S. foreign policy can lead to a reinvigorated American commitment to stated principles of upholding liberal democratic values, at home or abroad. The ability and the propensity of U.S.-based diasporas to support and export "classical American" values is negligible, as the U.S. government and its foreign-policy processes are not truly open to diasporic input, and diaspora members who do gain access to decision-making circles are no more likely to have a genuine commitment to such high-minded principles than "stay-at-home" compatriots. Robbins asserts that to believe otherwise is to disparage the political maturity and sovereignty of those who have not lived the diasporic experience, and glosses over the faults and potential political dangers (to the United States and other countries) of diasporic activists in the United States. North America does not have this kind of "unique civilizing influence,"[18] says Robbins. On the contrary, it corrupts and assimilates and causes immigrants to forsake their heritage in favor of becoming mere reflections of mainstream Anglo-America. Even if this pernicious influence is disregarded, it cannot be said that transnational Americans are reliable guides to the politics of their homelands, as they lack the accurate knowledge and more recent experience of domestic matters of those who have stayed in "home countries," and they typically pursue narrow and self-interested political agendas. These diasporic activists and pro-interventionists among U.S. government policy makers develop a symbiotic relationship wherein the former receive backing for intervention abroad in accordance with their agendas, while the latter can seek ethical justification "projecting American pluralism outward in such a way as to guarantee the supposed multicultural impartiality behind [such] intervention."[19] A government heeding the voices of diasporic activists is just as likely as previous governments to use "political democracy and human rights" as an excuse to "defend or expand a partisan view of its national interest abroad."[20]

Robbins's analysis of diasporic involvement in U.S. foreign policy displays many of the internal contradictions characteristic of contemporary "ultraleft" scholarship on U.S. ethnic affairs. While insisting on a greater ethnic role in American politics and society, Robbins simultaneously discredits ethnic voices by indicating that their contributions to U.S. foreign policy debates are suspect. Diasporic information or opinions on homeland affairs are seen as being less reliable because these individuals have split their lives between two countries. Ironically, this position sits well with the traditional nativist Anglo-Saxon American viewpoint on foreign affairs that theirs is the only voice to be trusted in determining national policy, since they have no transnational affiliations. On the one hand, people like Robbins decry the disempowerment of ethnic Americans and the disregard for their cultures. On the other, Robbins claims that by the time ethnic voices are heard, they are almost by definition no longer authentically "ethnic," so their "value" has been lost. Robbins, who is assisted in his arguments by Edward Said's critique of Western "orientalism," may wish to review his position in light of Said's own Western-style call on Arab-Americans to benefit from their U.S. experience and hold Arab leaders and governments to account for their actions and inaction on important issues.[21]

Samuel Huntington argues that in the era of transnationalism the United States is most affected by the "shifts from assimilation to diversity and from ethnic group to diaspora." In his critique of decision makers who accept the validity of multiculturalism by heeding ethnic voices, he goes so far as to blame foreign-policy makers for accepting the proposition that multiculturalism in society must be reflected in a voice in foreign policy, a position he believes leads to incoherence. He disputes even the possibility that ethnic groups could represent the "real" American national interest, although he admits that diasporas may often adopt causes abroad which *coincide* with the national interest. Since U.S. foreign policy is in a state of confusion after the cold war, he advises "a policy of restraint and reconstitution aimed at limiting the diversion of American resources to the service of particularistic subnational, transnational, and non-national interests. The national interest is national restraint, and that appears to be the only national interest the American people are willing to support at this time in their history."[22]

The idea of restraint is presented as a counter to the supposed efforts of ethnics to compromise the American national interest in the name of particularist "commercial and ethnic interest[s]." As mentioned earlier, however, such arguments about the confusion of the national interest by ethnic groups did not originate with the end of the cold war. Even during the early Reagan era, a period of relative ideological clarity and intense Soviet-American antagonism, commentators pointed to the damaging effects of ethnicity on foreign and domestic policy. Observers like Senator Charles Mathias claimed that "the loss of cohesion in [U.S.] foreign policy and the derogation from the national interest [are the result of diasporic] factions among us [which] lead the nation toward excessive foreign attachments or animosities."[23]

Although Huntington himself offers no new definition of the national interest, he is quick to follow nativists in condemning ethnic involvement in the current foreign-policy debate. This raises the question of just who *is* competent or worthy enough to participate in formulating U.S. foreign policy in general and in defining the national interest in particular. Huntington's answer seems to be that the Anglo-American establishment of the cold war years should be restored to its former glory and left to work out its foreign policy positions undisturbed by other influences. While the left holds ethnics suspect because they are too easily manipulated by Anglo-American elites, and too readily co-opted into American interventionist ideology, Huntington, representing a conservative view, does not trust the mainstream to withstand the manipulative influences of multiculturalism. The fact that American ethnic diasporas remain suspect for mutually contradictory reasons is perhaps an indication that a reassessment of the entrenched biases of both sides on this subject is in order.

To some extent, policy makers in countries of origin have been undergoing their *own* processes of reassessment, developing in many cases a more realistic approach toward the position of their diasporas inside the United States than their American decision-making counterparts. Many of the older source countries of American immigration have come to appreciate their diasporas' financial and political power and wish to use it to their own advantage. They are more prepared than in the past to forgo or minimize less tangible emotional or nationalistic considerations in order to benefit from practical benefits, such as trade enhancements or political lobbying on matters of national importance. Some homelands are also grasping the American reality in which, over time, their former citizens cannot be expected to maintain the same level of attachment to home countries, as they become more interested in making their mark *inside* the United States. They also understand that diasporic mobilization in the service of the homeland must be done in a careful manner that does not compromise the diaspora's position inside the United States.

The recent trend of home countries allowing their nationals residing in the United States the right to hold dual citizenship and even to vote without returning home (or even to run for office from the United States) is certainly an indication of growing transnationalism, but this does not necessarily signal the development or the persistence of divided loyalties. It is first and foremost a sober recognition by home countries (like Mexico, the Dominican Republic, and Israel) that their kin diasporas do not intend to return "home," that they have "normalized" their lives in America, and that their minds are focused on their countries of domicile. It is also apparent that their diasporas' ethnocultural concerns are being expressed as part of (rather than separate from) their American identity, as was the case with previously integrated immigrant communities. Thus, even when home countries accord their diasporas formal membership at home, by allowing dual citizenship or voting rights, they do not perceive members of these communities as *theirs* in the same way as their resident nationals. Rather, they wish to maintain a cultural, financial, or political tie as long as possible before the forces of distance and time inevitably erode their influence to the point of nonexistence.

This growing (though not universal) homeland recognition of the potential of diasporic power is largely the result of the successful American story of diversity and inclusion. Countries of origin of previously weak diasporic communities, or countries whose ideology had contributed to resentment of their kin's success abroad, have in many cases come to appreciate that the process of upward mobility for American-based diasporas cuts across the ethnic spectrum, even if not all groups proceed at the same pace.

The "era of multiculturalism" in the United States, which signals the empowerment of non-European ethnic groups, not only in American civic culture but also in foreign affairs, is a clear manifestation of the strength of American society's integrative processes. Indeed, one can argue that the highly vocal nativist and ideological rejection of cultural pluralism earlier in this century did not stop the evolution of a pluralist society. As one student of American ethnicity has observed,

> In fact, hostility from the larger American society has often served to reenforce [sic] the cultural identity of ethnic groups rather than eliminate it. While the United States has not always upheld a principled commitment to the cultivation of cultural pluralism, it has usually settled on a de facto acceptance of it. This has provided a space for ethnic groups to exercise a significant measure of cultural autonomy and self-definition.[24]

What we have been witnessing in recent years is not a major shift in the American reality, suddenly giving ethnoracial groups permission to organize and mobilize politically. Rather, change has come mainly in terms of the composition of ethnicity (and the primary sources of immigration) – which may seem to some to be a critical qualitative change in American culture and identity. Thus, the most significant development of the past three or so decades has in fact been a greater synchronization between "the de facto acceptance of cultural pluralism and the promise of economic gain,"[25] which has characterized American life at least since the beginning of this century, with a de jure acceptance of a pluralist society in which ethnoracial affiliation and ethnically organized politics (including non-European) are accepted as legitimate, even at the "national interest" level.

As this book has shown, the implications of this dynamic of newly acquired legitimacy are not negative or damaging to the American national fabric or to the national interest, as many have asserted, and in fact have some beneficial effects, strengthening America's ability to integrate previously disenfranchised minorities while preserving the basic liberal tenets of a pluralist society. The process of moving ethnic elites from total preoccupation with distinct ethnocultural activities in their own groups to greater interaction with American institutions as well as other groups in society helps to facilitate transformation of the ethnic operational code, directing it into a more universalist national perspective. This general integrationist dynamic has far-reaching consequences not only inside the United States, but also in many countries of origin in which American diasporas are increasingly becoming important vehicles of social, political, and value change.

Notes

Chapter 1. U.S. Diasporas and Homelands in the Era of Transnationalism

1. Lawrence H. Fuchs, "Minority Groups and Foreign Policy," *Political Science Quarterly* 74.2 (1959): 165–75; Abdul Aziz Said, ed., *Ethnicity in U.S. Foreign Policy* (New York: Praeger Publishers, 1977).
2. Lawrence H. Fuchs, *The American Kaleidoscope: Race, Ethnicity, and the Civic Culture* (Hanover, N.H.: University Press of New England, 1990); and Alexander DeConde, *Ethnicity, Race, and American Foreign Policy: A History* (Boston: Northeastern University Press, 1992).
3. Louis L. Gerson, *The Hyphenate and Recent American Politics and Diplomacy* (Lawrence: University of Kansas Press, 1964), 235.
4. Louis L. Gerson, "The Influence of Hyphenated Americans on U.S. Diplomacy," *Ethnicity and U.S. Foreign Policy*, ed. Abdul Aziz Said (New York: Praeger, 1977), 47.
5. See, for example, *U.S. News and World Report*, April 26, 1993, 21–31.
6. Tamar Jacoby, "Roundtable: Beyond Crown Heights – Strategies for Overcoming Anti-Semitism and Racism in New York," *Tikkun* 8.1 (January–February 1993): 61.
7. See Fuchs, "Minority Groups."
8. *New York Times*, June 20, 1993, 27.
9. Charles S. Maier, "Unsafe Haven," *New Republic*, October 14, 1992, 21.
10. Myron Weiner, *The Global Migration Crisis: Challenge to States and to Human Rights* (New York: HarperCollins, 1995), 85.
11. Jack Miles, "Blacks vs. Browns," in *Arguing Immigration: The Debate over the Changing Face of America*, ed. Nicolaus Mills (New York: Simon and Schuster, 1994), 101.
12. Weiner, *The Global Migration Crisis*, 12n17.
13. Miles, "Black vs. Brown," 101.
14. Cited in Weiner, *The Global Migration Crisis*, 84–85n15.
15. Leo R. Chavez, "Immigration Reform and Nativism: The Nationalist Response to the Transnationalist Challenge," in *Immigrants Out! The*

New Nativism and the Anti-Immigrant Impulse in the United States, ed. Juan F. Perea (New York: New York University Press, 1996), 62.

16. See Nancy Abelmann and John Lie, *Blue Dreams: Korean-Americans and the Los Angeles Riots* (Cambridge, Mass.: Harvard University Press, 1995), 26–27.

17. "New Law in Mexico Allows Emigrés to Call Two Nations Home," *Washington Post*, May 31, 1998.

18. Noah M. J. Pickus, " 'True Faith and Allegiance': Immigration and the Politics of Citizenship" (Ph.D. diss., Princeton University, 1995), 4; and Pickus, "Does Immigration Threaten Democracy? Right Restriction and the Meaning of Membership," in *Democracy: The Challenges Ahead*, ed. Yossi Shain and Aharon Klieman (London: Macmillan, St. Antony's Series, 1997), 130–45.

19. Noah M. J. Pickus, "Becoming American/America Becoming," Duke University Workshop on Immigration and Citizenship, November 1997, 22.

20. Chavez, "Immigration Reform and Nativism," 62.

21. Khachig Tölölyan, "Uprooted Peoples Enter a New Age of Migration," *Newsday*, September 8, 1991, 36.

22. "New Law in Mexico," *Washington Post*, May 31, 1998.

23. Adam Nagourney, "Messinger Goes Far Afield to Campaign for New York Mayoral Election," *New York Times*, December 4, 1996.

24. See Samuel P. Huntington, *The Clash of Civilizations and the Remaking of World Order* (New York: Simon and Schuster, 1996), 272–91.

25. See Francis Fukuyuma, "Immigrants and Family Values," in Mills, *Arguing Immigration*, 151.

26. Samuel P. Huntington, "If Not Civilizations, What?: Paradigms of the Post–Cold War World," *Foreign Affairs* 72.5 (November–December 1993): 180.

27. See Yossi Shain, *The Frontier of Loyalty: Political Exiles in the Age of the Nation-State* (Middletown, Conn.: Wesleyan University Press, 1989), 51–52. The traditional definition of diaspora applied to Jews who after the Babylonian captivity were scattered among the heathens. Today, many scholars use "diaspora" in a broader sense as a term that "shares meaning with a larger semantic domain that includes words like immigrant, expatriate, refugee, guest-workers, exile community, overseas community, ethnic community." See Khachig Tölölyan, "The Nation-State and Its Others: In Lieu of a Preface," *Diaspora* 1 (Spring 1991): 4–5. Also see Gabriel Sheffer, ed., *Modern Diasporas in International Politics* (New York: St. Martin's, 1986).

28. See David Vital, *The Future of the Jews* (Cambridge, Mass.: Harvard University Press, 1990), 136; also see Arthur Hertzberg, "Showdown," *New York Review of Books*, October 24, 1991, 23–24.

29. See Chapter 4 on the transnational impact of black-Jewish relations.

30. Laurence Kotler-Berkowitz, "Ethnic Cohesion and Division among

American Jews: The Role of Mass-Level and Organizational Politics," *Ethnic and Racial Studies* 20.4 (October 1997): 799.

31. L. Ling-chi Wang, "Roots and Changing Identity of the Chinese in the United States," *Daedalus* 120 (Spring 1991): 205.

32. Kotler-Berkowitz, "Ethnic Cohesion and Division among American Jews," 800.

33. Cited in Alejandro Portes and Ruben G. Rumbaut, *Immigrant America: A Portrait* (Berkeley: University of California Press, 1990), 107.

34. See Victor Wolfgang Von Hagen, *The Germanic People in America* (Norman: University of Oklahoma Press, 1976), 374–80.

35. Alicja Iwańska, *Exiled Governments: Spanish and Polish* (Cambridge, Mass.: Schenkman, 1981), 43–44.

36. Cited in Richard D. Alba, *Ethnic Identity: The Transformation of White America* (New Haven: Yale University Press, 1990), 151.

37. Rogers M. Smith, "Beyond Tocqueville, Myrdal, and Hartz: The Multiple Traditions in America," *American Political Science Review* 87.3 (1993): 549.

38. DeConde, *Ethnicity, Race, and American Foreign Policy: A History*, 10–26.

39. Michael Lind, *The Next American Nation: The New Nationalism and the Fourth American Revolution* (New York: Simon and Schuster, 1995), 27.

40. Bowyer J. Bell, "The Transcendental Irish Republic: The Dream of Diaspora," in *Governments-in-Exile in Contemporary World Politics*, ed. Yossi Shain (New York: Routledge, 1991), 204.

41. Cited in David Carroll Cochran, "Ethnic Diversity and Democratic Stability: The Case of Irish Americans," *Political Science Quarterly* 110.4 (Winter 1995–96): 590.

42. Jonathan Freedland, "Irish Americans Break Taboo to Talk of the Blight They Survived," *Guardian*, June 7, 1995, 9.

43. Lind, *The Next American Nation: The New Nationalism and the Fourth American Revolution*, 32.

44. Ibid., 34. As late as the 1860 U.S. census, the Irish were still regarded as a distinct "race" (p. 53), but the Civil War eroded Anglo-American nativism and led to an official redefinition of the white race that made people of Irish descent "honorary Saxons" (p. 84).

45. Paul Arthur, "Diasporan Intervention in International Affairs: Irish America as a Case Study," *Diaspora* 1 (1991): 144.

46. Ibid., 145.

47. Joseph O'Grady, "An Irish Policy Born in the U.S.A.: Clinton's Break with the Past," *Foreign Affairs* 75.3 (May–June 1996): 2.

48. Ibid.

49. Ibid.

50. DeConde, *Ethnicity, Race, and American Foreign Policy: A History*, 89.

51. Portes and Rumbaut, *Immigrant America: A Portrait*, 104–6; also see Antanas J. Van Reenen, *Lithuanian Diaspora: Konigsberg to Chicago* (Lanham, Md.:University Press of America, 1990).

52. William Safire, "On Language: The Prep-Droppers," *New York Times Magazine*, July 28, 1991.
53. John Bodnar, "Ethnicity and Nationalism before Multiculturalism," *American Quarterly* 48.4 (December 1996): 718.
54. John Bodnar, *Remaking America: Public Memory, Commemoration, and Patriotism in the Twentieth Century* (Princeton: Princeton University Press, 1992), 57.
55. Portes and Rumbaut, *Immigrant America: A Portrait*, 108.
56. Michael H. Hunt, *Ideology and U.S. Foreign Policy* (New Haven: Yale University Press, 1987), 139.
57. Rogers M. Smith, "The 'American Creed' and American Identity: The Limits of Liberal Citizenship in the United States," *Western Political Quarterly* 41.2 (1988): 232.
58. Smith, "Beyond Tocqueville, Myrdal, and Hartz," 560; see also Ronald Takaki, ed., *From Different Shores: Perspectives on Race and Ethnicity in America*, 2nd ed. (Oxford: Oxford University Press), 1994.
59. Pickus, " 'True Faith and Allegiance': Immigration and the Politics of Citizenship," 84.
60. Ibid.
61. Bourne, "Transnational America," in *War and the Intellectuals: Essays, 1915–19*, ed. Carl Resek (New York: Harper and Row, 1964), 109.
62. Ibid., 113–14.
63. Ibid., 110.
64. Ibid., 117.
65. See John Gerard Ruggie, "The Past as Prologue? Interests, Identity and American Foreign Policy," *International Security* 21.4 (Spring 1997): 111–12.
66. Smith, "Beyond Tocqueville, Myrdal, and Hartz," 560.
67. Lind, *The Next American Nation: The New Nationalism and the Fourth American Revolution*, 85.
68. Michael Walzer, "Multiculturalism and Individualism: Principles of Government," *Dissent* (Spring 1994): 185.
69. Bodnar, *Remaking America*, 171.
70. Ibid., 100.
71. Hunt, *Ideology and U.S. Foreign Policy*, 139; Joe R. Feagin, *Racial and Ethnic Relations*, 2nd ed. (Englewood Cliffs, N.J.: Prentice-Hall, 1984), 60.
72. David S. Wyman, *The Abandonment of the Jews: America and the Holocaust, 1941–1945* (New York: Pantheon Books, 1984), 6–12.
73. Gerson, *The Hyphenate and Recent American Politics and Diplomacy*, 137.
74. Don. T. Nakinishi, "Surviving Democracy's 'Mistake': Japanese Americans and Executive Order 9066" (paper presented at the International Conference on Political Identity in American Thought, Whitney Humanities Center, Yale University, April 19–21, 1991). Takaki has argued that the harsh treatment of Japanese-Americans was largely motivated by racism. "Japanese in America were not regarded as 'free individuals'

but as members of a polity simply because of their Japanese ancestry. In the camps, draft-age Nisei men were required to fill out and sign a loyalty questionnaire. . . . Young men of Italian or German ancestry were not subjected to such a 'loyalty' test." Takaki, "Reflections on Racial Patterns in America," in Takaki, *From Different Shores,* 27–28. In fact, Takaki's claim of Japanese-American exclusivity is not entirely correct. There were Italian-Americans who were relocated from their homes during the war, whose property was confiscated, and whose movements were restricted. "Even the fisherman father of baseball great Joe DiMaggio . . . was told he could not fish San Francisco Bay or visit the city." " 'Secret' of WWII: Italian-Americans Forced to Move" (CNN website, www.cnn.com, September 21, 1997).

75. Morton Grodzins, *Americans Betrayed: Politics and the Japanese Evacuation* (Chicago: University of Chicago Press, 1949), 147–48.
76. Ibid., 149.
77. Ibid.
78. Ibid., 150–51.
79. Ibid., 154.
80. Pickus, "Becoming American," 23.
81. Ibid., 24.
82. Hunt, *Ideology and U.S. Foreign Policy,* 161.
83. Irving Howe, "A Fear beyond Escaping," in *Bridges and Boundaries: African Americans and American Jews,* ed. Jack Salzman et al. (New York: Braziller and the Jewish Museum, 1992), 70.
84. For this information, I am indebted to University of Tel-Aviv professor Abraham Ben-Zvi; also see Charles Lipson, "American Support for Israel: History, Sources, Limits," *Israel Affairs* 2.3–4 (Spring–Summer 1996): 138.
85. Ned Lebow, "Psychological Dimensions of Post–Cold War Foreign Policy," *Israel Affairs* 2.3–4 (Spring–Summer 1996): 48.
86. Ibid., 48–49.
87. John Higham, "Multiculturalism and Universalism: A History of Critique," *American Quarterly* 45 (1993): 206.
88. Philip V. White, "The Black American Constituency for Southern Africa," *The American People and South Africa,* ed. Alfred O. Hero Jr. and John Barratt (Lexington, Mass.: Lexington, 1981), 83.
89. Noah M. J. Pickus, "Creating Citizens: Americanization and the Transformation of National Identity" (paper presented at the annual meeting of the American Political Science Association. Washington, August 29, 1991), 17; see also Will Kymlicka, *Multicultural Citizenship: A Liberal Theory of Minority Rights* (Oxford: Clarendon Press, 1995), 14.
90. Alan Dowty, *Closed Borders: The Contemporary Assault on Freedom of Movement* (New Haven: Yale University Press, 1987), 234.
91. See Deborah Scroggins, "Making Themselves Heard: Blacks Gain Foreign Policy Clout," *Atlanta Journal/Atlanta Constitution,* May 31, 1994, A9.

92. Nathan Glazer, "New Rules of the Game," in *Immigration and US Foreign Policy*, ed. Robert W. Tucker et al. (Boulder, Colo.: Westview Press, 1990), 19.

93. Carlos Gonzalez Gutierrez, "Decentralized Diplomacy: The Role of Consular Offices in Mexico's Relations with Its Diaspora," in *Bridging the Border: Transforming Mexico-US Relations*, ed. Rodolfo O. de la Garza and Jesus Velasco (Lanham, Md.: Rowman & Littlefield Publishers, 1997), 54, 57.

94. Ibid., 56–57.

95. Ibid., 57.

96. Martin Kilson, "African Americans and Africa: A Critical Nexus," *Dissent* (Summer 1992): 367.

97. DeConde, *Ethnicity, Race and American Foreign Policy: A History*, 200.

98. Ibid., 199.

99. Ibid., 193.

100. Jason McDonald, "Conceptual Metaphors for American Ethnic Formations," in *Representing and Imagining America*, ed. Philip J. Davies (Keele: Keele University Press, 1996), 88.

101. Michael Walzer, "Comment," in *Multiculturalism and "The Politics of Recognition": An Essay by Charles Taylor*, ed. Amy Gutman (Princeton: Princeton University Press, 1992), 101.

102. Steven C. Rockefeller, "Comment," in ibid., 89 (emphasis added).

103. Jeff Spinner, *The Boundaries of Citizenship* (Baltimore: Johns Hopkins University Press, 1994), 76.

104. Takaki, *From Different Shores*, 34.

105. Smith, "The 'American Creed' and American Identity," 247.

106. Joseph Raz, "Multiculturalism: A Liberal Perspective," *Dissent* (Winter 1994): 73.

107. Ibid., 74.

108. Jack Citrin et al., "Is American Nationalism Changing? Implications for Foreign Policy," *International Studies Quarterly* 38 (1994): 10.

109. Will Kymlicka, *Multicultural Citizenship*, 11.

110. See Glazer, "The Emergence of an American Ethnic Pattern," in Takaki, *From Different Shores*, 11.

111. Cited in McDonald, "Conceptual Metaphors for American Ethnic Formations," 85.

112. Lind, *The Next American Nation: The New Nationalism and the Fourth American Revolution* 98.

113. Peter Skerry, *Mexican Americans: The Ambivalent Minority* (New York: Free Press, 1993), 18.

114. Will Kymlica, "Social Unity in a Liberal State" (revised draft of a paper that was published later in *Social Philosophy and Policy* 13. 1 [Winter 1996]: 105–36). This quote is taken from the February 1995 draft, p. 7.

115. Christian Joppke, "Multiculturalism and Immigration: A Comparison

of the United States, Germany, and Great Britain," *Theory and Society* 25.4 (August 1996): 455.

116. Ibid., 454.
117. This point was made by the late Judith Shklar in her posthumously published essay "Obligation, Loyalty, Exile," *Political Theory* 21.2 (May 1993): 181–97.
118. Lawrence Wright, "One Drop of Blood," *New Yorker*, July 25, 1994, 52–53.
119. Bodnar, *Remaking America*, 71.
120. Kilson, "African Americans and Africa," 362.
121. Fuchs, *The American Kaleidoscope*, 81.
122. Elliot P. Skinner, *African Americans and U.S. Policy toward Africa, 1850–1924* (Washington, D.C.: Howard University Press, 1992), 470.
123. Ibid.
124. In his famous book *An American Dilemma* (1944) Gunnar Myrdal wrote: "In his allegiances the Negro is characteristically an American. He believes in the American creed and in other ideals held by most Americans, such as getting ahead in the world, individualism, the importance of education and wealth. He imitates the dominant culture as he sees it and insofar as he can adopt it under his conditions of life." Cited in Philip Mason, "The Revolt against Western Values," *Daedalus* 96.2 (Spring 1967): 331.
125. Cited in White, "The Black American Constituency for Southern Africa," 84–85.
126. Ibid., 84.
127. Martin Staniland, *American Intellectuals and African Nationalists, 1955–1970* (New Haven: Yale University Press, 1991), 193.
128. Herbert H. Haines, *Black Radicals and the Civil Rights Mainstream, 1954–1970* (Knoxville: University of Tennessee Press, 1988): 65.
129. Ibid.
130. Ibid., 555–56.
131. Kilson, "African Americans and Africa," 362.
132. Skinner, *African-Americans and U.S. Policy towards Africa, 1850–1924*, 10.
133. Cited in Fuchs, *The American Kaleidoscope*, 255.
134. Ignacio M. Garcia, *Chicanismo: The Forging of a Militant Ethos among Mexican Americans* (Tucson: University of Arizona Press, 1997), 13.
135. C. Eric Lincoln, "Color and Group Identity in the United States," *Daedalus* 96.2 (Spring 1967): 537.
136. Don Terry, "Black Muslims Enter Islamic Mainstream," *New York Times*, May 3, 1993, B7.
137. See Henry Kissinger, "Reflections on Containment," *Foreign Affairs* 73.3 (May–June 1994): 113–30.
138. Cecil V. Crabb Jr., *Policy-Makers and Critics: Conflicting Theories of American Foreign Policy* (New York: Praeger, 1976), 271.
139. Ibid., 270.

140. Hugh De Santis, *The Diplomacy of Silence: The American Foreign Service, the Soviet Union, and the Cold War, 1933–1947* (Chicago: University of Chicago Press, 1980), 4.
141. See Noam Chomsky, "Intervention in Vietnam and Central America: Parallels and Differences," *Monthly Review* 37.4 (September 1985): 1–29.
142. Crabb, *Policy-Makers and Critics*, 277.
143. Ibid., 278.
144. See Jeanne Kirkpatrick, "Dictatorships and Double Standards," *Commentary* 68.5 (November 1979): 34–45.
145. Silvia Pedraza-Bailey, *Political and Economic Migrants in America: Cubans and Mexicans* (Austin: University of Texas Press, 1985), 154.
146. George F. Kennan, *American Diplomacy: Expanded Edition* (Chicago: University of Chicago Press, 1985), 95.
147. Ibid.
148. Ibid., 101.
149. Stephen J. Stedman, "The New Interventionists," *Foreign Affairs* 72.1 (1992–93): 5.
150. Jack I. Garvey, "Repression of the Political Emigre – The Underground to International Law: A Proposal for Remedy," *Yale Law Journal* 90.78 (1980): 81, 84.
151. *Los Angeles Times*, March 15, 1984.
152. Fuchs, *The American Kaleidoscope*, 366–67.
153. Arthur M. Schlesinger Jr., *The Cycles of American History* (Boston: Houghton Mifflin, 1986), 99.
154. For an excellent analysis of Carter's failure to live up to his human rights credo, see Stanley Hoffmann, *Dead Ends: American Foreign Policy in the New Cold War* (Cambridge, Mass.: Ballinger Publishing, 1983), 67–83.
155. Schlesinger, *The Cycles of American History*, 104.
156. Ibid., 103.
157. Ibid., 103–4.
158. See Matthew Schatzman's "The Politics of Exile in the Democratization of South Korea" (unpublished manuscript, Yale University, January 1986).
159. Marvin Howe, "South Koreans in the U.S. Are Going Home," *New York Times*, July 19, 1987.
160. Kennan, *American Diplomacy: Expanded Edition*, vii.
161. Stephen J. Stedman, "The New Interventionists," 5.
162. Myron Weiner, "Asian Politics and US Foreign Policy," in Tucker et al., *Immigration and US Foreign Policy*, 207–8.
163. Yehuda Mirsky, "Democratic Politics, Democratic Culture," *Orbis* 37.4 (Fall 1993): 567.
164. Alan Tonelson, "Beyond Left or Right," *National Interest* 34–37 (Winter 1993–94): 8.
165. See, for example, speeches by James Baker and Bill Clinton cited in Mirsky, "Democratic Politics, Democratic Culture," 567, 575.

166. Tony Smith, "In Defense of Intervention," *Foreign Affairs* 73.6 (November–December 1994): 42.
167. Michael Mandelbaum, "Foreign Policy as Social Work," *Foreign Affairs* 75.1 (January–February 1996): 18.
168. David C. Hendrickson, "The Recovery of Internationalism," *Foreign Affairs* 73.5 (September–October 1994): 26.
169. George F. Kennan, "On American Principles," *Foreign Affairs* 74.2 (March–April 1995): 116–27.
170. Ibid., 62.
171. Michael Clough, "Grass-Roots Policymaking: Say Good-Bye to the 'Wise Men,' " *Foreign Affairs* 73.1 (January–February 1994): 2.
172. Ibid., 7.
173. Bruce D. Porter, "Can American Democracy Survive?" *Commentary* 96.5 (November 1993): 39.
174. Citrin et al., "Is American Nationalism Changing?" 26.
175. Tonelson, "Beyond Left or Right," 3.

Chapter 2. U.S. Ethnic Diasporas in the Struggle for Democracy and Self-Determination

1. See Nathan Glazer and Daniel Patrick Moynihan, eds., *Ethnicity: Theory and Experience* (Cambridge, Mass.: Harvard University Press, 1975), 23–24.
2. Charles S. Campbell, *The Transformation of American Foreign Relations, 1865–1900* (New York: Harper and Row, 1976), 8.
3. See J. Bowyer Bell, "The Transcendental Irish Republic: The Dream of Diaspora," in *Governments-in-Exile in Contemporary World Politics*, ed. Yossi Shain (New York: Routledge, 1991), 202–18.
4. See Campbell, *The Transformation of American Foreign Relations, 1865–1900*, 8.
5. See ibid., 334, and Charles McC. Mathias Jr., "Ethnic Groups and Foreign Policy," *Foreign Affairs* 59 (Summer 1981): 982. Also see Paul Arthur, "Diasporan Intervention in International Affairs: Irish America as a Case Study," *Diaspora* 1 (Fall 1991): 143–62.
6. For a more thorough account of the impact of Irish-American lobbying on President Clinton's Ireland policies, see Joseph O'Grady, "An Irish Policy Born in the U.S.A.: Clinton's Break with the Past," *Foreign Affairs* 75.3 (May–June 1996): 2–7.
7. Cited in ibid.
8. Ibid.
9. Ibid.
10. Monna Harrington, "Loyalties: Dual and Divided" in *The Politics of Ethnicity*, ed. Michael Walzer et al. (Cambridge, Mass.: Belknap Press of Harvard University Press, 1982), 122–23.
11. Helena Znaniecki Lopata, *Polish-Americans: Status Competition in an Ethnic Community* (Englewood Cliffs, N.J.: Prentice-Hall, 1976), 22.

12. Ibid., 22–23.
13. Ibid., 23.
14. Cited in ibid., 24.
15. Ibid., 25.
16. Ibid., 32. Over thirty thousand Polish immigrants arrived in Chicago, the largest Polish-American community, during the late 1970s and early 1980s. Many thousands cast absentee ballots in the 1989 Polish elections, when Solidarity participated in national elections for the first time. *New York Times*, June 5, 1989, and *Time*, November 27, 1989, 22–23.
17. Brian Knowlton, "All Abroad: A Surge in Expatriate Americans," *International Herald Tribune*, October 13, 1997.
18. See Robert A. Kann and Zdenek V. David, *The Peoples of the Eastern Hapsburg Lands, 1526–1918* (Seattle: University of Washington Press, 1984), 391; George J. Kovtun, *Masaryk and America: Testimony of a Relationship* (Washington, D.C.: Library of Congress, 1988), 11–27.
19. A copy of the petition is available upon request.
20. Mark Stolarik, "Adrift in the Velvet Revolution: Slovakia Six Months Later (1990)," *Literárny Týždenník* (Bratislava), August 3, 1990. Stolarik provided the English translation to the author.
21. Ibid., pp. 7–8.
22. Ibid., p. 8.
23. Mark Stolarik, Letter to the Editor, *Globe and Mail* (Toronto), July 25, 1992.
24. Author's telephone interviews with Mark Stolarik, October–November 1991.
25. See, for example, Petition to U.S. Congress to send a fact-finding mission to Slovakia and attached "One Thousand Words on Slovakia" by Igor Uhrik, submitted January 15, 1992.
26. Igor Uhrik, transcript of television program broadcast February 16, 1990, in both the Czech Republic and Slovakia. Uhrik claims that the chairman of Slovak TV had to override the refusal of Czech network executives to air the program.
27. Author's interview with Igor Uhrik, New York, September 6, 1995.
28. Igor Uhrik, "Vôľa žiť ako národ" (The will to live as a nation), *Literárny Týždenník*, April 6, 1990.
29. "Zvrchovanost ako výučný list," *Smena*, March 28, 1991.
30. Yossi Shain, "Ethnic Diasporas and U.S. Foreign Policy," *Political Science Quarterly* 109.5 (Winter 1994–95):
31. Henry Brandon, "Who Split Czechoslovakia?" *New York Times*, September 24, 1992.
32. Ibid.
33. Author's interview with Igor Uhrik, New York, September 6, 1995.
34. John Bondar, *Remaking America: Public Memory, Commemoration, and Patriotism in the Twentieth Century* (Princeton: Princeton University Press, 1992), 106.

35. See "Yugoslavia Is Such a Bother," *Economist*, June 29, 1991.

36. Cited in William Safire, "Ukraine Marches Out," *New York Times*, November 18, 1991.

37. See Andrew Rosenthal, "Aides Say Bush Is Shifting Focus to Relations among the Republics," *New York Times*, November 30, 1991.

38. "Diaspora Ukrainians Say 'The Thrill's Gone'," *Washington Post*, August 7, 1994.

39. See Romuald Misiunas, "Sovereignty without Government: Baltic Diplomatic and Consular Representation, 1940–1990" in Shain, *Governments-in-Exile*, 134–44.

40. The diasporan Dashnag Party became active in Karabagh where it had won the local elections; see Khachig Tölölyan, "National Self-Determination and the Limits of Sovereignty: Armenia, Azerbaijan and the Secession of Nagorno-Krabakh," *Nationalism and Ethnic Politics* 1.1 (Spring 1995): 86–110.

41. See Khachig Tölölyan, "Exile Governments in the American Polity," in Shain, *Governments-in-Exile*, 166–87, and his "Commentary," *Diaspora* 1 (Fall 1991): 225–28. I have also benefited from personal conversations with Tölölyan.

42. See Samuel P. Huntington, *The Clash of Civilizations and the Making of World Order* (New York: Simon and Schuster, 1996), 287.

43. See Paul Franklin Lytle, "Loyalty and Recognition under Challenge: The Yugoslav Case, 1941–1945" in Shain, *Governments-in-Exile*, 122.

44. Documents are available from the author upon request.

45. For the information on the activities of the Croatian diaspora, I am indebted to Nenad Bach (Irvington, N.Y.) and to Professor Paul Franklin Lytle. It has been argued that the strong German support of Croatia's independence can be attributed in part to the fact that Germany has a built-in lobby consisting of nearly 500,000 Croats living in the country. See Frederick Painton, "The Shock of Recognition," *Time*, December 30, 1991, 29.

46. See Michael Isikoff, "Member of Croatian Group Charged in Army Plot," *Washington Post*, August 13, 1991.

47. And their early 1990s political campaign against the former Yugoslav Republic of Macedonia.

48. See *Newsweek*, January 19, 1970, 36–37.

49. Gregory Jusdanis, "Greek Americans and the Diaspora," *Diaspora* 1 (Fall 1991): 218.

50. Panayiotis Ifestos, "Ethnic Lobbies and Foreign Policy: The American Experience" (draft paper, Panteion University, Athens, Greece, 1993), 10; and Christopher Hitchens, "Dead End: The Decline and Fall of the Greek Lobby in America," *Odyssey* (November–December 1995): 31.

51. John P. Paul, "The Greek Lobby and American Foreign Policy: A Transnational Perspective," in *Ethnic Identities in a Transnational World*, ed. John F. Stack Jr. (Westport, Conn.: Greenwood Press, 1990), 61–62.

52. See Alice Scourby, *The Greek Americans* (Boston: Twayne Publishers, 1984), 105; even this success, however, has been minimized by some authors who have written that other factors were just as important in the congressional decisions. These include Turkish use of weapons in Cyprus in contravention of legal commitments to the United States (Paul, "The Greek Lobby," 55), concerns over international aggression and the rule of law (Hitchens, "Dead End," 30; Ifestos, "Ethnic Lobbies," 11–12), and even a power struggle between the U.S. government's executive and legislative branches (Paul, "The Greek Lobby," 70–71). John P. Paul suggests that the Greek-American lobby's significance was overplayed at the time by all sides concerned, for their own reasons, and points out how easily Greek gains were subsequently rolled back ("The Greek Lobby," pp. 73–76).

53. "Compromise Likely to Take Macedonia into U.N.," *New York Times*, January 26, 1993; "Get Real in Macedonia," editorial in *Christian Science Monitor*, September 15, 1994, 18.

54. Hitchens, "Dead End," 31.

55. Benjamin Barber, "To Be an American: Identity as Citizenship in the New World" (paper presented at a conference on Political Identity in American Thought, Yale University, April 1991), 8.

56. See Thomas Sewell, *Ethnic America: A History* (New York: Basic Books, 1981), 65.

57. See Felicity Barringer, "With Loyalty Split, Arab-Americans Fault Hussein, but Question U.S. Too," *New York Times*, August 16, 1990.

58. See Trudy Rubin, "An American Is Best Hope for Battered Ex-Yugoslavia," *Philadelphia Inquirer*, October 9, 1992.

59. Chuck Sudetic, "Yugoslav Premier Ousted by Foes 6 Months after Return from U.S.," *New York Times*, December 30, 1992.

60. See Yossi Shain, *The Frontier of Loyalty: Political Exiles in the Age of the Nation-State* (Middletown, Conn.: Wesleyan University Press, 1989), 145–62.

61. For more details, see Robert Delfs, "Long-Arm Tactics," *Far Eastern Economic Review*, July 5, 1990, 10–11.

62. Jean Jean-Pierre, "The Tenth Department," *NACLA Report on the Americas* 27.4 (January–February 1994): 41–45.

63. See Elaine Ray, "In Another Country," *Boston Globe Magazine*, July 26, 1992, 14–27.

64. See David Malone, "Haiti and the International Community: A Case Study," *Survival* 39.2 (Summer 1997): 126–46.

65. *Los Angeles Times*, November 11, 1993, 12.

66. Ibid.

67. Christopher Caldwell, "Aristide Development," *American Spectator* (July 1994): 32–41, 74–77.

68. See Silvia Pedraza-Bailey, *Political and Economic Migrants in America: Cubans and Mexicans* (Austin: University of Texas Press, 1985), 29.

69. Ed Vulliamy, "Street War Splits Exiled Cubans in Little Havana," *Observer*, December 11, 1994.
70. Damian J. Fernandez, "From Little Havana to Washington, D.C.: Cuban-Americans and U.S. Foreign Policy," in *Ethnic Groups and U.S. Foreign Policy*, ed. Mohammed E. Ahrari (New York: Greenwood Press, 1987), 122–23.
71. Ibid., 116.
72. See Larry Rother, "The Cold War of Cuba and the Miami Exiles Heats Up," *New York Times*, January 16, 1992; James J. Guy, "Cuba: A Regional Power without a Region?" *World Today* 46.8–9 (August–September 1990): 165–66.
73. Tim Golden, "Mexico's Chief, in a Shift, Meets Two of Castro's Main Foes in Exile," *New York Times*, October 5, 1992.
74. See Larry Rother, "A Rising Cuban-American Leader: Statesman to Some, Bully to Others," *New York Times*, October 29, 1992. Also see Cathy Booth, "The Man Who Would Oust Castro," *Time*, October 26, 1992, 56.
75. Deborah Sontag, "The Lasting Exile of Cuban Spirits," *New York Times*, September 11, 1994, sec. 4, p. 7.
76. See Douglas Farah, "Cuba Admits U.S. Law Damages Economy," *International Herald-Tribune*, January 28, 1997, 2.
77. David Rieff, "From Exiles to Immigrants: The Miami Cubans Come 'Home,' " *Foreign Affairs* 74.4 (July–August 1995): 87.
78. Ibid., 89.
79. See Sontag, "The Lasting Exile of Cuban Spirits," 1, 5.
80. See Alicja Iwańska, "Modern Exiles: Spanish, Polish, American," *Polish Review* 23 (1978): 60.
81. Pedraza-Bailey, *Political and Economic Migrants in America*, 154.
82. Arthur M. Schlesinger Jr., *The Cycles of American History* (Boston: Houghton Mifflin, 1986), 95.
83. Henry Kissinger, *White House Years* (Boston: Little, Brown, 1979), 57.
84. See Jack I. Garvey, "Repression of the Political Emigré – The Underground to International Law: A Proposal for Remedy," *Yale Law Journal* 90 (November 1980): 78–120.
85. Cited in Daniel B. Schirmer and Stephen Rosskamm Shalom, eds., *The Philippines Reader* (Boston: South End Press, 1987), 227.
86. See Yossi Shain and Mark Thompson, "The Role of Political Exiles in Democratic Transitions: The Case of the Philippines," *Journal of Developing Societies* 6 (January–April 1990): 71–86.
87. Ibid., 80.
88. See Martin Tolchin, "High Profile for South Korean 'Embassy in Exile,' " *New York Times*, October 10, 1986.
89. See Ferdinand E. Marcos, "A Defense of My Tenure," *Orbis* 33 (Winter 1989): 94.
90. See Carlos B. Gil, "Cuauthémoc Cárdenas and the Rise of Transborder

Politics" in *Hopes and Frustration: Interviews with Leaders of Mexico's Political Opposition*, ed. Carlos B. Gil (Wilmington, Del.: Scholarly Resources, 1992), 298.

91. See Myron Weiner, "Asian Politics and US Foreign Policy," in *Immigration and US Foreign Policy*, ed. Robert W. Tucker et al. (Boulder, Colo.: Westview Press, 1990), 207–8.

92. See Antonio J. A. Pido, *The Filipinos in America: Macro/Micro Dimensions of Immigration and Integration* (New York: Center for Migration Studies, 1986), 55–56.

93. See Geremie Barmé, "Traveling Heavy: The Intellectual Baggage of the Chinese Diaspora," *Problems of Communism* 40 (January–April 1991): 98.

94. Lewis J. Edinger, *German Exile Politics: The Social Democratic Executive Committee in the Nazi Era* (Berkeley: University of California Press, 1956), viii.

95. See Lucian W. Pye, *Asian Power and Politics: The Cultural Dimensions of Authority* (Cambridge, Mass.: Belknap Press of Harvard University Press, 1985), 252.

96. See Barmé, "Traveling Heavy," 100.

97. See Madeleine Nash, "From Polonia with Love," *Time*, November 27, 1989, 22–23.

98. Edward Friedman, "The Diaspora and Why Taiwan's Future Matters So" (paper presented at University of California at Berkeley conference on Taiwan, September 28–29, 1996.

99. For an analysis of the growth and impact on U.S. policy toward South Africa of the American antiapartheid movement, see Donald R. Culverson, "The Politics of the Anti-Apartheid Movement in the United States, 1969–1986," *Political Science Quarterly* 111.1 (1996): 127–49.

100. George M. Frederickson, "America's Caste System: Will It Change?" *New York Review of Books*, October 23, 1997, 68.

101. See Randall Robinson, "After Sanctions: Apartheid and the African-American Collegian," *Black Collegian* (September–October 1991): 132–39.

102. Roger Wilkins, "What Africa Means to Blacks," *Foreign Policy* 15 (Summer 1974): 137.

103. Martin Weil, "Can the Blacks Do for Africa What the Jews Did for Israel?" *Foreign Policy* 15 (Summer 1974): 109.

104. Ibid., 127.

105. Ibid., 109.

106. See Peter J. Schraeder, "Speaking with Many Voices: Continuity and Change in U.S. Africa Policies," *Journal of Modern African Studies* 29 (September 1991): 398–406.

107. *Time*, July 2, 1990, 18.

108. Cited in Pauline Baker, "The Sanctions Vote: A G.O.P. Milestone," *New York Times*, August 26, 1986.

109. See *Time*, March 6, 1989, 32; Stephan Thernstrom, "Just Say Afro,"

New Republic, January 23, 1989, 10–12; *U.S. News and World Report*, October 30, 1989, 17; Doris Wilkinson, "Americans of African Identity," *Society* 27 (May–June 1990): 14–18.

110. Cited in *Newsweek*, January 2, 1989, 28.
111. *Time*, July 2, 1990, 16–17.
112. See "A 'Homecoming' for the Mayor," *New York Times*, November 17, 1991.
113. See Jim Hoagland, "Africans Are Now Uniting against Nigeria Tyranny," *International Herald-Tribune*, June 10–11, 1995, 6.
114. Adonis Hoffman, "Nigeria: The Policy Conundrum," *Foreign Policy* 101 (Winter 1995–96): 156.
115. Karen De Witt, "Black Group Begins Protest against Nigeria," *New York Times*, March 17, 1995. A10.
116. Cited in Yossi Shain, "Multicultural Foreign Policy," *Foreign Policy* 100 (Fall 1995): 85.

Chapter 3. Arab-American Identity and New Transnational Challenges

1. Earlier versions of this chapter appeared in *Foreign Policy* 100 (Fall 1995) and the *Journal of Palestine Studies* 26 (Winter 1995).
2. See Alixa Naff, *Becoming American: The Early Arab Immigrant Experience* (Carbondale: Southern Illinois University Press, 1985), 17.
3. See Amy Dockser Marcus, "Burden of Peace: American Jews Grapple with an Identity Crisis as Peril to Israel Ebbs," *Wall Street Journal*, September 14, 1994, 1. Also see Nathan Glazer, "The Jews," in *Ethnic Leadership in America*, ed. John Higham (Baltimore: Johns Hopkins University Press, 1978), 32–33.
4. Barry Rubin, *Assimilation and Its Discontents* (New York: Random House, 1995), 260.
5. See "American Jewish Attitudes towards Israel and the Peace Process," public opinion survey conducted for the American Jewish Committee, New York, by Market Facts, August 7–15 1995 (New York: American Jewish Committee, 1995).
6. In the mid-1980s Edward Said questioned whether an Arab-American culture could ever establish a real presence in the U.S. "[T]here isn't a tradition yet of Arab Americans who write, who are involved in the arts. Second, it's not perceived as particularly important. . . . But the question is, can you make an impression in the face of the dominant culture . . . [which is] in terms of imagination . . . largely Jewish." He further maintained that although an Arab-American mode is developing, it's still in a rudimentary stage. "It's not very strong: it doesn't make much of an impression on the American scene, culturally, politically, economically." Cited in Gregory Orfalea, *Before the Flames: A Quest for the History of Arab-Americans* (Austin: University of Texas Press, 1988), 159–60.

7. See Barbara C. Aswad, "The Lebanese Muslim Community in Dearborn, Michigan," in *The Lebanese in the World: A Century of Emigration*, ed. Albert Hourani and Nadim Shehadi (London: Center for Lebanese Studies and I. B. Tauris, 1992), 177.

8. See Gregory Orfalea, "Sifting The Ashes: Arab-American Activism during the 1982 Invasion of Lebanon," in *Arab-Americans: Continuity and Change*, ed. Baha Abu-Laban and Michael W. Suleiman (Belmont, Mass.: Association of Arab-American University Graduates, 1989), 208.

9. Shibley Telhami, "Arab Public Opinion and the Gulf War," *Political Science Quarterly* 108.3 (Fall 1993): 441.

10. Fawaz Turki, *Exile's Return: The Making of a Palestinian American* (New York: Free Press, 1994), 189.

11. Since the 1980s Muslims sympathetic to Iran's Islamic revolution have held demonstrations in cities across the United States commemorating the "Worldwide Day of al-Quds" on the last Friday of the Holy Month of Ramadan. See " 'The Struggle Is Now Worldwide': Hizballah and Iranian-Sponsored Terrorism," *ADL Special Report* (January 1995): 12–18.

12. See Yvonne Yazbeck Haddad, "American Foreign Policy in the Middle East and Its Impact on the Identity of Arab Muslims in the United States," in *The Muslims of America*, ed. Yvonne Yazbeck Haddad (New York: Oxford University Press, 1991), 227.

13. See Alixa Naff, "Lebanese Immigration into the United States: 1880 to the Present," in Hourani and Shehadi, *The Lebanese in the World*, 164.

14. For an account of these problems in other U.S. ethnic groups, see Glazer, "The Jews," 20. Also see Peter Skerry, *Mexican Americans: The Ambivalent Minority* (New York: Free Press, 1993), 368–69.

15. For these categories, see Alicja Iwańska, *Exiled Government: Spanish and Polish* (Cambridge, Mass.: Schenkman, 1981), 43–44.

16. Arab-American activists have exaggerated numbers as symbols of political strength. To the best of my knowledge there has been no conclusive study of the scope or distribution of the U.S. Arab community. The most common number to be cited by activists and writers is two to three million. Even the number of Palestinians in the United States, by all accounts a small portion and a more politically distinct segment of the Arab-American community, is unknown, and scholars have been talking about "educated guesses" in the 200,000 to 400,000 range. When it comes to political mobilization, leading Arab-American organizers have told me that they could depend on no more than 20,000 occasional members. See David J. Sadd and G. Neal Lendenmann, "Arab American Grievances," *Foreign Policy* 60 (Fall 1985): 19; Kathleen Christison, "The American Experience: Palestinians in the U.S.," *Journal of Palestine Studies* 18.4 (Summer 1989): 18.

17. The vast majority of the Christian Lebanese community is fully "Americanized." Its members have achieved prominence in all walks of life. They include former Senate majority leader George Mitchell, former

governor and White House chief of staff John Sununu, the famous diplomat Philip Habib, former senator James Abourezk, the founder of the ADC, and the recently elected Michigan senator Spence Abraham. One must remember that Lebanese Christians form one of the smallest of groupings in the Middle East.

18. The largest American organization that represents Palestinian localities is the Ramallah Federation, which has more than 20,000 members. The word "Palestine" was added to the federation name in the 1970s. See Christison, "The American Experience," 50–51, 35n29.

19. See Jacqueline S. Ismael and Tareq Y. Ismael, "The Holy Land: The American Experience: III. The Arab Americans and the Middle East," *Middle East Journal* 30.3 (Summer 1976): 402.

20. The early immigration wave of Arab Muslims left the Ottoman Empire at the turn of the twentieth century. In the United States many converted to Christianity to protect themselves in a society that "preached religious equality in public but was intolerant of it in private." See Kemal H. Karpat, "The Ottoman Emigration to America, 1860–1914," *International Journal of Middle East Studies* 17 (1985): 183.

21. Cited in Haddad, "American Foreign Policy in the Middle East," 234n41.

22. See Higham, *Ethnic Leadership in America*, 2.

23. The best review of the works on the rise of Arab-American identity is Theodore Pulcini, "Trend in Research on Arab Americans," *Journal of American Ethnic History* 12.4 (Summer 1993): 27–60. Also see Orfalea, *Before the Flames*, 178.

24. Author's interview with James Zogby, April 11, 1995.

25. Cited in Nabeel A. Khoury, "The Arab Lobby: Problems and Prospects," *Middle East Journal* 41.3 (Summer 1987): 382.

26. Cited in Pulcini, "Trend in Research on Arab-Americans," 42.

27. James Zogby, cofounder of the ADC, told me that even at the height of the war in Lebanon paid membership in the ADC never exceeded seven hundred. Interview, April 11, 1995.

28. Gregory Orfalea, "Sifting the Ashes: Arab-American Activism during the 1982 Invasion of Lebanon," 218, 222.

29. A 1994 study of Arab-Americans reports that "Americans of Arab origin are more educated, younger, and more affluent than the average American." See Samia El-Badry, "The Arab-American Market," *American Demographics* (January 1994): 22–31.

30. On the image of the Arab in the United States, see Michael Suleiman, "Americans' View of Arabs and its Impact on Arab-Americans" (in Arabic), *Al-mustaqbal al-àrabi* 177 (November 1993): 92–107.

31. See Elaine Hagopian, "Minority Rights in a Nation State: The Nixon Administration Campaign against Arab-Americans," *Journal of Palestine Studies* 5.1–2 (1975–76): 102–3.

32. See Jamin B. Raskin, "Remember Korematsu: The Predicament of Arab-Americans," *Nation*, February 4, 1991, 117.

33. Cited in James Brooke, "Amid Islam Growth in the U.S., Muslims Face a Surge in Attacks," *New York Times*, August 28, 1995, 1, B7.
34. See Dick Kirschten, "Shock Waves," *National Journal*, June 5, 1993, 1349–52; James L. Franklin, "Muslims in the US See a Setback," *Boston Globe*, March 5, 1993, 1.
35. See "The Bomb Threat," *New Republic*, March 29, 1993, 9.
36. Most recently Arab-Americans protested the depiction of Arabs in the Disney film *Aladdin* and in Arnold Schwarzenegger's *True Lies*. See *Los Angeles Times*, July 10, 1993, sec. F, p. 1; *Washington Post*, July 22, 1994, 23.
37. See Deborah Sontag, "Muslims in the United States Fear an Upsurge in Hostility," *New York Times*, March 7, 1993, 138.
38. See *Time*, May 1, 1995, 70.
39. Such concerns are typical to other ethnic groups in the United States. See Higham, *Ethnic Leadership in America*, 4.
40. This dependency proved to be damaging in the aftermath of the Gulf War when the Saudis and Kuwaitis pulled the plug on those who were slow to support their position.
41. See Nabeel Abraham, "Arab-American Marginality: Mythos and Praxis," *Arab Studies Quarterly* 11.2–3 (Spring–Summer, 1989): 17–43.
42. Cited in Steven Emerson, "The Other Fundamentalists," *New Republic*, June 12, 1995, 22.
43. Abraham, "Arab-American Marginality," p. 26.
44. See Ronald R. Stockton, "Arabs in America," in *Connections: Faculty Voices*, ed. Ted-Larry Pebworth and Claude Summers (Dearborn: University of Michigan, 1993), 41.
45. Ismael and Ismael, "The Holyland: The American Experience," 404.
46. Abdeen M. Jabara, "A Strategy of Political Effectiveness," in Abu-Laban and Suleiman, *Arab Americans*, 201–2.
47. See Hagopian, "Minority Rights in the Nation-State," 112–13.
48. See Lewis Young, "American Blacks and the Arab-Israeli Conflict," *Journal of Palestine Studies* 2.1 (Autumn 1972):70–85; Robert G. Newby, "Afro-Americans and Arabs: An Alliance in the Making," *Journal of Palestine Studies* 10.2 (Winter 1981): 50–58; Jake Miller, "Black Viewpoints on the Middle East Conflict," *Journal of Palestine Studies* 10.2 (Winter 1981): 41–42.
49. See Ismael and Ismael, "The Holyland: The American Experience," 396; also see Jeffrey Michels, "National Vision and the Negotiation of Narratives: The Oslo Agreement," *Journal of Palestine Studies* 24.1 (Autumn 1994): 28.
50. Turki, *Exile's Return*, 196.
51. Ibid., 196–200.
52. Ibid., 193.
53. Lewis A. Coser, *Refugee Scholars in America: Their Impact and Their Experiences* (New Haven: Yale University Press, 1984), 12.

54. Yet the image of Palestinians benefited mostly from the position taken by Israeli liberals and writers, like Amos Oz and David Grossman, who were most effective in bringing to the Palestinian cause its human face. They also drew the sympathy of the American public to the other face of Zionism. Fawaz Turki expressed his irritation with "the sweetness of Israeli intellectuals who . . . have only succeeded in robbing us of our right to be totally angry." See Turki, *Exile's Return*, 226.
55. Cited in Michels, "National Vision and the Negotiation of Narratives," 35.
56. See Orfalea, *Before the Flames*, 163.
57. For an extensive interview with Hisham Sharabi, see Judith Colp Rubin, "A Closer Look," *Jerusalem Post Magazine*, December 31, 1993, 10, 12–13.
58. He said, "Rejection of the agreement may appear to some the proof of ideological purity, to others it may be psychologically the most satisfying decision to take. But it is a Quixotic position at best and could be regarded as callous when the majority of the Palestinians who have carried the burden of struggle over these years have chosen to take the risk of the fait accompli." See Sharabi's address to the AAUG's annual convention, October 22–24, 1993. Cited in *AAUG Mideast Monitor* 9.1 (Winter 1994): 8.
59. Interview, with Hisham Sharabi, Washington, D.C., February 10, 1994.
60. Ibid.
61. Interview, with Hisham Sharabi, Washington, D.C., April 12, 1995. Also see proceedings of the conference on the Palestine National Authority: A Critical Appraisal, Center for Policy Analysis on Palestine, Washington, D.C., March 17, 1995.
62. On March 27, 1988, Said and Lughod met with then secretary of state George Schultz and were subsequently criticized by some members of the Palestine National Council.
63. See "Symbols versus Substance: A Year after the Declaration of Principles: An Interview with Edward W. Said," *Journal of Palestine Studies* 24.2 (Winter 1995): 64.
64. See Diana Jean Schemo, "America's Scholarly Palestinian Raises Volume against Arafat," *New York Times*, March 4, 1994. Also see Said's address to the AAUG's 26th Annual Convention, *AAUG Mideast Monitor* 9.1 (Winter 1994): 9–10. Said later preached that the role of intellectuals is to "approach everything with a critical stance, . . . to embrace positions on the margins of society, in isolation, and [never to] seek popularity . . . [or] be affiliated with any religion, organization or ideology." From Said's address at the Beirut Theater on December 27, 1994. Cited in "Said Revels in Outside Role," *Jerusalem Times*, January 6, 1995, 12.
65. AAUG's annual convention in October 1993 focused on the subject of democracy and human rights in the Arab world. AAUG's Second Inter-

national Conference, which was held in Amman, Jordan, in July 1994, denounced the submission of women throughout the Arab world. See AAUG *Newsletter* 25.1 (March 1994) and 25.2 (November 1994).

66. See Rashid Khalidi, *Under Siege: P.L.O. Decisionmaking during the 1982 War* (New York: Columbia University Press, 1986).

67. For an extensive interview with Khalidi, see *Ha'aretz* (Hebrew edition), December 10, 1993. For similar views see Elia Zureik, "What State Palestine?" *Dissent* (Winter 1994): 23–26.

68. See Dominique Schnapper, "Muslim Communities, Ethnic Minorities, and Citizens," in *Muslims in Europe*, ed. Bernard Lewis and Dominique Schnapper (London: Pinter, 1994), 149.

69. Most Muslims in the United States are African-Americans and South Asian immigrants from non-Arab Islamic countries. According to the American Muslim Council, in 1992 Arab Muslims comprised 12.4 percent of the U.S. Muslim population which was estimated at four to six million adherents. See Mary H. Cooper, "Muslims in America," *Congressional Quarterly*, April 30, 1993, 364, 369.

70. See Abdulaziz A. Sachedina, "A Minority within a Minority: The Case of the Shi'a in North America," in *Muslim Communities in North America*, ed. Yvonne Yazbeck Haddad and Jane Idleman Smith (Albany: State University of New York Press, 1994), 3–14.

71. See Ron Kelley, "Muslims in Los Angeles," in Haddad and Smith, *Muslim Communities in North America*, 145.

72. Haddad, "American Foreign Policy in the Middle East," 228–29. Haddad estimates that "only 5 to 10 percent of Muslims in America consider themselves to be religious." Cited in Cooper, "Muslims in America," 369.

73. Steve A. Johnson, "Political Activity of Muslims in America," in Haddad, *The Muslims of America*, 114.

74. See Cooper, "Muslims in America," 364.

75. The proliferation of small mosques and the countless splitting of Muslims is quite extraordinary in the heavily Shi'a community in Dearborn. A student of the Muslims in Los Angeles has written recently that "Despite predictions that Muslims will soon be the second largest religious community in the United States, they have been unable to unite as an effective lobbying force, relative to their large numbers. Often compared to American Jewish organizations, Muslims, as a political force, are comparatively invisible." See Kelly, "Muslims in Los Angeles," 144.

76. See John L. Esposito, *The Islamic Threat: Myth and Reality* (New York: Oxford University Press, 1993), 29.

77. See Oliver Roy, *The Failure of Political Islam*, trans. Carol Volk (London: I. B. Tauris, 1994), 39.

78. See Bernard Lewis, *The Political Language of Islam* (Chicago: University of Chicago Press, 1988), 106.

79. See Bernard Lewis, "Legal and Historical Reflections on the Positions

of Muslim Populations under Non-Muslim Rule," in Lewis and Schnapper, *Muslims in Europe*, 17.

80. See John Voll, "Islamic Issues for Muslims in the United States," in Haddad, *The Muslims of America*, 209.

81. Lewis, "Legal and Historical Reflections," 9.

82. See Roy, *The Failure of Political Islam*, 3; also see Voll, "Islamic Issues," 211.

83. Cited in Johnson, "Political Activity of Muslims in America," 114.

84. In an interview with Mary Anne Weaver, Sheikh Omar Abdel-Rahman alluded to this problem: "In Islam, we're permitted to take more than one wife – we can be polygamous. But American law prohibits this, and therefore we're punished, and prevented from practicing our own laws here." See "The Trail of the Sheikh," *New Yorker*, April 12, 1994, 88.

85. See Oliver Roy, "Islam in France: Religion, Ethnic Community or Social Ghetto?" in Lewis and Schnapper, *Muslims in Europe*, 58; also see Roy, *The Failure of Political Islam*, 13.

86. See Tamara Sonn, "Arab Americans in Education: Cultural Ambassadors?" in Abu-Laban and Suleiman, *Arab Americans*, 130–31.

87. See John L. Esposito, "Ismail R. Al-Faruqi: Muslim Scholar-Activist," in Haddad, *The Muslims of America*, 65–79.

88. For a similar analysis, see Roy, "Islam in France," 61.

89. Johnson, "Political Activity of Muslims in America," 112 (emphasis added).

90. Ibid., 112–113.

91. This point was stressed to me by Ismael Ahmed, executive director of the Arab Community Center for Economic and Social Services (AC-CESS) in Dearborn, and by Osama Siblani, publisher and editor in chief of the *Arab American News* (Dearborn). Author's Interviews, Dearborn, Mich., April 7 and 8, 1995 (respectively).

92. Metropolitan Detroit is considered to have the largest Middle Eastern community in the United States, with about 250,000 members. About half of them are Lebanese-Syrian Christians, 40,000 are Iraqi Chaldeans (many of them are reluctant to identify themselves as Arabs), 30,000 of Palestinian ancestry, and about 12,000 are Yemeni. The rest are Lebanese Shi'a, Jordanians, Egyptians, and people from other Arab countries. The community has many Arab clubs and centers and numerous churches and mosques. These numbers are estimates. See Thomas Gorguissian, "Detroit: Largest Arab Community Abroad" (in Arabic), *Al-Majal*, no. 271 (October 1993); Stockton, "Arabs in America," 39; Mary C. Sengstock, "Detroit's Iraqi-Chaldeans: A Conflicting Conception of Identity," in *Arabs in the New World: Studies on Arab American Communities*, ed. Sameer Y. Abraham and Nabeel Abraham (Detroit: Wayne State University Press, 1983), 136–44; "Metro Detroit's Middle Eastern Community," flyer adopted from *Detroit News*.

93. See Aswad, "The Lebanese Muslim Community in Dearborn, Michigan," 176–77.

94. See Emerson, "The Other Fundamentalists," 22; James Brooke and Elaine Sciolino, "U.S. Muslims Say Their Aid Pays for Charity, Not Terror," *New York Times*, August 16, 1995.
95. See Linda S. Walbridge, "The Shi'a Mosques and Their Congregations in Dearborn," in Haddad and Smith, *Muslim Communities in North America*, 337–57.
96. See Weaver, "The Trail of the Sheik," 71–89.
97. See Michael C. Dunn, "Islamic Activists in the West: A New Issue Produces Backlash," *Middle East Policy* 3.1 (1994): 140.
98. Martin Kramer, "Islam and the West (including Manhattan)," *Commentary* (October 1993): 35.
99. See "Jihad in America," a transcript of Emerson's PBS television report (SAE Productions, November 21, 1994). Ali A. Mazrui claims that Emerson has "a long record of hostility towards US Muslims," and calls him a "self-appointed crusader from the past." However, he does not challenge any of the claims made in Emerson's report. Mazrui, "Between the Crescent and the Star-Spangled Banner: American Muslims and US Foreign Policy," *International Affairs* 72.3 (1996): 499.
100. See *USA Today*, October 26, 1994, 4.
101. George Spectre, associate director of the Center of Public Policy of B'nai B'rith International, said that the alliance between American Jews and Arabs on the issue of Bosnia is unprecedented and yielded "a side benefit by helping both sides maintain a dialogue on the Middle East peace process." See *Times Union* (Albany, N.Y.), August 6, 1995, 10.
102. Cited in Cooper, "Muslims in America," 365, 378.
103. Cited in Afshin Molavi, "Alamoudi Critical of U.S. Approach to Muslim World," *Arab News*, February 8, 1995, 11. AMC's assistant executive director, Khaled Saffuri, told me that the AMC is highly involved in Arab-American affairs. Saffuri, a Palestinian-American, was the executive director of the American Task Force for Bosnia, a coalition of various American groups, including mainstream Jewish-American organizations, that advocated the lifting of the arms embargo against Bosnia. Saffuri also intimated that the AMC actively supports the Islamic opposition in Algeria. Interview, April 10, 1995. Also see the *AMC Report* 4.7 (Fall 1994): 1.
104. Helen Hatab Samhan, "Politics and Exclusion: The Arab American Experience," *Journal of Palestine Studies* 16.2 (Winter 1987): 16.
105. Ibid., 27.
106. See Naff, "Lebanese Immigration into the United States," 164.
107. Although Arab-American groups protested the "abusive" use of money by the pro-Israel lobby in pressuring Congress, they deliberately established themselves in the image of parallel Jewish organizations. In a 1982 interview with the *Wall Street Journal*, James Zogby, then a codirector of the ADC said: "We are operating in the same manner as the Jewish Anti-Defamation League when it first started." Cited in Ray Vicker, "U.S. Arabs, Adopting Tactics of Jewish Groups, Organize to

Aid Image, Exert Political Pressure," *Wall Street Journal*, July 29, 1982, 40. Also see Andrea Barron, "Jewish and Arab Diasporas in the United States and Their Impact on U.S. Middle East Foreign Policy," in *The Arab-Israeli Conflict: Two Decades of Change*, ed. Yehuda Lukas and Abdalla Battah (Boulder, Col.: Westview Press, 1988), 249.

108. Hagopian, "Minority Rights in the Nation State," 111.

109. See Sadd and Lendenmann, "Arab American Grievances," 29.

110. For an elaborate analysis of the NAAA, see Mitchell Geoffrey Bard, *The Water's Edge and Beyond: Defining the Limits to Domestic Influence on United States Middle East Policy* (New Brunswick, N.J.: Transaction, 1991), 14–18.

111. See Michael Lewis, "Israel's Critics: Trying to Adjust to New Realities," *Near East Report*, November 15, 1993, 204.

112. Kay Siblani wrote that "in the context of Arab world politics [ADC's] sympathies all lie with the Syrian Social Nationalist Party." See "As ADC Meets, It Stands at Crossroads," *Arab American News*, May 4–10, 1991, 1.

113. Cited in Helen Hatab Samhan, "Arab Americans and the Elections of 1988: A Constituency Comes of Age," *Arab Studies Quarterly* 11 (Spring–Summer 1989): 243.

114. See "The Anti-Israel Lobby Today: An Examination of the Themes and Tactics of an Evolving Propaganda Movement," *ADL Research Report* (1991): 13.

115. Philip Mattar, "The PLO and the Gulf Crisis," *Middle East Journal* 48.1 (Winter 1994): 31.

116. See "The Perils of Hyphenation," *Economist*, January 25, 1991, 24–25. Also see Nabeel Abraham, "The Gulf Crisis and Anti-Arab Racism in America," in *Collateral Damage: The New World Order at Home and Abroad*, ed. Cynthia Peters (Boston: South End Press, 1992), 225–278.

117. See Jose Miguel Sandoval and Mark Stephen Jendrysik, "Convergence and Divergence in Arab-American Public Opinion," *International Journal of Public Opinion Research* 5.4 (Winter 1993): 310–11.

118. Cited in Felicity Barringer, "With Loyalty Split, Arab-Americans Fault Hussein, but Question U.S. Too," *New York Times*, August 16, 1990, 16.

119. See Siblani, "As ADC Meets, It Stands at Crossroads," 1.

120. Ibid.

121. Ibid.

122. Mattar, "The PLO and the Gulf Crisis," 45.

123. See Rosalind Mandine, "Arab Americans Care about Racial Intolerance, Urban Issues," *USIA*, May 20, 1992.

124. See Robert Greenberger, "Levine and Zogby, Odd Couple on the Mideast, Seek Common Ground for Economic Development," *Wall Street Journal*, February 2, 1994, 2.

125. A New York–born Lebanese-American, Zogby described his own conversion to the Arab-American cause as a case of baptism by fire.

According to his account he was an assimilated college student who didn't reflect much on his ancestral roots until he was beaten by members of the Jewish Defense League in 1967. Seeing that his Arabic name was a liability, he maintained, he immersed himself in diaspora activity. See Vicker, "U.S. Arabs Adopting Tactics of Jewish Groups," 40.

126. When I brought up Zogby's name in an interview with ADC's former president, Albert Mokhiber (February 9, 1994), he dismissed him as a political opportunist who had nothing to do with the ADC. During my visit to Washington, D.C., in February 1994, I came across pamphlets that ridiculed Zogby's so-called opportunism and self-promotion.

127. See Christopher Madison, "Arab-American Lobby Fights Rearguard Battle to Influence U.S. Mideast Policy," *National Journal*, August 31, 1985, p. 1936.

128. Samhan, "Arab Americans and the Elections of 1988," 229.

129. Cited in Barron, "Jewish and Arab Diasporas in the United States," 252 n 66.

130. See Madison, "Arab-American Lobby," 1937.

131. See Samhan, "Politics and Exclusion," 27. Samhan's contention that "anti-Arab racism" radiates primarily from the Arab-Israeli conflict was challenged by Nabeel Abraham. He argued that the racism and violence affecting Arab-Americans, Muslims, and Middle Easterners in the United States are chiefly the result "of a volatile mixture of [American] jingoism combined with domestic racism." See Nabeel Abraham, "Anti-Arab Racism and Violence in the United States," in *The Development of Arab-American Identity*, ed. Ernest McCarus (Ann Arbor, University of Michigan Press, 1994), 179–80, 207.

132. Author's interview with Helen Hatab Samham, Washington, D.C., February 9, 1994.

133. See Barron, "Jewish and Arab Diasporas in the United States and Their Impact on U.S. Middle East Policy," 253.

134. Madison, "Arab-American Lobby," 1939. Zogby's campaign against the influence of "pro-Israeli money" won him the attention of Israel. See *Ha'aretz* (Hebrew edition), October 12, 1990.

135. See AAI's pamphlet "An Open Letter to American Jews," originally published in the *Jewish News* (Detroit), October 28, 1988.

136. See AAI's publication *The Arab American Agenda for the 1990s*, principal author Jean Abi Nader, September 18, 1993.

137. Samhan, "Politics of Exclusion," 22.

138. David Broder's article appeared in the *Washington Post*, December 13, 1992. The quotations are taken from James Zogby, "Arab American in the Clinton Administration," *Arab News*, December 21, 1992.

139. Ibid.

140. Zogby was quoted in the *Washington Post* as saying that overall, the Clinton Middle East team "is very good . . . and balanced" and condoned the selection. According to Zogby, Indyk, also a former director

of research for AIPAC, and Lewis, were "pragmatic problem solvers" who should not be dismissed by the Arab press automatically. They might, in fact, help to "move things forward and develop trust" in the peace process. See *Washington Post*, January 21, 1993.

141. Ghassan Bishara, "Pro-Israel Appointments Damage U.S. Credibility," *Al-Fajr*, February 1, 1993, 7.

142. Cited in Ghassan Bishara, "Arab Americans Sorry for Electing Clinton," *Al-Fajr*, February 8, 1993, 7–8.

143. See James Zogby, "Zogby: Face the Facts, Indyk Is In," *Al-Fajr*, March 22, 1993, 8–9, 15.

144. Ibid., 9.

145. See *An Arab American Domestic Agenda for the 1990s*.

146. Cited in Jane Friedman, "US Jews, Arabs Now find Some Common Ground," *Christian Science Monitor*, October 19, 1993, 2.

147. The initiative for "Builders for Peace" was advanced by President Clinton, who hosted Jewish and Arab-American leaders on the day the Declaration of Principles was signed (*New York Times*, September 14, 1993). On November 30, 1993, Vice-President Al Gore unveiled the enterprise. James Zogby and former congressman Mel Levine, an Arab and a Jew, were chosen copresidents. The stated aims of Builders for Peace are to "organize business leaders, especially those in the Arab American and American Jewish communities, to promote investment in the West Bank and Gaza. . . . The guiding rationale is that successful projects will demonstrate the benefits of the peace accord to both Palestinians and Israelis." The organization intended to "involve Arab Americans and American Jews to lend their experience in joint projects that will promote understanding, cooperation, and economic development. Not only will this promote prosperity and peace in the Middle East, this initiative will improve relations between these groups in the United States." See "Builders for Peace: Mission to the Middle East" (January 1994) (document available from the author upon request).

148. See Edward Said's address at the ADC's 11th National Convention, April 14–17, 1994. Cited in *ADC Times* 15.4 (May 1994): 11. After the Republican Party won the 1994 Congressional elections, Edward Said castigated Zogby for misinforming the Arab public about Clinton's declining power. He accused him of writing as a "presidential publicist." See Edward Said, "Changes for the Worse," *Al-Ahram*, November 24–30, 1994, 11.

149. When I interviewed Mokhiber he was concerned about Israel's conspiracy "to dominate the Arab economy." When I asked about his reluctance to support the Declaration of Principles, he replied: "Peace talks are not the main business of the ADC." Besides, "what is the big deal [of the accords] for refugees from Haifa?" Interview, Washington, D.C., February 9, 1994.

150. Arafat wrote a letter to Zogby and Levine praising them for their

efforts on behalf of the Palestinians in the territories. A copy of the letter is in the author's possession.

151. Author's interview with Albert Mokhiber, Washington, D.C., February 9, 1994.
152. Ibid.
153. See Richard Perez-Pena, "Demonstration and Protest; Arab, Jews," *New York Times*, March 7, 1996; Lisa Anderson, "As Peace Nears, the Spirit of Kahane Rears," *Chicago Tribune*, March 6, 1994.
154. See Melita Marie Garza, "A Fragile Link to West Bank, Gaza," *Chicago Tribune*, October 16, 1994, sec. 7, p. 4.
155. In the spring of 1995 the NAAA was considering a plan to redirect its energies toward Arab-American domestic affairs. Jahshan maintains that "The Arab governments have a simplistic and even racist view toward Arab-Americans." We have lost our role "at a time when Israeli Prime Minister Rabin is lobbying in Washington for economic assistance to Arafat and when Arab governments are appealing directly to Congress." Author's interview, Washington, D.C., April 10, 1995.
156. Author's interview with Osama Siblani, Dearborn, Mich., April 8, 1995.
157. Author's interview with Kay Siblani, Dearborn, Mich., April 8, 1995.
158. See *AAUG Mideast Monitor* 9.1 (Winter 1994): 1–2.
159. See *AAUG Newsletter* 26.1 (March 1995).
160. See "Symbols versus Substance: A Year after the Declaration of Principles: An Interview with Said," *Journal of Palestine Studies* 24.2 (Winter 1995): 70.
161. Cited in *ADC Times* 15.4 (May 1994): 12.
162. Most of the Arab-American board members of Builders for Peace are of Palestinian origin. Also see "Palestinian-American Brings Harvard Home," *Jerusalem Times*, May 26, 1995.
163. Cited in Garza, "A Fragile Link to West Bank and Gaza," sec. 7, p. 4.
164. See *Ha'aretz*, November 11, 1991.
165. See *USFI*, March 31, 1993.
166. *AAI Issues* (January–February 1994): 1.
167. See Yossi Shain, "Multicultural Foreign Policy," *Foreign Policy* 100 (Fall 1995): 87.
168. See AAI publication.
169. James Zogby, "One State's View of Arab Concerns," *Arab News*, February 20, 1995, 11.
170. Author's interview with James Zogby, Washington, D.C., April 11, 1995.
171. Author's interview with Khalil Jashan, Washington, D.C., April 10, 1995.
172. A column for *Al-Bostaan*, April 1, 1995, appeared on March 22 on PNet RAYHANANIA <pnet.listbanumusa.csl.uiuc.ed>. Also see "Lightner's Departure from ADC," *Arab American News*, March 25–31, 1994, 5.

173. Michael Lewis, "Israel's American Detractors – Back Again," *Middle East Quarterly* 4.4 (December 1997): 25–33. Lewis is director of policy analysis for the American Israel Public Affairs Committee.
174. Ray Hanania, Letter to the Editor, *New York Times*, March 10, 1996.
175. "Summit in Egypt: Appeals against Terrorism, Jointly and Individually by Former Adversaries,"*New York Times*, March 14, 1996.
176. Lewis, "Israel's American Detractors," 31.
177. Zogby has come under fire from Muslim-American and Arab-American critics who accuse him of seeking Jewish and governmental approval while turning his back on the community he purports to represent. The internet publication "Middle East Realities" headlined a 1996 quote of an American rabbi praising Zogby with the words "Just Call Me 'Uncle Jim.' " It goes on to claim that "Zogby has gained notoriety and wealth cooperating with the Zionist community throughout the years of the Intifada" (www.mideast.org/Zogby 1.html).
178. Muslim-American Advocacy Groups such as CAIR have lobbied government officials, religious leaders of other faiths, and other prominent U.S. groups and individuals on matters as diverse as housing discrimination, racial slurs (in one case, by televangelist Pat Robertson), the right of Muslim girls to wear veils at schools, and so on. "One Muslim worker . . . was recently awarded almost $3 million for discrimination in the workplace" (see CAIR website at www.cair-net.org). In another instance cited by CAIR, the organization's intervention led to a number of remedial measures at a Virginia school and an apology from a teacher who told a female Muslim student to "get your religious, upright, veil-wearing behind to class."
179. In addition to lobbying on broader policy questions such as U.S. relations with Israel and other Middle East nations, Muslim activists have mobilized on behalf of individuals arrested in the United States and/or being threatened with deportation. Among these individuals was Hamas leader Musa Abu Marzuq, who directed and channeled funds to operatives to carry out terrorist acts against Israelis at least as late as 1993. "At the time of his arrest, [he] was a permanent resident alien of the United States" (Anti-Defamation League Report, "Terror for a 'Noble' Cause: The Case against Hamas Leader Musa Abu Marzuq," n.d.). Marzuq was later deported to Jordan, rather than Israel, which had originally requested his extradition.
180. White House, Office of the Press Secretary, www.pub.whitehouse.gov/ uri-res/I2R?urn:pdi://oma.eop.gov.us/1998/5/12/8.text.

Chapter 4. Transnational Influences on Ethnoracial Relations in the United States: The Case of Black-Jewish Disputes

1. Samuel P. Huntington, "The Erosion of American National Interests," *Foreign Affairs* 76.5 (September–October 1997):32.

2. The enmity between members of the two communities reached violent extremes during the riots that shook the Brooklyn neighborhood of Crown Heights in August 1991.

3. Among the many writings on this subject, see Jonathan Kaufman, *Broken Alliance: The Turbulent Times between Blacks and Jews in America* (New York: Scribner's, 1988); Murray Friedman, *What Went Wrong: The Creation and Collapse of the Black-Jewish Alliance* (New York: Free Press, 1995).

4. Friedman, *What Went Wrong*, 351.

5. Nathan Glazer, who was one of the leading Jewish intellectual voices in opposition to affirmative action in its first years, has revisited his own opposition in his latest book, *We Are All Multiculturalists Now* (Cambridge, Mass.: Harvard University Press, 1997), 151–52. For his earlier view, see *Affirmative Discrimination: Ethnic Inequality and Public Policy* (New York: Basic Books, 1975).

6. Letty Cottin Progrebin, "Blacks and Jews: Different Kinds of Survival," *Nation*, September 23, 1991, 332–36. Indeed, some "aspirants to power in the largely Black inner cities continue to find the increasingly distant image of Jews a useful target for expressing the rage of the young and the poor and for gaining attention"; Milton D. Morris and Gary E. Rubin, "The Turbulent Friendship: Black-Jewish Relations in the 1990s." *Annals of the American Academy* 530 (November 1993): 46. Black anti-Semitism is most noticeable in the oratory of Louis Farrakhan and his disciples in the Nation of Islam, and in the claims made by Afrocentrists who have fabricated history to make Jews responsible for blacks' misfortune in America, including charges of Jewish responsibility for the slave trade; Marc Caplan, *Jew-Hatred as History: The Nation of Islam's "Secret Relationship between Blacks and Jews"* (New York: Anti-Defamation League, 1993). According to a 1994 Time/CNN poll, 63 percent of African-Americans surveyed agreed that Farrakhan "speaks the truth." Only 34 percent characterize him as "a bigot and a racist." (*Time*, February 28, 1994, 22; *Commentary*, April 1994, 21). See David Brion Davis, "The Slave Trade and the Jews," *New York Review of Books*, December 22, 1994, 14–16.

7. Earl Ofari Hutchinson, "Who Will Win the Battle for the Soul of a Divided Black America?" *Chicago Tribune*, March 18, 1994; Martin Kilson, "Paradoxes of Black Leadership," *Dissent* (Summer 1995): 368–72. In the 1960s black "radicals" and "moderates" – terms referring to the groups' position during the civil rights struggle – were divided between supporters of Israel and supporters of the Arabs. The spectrum of responses among moderate groups, which supported Israel – such as the NAACP, the Urban League, and the Southern Christian Leadership Conference (SCLC) – ranged from genuine commitment to calculated support in order to retain the Jewish alliance; Lewis Young, "American Blacks and the Arab-Israeli Conflict," *Journal of Palestine Studies* 2.1 (Autumn 1972): 70–85. In the late 1970s and 1980s mainstream black leaders were split over fraternization with the Palestine Liberation Organization (PLO). In recent years, when many wonder who should speak for black

America, the Jewish–black acrimony has pervaded the intrablack debate (Hutchinson, "Who Will Win"). In February 1994, the forty members of the CBC severed their ties with Farrakhan and the Nation of Islam in reaction to their anti-Semitic demagoguery; *New York Times*, March 2, 1994, A14.

8. Israel Elman, "The Relations between Jews and Other Ethnic Groups in the United States" (in Hebrew), *Gesher: Journal of Jewish Affairs* 40.129 (1994): 40.

9. Alexander DeConde, *Ethnicity, Race and American Foreign Policy: A History* (Boston: Northeastern University Press, 1992); Yossi Shain, "Ethnic Diasporas and U.S. Foreign Policy," *Political Science Quarterly* 109.5 (Winter 1994–95): 811–41. See Chapter 5 regarding the evolving Mexican-American–Mexican relationship, and the desire to have Mexicans in the United States become "like the Jewish lobby in the US for Israel" (Dianna Solis, "US Hispanics Flex Political Muscles as Mexico Lobbies for NAFTA Support," *Wall Street Journal*, March 3, 1993, 10).

10. Nathan Glazer, "The Jews," in *Ethnic Leadership in America*, ed. John Higham (Baltimore: Johns Hopkins University Press, 1978), 33.

11. See, for example, Mitchell Geoffrey Bard, *The Water's Edge and Beyond: Defining the Limits to Domestic Influence on United States Middle East Policy* (New Brunswick, N.J.: Transaction, 1991).

12. Raphael Israeli, "From Commitment to Zionism," *Forum: On the Jewish People, Zionism and Israel* 62 (Winter–Spring 1989): 51–59.

13. Kenneth Longmyer, "Black American Demands," *Foreign Policy* 60 (Winter 1985):7.

14. Yekutiel Gershoni, *Africans on African-Americans: The Creation and Uses of an African-American Myth* (New York: New York University Press, 1997), 7.

15. Ibid., 19.

16. Ibid., 30.

17. Ibid., 23.

18. See Alfred O. Hero Jr., "American Negroes and U.S. Foreign Policy: 1937–1967," *Journal of Conflict Resolution* 13.2 (June 1969): 222–23.

19. Kitty O. Cohen, "Black-Jewish Relations in 1984: A Survey of Black US Congressmen," *Patterns of Prejudice* 19.2 (1985): 12.

20. Elliott P. Skinner, *African Americans and US Policy toward Africa, 1850–1924* (Washington, D.C.: Howard University Press, 1992), 10.

21. Martin Kilson, "African Americans and Africa: A Critical Nexus," *Dissent* (Summer 1992): 361.

22. Yvonne D. Newsome, "International Issues and Domestic Ethnic Relations: African Americans, American Jews and the Israel–South Africa Debate," *International Journal of Politics, Culture, and Society* 5.1 (1991): 42.

23. Skinner, *African Americans and US Policy toward Africa*, 12.

24. Bernard M. Magubane, *The Ties That Bind: African-American Consciousness of Africa* (Trenton, N.J.: Africa World Press, 1987), 72–77.

25. Skinner, *African Americans and US Policy toward Africa*, 12; Lawrence H. Fuchs, *The American Kaleidoscope: Race, Ethnicity, and the Civic Culture* (Hanover, N. H.: University Press of New England, 1990), 179.
26. Glazer, *We Are All Muliticulturalists Now*.
27. Gunnar Myrdal, *An American Dilemma: The Negro Problem and Modern Democracy* (New York: Harper and Brothers, 1944), 28–29.
28. Fuchs, *The American Kaleidoscope*, 175.
29. DeConde, *Ethnicity, Race and American Foreign Policy*, 130–31.
30. Jake C. Miller, "Black Viewpoints on the Mid-East Conflict," *Journal of Palestine Studies* 10.2 (Winter 1981): 38; Friedman, *What Went Wrong*, 4.
31. J. J. Goldberg, "Gestures of Friendship," *Jerusalem Report*, March 11, 1993, 23–32. In fact, Jews accounted for the majority of white volunteers who went south during the freedom summer of 1964 and Jewish contributions totaled more than half of the money raised by the civil rights organizers. See Ronald Takaki, ed., *From Different Shores: Perspectives on Race and Ethnicity in America*, 2nd ed. (Oxford: Oxford University Press, 1994); Paul Berman, "The Other and Almost the Same," *New Yorker*, February 28, 1994, 61–71; Leslie W. Dunbar, "Blacks and Jews: On the Margins of Captivity," *Social Policy* 11.1 (May–June 1980): 54–58.
32. Irving Howe, "A Fear beyond Escaping," in *Bridges and Boundaries: African Americans and American Jews*, ed. Jack Salzman et al. (New York: George Braziller and the Jewish Museum, 1992), 72.
33. Longmyer, "Black American Demands," 8.
34. Herbert H. Haines, *Black Radicals and the Civil Rights Mainstream, 1954–1970* (Knoxville: University of Tennessee Press, 1988), 57–59.
35. Berman, "The Other and Almost the Same," 66.
36. Michael Feher, "The Schisms of '67: On Certain Restructurings of the American Left, from the Civil Rights Movement to the Multiculturalist Constellation," in *Blacks and Jews: Alliances and Arguments*, ed. Paul Berman (New York: Delacorte Press, 1994), 278. The idea behind black separatism was, in the words of black poet Imamu Baraka (formerly Leroi Jones), that "Western culture is and has been destructive to Black people all over the world. No movement shaped or contained by Western culture will ever benefit Black people." Cited in John T. McCartney, *Black Power Ideologies: An Essay in African-American Political Thought* (Philadelphia: Temple University Press, 1992), 171. Stokely Carmichael, a leading activist of the Student Nonviolent Coordinating Committee (SNCC), announced, "We don't need white liberals. We have to make integration irrelevant." Cited in Haines, *Black Radicals and the Civil Rights Mainstream*, 62.
37. Taylor Branch, "Blacks and Jews: The Uncivil War," in Salzman et al., eds., *Bridges and Boundaries*, 56; Kaufman, *Broken Alliance*, 200–2.
38. Kaufman, *Broken Alliance*, 208.
39. Alan M. Dershowitz, *Chutzpah* (New York: Simon and Schuster, 1991), 80.

40. Kaufman, *Broken Alliance*, 202.
41. Max Beloff, "The Diaspora and the Peace Process," *Israel Affairs* 1.1 (Autumn 1994): 33.
42. Peter J. Schraeder, "Speaking with Many Voices: Continuity and Change in U.S. Africa Policies," *Journal of Modern Africa Studies* 29 (September 1991): 406.
43. Young, "American Blacks and the Arab-Israeli Conflict." Even before the 1967 war, Malcolm X, who was assassinated in 1965, already depicted American support for Israel as a larger ploy to exploit blacks inside the United States: "In America the Jews sap the very life-blood of the so-called Negroes to maintain the state of Israel, its armies and its continued aggression against our brothers in the East." Cited in Miller, "Black Viewpoints on the Mid-East Conflict," 41.
44. In the early 1970s a movement of young Israeli Sephardic Jews (of North African and Middle Eastern origin) shook the Israeli establishment with its unconventional protest against the poverty and deprivation of oriental Jews. They adopted the name the Black Panthers (as a reference to the American group) for dramatic effect, emphasizing that "[we] will be like the [American] Black Panthers in the sense of being militant and frightening the establishment." Although they did not represent the majority of Sephardic Jews and were not able to mobilize the downtrodden, they were effective in raising their issues to the top of the Israeli political agenda; Deborah Bernstein, "Conflict and Protest in Israeli Society: The Case of the Black Panthers of Israel," *Youth and Society* 16.2 (December 1984): 129–52.
45. Berman, "The Other and Almost the Same," 68.
46. Cited in Takaki, *From Different Shores*, 408.
47. Dershowitz, *Chutzpah*, 82.
48. Kaufman, *Broken Alliance*, 208–10; Takaki, *From Different Shores*, 408–73.
49. Dershowitz, *Chutzpah*, 224.
50. Friedman, *What Went Wrong*, 2.
51. Adolph L. Reed Jr., *The Jesse Jackson Phenomenon: The Crisis of Purpose in Afro-American Politics* (New Haven: Yale University Press, 1986), 94, 97.
52. Kaufman, *Broken Alliance*, 220.
53. Lenni Brenner, "The Misguided Search for Black/Jewish Unity," *Freedomways* 24.2 (1984), 119–20.
54. David T. Canon, "Redistricting and the Congressional Black Caucus," *American Politics Quarterly* 23.2 (April 1995): 159–89.
55. Nathan Irvin Huggins, "Afro-Americans," in *Ethnic Leadership in America*, ed. John Higham (Baltimore: Johns Hopkins University Press, 1978), 114.
56. Donald R. Culverson, "The Politics of the Anti-Apartheid Movement in the United States, 1969–1986," *Political Science Quarterly* 111.1 (1996): 134–35.

57. Martin Weil, "Can the Blacks Do for Africa What the Jews Did for Israel?" *Foreign Policy* 15 (Summer 1974): 109.
58. Kilson, "African Americans and Africa," 368.
59. As early as March 1971, the CBC pressed President Nixon to impose economic sanctions on South Africa's minority white regime; DeConde, *Ethnicity, Race and American Foreign Policy*, 178.
60. Schraeder, "Speaking with Many Voices," 398–406; Shain, "Ethnic Diasporas and U.S. Foreign Policy"; Culverson, "The Politics of the Anti-Apartheid Movement."
61. DeConde, *Ethnicity, Race and American Foreign Policy*, 179.
62. Prior to his removal, Young had been a charter member of Black Americans for Support of Israel (BASIC) and a cosponsor of a resolution that called for the United States to reconsider its membership in the United Nations if the body excluded Israel. He had also castigated PLO terrorism; David Schoenbaum, *The United States and the State of Israel* (New York: Oxford University Press, 1993), 270.
63. Dunbar, "Blacks and Jews."
64. Ibid.
65. Thomas H. Landess and Richard M. Quinn, *Jesse Jackson and the Politics of Race* (Ottawa, Ill.: Jameson Books, 1985), 131.
66. Vernon Jordan of the National Urban League warned at the time that the flirtation with Arafat played into the hands "of cross burners and bomb throwers." He called on other black leaders to build on "the traditional fruitful alliance between the black community," and was subsequently labeled by some blacks as a hostage of Jewish financial support; Miller, "Black Viewpoints on the Mideast Conflict," 45–49.
67. Ze'ev Chafets, "Doing the Right Thing," *Jerusalem Report*, March 11, 1993, 33.
68. Miller, "Black Viewpoints on the Mideast Conflict," 45.
69. Landess and Quinn, *Jesse Jackson and the Politics of Race*, 129–55.
70. Reed, *The Jesse Jackson Phenomenon*, 92.
71. Ibid.
72. Adolph L. Reed Jr., "What Are the Drums Saying, Booker? The Current Crisis of the Black Intellectual," *Village Voice*, April 11, 1995, 34.
73. Friedman, *What Went Wrong*, 38–39.
74. Marshall Frady, *Jesse: The Life and Pilgrimage of Jesse Jackson* (New York: Random House, 1996), 297.
75. Chafets, "Doing the Right Thing," 33.
76. Reed, *The Jesse Jackson Phenomenon*, 92.
77. Glenn C. Loury, "Behind the Black-Jewish Split," *Commentary* 81.1 (January 1986):26.
78. David A. Coolidge Jr., "Prophet without Honor?: The Reverend Jesse Jackson and the Palestinian Question," *Journal of Religious Thought* 43.2 (1986):51–62.

79. Steve A. Johnson, "Political Activity of Muslims in America," in *The Muslims of America*, ed. Yvonne Yazbeck Haddad (New York: Oxford University Press, 1991), 115.
80. Reed, *The Jesse Jackson Phenomenon*, 101.
81. The perception among diasporic Jews that black criticism of Israel was malevolent and racially motivated was strengthened by a 1983 poll showing blacks to be "the most hostile to Israel of fifteen groups surveyed. They were also among the groups holding the highest percentage of anti-Semitic attitudes"; Kaufman, *Broken Alliance*, 229.
82. Curtina Moreland-Young, "A View from the Bottom: A Descriptive Analysis of the Jackson Platform Efforts," in *Jesse Jackson's 1984 Presidential Campaign: Challenge and Change in American Politics*, ed. Lucius J. Barker and Ronald W. W. Walters (Urbana: University of Illinois Press, 1989), 154–56.
83. Richard Cohen, "Blacks, Jews and the Mideast," *Washington Post*, September 16, 1993, 29.
84. Newsome, "International Issues and Domestic Ethnic Relations," 41.
85. Charles Whitaker, "First African/African-American Summit," *Ebony* 46.10 (August 1991), 118.
86. Kilson, "African Americans and Africa," 369.
87. See Yossi Shain, "Multicultural Foreign Policy," *Foreign Policy* 100 (Fall 1995): 69–87 and Yossi Shain and Martin Sherman, "Dynamics of Disintegration: Diaspora, Secession and the Paradox of Nation-States" (paper presented at the Harvard-MIT MacArthur Seminar, Boston, March 6, 1996).
88. Culverson, "The Politics of the Anti-Apartheid Movements," 45.
89. Mordechai Tomarkin, "Israel–South Africa Relations" (in Hebrew), *Monthly Review* 12 (December 1980): 17–24.
90. Cited in Samuel Decalo, "Afro-Israel Technical Cooperation: Patterns of Setbacks and Successes," in *Israel in the Third World*, ed. Michael Curtis and Susan Aurelia Gitelson (New Brunswick, N.J.: Transaction, 1976), 81.
91. Aaron S. Klieman, *Israel and the World after 40 Years* (Washington, D.C.: Pergamon-Brassey's, 1990), 174.
92. See Tomarkin, "Israel–South Africa Relations."
93. Dan Sagir, "The Procession" (in Hebrew), *Politica* 12 (January 1987): 34.
94. Cited in Newsome, "International Issues and Domestic Ethnic Relations," 31.
95. Author's interview with Dr. Shimshon Zelniker, Tel Aviv, July 16, 1996.
96. *Yediot Aharonot*, December 13, 1996. Yossi Beilin was the driving force behind the change, though his work was made difficult due to the position of the Israel defense establishment with its own agenda of promoting arms sales (Klieman, *Israel and the World after 40 Years*, 151).
97. Author's telephone interview with Ran Kuriel, July 18, 1996.

98. In August 1988, Jesse Jackson met with the Israeli ambassador to Washington, Moshe Arad, and demanded that Israel immediately cut its ties to South Africa, including previously agreed-upon contracts (*Ha'aretz*, August 11, 1988).

99. Cited in Newsome, "International Issues and Domestic Ethnic Relations," 39.

100. Allan L. Kagedan, "Israel and South Africa: The Mythical Alliance," *Political Communication and Persuasion* 4.4 (1987): 322.

101. Nancy Abelmann and John Lie, *Blue Dreams: Korean-Americans and the Los Angeles Riots* (Cambridge, Mass.: Harvard University Press, 1995), 26–29.

102. *Jewish Week*, May 11, 1990.

103. Official document translated from Hebrew by the author (Israeli Foreign Ministry Communications).

104. Economic "envy which generates anger and hostility"; continued "emphasis on Jewish historical suffering and the Holocaust," while "disregarding Black historical anguish"; Jewish "opposition to affirmative action" and the general perception that Jewish dedication to Israel comes at the expense of the upward mobility of blacks inside the United States are cited as the primary reasons for black opposition to the Jewish state (official document, ibid.).

105. Official document; ibid.

106. Author's telephone interview with Israel Peleg, June 27, 1996.

107. *New York Times*, June 30, 1991.

108. Author's telephone interview with Yehudit Katz-Carmieli, July 4, 1996.

109. Ibid.

110. *New York Times*, July 16, 1994.

111. Author's interview with Yossi Beilin, Tel Aviv, July 11, 1996.

112. See Shain and Sherman, "Dynamics of Disintegration."

113. Jean-Paul Sartre, *Anti-Semite and Jew*, trans. George J. Becker (New York: Schocken Books, 1948), 91.

114. Robert A. Rockaway, " 'The Jews Cannot Defeat Me': The Anti-Jewish Campaign of Louis Farrakhan and the Nation of Islam" (essay published by the Lester and Sally Entin Faculty of Humanities, Tel-Aviv University, November 1995).

115. Cited in *Israel Outreach 2*, Special Edition, July 1991.

116. *Boston Globe*, February 14, 1996.

117. *ADL Newsletter, Dream Team 1995*.

118. Cited in Ron Zohara, "Ethiopians in the Ghetto of Los Angeles" (in Hebrew), *Ha'ir*, December 31, 1993, 57.

119. David Vital, *The Future of the Jews* (Cambridge, Mass.: Harvard University Press, 1990), 136.

120. *Boston Globe*, February 14, 1996.

121. *Newsweek*, February 12, 1996.

122. *Yediot Aharonot*, July 24, 1996.

123. Cornel West, *Race Matters* (Boston: Beacon Press, 1993), 74.

124. Friedman, *What Went Wrong*, 348.
125. Berman, "The Other and Almost the Same," 71.
126. *Jerusalem Report*, March 11, 1993.
127. Paul Robertson Jr., *Paul Robertson Jr. Speaks to America* (New Brunswick, N.J.: Rutgers University Press, 1993), 189. Paul Berman was less generous ("The Other and Almost the Same," p. 71). He remarked that "the evolution in Jesse Jackson's description of Zionism – from 'a kind of poisonous weed' (in a speech to an American Palestinian group in 1980) to a 'liberation movement' . . . no doubt reflected personal development; but man and Zeitgeist have always been intertwined in the person of Jesse Jackson."
128. *Jerusalem Report*, November 3, 1993.
129. Cohen, "Blacks, Jews and the Mideast," 29.
130. *Ha'aretz*, April 13, 1994.
131. Cited in Frady, *Jesse*, 438.
132. Ibid.
133. Morris and Rubin, "The Turbulent Friendship," 60.
134. Charles B. Keely, "The Effects of International Migration on US Foreign Policy," in *Threatened Peoples, Threatened Borders: World Migration and US Policy*, ed. Michael S. Teitelbaum and Myron Weiner (New York: W. W. Norton, 1995), 233–39.
135. Abelmann and Lie, *Blue Dreams*, 162–67.
136. Peter Beinart, "New Bedfellows: The New Latino-Jewish alliance," *New Republic*, August 11 and 18, 1997, 23.
137. Progrebin, "Blacks and Jews," 334.
138. See Ilan Shahar, "A Tale of Two Movements," *Ha'aretz* (English edition), October 10, 1997, and Avirama Golan, "Conditional Jews," *Ha'aretz* (English edition), October 22, 1997.
139. See Arthur Hertzberg, "Showdown," *New York Review of Books*, October 24, 1991, and Amy Dockser Marcus, "Burden of Peace: American Jews Grapple with an Identity Crisis as Peril to Israel Ebbs," *Wall Street Journal*, September 14, 1994.
140. Deborah Scroggins, "Making Themselves Heard: Blacks Gain Foreign Policy Clout," *Atlanta Journal/Atlanta Constitution*, May 31, 1994. Even on America's intervention in Somalia, African-American leaders were split on whether to continue the mission when television images of Somalis celebrating the death of American soldiers shook the American public and brought cries for a quick withdrawal. The black chairman of the Armed Services Committee at the time, Ronald V. Dellums, remarked: "At the end of the day, [the black] caucus members are elected officials like everybody else. They respond to public opinion too."
141. Gates expressed this view during a public lecture at Tel-Aviv University on May 18, 1994, as a direct answer to a question posed by the author.
142. *New Republic* web site, www.thenewrepublic.com/magazines/tnr.

143. Ibid., see also "African Trade-Offs," *The Black World Today* web site, www.tbwt.com, March 24, 1998.
144. Kilson, "Paradoxes of Black Leadership," 372.

Chapter 5. "Go, but Do Not Forget Me": Mexico, the Mexican Diaspora, and U.S.-Mexican Relations

1. The quotation in the title – "Veto pero no me olvides" – is taken from Richard Rodriguez's *Days of Obligation: An Argument with My Mexican Father* (New York: Viking, 1992), 50.
2. See Alexander DeConde, *Ethnicity, Race and American Foreign Policy: A History* (Boston: Northeastern University Press, 1992).
3. See Robert Smith, "De-Territorialized Nation Building: Transnational Migrants and the Re-Imagination of the Political Community by Sending States" (paper presented at the annual meeting of the American Political Science Association, Washington, D.C., September 2–5, 1993).
4. See Yossi Shain, *The Frontier of Loyalty: Political Exiles in the Age of the Nation-State* (Middletown, Conn.: Wesleyan University Press, 1989).
5. Philip Cannistraro and Gianfausto Rosoli, "Fascist Emigration Policy in the 1920s: An Interpretive Framework," *International Migration Review* 13 (1979): 680.
6. Ibid., 676.
7. Ibid., 686–87.
8. Charles F. Delzell, "The Italian Anti-Fascist Emigration, 1922–1943," *Journal of Central European Affairs* 12 (1952): 21.
9. Douglas B. Klusmeyer, "Aliens, Immigrants and Citizens: The Politics of Inclusion in the Federal Republic of Germany," *Daedalus* 12.3 (1993): 84–85.
10. Ephraim Ya'ar, "Emigration as a Normal Phenomenon," *New Outlook* 31.1 (January 1988): 14.
11. Yael Har Even, "Hayeridah Keba'aya Hevratit" (M.A. thesis, Tel-Aviv University, 1989).
12. Ya'ar, "Emigration as a Normal Phenomenon," 17.
13. N. Bar Yaacov, *Dual Nationality* (London: Stevens and Sons, 1961), 145.
14. Morton Grodzin, *The Loyal and the Disloyal: Social Boundaries of Patriotism and Treason* (Chicago: University of Chicago Press, 1956), 213. Expatriates may be deprived of their citizenship and labeled as traitors, but home regimes have often made conciliatory gestures and used various means of propaganda to try to convince kindred diaspora, and even exiles who may have developed second thoughts about their struggle, to return home and cooperate with the existing power for the "benefit of the nation." Cuban exiles in the United States who met with Castro in 1978, in what became known as the "diálogo," ceased to be regarded as "traitors" and became "members of the Cuban community abroad." Cited in Shain, *Frontier of Loyalty*, 150.

15. See Jack I. Garvey, "Repression of the Political Emigre – The Underground to International Law: A Proposal for Remedy," *Yale Law Journal* 90 (1980): 79.
16. Myron Weiner, *The Global Migration Crisis: Challenge to State and to Human Rights* (New York: HarperCollins 1995), 37.
17. Alejandro Portes and Ruben G. Rumbaut, *Immigrant America: A Portrait* (Berkeley: University of California Press, 1990), 110.
18. Cited in ibid., 111.
19. See Nancy Abelmann and John Lie, *Blue Dreams: Korean Americans and the Los Angeles Riots* (Cambridge, Mass.: Harvard University Press, 1995), 10–35, 184–92.
20. See Alexander Kitroeff, "Continuity and Change in Contemporary Greek Historiography," in *Modern Greece: Nationalism and Nationality*, ed. Martin Bilinkhorn and Thanos Veremis (Athens: Sage-Eliamep, 1990), 170–71.
21. "In the Name of His Masters" (in Hebrew), *Ha'aretz*, September 27, 1996.
22. *New York Times*, June 29, 1996.
23. *New York Times*, October 12, 1996.
24. Deborah Sontag and Larry Rother, "Dominicans May Allow Voting Abroad, Empowering New York Bloc," *New York Times*, November 15, 1997.
25. Dianna Solis, "U.S. Hispanics Flex Political Muscles as Mexico Lobbies for NAFTA Support," *Wall Street Journal*, March 3, 1993, 10.
26. Morris Janowitz, *The Reconstruction of Patriotism: Education for Civic Consciousness* (Chicago:University of Chicago Press, 1983), 128–38.
27. Rodriguez, *Days of Obligation*, 57.
28. Peter Skerry, *Mexican Americans: The Ambivalent Minority* (New York: Free Press, 1993), 43.
29. Carlos Gonzalez Gutierrez, "The Mexican Diaspora in California: Limits and Possibilities for the Mexican Government," in *The California Mexican Connection*, ed. Abraham F. Lowenthal and Katrina Burgess, (Stanford, Calif.: Stanford University Press, 1993), 230.
30. Ibid., 231.
31. See Secretaria de relaciones exteriores, "Program Para Las Comunidades Mexicanas En El Externjero," Mexico, September 1995.
32. Rodolfo O. de la Garza, "Mexico, Mexicans and Mexican-Americans, in U.S.-Mexican Relations" (Center for Mexican American Studies, University of Texas at Austin, 1989), 8.
33. Rodolfo O. de la Garza et al., *Latino Voices: Mexican, Puerto Rican, and Cuban Perspectives on American Politics* (Boulder, Colo.: Westview Press, 1992), 104.
34. Rodolfo O. de la Garza, "Mexican-Americans and U.S. Foreign Policy: The Future of Mexican-American–Mexican Relations," *Western Political Quarterly* 33 (December 1980): 579.
35. As Antonia Hernandez, MALDEF president, stated: "[Members of the

Salinas administration] have come a long way to understand that we are Americans first of Mexican descent – that we care about democracy and that at times we're very critical of the lack of political openness there [in Mexico]. A relationship as complex as this one is going to have to develop over time. But they are beginning to see that it might be in their self-interest to better understand us." Cited in Tim Golden, "Mexico Is Trying Hard to Lift Its Profile in the US," *New York Times*, December 30, 1991, 1, 4.

36. Lawrence H. Fuchs, *The American Kaleidoscope: Race, Ethnicity and the Civic Culture* (Hanover, N.H.: University Press of New England, 1990), 110–11.

37. Linda B. Hall and Don M. Coerver, *Revolution on the Border: The United States and Mexico, 1910–1920* (Albuquerque: University of New Mexico, 1988), 12.

38. Ibid.; also see Ronald Takaki, *A Different Mirror: A History of Multicultural America* (Boston: Little, Brown, 1993), 313.

39. Cited in Hall and Coerver, *Revolution on the Border*, 8.

40. Hall and Coerver, *Revolution on the Border*, 26, 138.

41. Skerry, *Mexican Americans*, 22.

42. See Fuchs, *The American Kaleidoscope*, 141.

43. See Noah M. J. Pickus, " 'True Faith and Allegiance': Immigration and the Politics of Citizenship" (Ph.D. diss., Princeton University, 1995), 86.

44. Calavita, "U.S. Immigration and Policy Responses: The Limits of Legislation," in *Controlling Immigration: A Global Perspective*, ed. A. Cornelius, Philip L. Martin, and James F. Hollifield (Stanford, Calif.: Stanford University Press, 1994), 63.

45. See Jorge Hernandez-Diaz, "National Identity and Indigenous Ethnicity in Mexico," *Canadian Review of Studies in Nationalism* 21.1–2 (1994): 72–73.

46. A latter-day parallel of the Mexican government's endeavors in this regard can be found in the recent Irish government effort to repatriate skilled and successful emigrants from overseas in order to maintain and further Ireland's recent record of rapid growth and modernization. As one member of the Irish Senate commented in March 1997, these returnees "bring back a message that they went abroad and found that the Irish could be competitive." Warren Hoge, "Opportunity Knocks in Ireland, Calling Its Flock Back Home," *International Herald-Tribune*, March 24, 1997.

47. George J. Sanchez, *Becoming Mexican American: Ethnicity, Culture and Identity in Mexican-American Los Angeles, 1900–1945* (New York: Oxford University Press, 1993), 120.

48. Ibid., 123.

49. Ibid., 113.

50. Ibid., 114.

51. Ibid., 213.

52. Rodolfo O. de la Garza and Claudio Vargas, "The Mexican-Origin Population of the United States as a Political Force in the Borderlands," in *Changing Boundaries in the Americas: New Perspectives on the U.S. Mexican, Central American, and South American Borders*, ed. Lawrence A. Herzog (San Diego: Center for the U.S.-Mexican Studies, University of California, 1992), 91.

53. Fuchs, *The American Kaleidoscope*, 145. Also see Cynthia E. Orozco, "The Origins of the League of United Latin American Citizens (LU-LAC) and the Mexican American Civil Rights Movement in Texas with an Analysis of Women's Political Participation in a Gendered Context, 1910–1929" (Ph.D. diss., University of California at Los Angeles, 1992).

54. See Jose Angel Gutierrez, "The Mexican-American in Mexico – Norte Americano Foreign Relations," in *Chicano-Mexicano Relations*, ed. Tatcho Mindiola Jr. and Max Martinez (Houston: Mexican American Studies, University of Houston, 1986), 22.

55. Cited in Sanchez, *Becoming Mexican American*, 254.

56. Ibid., 124.

57. Gutierrez, "The Mexican-American in Mexico," 47.

58. Octavio Paz, *The Labyrinth of Solitude* (New York: Grove Press, 1950), 14–15.

59. See Arturo Madrid-Barela, "Pochos: The Different Americans, an Interpretive Essay, Part 1," *Aztlan* 7.1 (Spring 1976): 52.

60. Jorge A. Bustamante, "Chicano-Mexicano Relations: From Practice to Theory," in Mindiola and Martinez, *Chicano-Mexicano Relations*, 9.

61. Earl Shorris, *Latinos* (New York: W. W. Norton, 1992), 169.

62. Ibid., p. 170. See also Richard Rodriguez, *Hunger of Memory* (Boston: Godine Publishing, 1982).

63. See Denise Dresser, "Exporting Conflict: Transboundary Consequences of Mexican Politics," in *The California Mexican Connection*, ed. Abraham F. Lowenthal and Katrina Burgess (Stanford, Calif.: Stanford University Press, 1993), 98.

64. Shorris, *Latinos*, 170.

65. De la Garza, "Mexican-Americans and U.S. Foreign Policy," 573n8.

66. Albert O. Hirschman, *Exit, Voice and Loyalty: Responses to Decline in Firms, Organizations and States* (Cambridge, Mass.: Harvard University Press, 1970), 96.

67. Rodriguez, *Days of Obligation*, 50.

68. Madrid-Barela articulates the internalization of the *pocho* stereotype in "Pochos, the Different Mexicans": "We either had never or no longer lived the Mexican national experience, had never or no longer shared in the cultural goals of Mexican society. And as our hermanos mexicanos came north to swell the numbers of the mexicanos de aca de este lado, to become Mexican-Americans, they too came to share in our disgrace" (p. 52).

69. Shorris, *Latinos*, 171. For an excellent discussion on this subject, see also Aida Hurtado and Carlos H. Arce, "Mexicans, Mexican-Americans, or

Pochos ... Que somos? The Impact of Language and Nativity on Ethnic Labelling," *Aztlan* 17.1 (Spring 1986): 103–30.

70. Jorge G. Castaneda, "From Mexico Looking Out," in *The United States and Mexico*, ed. Robert A. Pastor and Jorge G. Castaneda (New York: Knopf, 1988), 58.

71. Gutierrez, "The Mexican-American Elite in Mexican-American–Mexican Relations," in Mindiola and Martinez, *Chicano-Mexicano Relations* 50–51.

72. See David R. Maciel and Angelica Casillas, "Aztlan en Mexico: perspectives Mexicanas sobre el Mexican-American," *Aztlan* 11.1 (1980): 133–35.

73. Jorge G. Castaneda, "Mexico's Circle of Misery," *Foreign Affairs* 75.4 (July–August 1996): 95.

74. A major impetus for change in Mexico was the 1975 amendment of the VRA enacted in 1965 to ensure that minorities, especially blacks, were no longer denied their right to participate in the electoral process. The 1975 amendments extended the act's coverage to 375 new jurisdictions and "to four 'language-minorities,' including Hispanics, who were granted the right to cast ballots printed in their native language." See Christian Joppke, "Multiculturalism and Immigration: A Comparison of the United States, Germany, and Great Britain," *Theory and Society* 25.4 (August 1996): 458. The new VRA also improved minority representation in government, mandating "ethnic majority, 'single member electoral districts' that virtually guaranteed ethnic office-holding" (ibid.). These changes were based on the assumption that individuals vote along racial and ethnic lines, and that racial and ethnic groups share common problems and interests. See de la Garza, "The Effects of Primordial Claims, Immigration and the Voting Rights Act on Mexican Sociopolitical Incorporation" (paper presented at the annual meeting of the American Political Science Association, 1994, 6–7).

75. De la Garza, "The Effects of Primordial claims," 8–23.

76. Cited in DeConde, *Ethnicity, Race and American Foreign Policy*, 160.

77. *New York Times*, December 30, 1991; January 2 and October 4, 1992.

78. Martin Torres, "Con los mexicanos de alla," *Examen* 5.56 (January 1994). See de la Garza, "Mexico, Mexicans and Mexican-Americans in U.S.-Mexican Relations," 8–9.

79. Mark Fineman, "Mexico Strives to Hold On to Its Past," *Los Angeles Times*, September 27, 1994, H2.

80. Smith, "De-Territorialized Nation Building," 7.

81. See Gutierrez, "The Mexican Diaspora in California," 226–30.

82. Rodolfo O. de la Garza et al., "Will the Real Americans Please Stand Up: Anglo and Mexican American Support of Core American Political Values," *American Journal of Political Science* 40.2 (1996): 346–51.

83. De la Garza et al., *Latino Voices*, 103.

84. Ibid.

85. Ibid., 85. See also Carlos B. Gil, "Cuauhotémoc Cárdenas and the Rise

of Transborder Politics," in *Hope and Frustration: Interviews with Leaders of Mexico's Political Opposition*, ed. Carlos B. Gil (Wilmington, Del.: Scholarly Resources, 1992), 291–97.

86. Dresser, "Exporting Conflict," 98.
87. Cited in ibid., 89.
88. See "The Trading Game: Inside Lobbying for the American Free Trade Agreement" (Center for Public Integrity, Washington D.C., 1993), 17, 26.
89. Ibid., 19, 22, 32.
90. Rodolfo O. de la Garza, "The Domestic and Foreign Policy Consequences of the Program for Mexicans Living in Foreign Countries" (draft paper, quoted with permission of the author).
91. Silvana Paternostro, "Mexico as a Narco-Democracy," *World Policy Journal* 12.1 (Spring 1995): 46.
92. Cited in Fineman, "Mexico Strives to Hold On to Its Past," H2.
93. Author's interviews with Jorge Alberto Lozoya, Tel Aviv.
94. *Examen*, Ano 5, no. 52 (September 1993).
95. Cited in Solis, "U.S. Hispanics Flex Political Muscles," 10.
96. *La Jornada*, October 20, 1995.
97. See Mario Moya Palencia, "La Doble Nacionalidad," *Voz de Mexico*, October 31, 1995.
98. *Economist*, November 12, 1994, 60.
99. Time, November 21, 1994, 53.
100. For survey data on this and other matters related to Mexican-American attitudes toward Mexico, see Rodolfo O. de la Garza and Louis De-Sipio, "Interests Not Passions: Mexican American Attitudes toward Mexico and Issues Shaping U.S.-Mexico Relation" (unpublished manuscript, 1997). The author thanks Rodolfo O. de la Garza for supplying this information during revision of this chapter.
101. *Examen*, Ano 5, no. 52 (September 1993).
102. *Economist*, March 19, 1994, 56.
103. *Economist*, February 19, 1994, 45.
104. Andrew Reding, "The Next Mexican Revolution," *World Policy Journal* 13.3 (Fall 1996): 69.
105. Interview with Andres Rozental, Oxford, May 26, 1995.
106. Cited in Secretaria de relaciones exteriores, *Programa para las Comunidades Mexicanas en el Extranjero* (February 1995), 3. Reproduced from *La Jornada*, January 28, 1995.
107. Carlos Fuentes, *La frontera de cristal* (Mexico, DF.: Alfaguara, 1995), 115.
108. De la Garza and DeSipio, "Interests Not Passions."
109. *Los Angeles Times*, February 21, 1994, B3.
110. Cited in de la Garza and DeSipio, "Interests Not Passions," 17.
111. Paternostro, "Mexico as a Narco-Democracy."
112. Reding, "The Mexican Revolution," 61.
113. Ibid.

114. Andrew Phillips, "Change in the Wind: Mexico's Ruling Party Faces a Strong Challenge," *Maclean's*, July 7 1997, 35.
115. Alfredo Corchado and Laurence Iliff, "Mexico's Ruling Party Suffers Worst Loss Ever," *Dallas Morning News*, July 8, 1997. This was the first occasion under PRI rule that the mayor was elected, rather than appointed.
116. Ibid.
117. Yossi Shain, "Marketing the American Creed Abroad: US Diasporas in the Era of Multiculturalism," *Diaspora* 4.1 (Spring 1994): 85–111.
118. On the impact of globalization on Mexico's "new nationalism," see Miriam C. Alfie, "El proceso de globalizacion y los nuevos nacionalismos: la herencia del fin de la guerra fria," *Sociologica* 8 (January–April 1993): 237–54. Other articles in this issue also deal with the redefinition and the changing perceptions of "Mexican-ness" in the context of globalization.
119. Enrique R. Lamadrid, "Ariel y Caliban: el reencuentro desdoblado de Mexican-Americans y mexicanos," *Cuadernos Americanos – Nueva Epoca*, Ano X,/1.55 (January–February 1996): 108.
120. Paz, *The Labyrinth of Solitude*, 9.

Conclusion: Diasporas and the American National Interest

1. Nathan Glazer, *We Are All Multiculturalists Now* (Cambridge, Mass.: Harvard University Press, 1997), 147.
2. Nathan Glazer, "The Hard Questions: The Citizenship Boom," *New Republic*, April 7, 1997, 25.
3. Cited in John F. Harris, "Clinton Assails State Restrictions on Immigrants as 'Un-American,'" *International Herald-Tribune*, June 15, 1998.
4. Khachig Tölölyan, "The Impact of Diasporas on US Foreign Policy," in *Ethnic Conflict and Regional Instability: Implications for U.S. Policy and Army Roles and Missions*, ed. Robert L. Pfaltzgraff Jr. and Richard H. Shultz Jr. (Washington, D.C.: U.S. Army, 1994), 156.
5. Cited in Mitchell Geoffrey Bard, *The Water's Edge and Beyond: Defining the Limits to Domestic Influence on United States Middle East Policy* (New Brunswick, N.J.: Transaction, 1991), 303.
6. Dan Morgan and Kevin Merida, "America's New Ethnic Powers Engage in Big-Bucks Politics," *International Herald-Tribune*, March 25, 1997, 3.
7. Ibid.
8. Eugene R. Wittkopf, "What Americans Really Think about Foreign Policy," *Washington Quarterly* (Summer 1996): 104.
9. See Michael Walzer et al., *The Politics of Ethnicity* (Cambridge, Mass.: Belknap Press of Harvard University Press, 1982), 124.
10. I am grateful to Professor Abraham Ben-Zvi for his insights on this subject.
11. *International Herald-Tribune*, September 20–21, 1997, 1.

12. Ibid.
13. *New York Times*, October 8, 1997.
14. John Gerard Ruggie, "The Past as Prologue? Interests, Identity, and American Foreign Policy," *International Security* 21.4 (Spring 1997): 111.
15. Ibid., 112.
16. Ibid., 113.
17. Bruce Robbins, "Some Versions of U.S. Internationalism," *Social Text* 45 (Winter 1995): 98.
18. Ibid., 99.
19. Ibid.
20. Ibid., 98.
21. See *ADC Times* 15.4 (May 1994): 12.
22. Samuel P. Huntington, "The Erosion of American National Interests," *Foreign Affairs* 76.5 (September–October 1997): 49.
23. Charles McC. Mathias Jr., "Ethnic Groups and Foreign Policy," *Foreign Affairs* 59.5 (Summer 1981): 981.
24. David Carroll Cochran, "Ethnic Diversity and Democratic Stability: The Case of Irish Americans," *Political Science Quarterly* 110.4 (Winter 1995–96): 591.
25. Ibid., 599.

Bibliography

Books, Articles, and Papers

Abelmann, Nancy, and John Lie. *Blue Dreams: Korean-Americans and the Los Angeles Riots*. Cambridge, Mass.: Harvard University Press, 1995.

Abraham, Nabeel. "Anti-Arab Racism and Violence in the United States." In *The Development of Arab-American Identity*, edited by Ernest McCarus, 155–214. Ann Arbor: University of Michigan Press, 1994.

——— "Arab-American Marginality: Mythos and Praxis." *Arab Studies Quarterly* 11.2–3 (Spring–Summer 1989): 17–43.

——— "The Gulf Crisis and Anti-Arab Racism in America." In *Collateral Damage: The New World Order at Home and Abroad*, edited by Cynthia Peters. Boston: South End Press, 1992.

Alba, Richard D. *Ethnic Identity: The Transformation of White America*. New Haven: Yale University Press, 1990.

Alfie, Mariam C. "El Proceso de globalizacion y los nuevos nacionalismos: la herencia del fin de la guerra fria." *Sociologica* 8.21 (January–April 1993): 237–54.

Alston, Ona. "Promoting an African American Foreign Policy Agenda: A Municipal Strategy." *Urban League Review* 16.1 (1993): 45–50.

American Jewish Committee. *American Jewish Attitudes towards Israel and the Peace Process*. Public opinion survey conducted by Market Facts, August 7–15, 1995. New York: American Jewish Committee, 1995.

Anti-Defamation League. "The Anti-Israel Lobby Today: An Examination of the Themes and Tactics of an Evolving Propaganda Movement." *ADL Research Report* (1991).

——— " 'The Struggle Is Now Worldwide': Hizballah and Iranian-Sponsored Terrorism." *ADL Special Report* (January 1995).

——— "Terror for a 'Noble' Cause: The Case against Hamas Leader Musa Abu Marzuq." New York, n.d.

Arthur, Paul. "Diasporan Intervention in International Affairs: Irish America as a Case Study." *Diaspora* 1.2 (Fall 1991): 143–62.

Aswad, Barbara C. "The Lebanese Muslim Community in Dearborn, Michigan." In *The Lebanese in the World: A Century of Emigration*, edited by Albert Hourani and Nadim Shehadi, 167–88. London: Center for Lebanese Studies and I. B. Tauris, 1992.

Baker, Pauline. "The Sanctions Vote: A G.O.P. Milestone." *New York Times*, August 26, 1986.

Barber, Benjamin. "To Be an American: Identity as Citizenship in the New World." Paper presented at Conference on Political Identity in American Thought, Yale University, April 1991.

Barmé, Geremie. "Traveling Heavy: The Intellectual Baggage of the Chinese Diaspora." *Problems of Communism* 40 (January–April 1991): 94–112.

Barnes, Fred. "Viva Haiti." *New Republic*, May 30, 1994, 16–17.

Bard, Mitchell Geoffrey. *The Water's Edge and Beyond: Defining the Limits to Domestic Influence on United States Middle East Policy*. New Brunswick, N.J.: Transaction, 1991.

Barringer, Felicity. "With Loyalty Split, Arab-Americans Fault Hussein, but Question U.S. Too." *New York Times*, August 16, 1990.

Barron, Andrea. "Jewish and Arab Diasporas in the United States and Their Impact on U.S. Middle East Foreign Policy." In *The Arab-Israeli Conflict: Two Decades of Change*, edited by Yehuda Lukas and Abdalla Battah, 238–59. Boulder, Colo.: Westview Press, 1988.

Bar Yaacov, N. *Dual Nationality*. London: Stevens and Sons, 1961.

Beinart, Peter. "New Bedfellows." *New Republic*, August 11 and 18, 1997, 22–26.

Bell, Bowyer J. "The Transcendental Irish Republic: The Dream of Diaspora." In *Governments-in-Exile in Contemporary World Politics*, edited by Yossi Shain, 202–18. New York: Routledge, 1991.

Beloff, Max. "The Diaspora and the Peace Process." *Israel Affairs* 1.1 (Autumn 1994): 27–40.

Berman, Paul. "The Other and the Almost the Same." *New Yorker*, February 28, 1994, 61–71.

——. ed. *Blacks and Jews: Alliances and Arguments*. New York: Delacorte Press, 1994.

Bernstein, Deborah. "Conflict and Protest in Israeli Society: The Case of the Black Panthers of Israel." *Youth and Society* 16.2 (December 1984): 129–52.

Bishara, Ghassan. "Arab Americans Sorry for Electing Clinton." *Al-Fajr*, February 8, 1993, 7, 9.

——. "Pro-Israel Appointments Damage U.S. Credibility." *Al-Fajr*, February 1, 1993, 7.

Bodnar, John. "Ethnicity and Nationalism before Multiculturalism." *American Quarterly* 48.4 (December 1996): 716–23.

——. *Remaking America: Public Memory, Commemoration, and Patriotism in the Twentieth Century*. Princeton: Princeton University Press, 1992.

Booth, Cathy. "The Man Who Would Oust Castro." *Time*, October 26, 1992, 56–57.

Bourne, Randolph. "Transnational America." In *War and the Intellectuals: Essays, 1915–19*, edited by Carl Resek, 107–23. New York: Harper and Row, 1964.

Branch, Taylor. "Blacks and Jews: The Uncivil War." In *Bridges and Boundaries: African Americans and American Jews*, edited by Jack Salzman, Adina Black, and Gretchen Sullivan Sorin, 50–69. New York: George Braziller and the Jewish Museum, 1992.

Brenner, Lenni. "The Misguided Search for Black-Jewish Unity." *Freedomways* 24.2 (1984): 107–23.

Broder, Jonathan. "Arabs in America: On the Defensive." *Jerusalem Report*, August 26, 1993, 28–33.

"The Odd Couple." *Jerusalem Report*, March 24, 1994, 30–31.

Brooke, James. "Amid Islam Growth in the U.S., Muslims Face a Surge in Attacks." *New York Times*, August 28, 1995.

Brooke, James, and Elaine Sciolino. "U.S. Muslims Say Their Aid Pays for Charity, Not Terror." *New York Times*, August 16, 1995.

Bustamante, Jorge A. "Chicano-Mexicano Relations: From Practice to Theory." In *Chicano-Mexicano Relations*, edited by Tatcho Mindiola Jr. and Max Martinez, 8–19. Houston: Mexican American Studies, University of Houston, 1986.

Calavita, Kitty. "U.S. Immigration and Policy Responses: The Limits of Legislation." In *Controlling Immigration: A Global Perspective*, edited by Wayne A. Cornelius, Philip L. Martin, and James F. Hollifield, 55–82. Stanford, Calif.: Stanford University Press, 1994.

Caldwell, Christopher. "Aristide Development." *American Spectator* (July 1994): 32–41, 74–77.

Campbell, Charles S. *The Transformation of American Foreign Relations, 1865–1900*. New York: Harper and Row, 1976.

Cannistraro, Philip, and Gianfausto Rosoli. "Fascist Emigration Policy in the 1920s: An Interpretive Framework." *International Migration Review* 13.4 (1979): 673–92.

Canon, David T. "Redistricting and the Congressional Black Caucus." *American Politics Quarterly* 23.2 (April 1995): 159–89.

Caplan, Marc. *Jew-Hatred as History: The Nation of Islam's 'Secret Relationship between Blacks and Jews.'* New York: Anti-Defamation League, 1993.

Carmon, Eli. "The Farrakhan Visit: Political Ploy or Sincere Reconciliation?" *Ha'aretz* (English edition), December 10, 1997.

Castaneda, Jorge G. "From Mexico Looking Out." In *The United States and Mexico*, edited by Robert A. Pastor and Jorge G. Castaneda, 55–77. New York: Knopf, 1988.

"Mexico's Circle of Misery." *Foreign Affairs* 75.4 (July–August 1996): 92–105.

Center for Policy Analysis on Palestine. Proceedings of Conference on the Palestine National Authority: A Critical Appraisal, Washington, D.C., March 17, 1995.

Center for Public Integrity. "The Trading Game: Inside Lobbying for the American Free Trade Agreement." Washington, D.C., 1993.

Chafets, Ze'ev. "Doing the Right Thing." *Jerusalem Report*, March 11, 1993, 33.

Chavez, Leo R. "Immigration Reform and Nativism: The Nationalist Response to the Transnationalist Challenge." In *Immigrants Out! The New Nativism and the Anti-Immigrant Impulse in the United States*, edited by Juan F. Perea, 61–77. New York: New York University Press, 1996.

Chomsky, Noam. "Intervention in Vietnam and Central America: Parallels and Differences." *Monthly Review* 37.4 (September 1985): 1–29.

Christison, Kathleen. "The American Experience: Palestinians in the U.S." *Journal of Palestine Studies* 18.4 (Summer 1989): 18–36.

Citrin, Jack, Ernst B. Haas, Christopher Muste, and Beth Reingold. "Is American Nationalism Changing? Implications for Foreign Policy." *International Studies Quarterly* 38 (1994): 1–31.

Clough, Michael. "Grass-Roots Policymaking: Say Good-Bye to the 'Wise Men.'" *Foreign Affairs* 73.1 (January – February 1994): 2–7.

Cochran, David Carroll. "Ethnic Diversity and Democratic Stability: The Case of Irish Americans." *Political Science Quarterly* 110.4 (Winter 1995–96): 587–604.

Cohen, Kitty O. "Black-Jewish Relations in 1984: A Survey of Black US Congressmen." *Patterns of Prejudice* 19.2 (1985): 3–18.

Cohen, Richard. "Blacks, Jews and the Mideast." *Washington Post*, September 16, 1993.

Colton, Elizabeth O. *The Jackson Phenomenon: The Man, the Power, the Message*. New York: Doubleday, 1989.

Coolidge, David A., Jr. "Prophet without Honor?: The Reverend Jesse Jackson and the Palestinian Question." *Journal of Religious Thought* 43.2 (1986): 51–62.

Cooper, Mary H. "Muslims in America." *Congressional Quarterly*, April 30, 1993, 363–72.

Corchado, Alfredo, and Laurence Iliff. "Mexico's Ruling Party Suffers Worst Loss Ever." *Dallas Morning News*, July 8, 1997.

Coser, Lewis A. *Refugee Scholars in America: Their Impact and Their Experiences*. New Haven: Yale University Press, 1984.

Crabb, Cecil V., Jr. *Policy-Makers and Critics: Conflicting Theories of American Foreign Policy*. New York: Praeger, 1976.

Culverson, Donald R. "The Politics of the Anti-Apartheid Movement in the United States, 1969–1986." *Political Science Quarterly* 111.1 (1996): 127–49.

Decalo, Samuel. "Afro-Israel Technical Cooperation: Patterns of Setbacks and Successes." In *Israel in the Third World*, edited by Michael Curtis and Susan Aurelia Gitelson, 81–117. New Brunswick, N.J.: Transaction, 1976.

DeConde, Alexander. *Ethnicity, Race and American Foreign Policy: A History*. Boston: Northeastern University Press, 1992.

de la Garza, Rodolfo O. "Chicanos and U.S. Foreign Policy: The Future of Mexican-American–Mexican Relations." *Western Political Quarterly* 33 (December 1980): 571–82.

———. "Chicanos as an Ethnic Lobby: Limits and Possibilities." In *Chicano-Mexicano Relations*, edited by Tatcho Mindiola Jr. and Max Martinez, 35–59. Houston: Mexican American Studies, University of Houston, 1986.

———. "The Effects of Primordial Claims, Immigration and the Voting Rights Act on Mexican Sociopolitical Incorporation." Paper presented at the annual meeting of the American Political Science Association, New York, 1994.

de la Garza, Rodolfo O., Louis DeSipio, F. Chris Garcia, John Garcia, and Angelo Falcon. *Latino Voices: Mexican, Puerto Rican, and Cuban Perspectives on American Politics*. Boulder, Colo.: Westview Press, 1992.

de la Garza, Rodolfo O., Angelo Falcon, and F. Chris Garcia. "Will the Real Americans Please Stand Up: Anglo and Mexican American Support of Core American Political Values." *American Journal of Political Science* 40.2 (1996): 335–51.

de la Garza, Rodolfo O., and Claudio Vargas. "The Mexican-Origin Population of the United States as a Political Force in the Borderlands." In *Changing Boundaries in the Americas: New Perspectives on the U.S.-Mexican, Central American and South American Borders*, edited by Lawrence A. Herzog, 89–111. San Diego: Center for U.S.-Mexican Studies, University of California, 1992.

Delfs, Robert. "Long-Arm Tactics." *Far Eastern Economic Review*, July 5, 1990, 10–11.

Delzell, Charles F. "The Italian Anti-Fascist Immigration, 1922–1943." *Journal of Central European Affairs* 12 (1952): 20–55.

Dershowitz, Alan M. *Chutzpah*. New York: Simon and Schuster, 1991.

De Santis, Hugh. *The Diplomacy of Silence: The American Foreign Service, the Soviet Union, and the Cold War, 1933–1947*. Chicago: University of Chicago Press, 1980.

De Witt, Karen. "Black Group Begins Protest against Nigeria." *New York Times*, March 17, 1995.

Dickstein, Morris. "After the Cold War: Culture as Politics, Politics as Culture." *Social Research* 60.3 (Fall 1993): 531–44.

Dowty, Alan. *Closed Borders: The Contemporary Assault on Freedom of Movement*. New Haven: Yale University Press, 1987.

Dresser, Denise. "Exporting Conflict: Transboundary Consequences of Mexican Politics." In *The California Mexican Connection*, edited by Abraham F. Lowenthal and Katrina Burgess, 82–112. Stanford, Calif.: Stanford University Press, 1993.

Dunbar, Leslie W. "Blacks and Jews: On the Margins of Captivity." *Social Policy* 11.1 (May–June 1980): 54–58.

Dunn, Michael C. "Islamic Activists in the West: A New Issue Produces Backlash." *Middle East Policy* 3.1 (1994): 137–45.

Edinger, Lewis J. *German Exile Politics: The Social Democratic Executive Committee in the Nazi Era.* Berkeley: University of California Press, 1956.

Eizenstat, Stuart E. "Loving Israel – Warts and All." *Foreign Policy* 81 (Winter 1990–91): 87–105.

El-Badry, Samia. "The Arab-American Market." *American Demographics* (January 1994): 22–31.

Elman, Israel. "The Relations between Jews and Other Ethnic Groups in the United States" (in Hebrew). *Gesher: Journal of Jewish Affairs* 40.129 (1994): 36–44.

Emerson, Steven. "Jihad in America." PBS News Transcript, SAE Productions, November 21, 1994.

"The Other Fundamentalists." *New Republic*, June 12, 1995, 21–30.

Escobar, Edward J. "Mexican Revolutionaries and Los Angeles Police: Harassment of the Partido Liberal Mexicano, 1907–1910." *Aztlan* 17.1 (1987): 1–46.

Esman, Milton J. "Ethnic Pluralism and International Relations." *Canadian Review of Studies in Nationalism* 17.1–2 (1990): 83–93.

Esposito, John L. *The Islamic Threat: Myth and Reality.* New York: Oxford University Press, 1993.

"Ismail R. Al-Faruqi Muslim Scholar-Activist." In *The Muslims of America*, edited by Yvonne Yazbeck Haddad, 65–79. New York: Oxford University Press.

Farah, Douglas. "Cuba Admits U.S. Law Damages Economy." *International Herald-Tribune*, January 28, 1997.

Feagin, Joe R. *Racial and Ethnic Relations.* 2nd ed. Englewood Cliffs, N.J.: Prentice-Hall, 1984.

Feher, Michel. "The Schisms of '67: On Certain Restructurings of the American Left, from the Civil Rights Movement to the Multiculturalist Constellation." In *Blacks and Jews: Alliances and Arguments*, edited by Paul Berman, 263–85. New York: Delacorte Press, 1994.

Fernandez, Damian J. "From Little Havana to Washington D.C.: Cuban-Americans and U.S. Foreign Policy." In *Ethnic Groups and U.S. Foreign Policy*, edited by Mohammed E. Ahari, 115–34. New York: Greenwood Press, 1987.

Fineman, Mark. "Mexico Strives to Hold On to Its Past." *Los Angeles Times*, September 27, 1994.

Frankel, Matthew. "The $10 Billion Question: AIPAC and the Loan Guarantees to Israel." *Fletcher Forum* (Winter–Spring 1995): 153–70.

Franklin, James L. "Muslims in the US See a Setback." *Boston Globe*, March 5, 1993.

Fredrickson, George M. "America's Caste System: Will It Change?" *New York Review of Books*, October 23, 1997, 68–75.

Freedland, Johnathan. "Irish Americans Break Taboo to Talk of the Blight They Survived." *Guardian*, June 7, 1995.

Friedman, Edward. "The Diaspora and Why Taiwan's Future Matters So."

Paper presented at University of California at Berkeley conference on Taiwan, September 28–29, 1996.

Friedman, Murray. "Going Our Own Ways." *Moment* (June 1994): 36–39, 72.

What Went Wrong: The Creation and Collapse of the Black-Jewish Alliance. New York: Free Press, 1995.

Fuchs, Lawrence H. *The American Kaleidoscope: Race, Ethnicity, and the Civic Culture.* Hanover, N.H.: University Press of New England, 1990.

"Minority Groups and Foreign Policy." *Political Science Quarterly* 74.2 (June 1959): 165–75.

Fuentes, Carlos. *La frontera de cristal.* Mexico, D.F.: Alfaguara, 1995.

Fukuyama, Francis. "Immigrants and Family Values." In *Arguing Immigration: The Debate over the Changing Face of America*, edited by Nicolaus Mills, 151–68. New York: Simon and Schuster, 1994.

Garcia, Ignacio M. *Chicanismo: The Forging of a Militant Ethos among Mexican Americans.* Tucson: University of Arizona Press, 1997.

Garvey, Jack I. "Repression of the Political Emigré – The Underground to International Law: A Proposal for Remedy." *Yale Law Journal* 90.78 (1980): 78–120.

Gates, Henry Louis, Jr. "Black Intellectuals, Jewish Tensions." *New York Times*, April 14, 1993.

Gershoni, Yekutiel. *Africans on African-Americans: The Creation and Uses of an African-American Myth.* New York: New York University Press, 1997.

Gerson, Louis L. *The Hyphenate and Recent American Politics and Diplomacy.* Lawrence: University of Kansas Press, 1964.

"The Influence of Hyphenated Americans on U.S. Diplomacy." In *Ethnicity and U.S. Foreign Policy*, edited by Abdul Aziz Said, 46–58. New York: Praeger, 1977.

Gil, Carlos B. "Cuauthémoc Cárdenas and the Rise of Transborder Politics." In *Hopes and Frustrations: Interviews with Leaders of Mexico's Political Opposition*, edited by Carlo B. Gil, 287–303. Wilmington, Del.: Scholarly Resources, 1992.

Glazer, Nathan. "The Emergence of an American Ethnic Pattern." In *From Different Shores: Perspectives on Race and Ethnicity in America*, 2nd ed., edited by Ronald Takaki, 11–23. Oxford: Oxford University Press, 1994.

"The Hard Questions: The Citizenship Boom." *New Republic*, April 7, 1997, 25.

"The Jews." In *Ethnic Leadership in America*, edited by John Higham, 19–35. Baltimore: Johns Hopkins University Press, 1978.

"New Rules of the Game." In *Immigration and US Foreign Policy*, edited by Robert W. Tucker, Charles B. Keely, and Linda Wrigley. Boulder, Colo.: Westview, 1990.

We Are All Multiculturalists Now. Cambridge, Mass.: Harvard University Press, 1997.

Glazer, Nathan, and Daniel Patrick Moynihan, eds. *Ethnicity, Theory and Experience*. Cambridge, Mass.: Harvard University Press, 1975.

Golan, Avirama. "Conditional Jews." *Ha'aretz* (English edition), October 22, 1997.

Goldberg, J. J. "Gestures of Friendship." *Jerusalem Report*, March 11, 1993, 23–32.

Golden, Tim. "Mexico Is Trying Hard to Lift Its profile in the U.S." *New York Times*, December 30, 1991.

"Mexico's Chief, in a Shift, Meets Two of Castro's Main Foes in Exile." *New York Times*, October 5, 1992.

Gonzalez, David. "From Israel, an Envoy to Blacks." *New York Times*, July 16, 1994.

Gorguissian, Thomas. "Largest Arab Community Abroad" (in Arabic). *Al-Majal*, no. 271 (October 1993).

Gray, Kenneth R., and Robert E. Karp. "An Experiment in Exporting U.S. Values Abroad: The Sullivan Principles and South Africa." *International Journal of Sociology and Social Policy* 13.7 (1993): 1–14.

Greenberger, Robert. "Levine and Zogby, Odd Couple on the Mideast, Seek Common Ground for Economic Development." *Wall Street Journal*, February 2, 1994.

Grodzins, Morton. *Americans Betrayed: Politics and the Japanese Evacuation*. Chicago: University of Chicago Press, 1949.

The Loyal and the Disloyal: Social Boundaries of Patriotism and Treason. Chicago: University of Chicago Press, 1956.

Guest, Iain. *Behind the Disappearances: Argentina's Dirty War against Human Rights and the United Nations*. Philadelphia: University of Pennsylvania Press, 1990.

Gutierrez, Armando. "The Chicano Elite in Chicano-Mexican Relations." In *Chicano-Mexicano Relations*, edited by Tatcho Mindiola Jr. and Max Martinez, 47–59. Houston: Mexican American Studies, University of Houston, 1986.

Gutierrez, Carlos Gonzalez. "Decentralized Diplomacy: The Role of Consular Offices in Mexico's Relations with Its Diaspora." In *Bridging the Border: Transforming Mexico-US Relations*, edited by Rodolfo O. de la Garza and Jesus Velasco, 49–67. Lanhan, Md.: Rowman and Littlefield, 1997.

"The Mexican Diaspora in California: Limits and Possibilities for the Mexican Government." In *The California Mexican Connection*, edited by Abraham F. Lowenthal and Katrina Burgess, 221–35. Stanford, Calif.: Stanford University Press, 1993.

Gutierrez, Jose Angel. "The Mexican-American in Mexico – Norte Americano Foreign Relations." In *Chicano-Mexicano Relations*, edited by Tatcho Mindiola Jr. and Max Martinez, 20–34. Houston: Mexican American Studies, University of Houston, 1986.

Guy, James J. "Cuba: A Regional Power without a Region?" *World Today* 46.8–9 (August–September 1990): 165–69.

Haddad, Yvonne Yazbeck. "American Foreign Policy in the Middle East and Its Impact on the Identity of Arab Muslims in the United States." In *The Muslims of America*, edited by Yvonne Yazbeck Haddad, 217–35. New York: Oxford University Press, 1991.

Hagopian, Elaine. "Minority Rights in a Nation State: The Nixon Administration Campaign against Arab–Americans." *Journal of Palestine Studies* 5.1–2 (1975–76): 97–114.

Haines, Herbert H. *Black Radicals and the Civil Rights Mainstream, 1954–1970*. Knoxville: University of Tennessee Press, 1988.

Hall, Linda B., and Don M. Coerver. *Revolution on the Border: The United States and Mexico, 1910–1920*. Albuquerque: University of New Mexico Press, 1988.

Har Even, Yael. "Hayeridah Keba'aya Hevratit." M.A. thesis, Tel-Aviv University, 1989.

Harrington, Monna. "Loyalties: Dual and Divided." In *The Politics of Ethnicity*, edited by Michael Walzer, Edward T. Kantowicz, John Higham, and Monna Harrington, 93–138. Cambridge, Mass.: Belknap Press of Harvard University Press, 1982.

Hendrickson, David C. "The Recovery of Internationalism." *Foreign Affairs* 73.5 (September – October 1994): 26–43.

Henry, William A., III. "Pride and Prejudice." *Time*, February 28, 1994, 21–27.

Hertzberg, Arthur. "Showdown." *New York Review of Books*, October 24, 1991, 23–24.

Higham, John. "Multiculturalism and Universalism: A History of Critique." *American Quarterly* 45.2 (1993): 195–219.

——— ed. *Ethnic Leadership in America*. Baltimore: Johns Hopkins University Press, 1978.

Hirschman, Albert O. *Exit, Voice and Loyalty: Responses to Decline in Firms, Organizations and States*. Cambridge, Mass.: Harvard University Press, 1970.

Hitchens, Christopher. "Dead End: The Decline and Fall of the Greek Lobby in America." *Odyssey* (November–December 1995): 30–33.

Hoagland, Jim. "Africans Are Now Uniting against Nigerian Tyranny." *International Herald-Tribune*, June 10–11, 1995.

Hoffman, Adonis. "Nigeria: The Policy Conundrum." *Foreign Policy* 101 (Winter 1995–96): 146–48.

Hoffman, Stanley. *Dead Ends: American Foreign Policy in the New Cold War*. Cambridge, Mass.: Ballinger Publishing, 1983.

Hoge, Warren. "Opportunity Knocks in Ireland, Calling Its Flock Back Home." *International Herald-Tribune*, March 24, 1997.

Holmes, Steven A. "U.S. Blacks Battle Nigeria over Rights Issue." *New York Times*, June 15, 1995.

Howe, Irving. "The Fear beyond Escaping." In *Bridges and Boundaries: Af-*

rican Americans and American Jews, edited by Jack Salzman, Adina Black, and Gretchen Sullivan Sorin, 70–73. New York: George Braziller and the Jewish Museum, 1992.

Howe, Marvin. "South Koreans in the U.S. Are Going Home." *New York Times*, July 19, 1987.

Huggins, Nathan Irvin. "Afro-Americans." In *Ethnic Leadership in America*, edited by John Higham, 91–118. Baltimore: Johns Hopkins University Press, 1978.

Hunt, Michael H. *Ideology and U.S. Foreign Policy*. New Haven: Yale University Press, 1987.

Huntington, Samuel P. *The Clash of Civilizations and the Remaking of World Order*. New York: Simon and Schuster, 1996.

"The Erosion of American National Interests." *Foreign Affairs* 76.5 (September – October 1997): 28–49.

"If Not Civilizations What? Paradigms of the Post–Cold War World." *Foreign Affairs* 72 (1993): 186–94.

Hurtado, Aida, and Carlos H. Arce. "Mexicans, Mexican-Americans, Mexican Americans, or Pochos . . . Que somos? The Impact of Language and Nativity on Ethnic Labelling." *Aztlan* 17.1 (Spring 1986): 103–30.

Hutchinson, Earl Ofari. "Who Will Win the Battle for the Soul of a Divided Black America?" *Chicago Tribune*, March 18, 1994.

Ifestos, Panayiotis. "Ethnic Lobbies and Foreign Policy: The American Experience." Draft paper, Panteion University, Athens, Greece, 1993.

Ilan, Shahar. "A Tale of Two Movements." *Ha'aretz* (English edition), October 10, 1997.

Isikoff, Michael. "Member of Croatian Group Charged in Army Plot." *Washington Post*, August 13, 1991.

Ismael, Jacqueline S., and Tareq Y. Ismael. "The Holy Land: The American Experience: III. The Arab Americans and the Middle East." *Middle East Journal* 30.3 (Summer 1976): 390–405.

Israeli, Raphael. "From Commitment to Zionism." *Forum: On the Jewish People, Zionism and Israel* 62 (Winter–Spring 1989): 51–59.

Iwańska, Alicja. *Exiled Governments: Spanish and Polish*. Cambridge, Mass.: Schenkman, 1981.

"Modern Exiles: Spanish, Polish, American." *Polish Review* 23 (1978): 47–61.

Jabara, Abdeen M. "A Strategy of Political Effectiveness." In *Arab Americans: Continuity and Change*, edited by Baha Abu-Laban and Michael W. Suleiman, 201–5. Belmont, Mass.: Association of Arab American University Graduates, 1989.

Jacoby, Tamar. "Roundtable: Beyond Crown Heights – Strategies for Overcoming Anti-Semitism and Racism in New York." *Tikkun* 8.1 (January–February 1993): 59–62, 78–80.

Janowitz, Morris. *The Reconstruction of Patriotism: Education for Civic Consciousness*. Chicago: University of Chicago Press, 1983.

Jean-Pierre, Jean. "The Tenth Department." *NACLA Report on the Americas* 27.4 (January–February 1994): 47–55.

Johnson, Steve A. "Political Activity of Muslims in America." In *The Muslims of America*, edited by Yvonne Yazbeck Haddad, 111–24. New York: Oxford University Press, 1991.

Joppke, Christian. "Multiculturalism and Immigration: A Comparison of the United States, Germany, and Great Britain." *Theory and Society* 25.4 (August 1996): 449–500.

Jusdanis, Gregory. "Greek Americans and the Diaspora." *Diaspora* 1.2 (Fall 1991): 209–23.

Kagedan, Allan L. "Israel and South Africa: The Mythical Alliance." *Political Communication and Persuasion* 4.4 (1987): 317–24.

Kann, Robert A., and Zdenek V. David. *The Peoples of the Eastern Hapsburg Lands, 1526–1918*. Seattle: University of Washington Press, 1984.

Karpat, Kemal H. "The Ottoman Emigration to America, 1860–1914." *International Journal of Middle East Studies* 17 (1985): 175–209.

Kaufman, Jonathan. *Broken Alliance: The Turbulent Times between Blacks and Jews in America*. New York: Scribner's, 1988.

Keely, Charles B. "The Effects of International Migration on US Foreign Policy." In *Threatened Peoples, Threatened Borders: World Migration and US Policy*, edited by Michael S. Teitelbaum and Myron Weiner, 215–43. New York: W. W. Norton, 1995.

Kelly, Ron. "Muslims in Los Angeles." In *Muslim Communities in North America*, edited by Yvonne Yazbeck Haddad and Jane Idleman Smith. Albany: State University of New York Press, 1994.

Kempster, Norman. "Use Force in Haiti, Black Americans Urge." *Los Angeles Times*, November 11, 1993.

Kennan, George F. *American Diplomacy: Expanded Edition*. Chicago: University of Chicago Press, 1985.

———. "On American Principles." *Foreign Affairs* 74.2 (March–April 1995): 116–27.

——— ("X"). "The Sources of Soviet Conduct." *Foreign Affairs* 26.3 (July 1947): 567–82.

Khalidi, Rashid. *Under Siege: P.L.O. Decisionmaking during the 1982 War*. New York: Columbia University Press, 1986.

Khoury, Nabeel A. "The Arab Lobby: Problems and Prospects." *Middle East Journal* 41.3 (Summer 1987): 379–95.

Kilson, Martin. "African Americans and Africa: A Critical Nexus." *Dissent* (Summer 1992): 361–69.

———. "Colin Powell: A Flight from Power?" *Dissent* (Spring 1986): 71–84.

———. "Paradoxes of Black Leadership." *Dissent* (Summer 1995): 368–72.

Kirkpatrick, Jeanne. "Dictatorships and Double Standards." *Commentary* 68.5 (November 1979): 34–45.

Kirschten, Dick. "Shock Waves." *National Journal*, June 5, 1993, 1349–52.

Kissinger, Henry. "Reflections on Containment." *Foreign Affairs* 73.3 (May–June 1994): 113–30.

White House Years. Boston: Little, Brown, 1979.

Kitroeff, Alexander. "Continuity and Change in Contemporary Greek Historiography." In *Modern Greece: Nationalism and Nationality*, edited by Martin Bilinkhorn and Thanos Veremis, 143–72. Athens: Sage-Eliamep, 1990.

Klieman, Aaron S. *Israel and the World after 40 Years.* Washington, D.C.: Pergamon-Brassey's, 1990.

Israel's Global Reach: Arms Sales as Diplomacy. Washington, D.C.: Pergamon-Brassey's, 1985.

Klusmeyer, Douglas B. "Aliens, Immigrants and Citizens: The Politics of Inclusion in the Federal Reublic of Germany." *Daedalus* 122.3 (1993): 81–114.

Knowlton, Brian. "All Abroad: A Surge in Expatriate Americans." *International Herald-Tribune*, October 13, 1997.

Kotler-Berkowitz, Laurence A. "Ethnic Cohesion and Division among American Jews: The Role of Mass-Level and Organizational Politics." *Ethnic and Racial Studies* 20.4 (October 1997): 797–829.

Kovtun, George J. *Masaryk and American: Testimony of a Relationship.* Washington, D.C.: Library of Congress, 1988.

Kramer, Martin. "Islam and the West (including Manhattan)." *Commentary* (October 1993): 33–37.

Kymlicka, Will. *Multicultural Citizenship: A Liberal Theory of Minority Rights.* Oxford: Oxford University Press, 1995.

"Social Unity in a Liberal State." Revised draft paper, February 1995. Later published in *Social Philosophy and Policy* 13.1 (Winter 1996): 105–36.

Lamadrid, Enrique R. "Ariel y Caliban: el reencuentro desoblado de Mexican-Americans y mexicanos." *Cuadernos Americanos – Nueva Epoca*, Ano X/1.55 (January – February 1996): 89–109.

Landau, David. "The 'Who Is a Jew' Affair: An Example of Jewish-American Influence on Israel's Policies" (in Hebrew). American-Jewish Committee and Bar Ilan University, Ramat Gan, 1996.

Landess, Thomas H., and Richard M. Quinn. *Jesse Jackson and the Politics of Race.* Ottawa, Ill.: Jameson Books, 1985.

Lebow, Ned. "Psychological Dimensions of Post–Cold War Foreign Policy." *Israel Affairs* 2.3–4 (Spring–Summer 1996): 46–56.

Lewis, Anthony. "Misguided Immigration Reform." *International Herald-Tribune*, October 4–5, 1997.

Lewis, Bernard. "Legal and Historical Reflections on the Positions of Muslim Populations under Non-Muslim Rule." In *Muslims in Europe*, edited by Bernard Lewis and Dominique Schnapper, 1–18. London: Pinter, 1994.

The Political Language of Islam. Chicago: University of Chicago Press, 1988.

Lewis, Michael. "Israel's American Detractors – Back Again." *Middle East Quarterly* 4.4 (December 1997): 25–34.

"Israel's Critics: Trying to Adjust to New Realities." *Near East Report*, November 15, 1993, 204.

Lincoln, C. Eric. "Color and Group Identity in the United States." *Daedalus* 96.2 (Spring 1967): 527–41.

Lind, Michael. "Are We a Nation?" *Dissent* (Summer 1995): 355–62.

— *The Next American Nation: The New Nationalism and the Fourth American Revolution*. New York: Simon and Schuster, 1995.

Lipson, Charles. "American Support for Israel: History, Sources, Limits." *Israel Affairs* 2.3–4 (Spring–Summer 1996):128–46.

Longmyer, Kenneth. "Black American Demands." *Foreign Policy* 60 (Fall 1985): 3–17.

Lopata, Helena Znaniecki. *Polish-Americans: Status Competition in an Ethnic Community*. Englewood Cliffs, N.J.: Prentice-Hall, 1976.

Loury, Glenn C. "The Alliance Is Over." *Moment* (June 1994): 32–35, 68–71.

— "Behind the Black-Jewish Split." *Commentary* 81.1 (January 1986): 23–27.

Lytle, Paul Franklin. "Loyalty and Recognition under Challenge: The Yugoslav Case, 1941–1945." In *Governments-in-Exile in Contemporary World Politics*, edited by Yossi Shain, 117–33. New York: Routledge, 1991.

Maciel, David R., and Angelica Casillas. "Aztlan en Mexico: perspectives Mexicanas sobre el Mexican-American." *Aztlan* 11.1 (1980): 133–35.

Madison, Christopher. "Arab American Lobby Fights Reaerguard Battle to Influence U.S. Mideast Policy." *Foreign Policy Report* 17, August 31, 1985, 1934–39.

Madrid-Barela, Arturo. "Pochos: The Different Americans, an Interpretive Essay, Part I." *Aztlan* 7.1 (Spring 1976): 51–64.

Magubane, Bernard M. *The Ties That Bind: African-American Consciousness of Africa*. Trenton, N.J.: Africa World Press, 1987.

Maier, Charles S. "Unsafe Haven." *New Republic*, October 12, 1992, 20–21.

Malone, David. "Haiti and the International Community: A Case Study." *Survival* 39.2 (Summer 1997).

Mandelbaum, Michael. "Foreign Policy as Social Work." *Foreign Affairs* 75.1 (January–February 1996): 16–32.

Mandine, Rosalind. "Arab Americans Care about Racial Intolerance, Urban Issues." *USIA*, May 20, 1992.

Marcos, Ferdinand E. "A Defense of My Tenure." *Orbis* 33.1 (Winter 1989): 91–96.

Marcus, Amy Dockser. "Burden of Peace: American Jews Grapple with an Identity Crisis as Peril to Israel Ebbs." *Wall Street Journal*, September 14, 1994.

Martin, Ben L. "From Negro to Black to African American: The Power of Names and Naming." *Political Science Quarterly* 106.1 (January–March 1991): 83–107.

Mason, Philip. "The Revolt against Western Values." *Daedalus* 96.2 (Spring 1967): 328–52.

Mathias, Charles McC., Jr. "Ethnic Groups and Foreign Policy." *Foreign Affairs* 59.5 (Summer 1981): 975–98.

Mattar, Philip. "The PLO and the Gulf Crisis." *Middle East Journal* 48.1 (Winter 1994): 31–46.

Mazrui, Ali A. "Between the Crescent and the Star-Spangled Banner: American Muslims and US Foreign Policy." *International Affairs* 72.3 (1996): 493–506.

McCartney, John T. *Black Power Ideologies: An Essay in African-American Political Thought*. Philadelphia: Temple University Press, 1992.

McDonald, Jason. "Conceptual Metaphors for American Ethnic Formations." In *Representing and Imagining America*, edited by Philip J. Davies, 84–91. Keele University Press, 1996.

Michels, Jeffrey. "National Vision and the Negotiation of Narratives: The Oslo Agreement." *Journal of Palestine Studies* 24.1 (Autumn 1994): 28–38.

Miles, Jack. "Black vs. Browns." In *Arguing Immigration: The Debate over the Changing Face of America*, edited by Nicolaus Mills, 101–42. New York: Simon and Schuster, 1994.

Miller, Jake C. "Black Viewpoints on the Mid-East Conflict." *Journal of Palestine Studies* 10.2 (Winter 1981): 37–49.

Mirsky, Yehuda. "Democratic Politics, Democratic Culture." *Orbis* 37.4 (Fall 1993): 567–80.

Misiunas, Romuald. "Sovereignty without Government: Baltic Diplomatic and Consular Representation, 1940–1990." In *Governments-in-Exile in Contemporary World Politics*, edited by Yossi Shain, 134–44. New York: Routledge, 1991.

Molavi, Ashfin. "Alamoudi Critical of U.S. Approach to Muslim World." *Arab News*, February 8, 1995, 11.

Moreland-Young, Curtina. "A View from the Bottom: A Descriptive Analysis of the Jackson Platform Efforts." In *Jesse Jackson's 1984 Presidential Campaign: Challenge and Change in American Politics*, edited by Lucius J. Barker and Ronald W. W. Walters, 149–59. Urbana: University of Illinois Press, 1989.

Morgan, Dan, and Kevin Merida. "America's New Ethnic Powers Engage in Big-Bucks Politics." *International Herald-Tribune*, March 25, 1997.

Morris, Milton D., and Gary E. Rubin. "The Turbulent Friendship: Black-Jewish Relations in the 1990s." *Annals of the American Academy* 530 (November 1993): 42–60.

Muravchik, Joshua. "Facing Up to Black Anti-Semitism." *Commentary* 100.6 (December 1995): 26–30.

Myrdal, Gunnar. *An American Dilemma: The Negro Problem and Modern Democracy*. New York: Harper and Brothers, 1944.

Naff, Alixa. *Becoming American: The Early Arab Immigrant Experience*. Carbondale: Southern Illinois University Press, 1985.

"Lebanese Immigration into the United States: 1880 to the Present." In

The Lebanese in the World: A Century of Emigration, edited by Albert Hourani and Nadim Shehadi, 141–66. London: Center for Lebanese Studies and I. B. Tauris, 1992.

Nagourney, Adam. "Messinger Goes Far Afield to Campaign for New York Mayoral Election." *New York Times*, December 4, 1996.

Nakinishi, Don T. "Surviving Democracy's 'Mistake': Japanese Americans and Executive Order 9066." Paper presented at the International Conference on Political Identity in American Thought, Whitney Humanities Center, Yale University, April 19–21, 1991.

Nash, Madeleine. "From Polonia with Love." *Time*, November 27, 1989, 31.

Newby, Robert G. "Afro-Americans and Arabs: An Alliance in the Making." *Journal of Palestine Studies* 10.2 (Winter 1981): 50–58.

Newsome, Yvonne D. "International Issues and Domestic Ethnic Relations: African Americans, American Jews and the Israel-South Africa Debate." *International Journal of Politics, Culture, and Society* 5.1 (1991): 19–47.

O'Grady, Joseph. "An Irish Policy Born in the U.S.A.: Clinton's Break with the Past." *Foreign Affairs* 75.3 (May–June 1996): 2–7.

Orfalea, Gregory. *Before the Flames: A Quest for the History of Arab-Americans*. Austin: University of Texas Press, 1988.

——. "Sifting the Ashes: Arab-American Activism during the 1982 Invasion of Lebanon." In *Arab-Americans: Continuity and Change*, edited by Baha Abu-Laban and Michael W. Suleiman, 207–25. Belmont, Mass.: Association of Arab-American University Graduates, 1989.

Orozco, Cynthia E. "The Origins of the League of United Latin American Citizens (LULAC) and the Mexican American Civil Rights Movement in Texas with an Analysis of Women's Political Participation in a Gendered Context, 1910–1929." Ph.D. dissertation, University of California at Los Angeles, 1992.

Palencia, Mario Moya. "La Double Nacionalidad." *Voz de Mexico*, October 31, 1995.

Paternostro, Silvana. "Mexico as a Narco-Democracy." *World Policy Journal* 12.1 (Spring 1995): 41–47.

Paul, John P. "The Greek Lobby and American Foreign Policy: A Transnational Perspective." In *Ethnic Identities in a Transnational World*, edited by John F. Stack Jr., 47–48. Westport, Conn.: Greenwood Press, 1990.

Paz, Octavio. *The Labyrinth of Solitude*. New York: Grove Press, 1950.

Pedraza-Bailey, Silvia. *Political and Economic Migrants in America: Cubans and Mexicans*. Austin: University of Texas Press, 1985.

Perez-Pena, Richard. "Demonstration and Protest: Arabs, Jews." *New York Times*, March 7, 1996.

Phillips, Andrew. "Change in the Wind: Mexico's Ruling Party Faces a Strong Challenge." *Maclean's*, July 7, 1997, 35–37.

Pickus, Noah M. J. " 'Before I Built A Wall' – Jews, Religion and American Public Life." *This World* 15 (Fall 1986): 28–43.

"Creating Citizens: Americanization and the Transformation of National Identity." Paper presented at the annual meeting of the American Political Science Association. Washington, D.C., August 29, 1991.

"Does Immigration Threaten Democracy? Right Restriction and the Meaning of Membership." In *Democracy: The Challenges Ahead*, edited by Yossi Shain and Aharon Klieman, 130–45. London: Macmillan, St. Antony's Series, 1997.

" 'True Faith and Allegiance': Immigration and the Politics of Citizenship." Ph.D. dissertation, Princeton University, 1995.

Pido, Antonio J. A. *The Filipinos in America: Macro/Micro Dimensions of Immigration and Integration.* New York: Center for Migration Studies, 1986.

Porter, Bruce D. "Can American Democracy Survive?" *Commentary* 96.5 (November 1993): 37–40.

Portes, Alejandro, and Ruben G. Rumbaut. *Immigrant America: A Portrait.* Berkeley: University of California Press, 1990.

Progrebin, Letty Cottin. "Blacks and Jews: Different Kinds of Survival." *Nation*, September 23, 1991, 332–36.

Puddington, Arch. "Black Anti-Semitism and How It Grows." *Commentary* 97.4 (April 1994): 19–24.

"Speaking of Race." *Commentary* 100.6 (December 1995): 21–25.

Pulcini, Theodore. "Trend in Research on Arab Americans." *Journal of American Ethnic History* 12.4 (Summer 1993): 27–60.

Pye, Lucian W. *Asian Power and Politics: The Cultural Dimension of Authority.* Cambridge, Mass.: Belknap Press of Harvard University Press, 1985.

Raskin, Jamin B. "Remember Korematsu: The Predicament of Arab-Americans." *Nation*, February 4, 1991, 117.

Ray, Elaine. "In Another Country." *Boston Globe Magazine*, July 26, 1992, 14–27.

Raz, Joseph. "Multiculturalism: A Liberal Perspective." *Dissent* (Winter 1994): 67–79.

Reding, Andrew. "The Next Mexican Revolution."*World Policy Journal* 13.3 (Fall 1996): 61–70.

Reed, Adolph L., Jr. *The Jesse Jackson Phenomenon: The Crisis of Purpose in Afro-American Politics.* New Haven: Yale University Press, 1986.

"What Are the Drums Saying, Booker? The Current Crisis of the Black Intellectual." *Village Voice*, April 11, 1995, 31–36.

Rieff, David. "From Exiles to Immigrants: The Miami Cubans Come 'Home.' " *Foreign Affairs* 74.4 (July–August 1995): 76–89.

"The Rift Between Blacks and Jews." *Time*, February 28, 1994, 28–34.

Robbins, Bruce. "Some Versions of U.S. Internationalism." *Social Text* 45 (Winter 1995): 97–123.

Robertson, Paul, Jr. *Paul Robertson Jr. Speaks to America.* New Brunswick, N.J.: Rutgers University Press, 1993.

Robinson, Randall. "After Sanctions: Apartheid and the African-American Collegian." *Black Collegian* (September–October 1991): 132–39.

Rockaway, Robert A. " 'The Jews Cannot Defeat Me': The Anti-Jewish Campaign of Louis Farrakhan and the Nation of Islam." Essay published by the Lester and Sally Entin Faculty of Humanities, Tel Aviv University, November 1995.

Rockefeller, Steven C. "Comment." In *Multiculturalism and "The Politics of Recognition": An Essay by Charles Taylor*, edited by Amy Gutman, 87–98. Princeton: Princeton University Press, 1992.

Rodriguez, Richard. *Days of Obligation: An Argument with My Mexican Father*. New York: Viking, 1992.

Hunger of Memory. Boston: Godine Publishing, 1982.

Ron, Zohara. "Ethiopians in the Ghetto of Los Angeles" (in Hebrew). *H'air*, December 31, 1993, 51–61.

Rosenthal, Andrew. "Aides Say Bush Is Shifting Focus to Relations among the Republics." *New York Times*, November 30, 1991.

Rother, Larry. "The Cold War of Cuba and the Miami Exiles Heats Up." *New York Times*, January 26, 1992.

"A Rising Cuban-American Leader: Statesman to Some, Bully to Others." *New York Times*, October 29, 1992.

"In Spanish, It's Another Story." *New York Times*, December 15, 1996.

Roy, Oliver. *The Failure of Political Islam*. Translated by Carol Volk. London: I. B. Tauris, 1994.

"Islam in France: Religion, Ethnic Community or Social Ghetto?" In *Muslims in Europe*, edited by Bernard Lewis and Dominique Schnapper, 54–66. London: Pinter, 1994.

Rubin, Judith Colp. "A Closer Look." *Jerusalem Post Magazine*, December 31, 1993, 10, 12–13.

Rubin, Trudy. "An American Is Best Hope for Battered Ex-Yugoslavia." *Philadelphia Inquirer*, October 9, 1992.

Ruggie, John Gerard. "The Past as Prologue? Interests, Identity and American Foreign Policy." *International Security* 21.4 (Spring 1997): 89–125.

Sachedina, Abdulaziz A. "A Minority within a Minority: The Case of the Shi'a in North America." In *The Muslim Communities in North America*, edited by Yvonne Yazbeck Haddad and Jane Idleman Smith, 3–15. Albany: State University of New York Press, 1994.

Sadd, David J., and G. Neal Lendenmann. "Arab American Grievances." *Foreign Policy* 60 (Fall 1985): 17–30.

Safire, William. "On Language: The Prep-Droppers." *New York Times Magazine*, July 28, 1991.

"Ukraine Marches Out." *New York Times*, November 18, 1991.

Sagir, Dan. "The Procession" (in Hebrew). *Politica* 12 (January 1987): 32–34.

Said, Abdul Aziz, ed. *Ethnicity in U.S. Foreign Policy*. New York: Praeger, 1977.

Said, Edward. Address to AAUG 26th Annual Convention. *AAUG Mideast Monitor* 9.1 (Winter 1994): 9–10.

"Said Revels in Outside Role." *Jerusalem Times*, January 6, 1995, 12.

Samhan, Helen Hatab. "Arab Americans and the Elections of 1988: A Constituency Comes of Age." *Arab Studies Quarterly* 11.2–3 (Spring–Summer 1989): 227–49.

"Politics and Exclusion: The Arab American Experience." *Journal of Palestine Studies* 16.2 (Winter 1987): 11–28.

Sanchez, George J. *Becoming Mexican-American: Ethnicity, Culture and Identity in Mexican-American Los Angeles, 1900–1945.* New York: Oxford University Press, 1993.

Sandoval, Jose Miguel, and Mark Stephen Jendrysik. "Convergence and Divergence in the Arab-American Public Opinion." *International Journal of Public Opinion Research* 5.4 (Winter 1993): 303–14.

Sartre, Jean-Paul. *Anti-Semite and Jew.* Translated by George J. Becker. New York: Schocken Books, 1948.

Schemo, Diana Jean. "America's Scholarly Palestinian Raises Volume against Arafat." *New York Times*, March 4, 1994.

Schirmer, Daniel B., and Stephen Rosskamm Shalom, eds. *The Philippines Reader.* Boston: South End Press, 1987.

Schlesinger, Arthur M., Jr. *The Cycles of American History.* Boston: Houghton Mifflin, 1986.

The Disuniting of America: Reflections on a Multicultural Society. New York: W. W. Norton, 1992.

Schnapper, Dominique. "Muslim Communities, Ethnic Minorities, and Citizens." In *Muslims in Europe*, edited by Bernard Lewis and Dominique Schnapper, 148–60. London: Pinter, 1994.

Schoenbaum, David. *The United States and the State of Israel.* New York: Oxford University Press, 1993.

Schraeder, Peter J. "Speaking with many Voices: Continuity and Change in U.S. Africa Policies." *Journal of Modern Africa Studies* 29 (September 1991): 373–412.

Scourby, Alice. *The Greek Americans.* Boston: Twayne Publishers, 1984.

Scroggins, Deborah. "Making Themselves Heard: Blacks Gain Foreign Policy Clout." *Atlanta Journal-Atlanta Constitution*, May 31, 1994.

Secretaria de relaciones exteriores. "Programa Para Las Communidades Mexicanas En El Externjero." Government of Mexico, February and September, 1995.

Sengstock, Mary C. "Detroit's Iraqi-Chaldeans: A Conflicting Conception of Identity." In *Arabs in the New World: Studies on Arab American Communities*, edited by Sameer Y. Abraham and Nabeel Abraham, 136–47. Detroit: Wayne State University Press, 1983.

Sewell, Thomas. *Ethnic America: A History.* New York: Basic Books, 1981.

Shain, Yossi. "Democrats and Secessionists: US Diasporas as Regime Destabilizers." In *International Migration and Security*, edited by Myron Weiner, 287–322. Boulder, Colo.: Westview Press, 1993.

"Ethnic Diasporas and U.S. Foreign Policy." *Political Science Quarterly* 109.5 (Winter 1994–95): 811–41.

"The Foreign Policy Role of US Diasporas and Its Domestic Consequences." In *Representing and Imagining America*, edited by Philip John Davies, 101–14. Keele: Keele University Press, 1996.

The Frontier of Loyalty: Political Exiles in the Age of the Nation-State. Middletown, Conn.: Wesleyan University Press, 1989.

"Marketing the American Creed Abroad: US Diasporas in the Era of Multiculturalism." *Diaspora* 4.1 (Spring 1994): 85–111.

"Multicultural Foreign Policy." *Foreign Policy* 100 (Fall 1995): 69–87.

Shain, Yossi, and Martin Sherman. "Dynamics of Disintegration: Diaspora, Secession and the Paradox of Nation-States." Paper presented at the Harvard – MIT MacArthur Seminar, Boston, March 6, 1996.

Shain, Yossi, and Mark Thompson. "The Role of Political Exiles in Democratic Transitions: The Case of the Philippines." *Journal of Developing Societies* 6 (January–April 1990): 71–86.

Sharabi, Hisham. Address to AAUG 26th Annual Convention. *AAUG Mideast Monitor* 9.1 (Winter 1994): 7–8.

Sheffer, Gabriel, ed. *Modern Diasporas in International Politics*. New York: St. Martin's, 1986.

Shklar, Judith. "Obligation, Loyalty, Exile." *Political Theory* 21.2 (May 1993): 181–97.

Shorris, Earl. *Latinos*. New York: W. W. Norton, 1992.

Siblani, M. Kay. "As ADC Meets, It Stands at Crossroads." *Arab American News*, May 4–10, 1991.

Skerry, Peter. *Mexican Americans: The Ambivalent Minority*. New York: Free Press, 1993.

Skinner, Elliot P. *African Americans and U.S. Policy toward Africa, 1850–1924*. Washington, D.C.: Howard University Press, 1992.

Smith, Robert. "De-Territorialized Nation Building: Transnational Migrants and the Re-Imagination of the Political Community by Sending States." Paper presented at the annual meeting of the American Political Science Association, Washington, D.C., September 2–5, 1993.

Smith, Rogers M. "The 'American Creed' and American Identity: The Limits of Liberal Citizenship in the United States." *Western Political Quarterly* 41.2 (1988): 225–50.

"Beyond Tocqueville, Myrdal and Hartz: The Multiple Traditions in America." *American Political Science Review* 87.3 (1993): 549–66.

Smith, Tony. "In Defense of Intervention." *Foreign Affairs* 73.6 (November–December 1994): 34–46.

Solis, Dianna. "U.S. Hispanics Flex Political Muscles as Mexico Lobbies for NAFTA Support." *Wall Street Journal*, March 3, 1993.

Sollors, Werner. *Beyond Ethnicity: Consent and Descent in American Culture*. New York: Oxford University Press, 1986.

Sonn, Tamara. "Arab Americans in Education: Cultural Ambassadors?" In *Arab Americans: Continuity and Change*, edited by Baha Abu-Laban and Michael W. Suleiman, 127–39. Belmont, Mass.: Association of Arab American University Graduates, 1989.

Sontag, Deborah. "The Lasting Exile of Cuban Spirits." *New York Times*, September 11, 1994.

"Muslims in the United States Fear an Upsurge in Hostility." *New York Times*, March 7, 1993.

Sontag, Deborah, and Larry Rother, "Dominicans May Allow Voting Abroad, Empowering New York Bloc." *New York Times*, November 15, 1997.

Sowell, Thomas. *Ethnic America: A History*. New York: Basic Books, 1981.

Spener, David. "U.S.-Mexico Relations: The Case of Tejuano Entrepreneurs and Trade with Mexico." Paper presented at the annual meeting of the American Political Science Association, San Francisco, August 31, 1996.

Spinner, Jeff. *The Boundaries of Citizenship*. Baltimore: Johns Hopkins University Press, 1994.

Staniland, *American Intellectuals and African Nationalists, 1955–1970*. New Haven: Yale University Press, 1991.

Stedman, Stephen J. "The New Interventionists." *Foreign Affairs* 72.1 (1992–93): 1–16.

Stepick, Alex. "Miami, Los Cubanos Han Ganado!" 26.2 (September 1992): 39–47.

Stockton, Ronald R. "Arabs in America." In *Connections: Faculty Voices*, edited by Ted-Larry Pebworth and Claude Summers, 37–44. Dearborn: University of Michigan, 1993.

Sudetic, Chuck. "Yugoslav Premier Ousted by Foes 6 Months after Return from U.S." *New York Times*, December 30, 1992.

Suleiman, Michael. "American's View of Arabs and Its Impact on Arab-Americans" (in Arabic). *Al-mustaqbal al-'arabi* (Beirut) 177 (November 1993): 92–107.

"Symbols versus Substance: A Year after the Declaration of Principles: An Interview with Edward W. Said." *Journal of Palestine Studies* 24.2 (Winter 1995): 60–72.

Takaki, Ronald. *A Different Mirror: A History of Multicultural America*. Boston: Little, Brown, 1993.

    ed. *From Different Shores: Perspectives on Race and Ethnicity in America*. 2nd ed. Oxford: Oxford University Press, 1994.

Telhami, Shibley. "Arab Public Opinion and the Gulf War." *Political Science Quarterly* 108.3 (Fall 1993): 437–52.

Terry, Don. "Black Muslims Enter Islamic Mainstream." *New York Times*, May 3, 1993.

Thernstrom, Stephan. "Just Say Afro." *New Republic*, January 23, 1989.

Tolchin, Martin. "High Profile for South Korean 'Embassy in Exile.' " *New York Times*, October 10, 1986.

Tölölyan, Khachig. "Commentary." *Diaspora* 1 (Fall 1991): 225–28.

    "Exile Governments in the American Polity." In *Governments-in-Exile in Contemporary World Politics*, edited by Yossi Shain, 167–87. New York: Routledge, 1991.

"The Impact of Diasporas on US Foreign Policy." In *Ethnic Conflict and Regional Instability: Implications for US Policy and Army Roles and Missions*, edited by R. L. Pfalzgraff Jr. and R. H. Shultz Jr., 147–60. Washington, D.C.: U.S. Army, 1994.

"National Self-Determination and the Limits of Sovereignty: Armenia, Azerbaijan and the Secession of Nagorno-Karabagh." *Nationalism and Ethnic Politics* 1.1 (Spring 1995): 86–110.

"The Nation-State and Its Others: In Lieu of a Preface." *Diaspora* 1.1 (Spring 1991): 3–7.

"Uprooted Peoples Enter a New Age of Migration." *Newsday*, September 8, 1991.

Tomarkin, Mordechai. "Israel–South Africa Relations" (Hebrew). *Monthly Review* 12 (December 1980): 17–24.

Tonelson, Alan. "Beyond Left or Right." *National Interest* 34–37 (Winter 1993–94): 3–18.

Turki, Fawaz. *Exile's Return: The Making of a Palestinian-American*. New York: Free Press, 1994.

Van Reenen, Antanas J. *Lithuanian Diaspora: Konigsberg to Chicago*. Lanham, Md.: University Press of America, 1990.

Vicker, Ray. "U.S. Arabs, Adopting Tactics of Jewish Groups, Organize to Aid Image, Exert Political Pressure." *Wall Street Journal*, July 29, 1982.

Vital, David. *The Future of the Jews*. Cambridge Mass.: Harvard University Press, 1990.

Voll, John. "Islamic Issues for Muslims in the United States." In *The Muslims of America*, edited by Yvonne Yazbeck Haddad, 205–16. New York: Oxford University Press, 1991.

Von Hagen, Victor Wolfgang. *The Germanic People in America*. Norman: University of Oklahoma Press, 1976.

Vulliamy, Ed. "Street War Splits Exiled Cubans in Little Havana." *Observer*, December 11, 1994.

Walbridge, Linda S. "The Shi'a Mosques and Their Congregations in Dearborn." In *Muslim Communities in North America*, edited by Yvonne Yazbeck Haddad and Jane Idleman Smith, 337–57. Albany: State University of New York Press, 1994.

Walzer, Michael. "Comment." In *Multiculturalism and "The Politics of Recognition": An Essay by Charles Taylor*, edited by Amy Gutman, 99–103. Princeton: Princeton University Press, 1992.

"Multiculturalism and Individualism: Principles of Government." *Dissent* (Spring 1994): 185–91.

Walzer, Michael, Edward T. Kantowicz, John Higham, and Mona Harrington. *The Politics of Ethnicity*. Cambridge, Mass.: Harvard University Press, 1982.

Wang, L. Ling-chi. "Roots and Changing Identity of the Chinese in the United States." *Daedalus* 120 (Spring 1991): 181–206.

Weaver, Mary Anne. "The Trail of the Sheikh." *New Yorker*, April 12, 1994, 71–89.

Weil, Martin. "Can the Blacks Do for Africa What the Jews Did for Israel?" *Foreign Policy* 15 (Summer 1974): 109–30.

Weiner, Myron. "Asian Immigrants and US Foreign Policy." In *Immigration and US Foreign Policy*, edited by Robert W. Tucker, Charles B. Keely, and Linda Wrigley, 192–213. Boulder, Colo.: Westview Press, 1990.

The Global Migration Crisis: Challenge to States and Human Rights. New York: HarperCollins, 1995.

"Nations without Borders." *Foreign Affairs* 75.2 (March–April 1996): 128–34.

West, Cornel. "How to End the Impasse." *New York Times*, April 14, 1993.

Race Matters. Boston: Beacon Press, 1993.

Whitaker, Charles. "First African/African-American Summit." *Ebony* 46.10 (August 1991): 116–22.

White, Philip V. "The Black American Constituency for Southern Africa." In *The American People and South Africa*, edited by Alfred O. Hero Jr. and John Barratt, 83–102. Lexington, Mass.: Lexington, 1981.

Wilkins, Roger. "What Africa Means to Blacks." *Foreign Policy* 15 (Summer 1974): 130–41.

Wilkinson, Doris. "Americans of African Identity." *Society* 27.4 (May–June 1990): 14–18.

Wittkopf, Eugene R. "What Americans Really Think about Foreign Policy." *Washington Quarterly* 19.3 (Summer 1996): 91–106.

Wright, Lawrence. "One Drop of Blood." *New Yorker*, July 25, 1994, 46–83.

Wyman, David S. *The Abandonment of the Jews: America and the Holocaust, 1941–1945*. New York: Pantheon Books, 1984.

Ya'ar, Ephraim. "Emigration as a Normal Phenomenon." *New Outlook* 31.1 (January 1988): 14–17.

Young, Lewis. "American Blacks and the Arab-Israeli Conflict." *Journal of Palestine Studies* 2.1 (Autumn 1972): 70–85.

Zogby, James. "Arab American in the Clinton Administration." *Arab News*, December 21, 1992.

"Creating Jobs First in Occupied Palestinian Lands." *Jerusalem Times*, February 11, 1994, 5.

"Zogby: Face the Facts, Indyk Is In." *Al-Fajr*, March 22, 1993, 8–9.

Zureik, Elia. "What State Palestine?" *Dissent* (Winter 1994): 23–26.

Newspapers, Magazines, and Newsletters

AAUG Newsletter
ADC Times
ADL Special Reports
AMC Report
Arab American News
Boston Globe
Christian Science Monitor

BIBLIOGRAPHY

Detroit News
Ebony
Economist
Examen
Ha'aretz (Israel)
International Herald-Tribune
Israel Outreach
Jerusalem Report
Jewish Week
La Jornada
Los Angeles Times
New Republic
New York Times
La Paloma (Mexico)
Siempre (Mexico)
Smena (Slovak journal)
Time
Times Union (Albany, N.Y.)
Newsweek
USA Today
U.S. News and World Report
Washington Post
Yediot Aharonot (Israel)

Internet Web Sites

CNN web site (www.cnn.com)
Council on American Islamic Relations web site (www.cair-net.org)
"Middle East Realities" web site (www.mideast.org)

277

Index

AAI. *See* Arab American Institute (AAI)
AAUG. *See* Association of Arab-American University Graduates (AAUG)
"The Abandonment of the Jews," 18
Abelmann, Nancy, 158
Abourezk, James, 98, 118, 127
Abraham, Nabeel, 101
Abraham, Spence, 111
Abu-Lughod, Ibrahim, 102, 103, 106
Adamkus, Valdas, 83
Adams, Gerry, 53–4
Adams, John Quincy, 48
ADC. *See* American Arab Anti-Discrimination Committee (ADC)
affirmative action
  in America, 164
  opposition of neoconservative Jews to, 133, 142
Africa
  See also Angola; Nigeria; Somalia; South Africa
  emergence of independent states in, 140–1
  myths about America and African-Americans in, 135–6
  as symbolic homeland, 90, 133–4, 136–9
African/African-American summit (1991), 148

African-Americans
  affinity with blacks everywhere, 133, 138
  Africa as symbolic homeland, 90, 133–4, 136–9
  as antipodal minority, 159
  civil rights alliance with Jewish-Americans, 133, 139
  conflict related to Hispanics, 3
  consolidation of black integrationists, 143–8
  discrimination against, 133, 136–40
  feuds with Jewish-Americans, 3, 133–4, 139–42, 144–5, 159–60
  identification with struggle of Palestinians, 141–2, 144–8
  influence on U.S foreign policy, 133, 143–4, 157, 162, 204–5
  influence on U.S. South African policy, 84–91
  integrationists, 143–4
  interest in Angola, 143
  interest in Nigeria, 32, 90, 203
  interest in Third World ideology, 133–4
  internationalism of, 22
  issue of American identity, 161–2
  knowledge of Africa, 33–4, 136
  perception of "Jewish power," 144–6
  radicals, 37, 86
  response to emerging independent African states, 34

African-Americans (*cont.*)
  slave history of, 32, 35–6
  society's reluctance to incorporate, 138, 140
  support for Haitian-Americans, 72
African Growth and Opportunity Act (1998), 164
Africans on African-Americans (Gershoni), 135
Africare, 86, 144
Akinyemi, Bolaji, 90
Alamoudi, Abdurahman, 99, 113
Al-Bostaan, 127
Albright, Madeleine, 38
Alianza, 36
America Israel Public Affairs Committee (AIPAC), 21
American-Arab Anti-Discrimination Committee (ADC), 98, 115–17, 122, 125, 127–8
American Committee on Africa, 87
American creed, 32
Americanization programs, 178–80
American Lebanese League, 95
American Muslim Council, 130
American principles, 42
American Revolution, 12
American Sroboran, 65
American values, x, 102
ancestral lands, 3
Anderson, Benedict, 11
Anglo-Americans
  as dominant population, 12–13
  Irish-Americans challenge hegemony of, 13
Anglo-Saxon culture
  adherents to, 101
  concept of individual law, 41
  domination of U.S. foreign policy, 25
  resistance to, 102
  view on foreign affairs, 205
Angola, 89, 143
anticommunism, American, 40
Anti-Defamation League (ADL), 154
"antipodal minorities," 159
anti-Semitism
  in America, 138
  of blacks, 133

interwar period in America, 18
Jewish-American perception of blacks, 141–2
in U.S. post–World War II period, 20–1
apartheid
  African-American campaign against, 143–4, 147–8
  antiapartheid movement, 85–9
Arab American Institute (AAI), 115–21
  Clinton speaks before, 131
  conference (1994), 127
Arab-American News, 117, 124
Arab-American politics
  integrationists in, 101–2, 113–16
  Islamic-leaning isolationists, 107–13
  left-leaning isolationists, 102–7
  Zogby's role, 116–21
Arab-Americans
  See also Islam; Muslim-Americans; Palestinian-Americans
  activism after Six Day War (1967), 97–8
  in American society, 99
  Christian Arabs, 124
  debates over Oslo Accord, 121–8
  effect of Gulf War on, 116–21
  export of American values and interests, 126–7
  idea of ethnic solidarity, 96–7
  Islamic-leaning isolationists, 107–13
  left-leaning isolationists, 102–7
  Muslims' conception of Palestinian cause, 90–2, 95
  during Persian Gulf War, 69, 116–21
  response to Israeli invasion of Lebanon (1982), 94, 98
  response to post-Oslo Israeli policies, 128–31
  response to World Trade Center bombing, 99–100
  vs. Jewish lobby, 113–16, 119–21
Arab-Israeli War (1967). *See* Six Day War (1967)
Arab-Israeli War (1973)
  African nations' response to, 149

black-Jewish relations in outcome of, 142
Arafat, Yasir, 95, 103, 105–6, 122, 125, 147
Aristide, Jean-Bertrand, 46, 71–3, 162
Armenian-Americans, 63–4
Armenians
  genocide against, 64
Asali, Ziad J., 125
Asian-Americans
  Chinese-Americans, 33
  Confucian values of, 159
  impact on U.S. foreign policy, 81
  Japanese-Americans, 19–20
  Korean-Americans, 5, 170
assimilation
  American cultural, xi, 15
  Anglo-Saxon demands related to, 16, 25, 32
  of Arab-Americans, 97, 99
  degrees of, 10
  of European immigrants, 17
  factors influencing, 5–6
  of Japanese-Americans, 19
  Muslims and Arab-Americans resisting, 102–3
  of Palestinian scholars into American society, 105
  shift to ethnic diversity from, 206
Association of Arab-American University Graduates (AAUG), 102–3, 105–6, 122, 125
asylum
  U.S. granting of, 40
Avital, Colette, 152

Baker, James, 62
balkanization, 2, 3, 4, 7, 8, 26, 31, 48
Baltic states, 63
Begin, Menahem, 145
Beilin, Yossi, 150, 153
Ben-Gurion, David, 21
Berisha, Sali, 82
Berman, Paul, 140, 141, 156
bilingual education, 5, 29, 192
Black Panther Party, 103
"Black Power" movement, 36, 103, 140
Blair, Tony, 54

Bourne, Randolph, 16–17
Brandon, Henry, 61
Broder, David, 120
Brown Berets, 36
Burciaga, José Antonia, 189
Bush, George, 62, 72, 76, 79, 126
Bush administration, 53, 62, 64
Bustamente, Jorge, 181

Caldwell, Christopher, 73
California Proposition 187, 4
"Can the Blacks Do for Africa What the Jews Did for Israel?" (Weil), 86
Cárdenas, Cuauhtémoc, 186–7, 193
Carranza, Venustiano, 177
Carter, Jimmy, 42–4, 78, 144
  "idealism" of, 43
  "strategic incoherence" of, 43
Carter administration
  pro-African interests of, 86–7, 143
Castro, Fidel, 73–77
Catholics, American, 13, 54
Center for Policy Analysis on Palestine, 105, 120
Chafets, Ze'ev, 145
Chazan, Naomi, 149
Chicanos, 36, 80
  See also Mexican-Americans
Chinese, overseas, 10, 71, 81–2
Chinese-Americans, 33
Chinese Exclusion Act (1882), 15
Chomsky, Noam, 38–9
Christopher, Warren, 126
Chun Doo Hwan, 44
citizenship
  acquisition of American, 169
  as definition of national membership, 167
  dual, 6, 11, 19, 207
  foreign consular involvement in U.S. in, 169–73
  immigrants adopting American, 196
  immigrants seeking U.S., 5–6
  Israeli, 168
  Japanese dual, 19–20
  Mexicans with American, 182, 190
  requirements in Germany, 167–8
  in United States, 169–73

citizens (native born), 6
Citrin, Jack, 49
civic culture, American, ix, x, 3, 8, 27, 158
civilizations (Huntington), 7
civil rights movement
  anti-apartheid element to, 87
  attitudes toward homelands during, 34–5
  cooperation of blacks and Jews during, 133, 139
  decline of Jewish-American interest in, 142
  immigration legislation as outcome of, 22
  influence of, 2, 97
Clinton, Bill
  on American nativist attitude, 197
  Arab-Americans in 1992 campaign, 120
  decisions related to Sinn Fein, 53–4
  meets with Arab-American lobby, 131
  as player in Northern Ireland's problems, 53–4
  pressured to intervene in Haiti, 72–3
  signs Helms-Burton law, 77
  visit to Africa, 90, 164
Clough, Michael, 48–9
cold war
  disintegrative effects of, 132
  post–cold war era, 46–7
  rhetoric of, 22
  U.S. inconsistent policy during, 41–4
color-blind, 33, 35, 196
Comprehensive Anti-Apartheid Act (1986), 85
Congressional Black Caucus (CBC), 72–3, 86, 90, 143–4, 146, 164, 204
containment, 21, 33–4, 39
Coser, Lewis, 104
Council on American Islamic Relations, 130
Council on Foreign Relations, Chicago, 38, 201
Croatian-Americans, 65–6

Croatian Democratic Union party, 65
Cuban American National Foundation (CANF), 74–6
Cuban-Americans, 3
  actions of political exiles, 73–7
  refugees, 40
Cyprus, 67–8
Czech- and Slovak-Americans, 57–62

Dashnag Party, Armenia, 64
Declaration of Principles (DOP), Israel-PLO (1993), 105, 107
DeConde, Alexander, 25, 31–2, 37
de la Garza, Rodolfo, 182, 192
de la Madrid, Miguel, 175
democracy
  American promotion of, x
  diasporic commitment to, 66–7
  Israeli, 93
  post–cold war importance of, 80
  in U.S. foreign relations, 78–81
Democratic Party, U.S.
  Jewish-black confrontation over party platform (1984), 147
Dershowitz, Alan, 140, 142
DeSipio, Louis, 192
diasporas
  See also homelands
  Americanized Mexican-American, 195
  attitudes of homelands toward, 166–9
  contribution to democratic change in homelands, 79
  defined, 8
  diaspora-homeland nexus, xi
  diasporic identity, 134–5, 160
  diasporic makeup, x, 10
  economic power and political strength of members, 171–2
  loyalty dilemma, 68–70
  militant groups in, 199
  as pawns, 9
  political exiles in, 70–7
  recently empowered, xi
diasporas, U.S.-based
  See also foreign policy, U.S.; homelands

Arab-American response to Gulf
War, 69, 116–21
character and size of Cuban-
American, 73–6
differences in older and more recent, 10–11
Dominican Republic, 172–3, 194
as force in countries of origin, 171
Haitian, 194
influence of Polish-American, 55–7
influence of Slovak-Americans on
independence of Slovakia, 57–62
influence on U.S. foreign relations,
ix–x
Irish-American, 12–13, 52–4
Israel as symbolic homeland for
Jews, 9, 133–4, 138–9
as legitimate foreign policy voice,
200
as messengers of American values,
50
Mexican, 23–4, 175–6, 183–9
mobilization of homeland, xi, 5
political contributions of Jews, 171
post–World War II Jewish-
American activities, 21
role in U.S. politics and foreign
policy, x–xi
transnational character of some,
194
Yugoslavian, 64–5
Díaz, Porfirio, 177
Dinkins, David, 88, 154
Dodd, Christopher, 72
Dole, Bob, 87
Dominican-Americans, 172–3
Douglass, Frederick, 139
Du Bois, W. E. B., 33, 136, 137

eastern Establishment, 38–9
East European-Americans
See also Czech- and Slovak-
Americans; Polish-Americans
lobbying during World War I, 55
lobbying for U.S recognition of
their homelands, 14
post–World War II disappointment, 21–2
Echeverría, Luis, 175
Eisenhower, Dwight D., 21–2, 22

elites
activist, 50
African-American, 37, 203
Anglo-American, 207
Anglo-Saxon, 12, 27, 38
Arab-American, 91
declining influence of, 51
diasporic, 11, 46, 200
Mexican diasporic, 174–5
use of homeland-related affairs by,
158
Emerson, Steven, 112–13
emigration
attitudes of homelands toward, 166–
70
of Irish to United States, 12–13
ethnic (diaspora) makeup, 3
ethnic groups
core, rearguard, and silent members, 96
electoral importance of ethnic vote
in United States, 6–7, 22
influence on U.S. foreign policy, ix–
x, 197–8
interaction among members of, 9–
10
interaction and cohesion of, 9–10
Israeli outreach to minorities in
United States, 151–3
politics in United States of, 1–2
ethnic integrationists
Arab-American, 113–16, 124, 126
conceptions of, 102
ethnic isolationists
Arab-American, 101–2
Islamic-leaning, 107–13
left-leaning, 102–7
ethnicity
change in composition of, 3–4,
208
critics of the rising tide, 2
difference from race, 35–6
German, 167–8
growing influence in United
States, 132
influence on U.S. foreign policy,
197–8
Jewish, 21
legitimization in American life of,
158

ethnicity (*cont.*)
  tolerance in United States of, 22
  U.S., 160
*Ethnicity, Race, and American Foreign
    Policy* (DeConde), 25
ethnic *vs.* diasporic, 31
"evil empire," 39
exile mentality, 50, 101, 104
exiles
  See also political exiles
  aberrant, 135
  among refugee scholars, 104
  Chinese, 81
  identification with Israel, 135
  inspiring radicalization of Ameri-
    can Muslims, 112
  political, 81–3

Farrakhan, Louis, 147, 162
Faruqi, Ismail R. al-, 110
Fenians, 13, 53
Fernandez, Damian J., 74
Fernández Peyma, Leonel, 172
foreign policy, U.S.
  Anglo-Saxon domination of, 12–
    13, 25, 38–40
  Arab-American lobby, 98
  during Bush administration, 53, 62–
    3, 68, 72, 75–6, 85
  during Carter administration, 43–
    4, 86–7
  during Clinton administration, 53–
    4, 72–3, 77
  during cold war, 38–44
  correlation with domestic politics,
    25
  criticism of, 38–40
  criticized by Arab-American isola-
    tionists, 101
  diasporic factor in, 199, 204–5
  focus in early twentieth century,
    40–2
  granting of asylum as, 78
  influence of African-Americans on,
    84–91, 133, 143–4, 157, 162,
    204
  influence of Cuban-Americans on,
    74–5
  influence of ethnic diversity on,
    204

  influence of ethnic groups on, ix–
    x, 7–8, 22–3, 197–8
  influence of Irish-Americans on,
    13, 53–4
  influence of Jewish-Americans on,
    21, 133, 157
  influence of Polish-Americans on,
    55–7
  influence of U.S.-based diasporas
    on, ix–x, 6–7, 22–3, 25, 49–91,
    197–9
  isolationism vs. interventionalism,
    47
  "Jewish power" in, 21, 65
  legalistic-moralistic approach
    (Kennan), 21, 41, 45, 48
  national interest in, 47–8
  under Nixon, Ford, and Kissinger,
    78
  during Nixon administration, 42,
    82
  post–cold war, 46–9
  post–cold war confusion in, 206
  post–cold war focus, 38, 40, 45–
    50
  pressures of ethnic lobbies on,
    158
  during Reagan administration, 44,
    78–9, 81
  recognition of Israeli state, 21
  related to containment of commu-
    nism, 21
  role of Congress in, 51–2, 80–1
Forster, John, 149
Fox, Vicente, 193
Frederickson, George, 84
Freedom Support Act (1992), United
    States, 64
Friedman, Murray, 133
Fuchs, Lawrence, 180, 198
Fuentes, Carlos, 191–2

Galut (exile), xii
Garvey, Marcus, 33, 35, 136, 137,
    138
Gates, Henry Louis, 162
General Bureau of Italians Abroad
    (Direzione Generale degli Itali-
    ani all'Estero), 167
Geneva Convention, 41

German-Americans
  pan-German movement, 10
  representation in United States, 12
  during World War I, 10–11, 15,
    69
  during World War II, 19
Gershoni, Yekutiel, 135–6
Gerson, Louis, 1–2
Glazer, Nathan, 28, 51, 134–5, 138,
    196
Gorbachev, Mikhail, 62
governments
  attitude toward diasporas, 166–7
  defining nationality, 167
  manipulating citizenship, 169–70
Gray, William, 73, 152
Great Depression, 18
Greek-Americans, 8, 14, 67–8
Green, Marjorie, 154
Guatemala, 39
Gulf War
  effect on Palestinians and other
    Arab-Americans, 69, 116–21

Habash, George, 105
Haddad, Yvonne, 95
Haiti, 32, 47, 71–3, 90, 133, 157,
    162, 203
Haitian-Americans, 71–3
Haleen, Amer, 109
Hallaj, Muhammad, 120
Hamas, 112–13
Hanania, Ray, 127, 129
Havel, Václav, 59, 61, 82
Helms-Burton law, 77
Hendrickson, David, 47
Hernandez, Antonia, 189, 190
Herschel, Abraham Joshua, 141
Hewko, John, 63
Hispanics, 3, 6, 31, 36, 151, 190, 201
Hizbullah, 112, 130
homelands
  Africa as African-American, 133–4,
    137
  ancestral, 66
  Arab-Americans identify with, 97–
    8
  attitudes toward diasporas, 166–9
  attitudes toward emigration, 166–
    70

  conceptions of immigration and
    diaspora, 166–73
  contributions of Czech and Slovak
    groups to independence in, 57–
    62
  diasporas trying to unseat authori-
    tarian regimes, 70–7
  Dominican Republic, 172–3
  as ethnic identification, 31
  Greece seeking support of Greek-
    Americans, 67
  immigrants' travel to and contacts
    with, 5
  influence of Czech- and Slovak-
    Americans on, 57–62
  influence of ethnic diasporas in, 49–
    50
  influence of Ukrainian and Arme-
    nian diasporas on, 62–4
  Israel as Jewish-American, 133–4,
    137–9
  as issue in United States, 158
  issues for African-Americans re-
    lated to, 136–9
  Japanese-American ties to, 19
  manipulation of citizenship, 169–70
    Mexico's relations with Mexi-
    can-Americans, 183–9
  perception of diasporas, 23
  perceptions of national identity, 23
  permitting dual citizenship and ab-
    sentee voting, 207–8
  Polish-Americans support for, 55–
    7
  used by black and Jewish groups in
    United States, 137
Hook, Benjamin, 154
Hoover, Herbert, 179
human rights, x, 37, 41–5
  as Anglo-Saxon ideal, 37
  in China, 48
  post–cold war importance of, 80
  U.S. adherence to idea of, 41–2
  in U.S. foreign policy, 46–8
Huntington, Samuel, 7, 204, 206–7
Hussein, Saddam, 69
*The Hyphenate and Recent American
  Politics and Diplomacy* (Gerson), 1–
  2
hyphenated Americans, 14–15, 88

identity
  African-American, 161–2
  American, 7, 29
  American ethnic, 26
  ancestral, xi, 15
  Arab-American, 97
  diasporic, 134–5, 160
  disappearance of German-
    American, 10–11
  immigrant groups, 14
  individual self-identification in
    United States, 11
  among Israeli Jews, 153–5
  national, 3, 23
  pan-Arab ethnic, 92, 94
"Imagined Community" (Anderson),
  11
immigrants
  California Proposition 187, 4, 190
  criticism of, 6
  with dual citizenship, 6
  fear in United States of, 4–5
  growing transnationalism of, 5
  identfication with homeland, 14
  from Poland to United States, 56
  pre–civil rights movement expecta-
    tions of, 32
  threat of transnational, 6
immigration, U.S.
  national origins quotas, 17
  as political issue, 4–5
  repeal of quota policy, 20
  statistics related to, 4
Immigration Act (1965), 22, 97
Immigration Reform and Control
  Act (1986), 24, 184
Indyk, Martin, 120
Institute of Palestinian Studies, 122
integration
  lack of African-American, 138,
    140
integrationists
  Arab-American, 113–16
  black, 36–7
  consolidation of black, 143–8
  ethnic, 34–5
  pluralist model, 26–8, 31
internationalists
  cultural, 22
  liberal, 38

Iranians
  exiles and the fall of the shah, 70
Ireland
  British concessions to, 54
Irish-Americans, 59
  as ethnic minority, 12–13
  famine and development of U.S.-
    based diaspora, 12
  influence on U.S. foreign policy,
    13, 52–4
  nationalists, 52
  political exiles, 12
Irish Republican Army (IRA)
  cease-fire vote (1994), 53
  Sinn Fein wing, 53–4
Islam
  See also Nation of Islam
  embraced by some blacks in Amer-
    ica, 37, 140
  law and traditional teachings, 108–
    10
  perceived Western assault on, 95
  revival among Arab-Muslims in
    United States, 111–12
Islam vs. Arab nationalism and diaspora, 108–11
Islamic Jihad, 112
isolationism
  of African-Americans, 37
  of Arab-American politics, 101–13
isolationists, 34–5
  Arab-American left-leaning, 102–7
  liberal, 39
  Muslim, 111
  U.S. ethnic, 101
Israel
  alliance with emerging African
    nations (1950s and 1960s), 148
  attack on Qana in Lebanon, 129–
    30
  commitment of Jewish-Americans
    to, 134–5, 140–2
  criticism by black radicals of, 37
  efforts to renew alliances with Af-
    rican nations, 150
  ethnofocal and ideofocal traits, 153
  as ethnofocal nation, 153
  experience of Ethiopian Jews in,
    153–5
  invasion of Lebanon (1982), 94, 98

Law of Return (1950), 168
outreach to U.S. ethnic minorities, 151–3
post-1973 relations with South Africa, 148–50
predominance of Orthodox Judaism in, 161
recent diverse Jewish-American opinion about, 202–3
reduces ties to South Africa (1987), 150
as symbolic homeland, 138
treatment of emigration, 168–9
Israeli-Jordanian peace treaty, 126
Israel-PLO accords. *See* Oslo Accords
Italian-Americans, 8, 19
Iwanska, Alicja, 11

Jackson, Jesse, 137
    ascendance of, 145–7
    as candidate for president, 111
    Clinton's trip to Africa with, 90
    declaration related to Zionism, 156
    Hymie and Hymietown slurs, 147
    interest in Middle East peace, 156–7
    rhetoric related to Jewish-black quarrel, 145
    on use of term African-American, 88
Jackson, Jesse, Jr., 164
Jackson-Vanik amendment, 82
Jacoby, Tamar, 2
Jahshan, Khalil, 120, 122, 124, 126
Janowitz, Morris, 174
Japan
    pre–World War II assistance to Japanese-American organizations, 19
Japanese-Americans, 33
    dual citizenship of, 19–20
    internment and relocation during World War II, 19
    relation to Pearl Harbor, 18–19
Jewish-Americans, 8, 59
    See also Israel; Judaism, Conservative and Reform; Judaism, Orthodox

connection and commitment to Israel, 93, 134–5
debate with orthodox Israeli Jews, 9
disputes with Israel, 161
feuds with African-Americans, 133–4, 139–42, 144–5, 159–60
impact on U.S. foreign policy, 21, 133, 157
internal conflict, 161
recent diversity of opinion about Israel, 202–3
relations with Israel, 9
support of world Jewry, 133–4
as targets of black isolationists, 37
Jews, Ethiopian
    airlifted to Israel, 153–4
    Jewish-American response to, 154
    rioting in Israel (1996), 155
    use made of, 155
Jews, Israeli
    adherence to Orthodox Judaism, 161
    ethnic cleavages among, 153
Johnson, Andrew, 13
Johnson, Tim, 198
Joppke, Christian, 30–1
Judaism, Conservative and Reform
    Israeli conversion debate related to, 161
    majority movements among American Jews, 161
    as minority in Israel, 9, 161
    struggle for official recognition in Israel, 9, 161
Judaism, Orthodox
    monopoly over religious services in Israel, 9, 161
    ultra-Orthodox American Jews, 163
    views on Conservative and Reform Judaism, 161

Kagedan, Allen, 150
Katz-Carmeli, Yehudit, 152
Kaufman, Jonathan, 142
Kennan, George, 21, 41, 45, 48
Kennedy, John F., 39
Kennedy, Joseph, Jr., 72
Khalidi, Rashid, 107

Kilson, Martin, 32–3
Kim Dae Jung, 44–5
kin-country, 7
King, Coretta Scott, 154
King, Martin Luther, Jr., 35, 43, 137, 139
Kirkpatrick, Jeane, 39
Kissinger, Henry, 42, 78
Klaus, Václav, 61
Korean-Americans, 5, 79
  as antipodal minority, 159
  as home-country colony, 170–1
  model minority, 159
  pro-democracy, 44
  response to Los Angeles riots (1992), 170
Kotler-Berkowitz, Laurence, 10
Kramer, Martin, 112
Kuriel, Ran, 150
Kymlicka, Will, 28, 30

The Labyrinth of Solitude (Paz), 194
La frontera de cristal (Fuentes), 191–2
Landsbergis, Vytautas, 82
Latinos, 39, 192
  See also Hispanics; Mexican-Americans
Lau, Meir, 157
Law of Return (1950), Israel, 168
Lebanon
  Israeli attack on Qana in, 129–30
  Israel's invasion of (1982), 94, 98
Lewis, Bernard, 109
Lewis, Samuel, 120
liberal-democratic ethos, American, 51
liberalism
  assumptions of, 26
  cold war liberals vs. Wilsonian liberals, 41–2, 45
Lie, John, 158
Lieberman, Joseph, 120
Lightner, Candace, 127
Lind, Michael, 29
Lithuania, 83
loyalty
  to Britain, 16–17
  cultural effects on, 81–4
  dilemma of diaspora, 68–70
  of ethnic Americans, 15

expectations of, 18
Greek-Americans, 67
homelands' building of U.S.-based, xi
as issue for ethnic isolationists, 34–5
loyalty baggage, 81
manipulation of boundaries of, 167
of Mexican-Americans, 180
multiple loyalties, 6
subnational, 7, 49
of U.S.-based diasporas, xi, 7
U.S. policies to promote, 18–19
Lozoya, Jorge Alberto, 189

Macedonia, 67–8
McKinney, Cynthia, 23, 204–5
Maier, Charles S., 3
Maksoud, Hala, 120
Malcolm X, 35, 137
Mandela, Nelson, 3, 85, 88, 136
Mandelbaum, Michael, 47
Marcos, Ferdinand, 78–80
Masaryk, Tomas, 57
Mas Canosa, Jorge, 75–6
Mathias, Charles, 207
Mattar, Philip, 107, 122
melting pot idea, 2, 16, 35
Mexican-American Legal Defense and Educational Fund (MALDEF), 189–90
Mexican-Americans, 33, 59
  See also Chicanos; Hispanics
  American-born leadership, 180, 184
  with American citizenship, 182, 190
  attitudes toward Mexico, 173–6
  concern related to Zapatista movement, 192–3
  el pocho, 181–3
  ethnic pride of, 175
  fear of Mexican immigrants, 182–3
  founding of League of United Latin American Citizens (LULAC), 180
  government manipulation of, 178–9
  importance of NAFTA to, 24
  integration of, 184, 186, 195

leadership during Great Depression of, 179–80
mistrust of homeland political system, 176
as mobilized diaspora, 174–6, 186–94
as pawns of Mexico and United States, 178–9
political opportunities, 184
political participation of, 184
relations with Mexico, 186–8
repatriation of, 178–9
response to 1988 elections, 186–8
Mexico
  attitude toward and relations with its diaspora, 165–6, 173–83
  attitude toward Mexican-American *el pocho*, 181–3
  Directorate General of Mexican Communities Abroad (DGMCA), 176
  elections (1988), 186–8
  elections (1994), 191–3
  immigration to United States from, 6
  legalized dual nationality, 5, 194–5
  manipulation of Mexican-Americans, 178–9, 184–5
  as a "narco-democracy," 193
  political parties in, 186–93
  Program for Mexican Communities Abroad (PCME), 176, 189–90
  Program for Mexican Communities Living in Foreign Countries (PMCLFC), 24
  reimagined Mexican nation, 23–4, 166
  relations with Mexican-American diaspora, 176–85, 195–6
  relations with United States, 176–7
  remittances from diaspora members, 175
  self-perception as a "global nation," 195
Mfume, Kweisi, 72, 204
Middle East issues
  See also Arab-Americans; Islam; Israel; Jewish-Americans; Lebanon; Palestinian-Americans

events since 1995, 128–31
influence on Arab- and Jewish-Americans, 92–3
intra-Arab enmities, 93–4
Israel-Palestine peace process and Israel-PLO accords, 92–3, 124–5
Six Day War (1967), 96–8, 140–2, 149
U.S. foreign policy, 101
Milošević, Slobodan, 69
miscegenation, 138
Mohammed, Warith Deen, 37
Mokhiber, Albert, 115, 122, 127
Monroe, President, 48
Morga, Eduardo, 184
"mosaic," 11, 29
Moynihan, Daniel Patrick, 51
multiculturalism, x, xi
  African-American perception of debate related to, 84
  in America, xi, 7, 25, 208
  concerns in United States related to, 7, 197–8
  cultural nationalism as, 29–31
  growth in United States, 114, 132
  in Israel, 152
  liberal, 28
  liberal pluralist version of, 27–8
  Mexican support for American, 190
  militant, 28
  nationalist, 28–32
  reconciling with liberal pluralism, 27–8
  as seen by African-Americans, 84
multilateralism
  of U.S. foreign policy, 204
Muslim-Americans
  as activists and lobbying force, 130–1
  American elections related to, 111
  da'wa, 109
  different denominations, 107
  the Hijra in relation to, 108–9
  ideal of, 110–11
  Judeo-Christian heritage related to, 108
  kufr, 111
  as lobbying force, 108

Muslim-Americans (*cont.*)
  mobilization of grass-roots support in, 113, 130
  radicals among, 111–12
  relation to Arab countries, 107–8
  resisting assimilation, 102
  terrorism related to, 112–13
  ummah, 108–10
Muslim Arab Youth Association (MAYA), 101, 111
Muslim organizations in United States
  as leaders in Arab diasporic activism, 130–1
  as lobbying force, 131
Muslim Public Affairs Committee, 130
Mussolini, Benito, 167
Myrdal, Gunnar, 138

NAAA. *See* National Association of Arab Americans (NAAA)
NAFTA. *See* North American Free Trade Agreement (NAFTA)
Nagorno-Karabakh, Azerbaijan, 64
National Association for the Advancement of Colored People (NAACP), 86, 144, 154
National Association of Arab Americans (NAAA), 98, 114– 15, 117, 124
national identity, 3
national interest, 1, 197–210
nationalism
  African, 135
  American, 17
  of African-Americans, 140–1
  black racial, 33–6
  conflict between Islam and Arab, 110
  cultural, 29
  homeland rhetoric of, 167
  of immigrant groups in United States, 14
  Irish, 13
  of Mexican-Americans, 36
  multicultural, 28–31
  of Palestinian- and Arab-Americans, 36
  pan-Arab, 114

nationality, dual, 20
national origins quota, 17, 22
Nation of Islam, 37, 103, 140, 162
nativism, American, 4, 14–15, 17–20
neo-Wilsonian values, x
Netanyahu, Benjamin, 129–30, 161, 171, 202
"New Jew," xii
Nigeria
  African-American help to, 203
  African-American opposition to dictatorship in, 32, 90
Nixon, Richard M., 42
Nixon administration, 99
North American Free Trade Agreement (NAFTA), 24, 175, 188, 192
Norwegian-Americans, 15
numerus clausus (affirmative action quotas equivalent to), 142
Nuremberg Trials, 41

Obregon, Alvaro, 179
Office of the Republic of Croatia, 65
O'Grady, Joseph, 54
Oklahoma City bombing, 20, 99
opposition, U.S.-based
  to affirmative action, 133
  dilemma of Philippine-Americans, 81
Orfalea, Gregory, 98
Oslo Accords
  Arab-American debates over, 121–8
  Declaration of Principles, 105, 107
  second Oslo agreement (1995), 128
Othman, Talat, 126
OTPOR (Croats), 66
Overseas students, 70–1

Palestine
  Arab-American identification with cause of, 90–2, 94, 123
Palestine Congress of North America (PCNA), 104
Palestine Liberation Organization (PLO)

See also Oslo Accords
relations with African-American leaders, 145–7
sponsors PCNA, 104
suppport of diaspora for, 94–5
Palestine National Council (PNC), 104
Palestinian-Americans
activism of, 94
factors influencing, 128
intelligentsia in United States, 107, 130
relations with PLO, 105–6
Palestinians
after Six Day War (1967), 97–8
response to opening of tunnel in Jerusalem, 171
sympathy of American blacks for, 146–7
pan-Africanism, 22, 33, 140
Panić, Milan, 69
PAN (Political Action Party), Mexico, 193
"pariah states" (Israel and South Africa), 149
Park Chung Hee, 44
Paz, Octavio, 181, 194–5
PCNA. *See* Palestine Congress of North America (PCNA)
Peleg, Israel, 152
Peña Gómez, José Francisco, 172
Peres, Shimon, 126
Peretz, Martin, 140
Pezzullo, Lawrence, 73
Pickus, Noah, 15
Pittsburgh Agreement (1918), 57
pluralism, x, 9
criticism of American, 27–9
cultural, 22, 25–32
internationalization of American, 32
in Israel, 168
liberal, 35, 162
pluralism, American
domestic, 26, 42
emergence of, 25–7
internationalization of, 32
nationalist ethnic, 28–9
Polish-Americans, 14, 55–7
post–World War, 56–7

political exiles
Aristide, 71–3
campaigns related to Cuba and Haiti, 70–7
Chinese-Americans, 81–2
Cuban-Americans, 73–7
diasporic elites as, 11
fleeing communism, 40
Greek, 67
Irish-Americans perceived as, 12–13
politics, diasporic
Arab-American, 96–131
Palestinian-Americans, 94–5
self-determination model of, 89
politics, home country
diasporic interest in, 8–12
Mexican diaspora interest in, 24
related to migration, 10
politics, U.S.
black domestic, 143
ethnic lobbies in, ix, xi, 1–2
homeland factor in, 158
influence through local government on, 23
Israeli outreach to ethnic minorities, 151–3
role of diasporas in, xi
polyethnic America, 28
Popular Front for the Liberation of Palestine (PFLP), 105
Porter, Bruce D., 49
PRD (Party of the Democratic Revolution), Mexico, 186–7, 193
Pressler, Larry, 198
PRI (Institutional Revolutionary Party), Mexico, 186–7, 191–3
Progrebin, Lettie, 160
Proposition 187, California, 4, 190
Psinakis, Steve, 79

Rabin, Yitzhak, 93, 95, 168
race
Anglo-Saxon, 12
difference from ethnicity, 35–6
race relations, 10
racism, 3
in America, 32–3, 35–6, 136, 139
anti-Arab, 115, 119–20
Chinese Exclusion Act, 15

racism (*cont.*)
  of ethnic isolationists, 35
  official, 20
  perceived expression of Jewish,
    144
  political, 114
  related to Japanese-Americans, 19–
    20
  in United States (1920s), 15–16
Raz, Joseph, 27–8
Reagan, Ronald, 39, 44, 74, 78
Reagan administration, 85, 87
Reed, Adolph, 142, 145–7
refugee policy, U.S., 40
religion
  revival among Arab-Muslims in
    United States, 111–12
  rift between Israeli and American
    Jews related to, 161
  in United States, 12–13
remittances from Mexican diaspora,
  175
Rhodesia, 143
Rieff, David, 77
Robbins, Bruce, 204–5
Robeson, Paul, Jr., 156
Robinson, Randall, 72, 86, 89–90,
  164
Rockefeller, Steven C., 26
Rodriguez, Richard, 174, 182
Rozental, Andres, 189
Ruggie, John Gerard, 17, 205

Said, Edward
  on Arab-American identity, 97
  attacks on Zogby, 122
  condemnation of Arab and Palesti-
    nian cultures, 125–6
  critique of Western orientalism,
    206–7
  as left-leaning isolationist, 102–
    6
  orientalism of, 36
Salem, George, 118
Salinas de Gortari, Carlos, 75, 175,
  186–7
Samhan, Helen Hatab, 114, 119
SAVAK, 42
Savir, Uriel, 151, 152
Schlesinger, Arthur, Jr., 1

self-definition
  American, xi, 18
  black, 147
self-determination, 51–91
self-perception, Mexican, 166
Serbian-Americans, 65, 69
Shalala, Donna, 120
Sharabi, Hisham, 102, 105–6
Shorris, Earl, 181–2
Siblani, Kay, 124
Siblani, Osama, 117, 124
Sikh separatists, 200
Sinn Fein, 53
Six Day War (1967)
  meaning for Jewish-Americans,
    140–2
  response of Arab-Americans to, 96–
    7
  South African perception of, 149
Skerry, Peter, 29–30, 177
Slovak-Americans, influence and in-
  put on homeland, 57–62
Slovakia's independence, 57–62
Slovak League of America, 57, 59–60
Smena, 60
Smith, Tony, 47
Solarz, Stephen, 198–9
Somalia, 133, 157, 203
South Africa, 133–4, 136
  influence of African-Americans on
    U.S. policy toward, 84–91
  perception of Six Day War, 149
  relations with Israel, 148–51
Soweto Uprising (1976), 143
state breakdown, 3
statistics
  political use of, 4
Stephanopolous, George, 73
Stolarik, Mark, 58, 59
Student Non-Violent Coordinating
  Committee, 103, 141

Takaki, Ronald, 27
terrorism
  Islamic, 99–100
  as issue for Arab-Americans, 99–
    100
  support for Hamas movement, 112–
    13
Terzi, Zehdi, 44

third wave (democratic transitions), 51
Third World
  African-American affinity for, 133
  ideologies, 34, 134
  liberation movements, 42
  Mexico's identification with causes of, 183
  movements, 36, 141
  refugees, 40
  revolutions, 39
  rhetoric of, 94
Third Worldism, 32, 45, 103, 105, 140, 156
TransAfrica, 72, 86–7, 89–90, 143–4, 164
"Transnational America" (Bourne), 16–17
transnationalism
  black, 136–8, 140
  effect of growth in, 165
  of immigrants, 5–6
  political implications of, 6–7
  of some U.S.-based diasporas, 194
  transnationalist threat, 7
  trend in, 207
  in United States, 6–7
Trefunonvic, Milos, 65
Truman, Harry S.
  decision to recognize Israel (1948), 21
  policy related to African-Americans, 33–4
Turkey, 67–8
Turki, Fawaz, 94–5, 103–4

Uhrik, Igor, 60, 61
Ukrainian-Americans, 62–3
United States
  See also foreign policy, U.S.
  Civil War, 52
  Defense Department, 38
  manipulation of Mexican-Americans, 178–9
  relations with Mexico, 176–7
  shift in racial composition, 198
  State Department, 38
Universal Negro Improvement Association (UNIA). See Garvey, Marcus

Vietnam, 39
Vietnam War, 42
Vital, David, 154
Vorspan, Albert, 142
voting patterns
  white ethnic, 22
voting rights
  of Mexican-Americans, 5, 184
  proposal for Dominican-Americans, 5, 172–3
  proposal related to Israeli emigrants, 5, 169
  of some diasporas, 5, 207
Voting Rights Act (amended), United States, 5, 183–4

Walesa, Lech, 82
Walzer, Michael, 17–18
War of 1812, 12
Washington, Booker T., 139
Watergate, 42
We Are All Multiculturalists Now (Glazer), 196
Weil, Martin, 86
Weiner, Myron, 4, 81
West, Cornel, 156
"White elites," 40
white ethnics, 22
Wilkins, Roy, 137
Wilson, Woodrow, 14, 55–6
Wilson administration, 18
World Trade Center bombing (1993), 20, 99–100
World War I
  See also Bourne, Randolph
  belief in American absorptive capacities, 14, 15–17
  East European-Americans lobbying during, 55–6
  German-Americans during, 69
  Zimmermann telegram (1916), 177
World War II, 56–7

Ya'ar, Ephraim, 168
Yom Kippur War (1973). See Arab-Israeli War (1973)
Young, Andrew, 43–4, 144–5

Yugoslavia, 64–6, 69
Yzaguirre, Raul, 189

Zangwill, Israel, 2, 15
Zedillo, Ernesto, 193
Zelniker, Shimshon, 150
Zimmermann, Arthur, 177
Zionism, xii, 103, 138, 141, 153, 156
  idea of, 168
  negation of diaspora related to,
    168
  Wilson's support for, 14
  yeridah (emigration) related to,
    168

Zogby, James
  on Arab issues in United States,
    98
  attacks on, in Arab-American com-
    munity, 121–2
  "Builders for Peace" enterprise,
    122–3
  as president of AAI, 116–18, 127,
    130
  relationship with Arafat, 122
  rise of, 116–21
  at signing of Israeli-Jordanian
    peace treaty, 126
Zoot Suit Riots (1943), 180–1